CRISIS AND CONFLICT IN ASIA
LOCAL, REGIONAL AND INTERNATIONAL RESPONSES

CRISIS AND CONFLICT IN ASIA
LOCAL, REGIONAL AND INTERNATIONAL RESPONSES

PURNENDRA JAIN, GREG O'LEARY AND FELIX PATRIKEEFF

Nova Science Publishers, Inc.
New York

Senior Editors: Susan Boriotti and Donna Dennis
Coordinating Editor: Tatiana Shohov
Office Manager: Annette Hellinger
Graphics: Wanda Serrano
Book Production: Matthew Kozlowski, Jonathan Rose and Jennifer Vogt
Circulation: Raymond Davis, Cathy DeGregory, Ave Maria Gonzalez,
Vladimir Klestov and Jonanthan Roque
Communications and Acquisitions: Serge P. Shohov

Library of Congress Cataloging-in-Publication Data
Available Upon Request

ISBN 1-59033-174-5.

227 Main Street, Suite 100
Huntington, New York 11743
Tele. 631-424-NOVA (6682) Fax 631-425-5933
E Mail: Novascience@earthlink.net
www.novapublishers.com

Printed in the United States of America

CONTENTS

About the Contributors

Sri Moertiningsih **Adioetomo** is Director of the Demographic Institute and Lecturer at the Faculty of Economics, University of Indonesia. Adioetomo is the author of articles in local and international journals and books, including 'Fertility and Family Planning: Prospects and Challenges for Sustainable Fertility Decline' in Gavin W. Jones and Terence H. Hull, eds, *Indonesia Assessment Population and Human Resources* (Singapore: RSPACS-ANU & ISEAS, 1997) and *The Impact of Economic Crisis on Reproductive Health and Family Planning in Indonesia* (New York: ANU & UNFPA, 1998).

Samina **Ahmed** is Research Fellow at the Belfer Center for Science and International Affairs, John F. Kennedy School of Government, Harvard University. Dr. Ahmed specialises in regional security, ethnic conflict and nuclear proliferation in South Asia.

Ikrar **Bhakti** is a researcher in the Center for Political and Regional Studies, Indonesian Institute of Sciences in Jakarta. Author of several book chapters, his articles have also appeared in *Tempo*, *Forum Keadilan*, *D&R*, *Kontan*, *The Strait Times,* and *Far Eastern Economic Review*.

Bob **Catley** is Professor and Chair of Political Studies at the University of Otago, New Zealand. He is the author, co-author or editor of thirteen books and seventy chapters/articles, most recently, 'Waltzing with Matilda: Should New Zealand Join Australia?' (Wellington, 2001). In January 2002 he becomes Foundation Professor of Governance in the University of the Northern Territory, Australia.

Brahma **Chellaney** is Professor of Security Studies at the Centre for Policy Research in New Delhi. Professor Chellaney has held appointments at the Brookings Institution, Harvard University, Australian National University and Johns Hopkins University. He is the author of three books and writes regularly for the *International Herald Tribune*, *Asian Wall Street Journal*, *The Japan Times*, *The Straits Times* and *The Hindustan Times*.

Sang-Hwa **Chung** is Research Professor at the Institute of East and West Studies, Yonsei University in Korea. He is a co-author of the *Korean Political Process* (Seoul: Bubmunsa), and has published several articles on the subjects of Asian political economy and Korean political processes.

Gareth **Evans,** QC, is President of the International Crisis Group in Brussels and is former Foreign Minister of Australia.

Akiko **Fukushima** is Adjunct Professor of Keio University and Head of Policy Research and Senior Fellow of the National Institute for Research Advancement in Tokyo, Japan. Her book *Japanese Foreign Policy: A Logic of Multilateralism* was published by Macmillan in 1999.

N. **Ganesan** is a Senior Lecturer in political science at the National University of Singapore where he has been since 1990. His teaching and research interests are in contemporary Southeast Asian politics and foreign policy. He regularly provides consultancy lectures and briefs for both the public and private sector.

Gerry **Groot** is a lecturer in Chinese Studies in the Centre for Asian Studies at Adelaide University. His major interests are in the means by which the Chinese Communist Party maintains its position and the role of the party's united front work in this.

Stuart **Harris** is Professor in the Department of International Relations in the Research School of Pacific and Asian Studies, Australian National University. He was Secretary of the Department of Foreign Affairs (subsequently Foreign Affairs and Trade) from 1984-88 while on leave from the University. He has written extensively in the fields of foreign economic, strategic and environment policy. His most recent book (with Greg Austin) is *Japan and Greater China: Political Economy and Military Power in the Asian Century* (London: Hurst and University of Hawaii Press, 2001).

Graeme **Hugo** is Professor of the Department of Geographical and Environmental Studies and Director of the National Key Centre in Research and Teaching in Social Applications of Geographical Information Systems at the University of Adelaide. He is the author of over two hundred books, articles in scholarly journals and chapters in books, as well as a large number of conference papers and reports. His books include *Australia's Changing Population* (Oxford University Press), *The Demographic Dimension in Indonesian Development* (with T.H. Hull, V.J. Hull and G.W. Jones, Oxford University Press), *International Migration Statistics: Guidelines for Improving Data Collection Systems* (with A.S. Oberai, H. Zlotnik and R. Bilsborrow, International Labour Office), *Worlds in Motion: Understanding International Migration at Century's End* (with D.S. Massey, J. Arango, A. Kouaouci, A. Pellegrino and J.E. Taylor, Oxford University Press).

Iyanatul **Islam** is Associate Professor in the School of International Business and Asian Studies at Griffith University in Australia. He has co-authored and co-edited seven books, a number of book chapters and has written extensively in international journals. A recent publication (with Anis Chowdhury) is *The Political Economy of East Asia: Post-Crisis Debates* (Oxford University Press, 2000). He has worked for UN agencies in Jakarta, Indonesia for two years (1999-2000) and acts regularly as a consultant for the Geneva-based International Labour Organization (ILO).

Purnendra **Jain** is Professor and Head of Asian Studies at Adelaide University in Australia. He is the author, editor and co-editor of eight books and more than two dozen book chapters and articles in international journals. His most recent co-edited book (with Takashi Inoguchi) is *Japanese Politics Foreign Policy Today* (New York: Palgrave, 2000).

Greg **O'Leary** has recently retired from his position as senior lecturer in international relations in the Department of Politics at Adelaide University. He is the author of various works on Chinese domestic and foreign policy and international relations. His most recent edited book is *Adjusting to Capitalism: Chinese Workers and the State* (New York: M.E. Sharpe, 1999.)

Felix **Patrikeeff** is a Lecturer in the Department of Politics at Adelaide University. He has also taught at the universities of Warwick, Oxford and Sydney. His publications include the book *Mouldering Pearl: Hong Kong at the Crossroads* (1989; London: Hodder and Stoughton, 1990), and numerous essays on Russia and East Asia.

Lesley **Potter** is Associate Professor in the Department of Geographical and Environmental Studies, Adelaide University. She has worked in Southeast Asia for over twenty years and has carried out many field-based studies, especially in Indonesia. She has published more than forty book chapters and articles in international journals, and one jointly authored book (with Harold Brookfield, assisted by Yvonne Byron) *In Place of the Forest: Socio-Economic and Environmental Transformations in Borneo and the Eastern Malay Peninsula* (Tokyo: United Nations University Press, 1995).

PART I. INTRODUCTION
REGIONAL CRISIS AND CONFLICT: CAUSES AND RESPONSES

Chapter 1

PERSPECTIVES ON CRISIS AND CONFLICT

Greg O'Leary and Purnendra Jain

Adelaide University
Australia

The severe economic and subsequent social and political difficulties experienced by various Asian countries from July 1997 have, somewhat inevitably, been referred to as crisis. Some four years later, the region continues to deal with the fall-out from these events and the countries involved have yet to return to their former economic growth and political stability. Despite significant economic recovery in some, especially in South Korea, the damage done to social and political institutions has left complex rebuilding tasks both within and between countries that may take decades to accomplish. Subsequent international developments, not least economic uncertainty, partially induced by terrorism, have further complicated recovery

While there remains disagreement as to the causes and triggers of the financial crisis and subsequent difficulties, most analysts, with the value of hindsight, generally concur that both domestic and international factors were involved. Among the domestic factors responsible were local institutional arrangements, including inadequate regulation and supervision of financial institutions. Heavy borrowing from abroad (much of it used in longer term loans and speculative or non-competitive investments) and access to credit based on family and other connections (especially in Indonesia), rather than appropriate risk assessment, were some of the additional factors. Exchange rates fixed to the US dollar exacerbated difficulties of adjustment when adjustment became paramount and prior to that created difficulties when the yen fell sharply against the dollar. External causes included continued investment and loans from abroad long after there were warnings of glutted export markets, overcapacity and unrealistic speculation (Pempel 1999; Jackson 1999) and the sharp appreciation of the dollar (Whitt 1999).

There were longer-term underlying causes related to the oversupply of similar export products from too many sources in the region and the consequent slowing of export growth from the mid-90s – although such issues have been much clearer in hindsight. In Thailand this should have been clear by 1997 as foreign exchange reserves were by then dependent on foreign borrowings rather than exports and warning signals have been posted (Jackson 1999).

The character and appropriateness of responses to the crisis, both regional and beyond, have also excited great attention, becoming the subject of conspiracy charges and political point scoring.[1] The IMF's initial responses which forced belt-tightening policies onto Thailand, Korea and Indonesia, despite their balanced budgets before the crisis, received widespread criticism, even from its sister organisation, the World Bank. Consumer demand was greatly reduced, recession followed and inter-Asian trade declined. While the IMF subsequently relaxed its budget-surplus requirements and made some of its decision-making more transparent, much damage had been done (World Bank 1998; Pempel 1999; Whitt 1999; Robison *et al.* 2000).

It is not our intention here to canvas these issues in any detail. Contributors to this book do so in the chapters that follow. We do, however, wish to note at the outset a few contextual issues that are of general relevance and provide a backdrop to the book. The first of these issues is the general position of Asia, most notably Southeast and East Asia in the world economy and international political perspectives.

The Background

By the mid-1990s, it seemed the Asian century was about to dawn. The drawn-out consequences of colonial presence and the Asia-Pacific War had been resolved or were no longer destabilising. The poverty that had long been the hallmark of the region was being countered by growth widely reported as miraculous and in turn provided a potential model for other third world countries in other parts of the world. The Cold War divisions that had wracked the region, drawn its member states into oppositional alliances and had profoundly affected domestic politics was over. With its passing, there were opportunities to realise finally the new and more independent national identities that were envisaged at the end of the Asia-Pacific War and to fashion regional institutions that reflected the new order.

There emerged also the possibility of China assuming an influential but cooperative regional role. While such an outcome was not assured, the People's Republic of China no longer felt threatened by the Soviet Union and what it perceived as Soviet hegemonic designs in the region and had achieved great economic success by rapidly expanding its economic exchanges with the rest of the world. In more positive terms, it had become cautiously engaged in greater regional and international security dialogue than it ever had before, and was becoming more integrated with the region economically.

Japan had, over half a century, become a world economic power second only to the US and demonstrated the kind of growth possible in the region. Its massive economic dominance of the region had led to widespread beneficial interaction with member states and its role as a model had assisted many other states in a similar process of economic growth – the 'Asian Tigers' being only the most celebrated among them. Japan also, despite slower domestic growth in the1990s, had demonstrated how a dominant regional power could be a force for stability as well as prosperity and had begun to take on wider international security responsibilities (World Bank 1993). That role would continue as the US reduced its influence in the region and Japan, it seemed, would take on greater responsibility for its own security interests. It also appeared that the lingering suspicions related to Japan's role in the Pacific War would finally be resolved by continued prosperity and the interaction Japan promised to promote. And the two future giants of the region, Japan and China, had established a cautious base for bilateral relations and regional cooperation that was underpinned by major and complex economic exchanges.

The Soviet Union had been removed from the region as a destabilising force and its Russian replacement was non-threatening and cooperative, being concerned essentially with rebuilding its ravaged economy and constructing viable domestic political institutions. The political forces it had inspired in the region had been undermined by the reduced credibility of socialism as well as the palpable success of Asian capitalism.

In so far as problems remained, they appeared as the detritus of previous conflicts that were not always of the region's making and that regional development would eventually dissolve.

The divisions in Korea, the tensions in the Taiwan Strait, the animosities of South Asia and the differential growth rates being experienced were the legacies of the Cold War and the period of colonialism. They would, it seemed, be swept away and probably soon, as the institutions and interests that had sustained them were removed or transformed into support for the powerful, regionally-centred interests that had emerged with such success. Regional institutions and proto-institutions and mechanisms had been established for the resolution of outstanding issues and the process of building confidence and trust between parties whose hostilities risked escalation was underway.

The ASEAN Regional Forum (ARF) as well as the Association of Southeast Asian Nations (ASEAN) appeared to be gaining credibility as forums for resolving difficult regional economic and strategic issues, even those involving non-ASEAN members, notably in its dealings with the Spratly Islands disputes. ASEAN itself, now fully expanded from its original 1967 membership, and the Asia Pacific Economic Cooperation (APEC) forum had increasingly become resilient and credible forums that provided the bases for cooperation within and beyond the region.

In terms of the strategic hot spots in the region, China and the US, as well as the parties directly involved, were engaged in discussions designed to engage North Korea in negotiations that would stabilise the Korean peninsula and ultimately reunify it. In South Asia, the opportunity had arisen for resolving long-standing territorial, cultural and political differences without the intrusion of Cold War dynamics. And in the Taiwan Strait, the Association for Relations Across the Taiwan Strait and the Straits Exchange Foundation had been established by Beijing and Taipei respectively to deal with ongoing difficult issues. Gone was the sabre rattling of 1996 when Beijing had tested missiles across the Strait in response to the Democratic Progressive Party's election promise to declare Taiwan's independence if it won.

These substantial efforts to forge an identity for Asia as a region and for its sub-regions, partly as a counter to regionalising forces elsewhere and partly to represent the collectively enjoyed benefits of recent years, had resulted in a growing degree of regional confidence and security (McGrew and Brook 1998). While there remained levels of significant distrust, and while Japan and China were still to find regional roles that were both commensurate with their power and acceptable to other nations, it seemed that continued prosperity would ensure a suitable environment for resolving these long-standing diplomatic and strategic difficulties. It would also continue to produce an outward looking middle class whose interests were in stability, cultural tolerance, liberal values and democratic structures.

But above all, what characterised the recent past and held such promise for the future for that third of humanity that lives in the region was its remarkable economic growth. This growth had not only raised living standards in the region dramatically, it had also integrated the region economically with the rest of the world through trade, investment and borrowing. Rapid economic growth had muted or removed hostile and militant opposition within most of the states concerned, as its benefits became more widely available. The consistently high and growing demand for goods and services from the west even served to reduce the oscillations of Western economies.

Rarely in recent history had Asia seemed so poised to enjoy a period of stability and growth. The Pacific Century was proposed as a period in which the population of the region would be matched by its economic strength and by the peace its title signified.

THE CRISIS

The Asian economic scenario changed dramatically on 2 July 1997 when the Thai currency nosedived and the contagion spread rapidly to many other countries in the region, including the Philippines, Indonesia, Malaysia and even Singapore (Sender 1997). South Korea, despite its extraordinary success over recent decades, also succumbed to its worst financial crisis ever and officially turned to the IMF for emergency help on 21 November 1997.

Within the space of a few years, Asia entered the twenty-first century with a great deal less optimism and with complex problems that are widely referred to as crises. The high rates of economic growth ceased in mid-1997 for almost all states that had enjoyed them and they have yet to return. For some, most notably Indonesia, the resultant political crises have undermined central state institutions, established patterns of internal cultural, religious and ethnic relations and even territorial integrity. And for most, there have been severe disruptions to the political process, to labour and capital markets, to financial institutions and to corporate activity.

For all of Southeast Asia and some of East Asia, severe currency and stock market declines have raised questions about the ability of the region to recapture and sustain the growth rates of the past. The region's credibility as a site for foreign investment and foreign credit has been damaged, trading patterns and initiatives have been disrupted and massive financial assistance from international agencies and governments has been required.

Indeed, such has been the success of Asia's development in recent decades that its current crises threaten not only its own future but also that of the rest of the world with which its economy has become highly integrated.

The politico-strategic consequences of the end of the Cold War have, since the onset of the economic difficulties in the region, become less obviously beneficial. China, free now of its northern threat, has adopted a more assertive role in the region – a role viewed with apprehension by many of its neighbours. Its long dormant demand for unification with Taiwan has been reactivated in ways that threaten regional stability and invoke the possibility of United States intervention. And its territorial assertion in the Spratly Islands has generated complex tensions in Southeast Asia. Its role during the crisis, particularly in not devaluing its currency and in the moderation of its support for the ethnic Chinese corporate sector in Southeast Asia when it came under attack, was carefully judged politically to enhance its regional support. In contrast, its increased hostility to the US and its heightened nationalism do little to garner regional support.

The great task of ensuring China and Japan assume roles in the region which are both commensurate with their status, acceptable to each other and to the region has become much more urgent as the US role in providing regional stability becomes more complex and attenuated. The process of regional and global integration has become much more fraught since the onset of the crisis.

The old tensions between India and Pakistan have also been reignited on a nuclear plane and the unresolved issues of sovereignty in Kashmir have resurfaced in destructive ways, including a mini-war in Kargill. Visits by the heads of state and summit meetings have not resulted in any confidence-building between the countries and historical stresses and strains continue to impede any progress.

The simmering secessionist tensions in many Asian states have been fuelled by the post Cold War climate – as they have elsewhere – and in East Timor have produced a dramatic outcome which seemingly demonstrates the possibility of success as well as the price to be paid for it. The East Timor outcome has also stiffened the resolve of many states in the region to prevent similar outcomes in their own territories. The cultural tolerance that had grown with economic success has been sorely tried in the wake of the financial crisis and is clearly in need of stronger affirmation at an institutional level.

Rapid growth was accompanied in Asia by significant ecological costs, the degree of which has not always been appreciated or that has been minimised. The fires that raged in parts of rural Indonesia as the financial crisis deepened were the most spectacular example of the regional implications of this neglect, but the extent of urban ecological problems throughout the region is also of great concern. The economic crisis resulted in diabolic difficulties in some countries, most notably Indonesia. The impact of the crisis has been obvious on population, migration and refugees, on farmers and forests, and on the general wellbeing of the Indonesian people.

Regional institutions, painstakingly and tentatively developed during the years of rising prosperity, most importantly ASEAN, proved ineffective in dealing with the crisis or its outcomes. The relevance, future and power of such institutions has been seriously undermined and they will require statesmanship from leaders already under severe pressure in order to recapture their momentum. As many observers have noted, the role of the major powers operating in the region has also been decisively altered by the crisis (Lam 2000; Naughton 1999; Pempel 1999; Ruland 2000).

Crisis is perhaps inevitably accompanied by conflict. Conflicts of various sorts have ensued within the countries of the region. While most of these are not of recent origin, the financial crisis reactivated ethnic, religious, national and social conflicts that had been subdued or deactivated by economic success in recent decades. Levels of cultural tolerance and acceptance have been lowered along with living standards, especially in Indonesia where the economic and political difficulties have been greatest. Many commentators predict that these conflicts may well produce regional destabilisation for decades and that they will not be confined to Indonesia.

While it is clear that the crisis has proved an unmitigated disaster for millions in the region, it is also apparent, however, that the severe pressure has, in most countries, effected the establishment of more sound institutions both political and economic, that should serve as the basis for more secure, if less rapid, growth prospects in the future. South Korea is perhaps the best example but all have been forced to initiate painful and serious institutional change that will remedy many of the worst institutions and regulatory arrangements. The economic and financial interaction of the region with the rest of the world has been so shocked that foreign investors and creditors are unlikely to act with the same lack of caution or oversight as previously. Multilateral agencies such as the IMF have introduced complexities into their crisis response that were not apparent at the outset.

Crisis Defined

There are fascinating issues related to the nature of crises that underpin these events. The term crisis is used widely and loosely to describe everything from a bout of depression at a personal level to a global economic meltdown. In the case of the events under consideration here, it was the term of first choice. Questions arise as to whether there is merit in attempting to define it and use it as an analytical tool and whether time spent in categorising the varieties of crises that affect international relations would be beneficial. The hope would be that such categorisation would lead to an understanding of responses that had proved most useful in various forms of crises.

The task is a daunting one. Crises might be considered according to such categories as the suddenness of their onset, their duration, the nature of the crisis (for example, economic, political, social, ecological, ethnic, class, cultural, religious), whether crises might be averted by local, regional or international responses, whether they involve military conflict or threats of conflict, etc. Even what constitutes a threshold for crisis is clearly contentious. When does a 'problem' or an 'issue' reach the critical point?

Serious attempts to undertake these tasks have been made. Richard N. Lebow, for example, made a comparative study of 26 historical crises since 1989, focusing on the origins and outcomes of crises, how the crises affected the subsequent relations between the protagonists and whether they intensified or ameliorated ongoing conflicts (Dougherty and Pfaltzgraff 1996, 480).

Michael Brecher, Jonathan Wilkenfeld and Sheila Moser assembled data about 278 crises for the 50-year period between 1929 and 1979 in a study of both micro and macro level crises. An international crisis is said to pose a challenge to the existing structure of the international system or the subsystem within which it takes place. These authors point out that crises were more frequent in Asia than in any other part of the world; such crises were longer, proportionately, than crises that took place in other regions. In contrast to the 69 crises that broke out in Asia, the Americas have had 33 crises, the smallest number of any region. Europe ranked behind Asia with 57 in those years. Most of the crises came after World War II and had varying levels of US and Soviet involvement. Africa, most of which gained independence in the 1960s, provided the setting for 64 crises, just behind Asia. More than half of these crises formed part of protracted conflicts (Dougherty and Pfaltzgraff 1996, 482-85).

Such categorisation may well prove useful and provide a background against which the 'Asian Crisis' might be evaluated, but like the Asian miracle, the 'Asian Crisis' has been such a unique phenomenon that comparisons with other events can only provide restricted insights.

Although we have discussed crisis and conflict in Asia in the wider context and include South Asia and draw comparisons from other parts of the world, this book focuses primarily on the events and consequences that followed the July 1997 collapse of the Thai baht. We do so in the belief that there has now been sufficient time for mature reflection on these regional events and the global responses made to them.

The contributions reflect the range in approach and focus of scholarship in the region. In the first section, Gareth Evans presents a detailed overview of the conflicts that the crisis has precipitated in the region, while Bob Catley outlines the post-Cold War strategic arrangements of the region and their implications. Sang-hwa Chung provides an outline of the economic crises experienced by the worst affected countries. Iyanatul Islam discusses the implications of the crisis from US perspectives and Western institutions.

In the second section, N. Ganesan, Ikrar Nusa Bhakti, Gerry Groot and Samina Ahmed examine political and strategic dimensions of the crises and the responses to them. In the third section, Stuart Harris, Akiko Fukushima, Felix Patrikeeff and Brahma Chellaney analyse territorial, sovereignty and nuclear issues arising from the crises. In the final section, Graeme Hugo, Lesley Potter and Sri Moertiningsih Adioetomo concentrate on the social, ecological and human aspects of the crises.

Participants in the symposium that generated this volume were invited to contribute from perspectives that reflected their own involvement or expertise, which in each case is very considerable. Their contributions are by no means uniform with respect to the assumptions or analyses they apply and it has not been the intention of the editors to impose conformity. Rather, the contributions reflect the diverse and, in some cases, incompatible, perspectives that continue to be brought to discussions of the Asian Crisis.

This book, as mentioned above, has its origin in an international symposium held at the University of Adelaide in February 2001. There are several key people and institutions whose assistance and generosity have been invaluable both in organising the symposium and for the completion of this book. The Japan Foundation Asia Centre, AusAID, the Kennedy Trust of Otago University, the Adelaide Research Centre for Humanities and Social Sciences (ARCHSS) and the Vice-Chancellor's Office of the University of Adelaide provided funding for the international symposium. Funding from ARCHSS and the Vice-Chancellor also helped us defray some of the publication costs. We would also like to thank Mr Ueno Kagefumi, Japan's Consul General in Melbourne, and the South Australian Branch of the Australian Institute of International Affairs for their support.

We are grateful to all the contributors for their cooperation in preparing work for this volume. Most presented draft papers at the symposium. Comments, suggestions, and feedback from the symposium, especially from discussants, have been useful to authors in revising their papers for publication. We thank all contributors for their contribution and cooperation. We are especially grateful to former Foreign Minister of Australia Gareth Evans who travelled from Brussels to present his keynote speech to the symposium and for his contribution to this volume. We thank Jenny Dorsett, Jan Holmes, Michelle Matthews, David Ellis, Greg de Cure and Peter Murdoch for their help with a range of organisational aspects of the symposium. Indu Jain and Sam Jain gave their support in various forms both at the time of the symposium and with the publication of the book. Both read the entire manuscript and drew the editors' attention to a number of stylistic inconsistencies. We also owe a debt of appreciation to Cally Guerin for her editorial assistance. Finally, we express our gratitude to Frank Columbus of Nova Science Publishers for his interest in our project and for his support at every stage of publishing this book.

REFERENCES

Dougherty, James E. and Robert L. Pfaltzgraff, Jnr., eds (1996) *Theories of Internantional Relations: A Comparative Survey*. 4th Ed. New York: Longman.

Jackson, Karl D., ed. (1999) *Asian Contagion: The Causes and Consequences of a Financial Crisis*. Singapore: Institute of Southeast Asian Studies.

Lam, Peng Er (2000) 'The Asian Financial Crisis and Its Impact on Regional Order: Opening Pandora's Box'. *The Journal of Pacific Asia* 6: 10.

McGrew, Anthony and Christopher Brook (1998) *Asia-Pacific in the New World Order*. London: Routledge.

Naughton, Barry (1999) 'China: Domestic Restructuring and a New Role in Asia'. In Pempel, *Politics of the Asian Economic Crisis*.

Pempel, T.J., ed. (1999) *Politics of the Asian Economic Crisis*. Ithaca and London: Cornell University Press.

Robison, Richard, Mark Beeson, Kanishka Jayasuriya and Hyuk-Rae Kim, eds (2000) *Politics and Markets of the Asian Crisis*. London and New York: Routledge.

Ruland, Jurgen (2000) 'ASEAN and the Asian Crisis: Theoretical Implications and Practical Consequences for Southeast Asian Regionalism'. *The Pacific Review* 13.

Sender, Henry (1997) 'Drop Everything'. *Far Eastern Economic Review* July 24.

Whitt, Joseph (1999) 'The Role of External Shocks in the Asian Financial Crisis'. *Economic Review* (Atlanta) 84, April.

World Bank (1993) *The East Asian Miracle: Economic Growth and Public Policy*. New York: Oxford University Press.

World Bank (1998) *East Asia: The Road to Recovery*. Washington, DC.

ENDNOTES

1 For example, Malaysia's Prime Minister Mahathir implied that George Soros had single-handedly undone the Asian miracle or alternatively that it was a 'Jewish plot' or 'a Western plot to keep Asia poor'.

Chapter 2

PREVENTING DEADLY CONFLICT (KEYNOTE ADDRESS)

Gareth Evans
International Crisis Group
Brussels

Asia made more than its fair share of contributions to the world's crises and conflicts in the twentieth century, and is perfectly capable of doing the same in the twenty-first. Just look around.

In *South Asia*, we have for a start what Bill Clinton accurately described, before his trip there in March 2000, as 'the most dangerous place' on earth. India and Pakistan have already fought three wars since 1947. In both of these states there are strong nationalist and confrontational forces still at work, both now having nuclear weapons, and the dispute over Kashmir remaining anything but resolved. In Sri Lanka, one of the world's ugliest little wars continues with no sign of lasting settlement.

In *Central Asia*, there is increasing anxiety about the spillover of the continuing war in Afghanistan into Uzbekistan, Krgyzstan and Tajikistan to the north, each of which have internal problems of their own, not least in the Ferghana Valley area where they meet – and where my International Crisis Group has last year established a field project.

In *East Asia*, the biggest question of all for international policymakers is, to quote former President Clinton again (this time during his visit to Australia in November 1996): 'how will the Chinese define their greatness in the twenty-first century'? Will it be in terms of realising their country's extraordinary economic and cultural potential, or will they define their greatness in terms of their ability to dominate others?

Two obvious arenas in which that question will be tested are the Straits of Taiwan and the South China Sea; another is the border with India, which has exploded before and could again. And, looking inward as well as outward, there is the continuing repression in Tibet and – in many ways even more ugly these days, with 200 executions of separatists in the last two years – Xinjiang.

Notwithstanding North Korea's recent graduation (at least under the Democrats) from 'rogue state' to 'state of concern', and the new Bush Administration's apparent determination to push on with both theatre and national missile defence systems (with the new Defence Secretary disparaging the ABM Treaty as 'old history'), this state has the potential to be profoundly destabilising for the whole East Asian region. It certainly has the capacity to trigger a new arms race as China and Japan eye each other's capacity for dominance in the new order.

In *South East Asia*, the biggest concern by far is Indonesia, where the country has lurched and muddled its way through a number of crises over the years, but now is closer to the edge than it has been for a long time. Let me spend just a little more time on the situation there, both because it's so close to home here, and because my International Crisis Group (ICG) has established a major project there.

The reasons for the massive disaffection with former President Abdurrahman Wahid are not hard to find. Gus Dur, as he used to be known with rather more affection than was latterly the case, gave Indonesians little reason to believe that the state would protect them from corruption, chaos and violence. The economy is still limping badly, with investor confidence negligible. There was (and is) no resolution in sight of the separatist conflicts in Aceh and Irian Jaya, and the Maluku communal conflict fuelled by the security forces taking sides. Despite rhetorical commitment, the record in bringing major human rights violators to justice has been unimpressive, with convictions in only four major cases since 1998 (and there are reservations widely felt about three of those). Corruption charges against Suharto were dismissed in 2000, and pursuit of other key figures has idled.

The immediate issue precipitating impeachment proceedings against him was Gus Dur's failure to provide a convincing explanation of his involvement in a financial scandal in which his masseur obtained, and apparently divided among figures linked to the President, US$4 million from a state food agency. A US$2 million dollar gift from the Sultan of Brunei intended for social welfare programs had also gone conspicuously astray. The sums involved were small compared to the plunder of state agencies carried out during the Suharto presidency, and the funds seem more likely to have benefited Wahid's party than him personally, but in the new reform era the public rightly expects much more of its leaders.

On the credit side, Gus Dur had maintained his lifelong commitment to the promotion of religious and ethnic tolerance. Political opponents were no longer detained, he had moved toward ending official discrimination against Indonesians of Chinese descent, and encouraged public debate, emphasising that differences of opinion are normal. And his open, casual and jokey style was personally engaging until the very end. But his friends and enemies alike wish that he would have behaved more like his country's President, and less like (with all due respect to the profession in which I now find myself!) an NGO leader. Wahid's public political battle ended in the parliament where Vice-President Megawati Sukarnoputri holds the key to his survival. As head of the biggest party, the Indonesian Democratic Party of Struggle (PDI-P), she controls 31 per cent of the seats and eventually (in August 2001) took control of the Presidency.

Waiting in the wings through all this, although weakened and demoralised, are the old political forces – those once allied with the Suharto regime and especially the military. In February 2001 Defence Minister Mohammed Mahfud told reporters that the armed forces could seize power if politicians fail to lead the country, or if chaos or anarchy cannot be controlled. Mahfud is a constitutional lawyer, not a general, and with his retreating from greater accountability for military crimes, and effective action against corruption, Indonesia's situation will become even more volatile and parlous.

Elsewhere in South East Asia, the potential for major conflict is not so alarming, but it is still there, and perhaps no more so than in Burma/Myanmar (also the site of a new ICG project) where the level of dissatisfaction bubbling both in the traditional areas of ethnic dissent and in the mainstream population has been concealed only by the extent of the military regime's repression. In most observers' judgement the current moves to reopen some dialogue with Daw Aung San Suu Kyi are no more than a cosmetic response to escalating international (and in particular ILO) pressure, but if they are no more than that, the regime certainly risks the lid blowing off again, as it last did in 1988.

In the *South Pacific*, to complete this less than optimistic picture of what conflict could flare up where, we have the unhappy emergence of what Ben Reilly has called the 'Africanisation' of the region, a phenomenon characterised by civil/military tension, weak institutions and the appearance of conflicts driven by a mixture of ethnic grievance and resource greed. As he puts it, 'the perception of the South Pacific has changed from an "oasis of democracy" to an "arc of instability", with the violent overthrow of the elected government in Fiji, an ethnic civil war...in the Solomon Islands, military insubordination in Vanuatu, on-going political instability in PNG, the killing of a cabinet minister in Samoa, and, most worryingly, an apparent demonstration effect at work, whereby extra-constitutional actions in one island group can, it seems, trigger similar activities in another' (Reilly 2000, 261).

Comparative Perspectives

All that said, it helps to keep things in perspective. Maybe that is a little easier from my present lofty and distant vantage points in Brussels and Washington, where I spend most of my time these days (hopefully not yet succumbing to the disease of those many trans-Atlantic policymakers whose indifference to the Asia Pacific, as I found all too often when I was Foreign Minister, was matched only by their ignorance).

As seen from Europe and North America, and I think it is fair to say from the viewpoints of many observers closer to home as well, none of the actual or potential conflicts which we can identify around this region (with the exception of what is happening now in Sri Lanka and what could all too easily happen in Indonesia) seems quite as ugly and intractable as the killing now going on in Chechnya, the Congo and Sudan; as capable of exploding again at any time as the violence in Israel and Palestine; and as difficult to resolve ultimately as the remaining issues in the Balkans, especially the situations in Kosovo and Bosnia. That may not be much source of comfort, but it's some, and given the history of this region, we should welcome it.

Another perspective which should immediately be brought to bear on the situation in Asia, because it brings me to the heart of what I want to discuss, is that what we can see around us today are a number of good examples (although we never seem to characterise them this way) of successful *conflict prevention*.

The quiescent situation in the South China Sea can certainly be characterised this way, with a great deal of the credit given to the rather maligned ASEAN Regional Forum as the vehicle for focusing concerned attention and stimulating the dialogue which has kept the gunboats quiet, even if the underlying tangle of overlapping sovereignty claims remain quite unresolved, and are perhaps unresolvable.

So too can the situation across the Strait of Taiwan, where some cool and deft diplomacy by the new Taiwanese President and his PRC counterparts has kept the lid firmly on – notwithstanding the disconcertingly-close-to-real missile-firing theatre that was played out in 1995-96, and the election to power since then of a party with, on the face of it, an even more provocative approach to the mainland.

But nowhere has the preventive diplomacy success been greater, although still only grudgingly acknowledged in many quarters, than on the Korean Peninsula – where successive US negotiators did a brilliant job in defusing the nuclear and missile crises of the mid-1990s, translating them (through the KEDO nuclear reactor and alternative energy exercise in which Australia participated) into a new foundation for dialogue, and creating the conditions in which Kim Dae Jung could take a quantum leap forward with his 'sunshine' policy of opening to the north. Maybe it was only Kim Jong Il's realisation of his utter helplessness in managing the horrendous food crisis afflicting his country that made the current optimistic environment really possible – but there are always multiple causes for any course of events, and there is no doubt that intelligent and effective preventive diplomacy was a necessary, if not sufficient, condition for the remarkable progress that has been made.

There is not much argument from anyone these days that prevention, with conflict as with so much else, beats the hell out of cure. But it is still far too often the case that the force of this proposition is honoured far more in the rhetoric than the action. What can we, who make up the international community (governments, intergovernmental organisations and, increasingly these days, international NGOs) do to make prevention work better, and do so more of the time?

Making Prevention Work

For effective conflict prevention, three essential conditions have to be met. There has to be knowledge of the fragility of the situation, and the risk of impending conflict, the so-called 'early warning'. There has to be a set of appropriate policy measures available that are capable of making a difference, the so-called 'preventive toolbox'. And there has to be the willingness to apply those measures, the issue of 'political will'.

Early Warning

So far as early warning is concerned, there is no doubt that governments and intergovernmental organisations need all the help that they can get. As budgets for foreign offices around the world tend to go on shrinking (and in my view, and I say this not only as a member of the ex-foreign ministers' club, that is bizarre and indefensible), there seems to be, even in large services like America's and Britain's, less capacity than ever to track and monitor fragile situations and crises, and conflicts in the making. There is a useful role, as a result, to be played here by non-government players including the media, and especially NGOs.

All that said, it is easy to exaggerate the extent to which lack of early warning is a serious problem. My own suspicion (and the recent pathbreaking reports on the Rwanda tragedy certainly support this) is that far too often it is an excuse rather than an explanation, and that the problem is not lack of warning but lack of timely response. Most of the time, key governments, the UN and certainly the major regional organisations, know perfectly well that there is a problem looming. They just hope that it will go away, or even if they know that it won't, they don't get around to doing anything about it because it is an iron law of both politics and the bureaucracy that the urgent always drives out the important.

The Preventive Toolbox

If governments and intergovernmental organisations are of the mind to do something about conflict prevention, what should they do? What are the measures available in the preventive toolbox? Exploring this issue in any useful detail would involve looking at much more than we have time for now – the different causes of conflict (grievance or something else) to which those tools may be responsive;[1] what kinds of measures may be appropriate when; and how those measures might most usefully be operationalised. All I can really do now is hint at the breadth and complexity of the options available by summarising under two headings: structural measures and direct measures, the most familiar preventive options available (Bjorkdahl 1999; Lund 1996).

Structural Measures

Political

Democratic institution – and capacity – building; constitutional power-sharing and redistribution arrangements; confidence building measures between different community groups; funding and training support for democratic opposition groups.

Economic

Development assistance and cooperation to address inequitable distribution of resources; promotion of economic growth and opportunity; aid made conditional on structural reform.

Legal

Building effective and non-corrupt judicial and police systems; formal protection of minority rights; establishment of local human rights commissions.

Military

Reform, professionalisation and civilian control of the military; encouragement of, and adherence to, arms control and disarmament regimes.

Direct Measures

Political/Diplomatic

Fact-finding missions; dialogue and mediation; international appeals (from subtle and encouraging to 'naming and shaming'); threat of political sanctions (diplomatic isolation, suspension of organisation membership); targeted personal sanctions (visas, bank accounts; non-official 'second track' dialogue and problem-solving workshops).

Economic

Threat of trade and financial sanctions; withdrawal of investment; threat of withdrawal of IMF or World Bank support; curtailment of economic aid.

Legal

Mediation; arbitration; adjudication; threat of application of international criminal process.

Military

Preventive deployment; threat of use of military force.

This list still only scratches the surface of discussing the range of options available, not only at the stage of preventing the initial *outbreak* of conflict, but also at the later stages of preventing its *escalation* and preventing its *recurrence*, bearing in mind that in these later stages of prevention many of the techniques available are indistinguishable from those involved in conflict resolution.

The question on which I do feel it is worth spending a little more time here – both because it is so important and because it is so often sped over – is the third condition for effective conflict prevention: the mobilisation of political will.

Mobilising Political Will

The difficulty with most discussions of political will is that we spend more time lamenting its absence than analysing what it means. We tend to talk about it as a single missing ingredient – the gelatine without which the dish won't set.

The trouble with this metaphor, or any other way of thinking about 'political will' as a single, simple factor in the equation, is that it understates the sheer complexity of what is involved. To mobilise political will does not mean just finding that elusive packet of gelatine, but rather working your way through a whole cupboardful of further ingredients. What, then, are those ingredients?

Institutional Measures

In the first place, some of these are institutional. There is a great deal to be said for having some institutionalisation and routinisation of prevention, someone or some group within the system whose responsibility it is to think about prevention, and devise and recommend, at the highest levels of power, appropriate policy responses. Another way of putting this is in terms of deliberately trying to build, through more focused arrangements of this kind, a 'culture of prevention'. There have been some encouraging recent developments of this kind in a number of foreign affairs and development bureaucracies, including those in Britain.

More substantial organisational innovations are also possible. Probably the most successful example of the approach of creating a new organisation on the principle that there is thereby a better chance of its functions being employed, has been the OSCE's appointment of a High Commissioner on National Minorities. Max Van der Stoel's full-time application over many years to the task of devising and encouraging preventive measures to stop ethnic communities tearing at each other's throats in many parts of Europe has been hugely more effective than a series of case-by-case diplomatic excursions is likely to have been.

If you are going to get things to happen in political and governmental systems, overcoming the inbuilt inertia which seems to afflict them all, the other crucial institutional element is some decision-forcing mechanism, something to bring the issue to the top of the decisionmaker's in-tray. In the case of conflict prevention, there is nothing as readily implementable as, for example, the agenda-forcing associated with the annual budget process, though regularly timetabled report and review sessions can work with the occasional idiosyncratic minister who happens to possess a disciplined cast of mind.

The best attention-getter and decision-forcer, apart from a real crisis itself, is likely to be media attention, and it is always a prime objective of those outside government, including NGOs, to concentrate the minds of the powerful in this way.

The Right Arguments for the Right People

Institutional innovations will only take one so far in mobilising the political will to get something done about prevention. From my own experience both in government and beating on the doors of governments, one just has to recognise that there are key individuals at or near the top of the food chains, and at the end of the day one has to find good arguments that will appeal to them. The well-equipped political-will-mobiliser needs to be armed, as I see it, with five different kinds of argument in favour of preventive action.

Moral Argument

However base and self-interested their actual motives may be, governments always like to be seen (both nationally and internationally) as acting from higher motives. Preventing human suffering, and all the catastrophic loss and misery associated with deadly conflict, can act as both an inspiring and a legitimising motive in almost any political context. Getting this moral motive to work means, however, being able to convey a sense of urgency and reality about the threat to human life involved in a particular situation – always difficult when there's no blood or amputees for CNN to film.

Financial Argument

The best financial argument for preventive action (whether through military action, humanitarian relief assistance, post-conflict reconstruction, or all three) is that it is likely to be cheaper, and by many orders of magnitude, than responding after the event.

This is not a hard argument to establish. For example, after the Gulf War I asked my Department to assess the cost to the allies of waging it, as compared with what the cost would have been in setting up a credible worldwide system of preventive diplomacy centres, staffed by professionals, which might conceivably have averted Iraq's invasion of Kuwait (still generally acknowledged to be one of history's best examples of missed opportunities for such diplomacy). The result? Cost of establishing the centres $21 million; material cost to the allies of fighting the war – not to Iraq, and leaving aside any calculation of human cost – $70 *billion*.

National Interest Argument

Preventive action can often serve a country's national interests as very narrowly and traditionally defined in security and economic terms. Avoiding the disintegration of a neighbour, with the refugee outflows and general regional security destabilisation associated with it, can be a compelling motive in many contexts. National economic interests can often be equally well served by keeping resource supply lines, trade routes and markets undisrupted. Whatever may have been the case in the past, these days peace is generally regarded as much better for business than war.

There is another dimension of the national interest which is highly relevant here. It is what I have been arguing for some years is every country's national interest in being, and being seen to be, a good international citizen. There is a great deal of direct reciprocal benefit to be gained in an interdependent, globalised world where nobody can solve all their own problems: my assistance for you today in solving your drugs and terrorism problem might reasonably lead you to be more willing to help solve my environmental problem tomorrow. The interest in being *seen* to be a good international citizen is simply the reputational benefit that a country can win for itself, over time, by being willing to pitch into international tasks regularly for motives that appear to be relatively self-less.

Domestic Politics Argument

Making an argument that will address domestic political concerns is a subtler business than just calculating what the majority reaction will be. Governments (even those directly dependent for their support on the ballot box) often do things without knowing what is the majority view, and in some cases even when they know that the majority sentiment might be against the proposed action. What matters more is that they have arguments that will appeal to, or at least not alienate, their own political support base; and that they have arguments that they can use to deflate, or at least defend against, the attacks of their political opponents.

A good deal of the political debate, when it comes to preventive measures, is really shadow play, in which it is enough that the government be seen to be acting competently and credibly. As often as not, there won't *be* a majority reaction to have to take into account, and if there is one, it will be muted. This is because few issues, when it comes to prevention, are really likely to have strong political salience, in the sense of directly winning or losing a government enough votes to be relevant to its survival.

The kind of arguments a government will find most useful in dealing with its supporters, and its opponents, will depend largely on what kind of government it is. Governments of a left-of-centre persuasion, if there are any these days, will by and large find more comfort with their support base in moral arguments, and in national interest arguments of the good international citizenship variety, while governments of the right have traditionally drawn more comfort from economic and security interest arguments.

Manageability Argument

There is one final kind of argument that it is very helpful to be able to make in advocating any kind of preventive strategy to any colour of government in the world, and that is that the commitment is somehow finite, and won't be the forerunner for more and more demands: in other words, that it is limited, and manageable.

It is not always easy to make this argument persuasively. It has to be acknowledged that prevention won't always be successful – and making an effort at prevention might be seen, reasonably, as implying a commitment to full-scale reactive response if prevention fails, although there will always be separate criteria to be applied, and separate arguments to be had, on that score. Certainly in the case of deterrent prevention by use of military threats, credibility can be maintained only if there is an absolute willingness to follow it through.

One of the biggest fears that all governments have is that of precedent: that having been drawn into a preventive response in this situation, what is to stop the country being drawn into a never-ending and ever-expanding set of such responses, in a world where conflict, and the threat of conflict, seem to be forever growing?

The best possible argument to be able to make in response to this fear is that which is suggested by the work of Ted Robert Gurr and his team at the University of Maryland – *viz.*, that notwithstanding appearances, conflict not only between states but also within states is declining, and there is every reason to believe that this trend will continue. In their just-published survey *Peace and Conflict 2001* (Gurr, Marshall and Khosla 2000),[2] which is formidably detailed and meticulous, the Gurr team concludes that while serious armed violence obviously persists in parts of the world, 'the turbulence that accompanied the end of the Cold War was largely contained by the end of 2000', and that the 'number and magnitude of armed conflicts within and among states have lessened since the early 1990s by nearly half'. This is extremely comforting for governments – and extremely useful as a result for those advocating higher government action profiles in the areas of potential conflict that do remain.

Generally, I do not think there is any reason for particular despair on the subject of political will. It is always going to be difficult to mobilise for the preventive causes we care about, but it is not impossible. There is a lesson here, and especially for NGOs – that we have to work much harder at advocacy than we have been, and adopt a much more extensive repertoire of arguments, and much more carefully targeted arguments, than we have been in the habit of doing.

The Role of NGOs – and the International Crisis Group

This is not the occasion to be waxing either lyrical or indignant about the growing place of non-governmental organisations in international affairs (*Economist* 2000; Falk and Strauss 2001). It is sufficient to say that the last time someone tried to count the number of these (for the Global Governance report in 1995), there were 29,000 of us operating internationally, and a lot more have been created since; that NGOs operate in as many different areas as life itself and defy easy classification; that we are no longer as easy to ignore as we used to be; and that by and large governments and intergovernmental organisations are seeing increasing virtue and utility in drawing upon the skills and experience that a great many NGOs can offer.

In the peace, security and human rights band of the spectrum, in which my own organisation, the International Crisis Group, is located, if one leaves aside the aid and humanitarian relief organisations (whose work does quite often overlap with what the others of us are doing), the most active, prominent and useful NGOs generally concentrate on one or other of three quite distinct kinds of activity, *viz.*, thinking, talking or doing.

The 'thinking' NGOs are by and large the research institutes and think tanks, whose product is books and papers, and who engage in data gathering, idea generating, network building, paper publishing and conference organising. Their rationale tends to be contributing to the ideas pool and general debate, though some are more sharply focused.

The 'talking' or advocacy NGOs (for example, Asia Watch and Amnesty International) engage in research and analysis, but their primary emphasis is on spotlighting governmental abuses and engaging in tom-tom beating advocacy accordingly.

The 'doing' NGOs (Search for Common Ground, International Alert and the Community of San Egidio are examples of these) tend to focus on field operations, which bring people together, build confidence and mediate disputes. They also tend to be greatly involved in improving governance through training and general capacity building programs.

My own organisation is something of a hybrid, but I think a good example of what NGOs can and should be doing to help the cause of conflict prevention. ICG concentrates essentially on conflict prevention and containment rather than on conflict resolution or peace-building more generally; and, while being very much field-based, engages in research, analysis and advocacy (that is, thinking and talking) rather than operationally doing things.

The group was formed in 1995 by a group of prominent internationalists and foreign policy specialists who wanted to create a wholly independent new organisation which might be capable of injecting (through high quality analysis, policy prescription and advocacy) a little more substance and responsiveness into the international conflict prevention effort.

ICG now has a team of 55 worldwide, with field operations in Africa, Asia and the Balkans and advocacy offices in Brussels (the headquarters), Washington, New York and Paris; and a budget of US$6 million, with 40 per cent of its funding coming from 16 governments, 44 per cent from major foundations and 16 per cent from individuals. Last year we produced and distributed in printed form and electronically, to many thousands of recipients, 49 reports and briefing papers on the prevention or containment of conflict in 18 countries; and had in the last 12 months 7 million hits on and half a million visitors to our website, www.crisisweb.org.

Measuring the impact and effectiveness of an organisation like ours is extremely difficult. One can measure a whole lot of easily quantifiable things, which will give one a picture of the level of output, of activity, of media exposure, of website access, of the number of supportive letters and comments from Foreign Ministers, or of the increase or decrease in funding support which all this is generating.

One can measure the extent to which one's policy recommendations bear fruit, in the sense of being implemented by someone, somewhere, at some time, wholly or in part, but that exercise has its limitations. We make hundreds of recommendations in the course of a year, ranging from the very narrowly focused (for example, local government administration in Mitrovica or Mostar) and others much larger, for example a security guarantee for Montenegro or a resetting of peace priorities in Central Africa. Many of them are implemented, but there is always the difficulty of establishing a cause-and-effect relationship when they are; and when they are not, there are often other good explanations than that they were wrong-headed, for example, that they were overtaken by events, or were seen as right but not yet timely, or affordable.

About the only personal contribution I think I can completely confidently claim to have made to the overthrow of Slobodan Milosevic last year, despite all my innumerable face-to-face meetings and speeches and print and electronic media excursions on the Balkans, was acknowledged in this letter I received in November, after addressing an Institute for International Mediation and Conflict Resolution (IIMCR) seminar in the Hague a few weeks earlier:

> One of our female students from Belgrade was particularly energised by your talk. As a leading member of Otpor, she served as the go-between in getting the gentleman to drive his construction crane into the parliament building.

There is no doubt that you need a certain masochistic streak to get involved in the conflict prevention and containment business. Because the blood is not yet running in the streets the media do not find it nearly as fascinating as conflict resolution, and the attention of decision-makers is hard to grab. The most frustrating thing of all is that when a government or an intergovernmental body, urged on by NGOs like mine, does actually put together a conflict-prevention or containment strategy which triumphantly succeeds, so that instead of the feared violence nothing at all happens, then you can be absolutely certain that nobody will notice. And, of course, for a politician to perform good works without anyone actually noticing is like having a tooth pulled without anaesthetic.

The frustrations notwithstanding, this is a deeply satisfying business to be in. Nothing is worse to contemplate, against the background of all the horror that has been wrought this last century, and all the avoidable horror of the last ten years, than the thought of the pain and terror and misery that lies ahead for so many men, women and children if we fail yet again to prevent what is preventable, and deadly conflict again breaks out. To play a part, however small, in making that horror just a little less likely is to be as richly rewarded as one could ever be.

References

Bjorkdahl, Annika (1999) 'Developing a Toolbox for Conflict Prevention'. Swedish Institute of International Affairs.

Economist (2000) 'NGOs: Sins of the Secular Missionaries'. January 29.

Falk, Richard and Andrew Strauss (2001) 'Toward Global Parliament'. *Foreign Affairs* 80: 1 January/February.

Gardner, Anne-Marie (2000) 'Putting Prevention on Solid Ground: Recent Findings from Studies of Conflict Trends and Causes'. Paper for IPA International Policy Conference *From Reaction to Prevention: Opportunities for the UN System in the New Millennium.* New York 13-14 April.

Gurr, Ted Robert, Monty G. Marshall and Deepa Khosla (2000) 'Peace and Conflict 2001: A Global Survey of Armed Conflicts, Self-Determination Movements and Democracy'. Center for International Development and Conflict Management, University of Maryland (*www.bsos.umd.edu/cidcm/peace.htm*).

Lund, Michael (1996) *Preventing Violent Conflicts.* Washington DC: USIP.

Reilly, Ben (2000) 'The Africanisation of the South Pacific'. *Australian Journal of International Affairs* 54: 3.

ENDNOTES

[1] One recent compilation of the relevant literature identified four distinct types of factors repeatedly occurring as prominent causes of conflict: insecurity (often linked to weak or collapsed state institutions); inequality (discrimination across recognised groups in society); private incentives (political or economic incentives for leaders and masses); and perceptions (group histories and myths, often used instrumentally by elites). See Gardner 2000.

[2] It should be acknowledged that while the Gurr team's findings have been widely cited and embraced, some other peace researchers, notably Peter Wallensteen (see Uppsala Conflict Data Project, www.pcr.uu.se/data.htm), are critical of its methodology and contest its conclusions.

Chapter 3

STRATEGIC DIMENSIONS OF THE CRISIS IN ASIA

Bob Catley
University of Otago
New Zealand

INTRODUCTION

In a realist analysis, the states of East Asia have emerged from the period of colonialism and Cold War to form a classic regional inter-state system in which each pursues its own interests within the confines established by the advantages of membership of the system itself. The partial exceptions to this are North Korea (Buzo 1999), which has recently shown quite strong indications of wanting to emerge from its isolationism, and Myanmar, which has tried to do the same thing. There are also residues of the Cold War in the form of several remaining communist regimes in North Korea, the PRC, Vietnam and Laos, and other governments with personnel whose careers were first forged during that contest, including the USA, South Korea and, arguably, Australia and New Zealand. What marks out the Asian regional international system from other regional systems in the contemporary world is that there is little by way of a generalised regional institutional architecture in the security, political or even economic sphere. The partial exceptions to this generalisation are limited in either geographic or functional scope.

The geographically based institutions include most notably the Association of South East Asian Nations (ASEAN). ASEAN was formed in 1967 and was until recently depicted as one of the world's most successful regional political associations. It ranked only perhaps behind the European Union in its historical record of producing cooperation and integration among its member states when previously there had been conflict and discord. During the last four years that record has come to look less impressive as the old long-term leadership personnel and regime structures of the member countries have changed, often as a result of the regional financial crisis and its knock on effects. The 'ASEAN way' of mutual admiration has given way to more determined pursuit of individual interest and, in some instances, ready criticism. In many respects this new openness may be no bad thing. But ASEAN is geographically limited.

Nonetheless, ASEAN did spawn in the 1990s the ASEAN Regional Forum (ARF), which expanded out of the dialogue partners' meetings to produce regular, annual contacts between the major powers of the region and then ASEAN plus three (PRC, Japan, South Korea). Coupled with other bilateral relationships, this has produced a growth in commitments to confidence building measures, such as publishing annual defence white papers to reassure other states about military intentions, dialogues about difficult issues like the South China Sea, cultural, educational and diplomatic exchanges, and even regular summit meetings to provide some person-to-person contacts. In the world of international power politics such developments of an international civil society can surely do no harm.

In contrast, the Asia Pacific Economic Cooperation (APEC) has proven to be almost entirely an instrument for economic liberalisation – and costume manufacture and distribution – but one that could not act in the face of a real economic/financial crisis for several of its members in 1997-98. Its inability to act even in its designated sphere – economics – left little confidence in its capacity to intervene in strategic issues. It was merely an accident of timing that enabled the New Zealand APEC summit of 1999 to be the site of important negotiations which produced the INTERFET intervention in East Timor.

This scant regional security architecture compares unfavourably with what has emerged in Europe since the end of the Cold War. There, the expansion of NATO and the European Union, both of which are still proceeding, promises to produce parallel, overlapping but differentiated mechanisms for economic, social, political and strategic integration and problem resolution. Neither ASEAN nor APEC have gone this far, nor seem likely to.

In the Asia Pacific region there are also a number of more limited multilateral organisations. These include: the US security agreements with South Korea and Japan; the emerging relationships between China and Russia and between China and Myanmar; the South Pacific Forum; and the ANZUS and ANZAC treaties. In the main, however, these are not so much systems of regional security as treaty relationships designed to pursue joint national interests. They are, in other words, with the partial exception of the South Pacific Forum, which is somewhat more than just an organisation for administering Australian regional hegemony, classical tools of power politics. The region of East Asia/western Pacific has an international system which has more in common with the world of nineteenth-century European power politics than it does with the twenty-first century Atlantic world of states being integrated into a larger political community.

In Asia, while it is the case that for most states of the region the problems of adjustment to the age of globalisation have replaced strategic issues as the dominant priority, national security always lurks near the surface of much state decision making.

In simple realist terms the major attributes of the region are:

1. a dominant great power, the US (which is also systemically hegemonic);
2. a declining great power, the Russian Federation;
3. two potentially rising great powers, in China and Japan;
4. a number of lesser powers with different interests to pursue like Thailand, Malaysia and Vietnam (some of which are quite large and potentially powerful, but temporarily disabled, like Indonesia, and a unified Korea);
5. many lesser states unlikely to be strategically important for the foreseeable future, like Laos, Cambodia, Brunei and East Timor;

6. and the mostly even smaller states of the western Pacific including Australia, Papua New Guinea, and New Zealand.

THE USA: THE HEGEMONIC POWER

Since its victory over the Soviet Union the United States has emerged as the hegemonic power in the international system. It is the dominant military, economic and political power in the global system and this applies regionally to East Asia and the entire Pacific (Mosler and Catley 2000).

The Presidency of Bill Clinton marked the transformation of an uncertain but victorious US finding it difficult to define its strategic goals as a hegemon, to an ascendant and confidant 'Global America' pursuing globalisation with considerable success. While much of this objective can be defined in terms of economics and then, to a lesser extent, culture, it has had to be buttressed by the application of state power. This has been most evident in the use of force against what were then and are now again, called 'rogue states' by the US. Military power was used directly against Iraq and Serbia, vicariously against Syria, Afghanistan and Sudan, and threatened against North Korea and even the PRC (Catley 1999).

The instruments of US power in East Asia are the global power projection capabilities which have been able to transform almost the entire US military structure into a medium time (about a month) deployment force; a naval and air power based military command which extends from California to the Persian Gulf; and pre-positioned forces and installations in states as diverse as Japan, South Korea and Australia. These forces have stood behind US political activities in the region for the last decade and are the foundations for its capacity to constrain China, deter North Korea and restructure East Timor (Weeks and Meconis 1999).

Does US policy look likely to continue in this vein under the new administration?

There are four main indicators for the direction of US policy under the new administration of President W. Bush: the stated policy intentions of its personnel; the existing DOD document, recently published in 2000 and not disowned; the inaugural Presidential address of 16 January; and the continuing interests of the US.

- The personnel of the new Bush administration are represented by its critics as being dominated by the staff of his father's team of the last stanza of the Cold War. There is of course much substance to this claim. As a result, it may be expected that some of the strains in relations with both Russia and China of a decade ago will re-emerge. This is particularly so over the issues of an anti-ballistic missile (ABM) defence system and Taiwan, although, in the latter case, a clearer US doctrine than 'strategic ambiguity' may well be an improvement.

Colin Powell, the Secretary of State, made his name during the application of US military power to the protection of access to that most important of tradeable commodities, oil, against the attempts of the Iraqi militarist regime to control half the world's known reserves. In this his career does not differ markedly from that of his predecessor who waged war against another militarist regime, that of Serbia, to establish US domination across the European continent via NATO. Kosovo was Madeleine's war.

According to the semi-official pen portrait in the *New York Times* (2000), Donald H. Rumsfeld began his first tour of duty as Secretary of Defense when the Vietnam War had just been lost. His supporters say Rumsfeld, 68, will not be stuck in the Cold War. His one-time protégé Dick Cheney, a former Defense Secretary under George Bush, is now the Vice-President. The Bush administration will seek to increase defence spending and win Congressional approval for a national missile defence program.

During his first stint at the Pentagon, Rumsfeld also tried to increase the defence budget, and re-emerged as a leading force in Republican circles on national security issues. He led an independent commission which in 1998 found that the ballistic missile threat from countries like North Korea and Iran was growing, and appeared more serious than the intelligence community had previously concluded.

Rumsfeld, Cheney and General Powell are all advocates of a strong US military force and substantial defence spending.

Condoleezza Rice, the new National Security Adviser, is less well known than many of her predecessors but has revealed some of her strategic thinking, particularly about Russia, her speciality. In 'Promoting the National Interest', in *Foreign Affairs* (Rice 2000), she wrote:

> Power matters, both the exercise of power by the United States and the ability of others to exercise it. Yet many in the United States are (and have always been) uncomfortable with the notions of power politics, great powers, and power balances. In an extreme form, this discomfort leads to a reflexive appeal instead to notions of international law and norms, and the belief that the support of many states – or even better, of institutions like the United Nations – is essential to the legitimate exercise of power. The 'national interest' is replaced with 'humanitarian interests' or the interests of 'the international community'.

She added:

> The Kosovo war was conducted incompetently, in part because the administration's goals kept shifting and in part because it was not, at the start, committed to the decisive use of military force....If it is worth fighting for, you had better be prepared to win. Also, there must be a political game plan that will permit the withdrawal of our forces – something that is still completely absent in Kosovo....The president must remember that the military is a special instrument. It is lethal, and it is meant to be. It is not a civilian police force. It is not a political referee. And it is most certainly not designed to build a civilian society....
>
> Foreign policy in a Republican administration will most certainly be internationalist....But it will also proceed from the firm ground of the national interest, not from the interests of an illusory international community. America can exercise power without arrogance and pursue its interests without hectoring and bluster.

- The Department of Defense annual report document of 2000 shows that under the Democrats the US was continuing its policy of essentially maintaining military superiority from California to the Gulf to the extent of the 'two and a half wars' doctrine. The Republicans only criticised this as being too little and under-resourced. We may expect US military capabilities in the Asia Pacific region, as elsewhere, to be augmented. To judge by other statements, however, notably those of Colin Powell, US forces would be used more specifically for US national interest purposes. Issues of humanitarian intervention would be downgraded and regional security issues hand-balled to allies wherever possible. The DOD Report already said:

East Asia and the Pacific Rim

U.S. Defense Objectives. The United States seeks a stable and economically prosperous East Asia that embraces democratic reform and market economics. Central to achieving this goal are the United States' strong alliance relationships within the region, especially with Japan, Australia, and the Republic of Korea (ROK). In addition, it is critical to continue to engage China so that it contributes to regional stability and acts as a responsible member of the international community. The United States desires a peaceful resolution of the Korean conflict resulting in a non-nuclear, democratic, reconciled, and ultimately reunified Peninsula, as well as the peaceful resolution of the region's other disputes, including that between Taiwan and the People's Republic of China. Successful counters to terrorism, illegal drug trafficking, and nuclear proliferation are also major U.S. goals for the region.

U.S. Regional Defense Posture and Activities. The United States is committed to maintaining its current level of military capability in East Asia and the Pacific Rim. This capability allows the United States to play a key role as security guarantor and regional balancer. The United States will continue a forward presence policy, in cooperation with its allies, that reflects its interests in the region and allows for adjustments in the U.S. force posture over time to meet the changing demands of the security environment. Today, the United States stations or deploys approximately 100,000 military personnel in the region. Of these personnel, over half are stationed in Japan and close to 40 per cent are in the ROK. The United States will seek to continue and build upon bilateral and multilateral exercises with key states in the region, including the ROK, Japan, Thailand, the Philippines, and Australia.

The most significant near-term danger in the region is the continuing military threat posed by the Democratic People's Republic of Korea. The United States remains fully committed to its treaty obligations to assist the ROK in defending against North Korean aggression. The United States also seeks a Korean Peninsula free of NBC weapons – a goal shared with the ROK and other allies and friends in the region. The U.S.-North Korean Agreed Framework froze North Korea's nuclear facilities at Yongbyon and Taechon under International Atomic Energy Agency inspection. The Agreed Framework still provides the best means to secure North Korean compliance with its non-proliferation commitment under the Nuclear Non-Proliferation Treaty. The Department is also working with its Pacific allies to enhance their collective capabilities to deter and defeat use of chemical or biological weapons.

The U.S. security alliance with Japan is the linchpin of its security policy in Asia and is key to many U.S. global objectives. Both nations have moved actively in recent years to strengthen this bilateral relationship and update the framework and structure of joint cooperation to reflect the security environment. U.S. efforts to build on strong alliances with other nations in the region, especially Australia, buttress the U.S. goal of ensuring stability in Southeast Asia, an area of growing economic and political importance. The continued strengthening of U.S. security dialogues and confidence-building measures with the members of the Association of Southeast Asian Nations (ASEAN) through the ASEAN Regional Forum is one of many ways in which the United States is working to enhance political, military, and economic ties with friends and allies in Southeast Asia. The Asia-Pacific Center for Security Studies is a key U.S. initiative that promotes mutual understanding and cooperation by providing an academic forum for military and civilian decision makers from the United States and Asia to exchange ideas and explore regional security challenges.

The Asian financial crisis has shaken the region's assumptions about uninterrupted economic development. Indonesia's economic and political difficulties in particular will pose challenges to the established order both internally and in the region. Continued U.S. engagement in Indonesia will help promote the stability necessary to manage this difficult period of change.

> Because of China's critical importance in the Asia-Pacific region, the United States is working to integrate China more deeply into the international community. Specifically, the United States engages China in order to promote regional stability and economic prosperity while securing China's adherence to international standards on weapons non-proliferation, international trade, and human rights. The United States also seeks greater transparency in China's defense program, including its planning and procurement processes, and will continue to engage China in dialogue aimed at fostering cooperation and confidence-building. Military exchange programs, port visits, and professional seminars contribute to this dialogue and are aimed at building lasting relationships that will foster cooperation and build confidence among U.S. and Chinese leaders. (US Department of Defense 2000a)

- During the 2000 US Presidential elections, less emphasis was placed on foreign policy than had been the case during the last five decades. In part, this was due to agreement on the major issue, globalisation. In his inauguration address President George W. Bush also placed little emphasis on foreign policy issues, although he stated:

> We will build our defenses beyond challenge, lest weakness invite challenge. We will confront weapons of mass destruction, so that a new century is spared new horrors.
> The enemies of liberty and our country should make no mistake, America remains engaged in the world, by history and by choice, shaping a balance of power that favors freedom. We will defend our allies and our interests. We will show purpose without arrogance. We will meet aggression and bad faith with resolve and strength. And to all nations, we will speak for the values that gave our nation birth. (*New York Times* 2001a)

- Finally, of course, US interests in the regional have not substantially changed because of a change in administration. In the past these have been described as including: over US$500 billion in trade (1998); the maintenance of open trade routes and Sea Lanes of Communication (SLOCs); extensive investments; the maintenance and expansion of open, growing, capitalist economies; and the prevention of a single power, or allied group of powers, establishing their control over the region. To that end, the US has maintained an extensive military presence in a command which stretches from California to the Gulf:

> US overseas presence in the Asia-Pacific region, including the continued maintenance of approximately 100,000 military personnel for the foreseeable future, will continue to promote regional strategic interests, and provide evidence of undiminished US commitment and engagement. Our force structure will continue to reflect our conception of regional strategic requirements and the capabilities necessary to support them, and remain the subject of continued consultation with our allies. In coming years, the United States will also examine new modes of sustaining and supporting this presence within the region. The continued development of support – outside the traditional basing structure – in such nations as Australia, Indonesia, Thailand, Malaysia, Brunei, Singapore and the Philippines will enhance US strategic interests in maintaining regional stability and a credible power projection capability in the region and beyond, including to the Arabian Gulf when necessary. (US Department of Defense 2000a)

In the substantial policy area of globalisation there seems little reason to believe that the Bush administration will differ much from that of Clinton. Indeed, it may be anticipated that with organised labour and protected industry supporting the Democrats – and in some instances Ralph Nader – Bush's pursuit of a free trading global economy may be even more determined than Clinton's. His personnel are otherwise even more oriented towards the national interest. The Democrats developed into a liberal, institution building and power projecting team under Clinton, and especially under Madeleine Albright in his second administration. As far as may be determined, Colin Powell, the Gulf War notwithstanding, is less keen on the use of force than Albright.

The thrust of the late Clinton administration was economic globalisation, although the threat or use of US military power was periodically deployed to achieve that outcome – as against North Korea, the PRC, Serbia, and Iraq. The Bush administration is more likely to be more geo-politically realist. Rumsfeld will probably be more committed to building greater US military power and expenditure than Cohen, Dick Cheney more oriented to geo-political power than the Internet and ecology than Al Gore, and Dr. Rice is more classical in her realist posture than Sandy Berger.

This provides a picture of a US which is likely to be more committed to: free trade and a liberal economy; the use of military power to pursue US national interests; a reduced inclination to act multilaterally; and a lesser inclination to use US power for systemic purposes depicted in Albright's phrase, 'the indispensable nation'. The new personnel are less ideological, less liberal, a trifle more isolationist and rhetorically more realist. But, of course, it is early days.

On specific issues, the Republicans seem less committed than the Clinton administration to the liberal belief that economic growth will produce political development, liberalisation and a greater harmony of interests with the old adversaries of the US in East Asia like China, North Korea and even Russia. They are more likely, therefore, to take out military insurance policies, like the regional anti-missile defence system. They are also likely to be more precise about their intention to use force in protection of their allies in Taiwan and South Korea, if this should become necessary. This may involve the abandoning of the doctrine of 'strategic ambiguity'. There will probably be less rhetoric and policy based on the idea that the more the PRC and North Korea can be brought into the community of nations, the better will regional security be served, and more emphasis placed on the need for the US to maintain its military superiority, in order, they may well believe, to avoid the need to use it.

This is not to say the Bush administration will not pursue a global economy; it is to suggest that this will be seen as a distinct agenda from that of regional stability, that will be regarded as more dependent on its strategic policies than on modernisation theory. In short, the basis for US hegemony in the system as a whole, and in East Asia in particular, will not be eroded by the new Republican administration. But it will be less likely to resort to the use of force in support of it.

Finally, the so-called unipolar moment of US power is now coupled with a less clearly dominant US electoral support for a coherent global role. The US Congress is now evenly divided, and thus is likely to be more resistant to (and the people are more sceptical about) Clinton's idea of a US global responsibility – or Albright's concept of the 'indispensable nation'. The US, it seems, is more interested on those inside its tent than outside. In this mood it may well expect friends and allies to do more as it has already made clear to both Australia, which seems likely to respond, and to New Zealand, which is unlikely to respond.

State Challengers to the US: The Russian Federation

There are three states which might have the capacity to pose a substantial challenge to US regional hegemony: the Russian Federation, the PRC and Japan.

The collapse of the Soviet Union in December 1991 marked the end of the Cold War. The decisiveness of this defeat was masked by the decision of the US not to celebrate its victory in order to support more readily the new Russian administration in Moscow headed by its ally/client, Boris Yeltsin. But the impact on the former client states of the Soviet Union in East Asia should not be underestimated. North Korea was most severely effected because its subsidised, cheap oil supply from the Soviet Union was cut off with considerable impact on its economic performance. Much of the North Korean economic collapse can be attributed to that cause (together with the inability of its rigid economy to adjust to it). Some of the Vietnamese problems of economic development also derive from its difficulty in adjusting a COMECON (Council for Mutual Economic Assistance; Communist Economic Conference) oriented economy to one located in a globalised world economy.

Russia no longer represents the failed ideal of communism and is merely the successor state of the Soviet Union. Its power is now based on a diminished economy still finding any growth difficult to achieve, a population halved and now shrinking, a military under-funded, poorly serviced and damaged by a succession of defeats, and an inability to project power even into its own near abroad (Mosler and Catley 2000, ch.6). During the Clinton administration this was somewhat offset by the determination of Washington to treat the Yeltsin and then Putin regimes as a co-superpower because of the Russian nuclear arsenal. This diplomacy got Moscow into the G-8 and other serious high level negotiations where it had otherwise little right to be.

The Republicans seem determined to treat Russia more as a rival than an ally. Dr. Rice has already suggested that the US has little interest in building the power of Russia in order that it may better rival US strategy. The commitment to continue with the ABM deployment is likely to produce greater Russian hostility amid claims that this breaks treaties which go back as far as 1972 and 1974. But in the end Russia can do little about it. Yeltsin was committed to containing Russian military expenditure to 3 per cent of GDP – a similar percentage to the US, pre-Bush. This will not produce a military machine to rival that of the US, nor indeed provide a significant power projection capability except where the Russian land forces can engage even weaker forces. This probably means only Central Asia. As a player in the wider diplomacy of East Asia, Russia is of extremely limited importance. As in the European theatre, Russia has demonstrated a model descent, achieved rapidly, and now shows no significant power projection capacity.

Under Boris Yeltsin, Moscow was committed to winding down its military forces to an expenditure level of under 4 per cent of GDP. Since the economy was in apparently permanent decline, this amounted to a rapid demobilisation of the kind that occurred throughout the 1990s. President Putin is unlikely to change this policy dramatically, although he is more dependent than his predecessor on military force for his legitimacy, having eased himself into power at the same time as finally achieving some sort of victory in Chechnya. Nonetheless, unlike its Soviet predecessor, the Russian Federation regime is not dependent on revolutionary ideology, global expansion or military might for its survival. As such, it is as likely as that of Yeltsin to continue to give highest priority to the economic reforms in the surviving hope that these will generate substantial growth. There is now some literature describing the failure of the rapid economic liberalisation of the early 1990s in Russia. There is also some by participants apologising for their rather over-enthusiastic application of the World Bank/IMF canon. Whatever their validity, it now seems that the creation of a successful, liberal democratic political and economic structure requires more than state deregulation. It may involve a broader range of sociological, cultural and legal artifices than have yet been obtainable in Russia.

Under Vladimir Putin, the dictatorial aspects of the Russian political system are commonly believed to be already more in evidence. The recreation of the capacity to project serious power is still far from the official Russian agenda, notwithstanding the recent despatch of a Russian naval flotilla into East Asian waters for probably the first time since the Cold War. While Russia may complain at US behaviour – over, for example, a missile defence system – it is difficult to envisage it putting these developments before US assistance for its economic plans, assistance which will be more difficult to win from a Bush administration if Dr. Rice's views are a guide. Even if it were to do so (and in 2001 there are signs of such action involving, particularly, weapons and technology transfers to the PRC and Iran), its power base is presently insufficient to mount a general or even regional strategic opposition to the US.

State Challengers to the US: The PRC and Japan

The PRC

In 1989 the People's Republic of China (PRC) turned from being a US ally in the global contest against Soviet-backed communism, to a more carefully scrutinised, old-style communist political dictatorship. The Tiananmen Square repression marked a key event in this transition. The regime itself, almost paradoxically, also changed its orientation, but away from Marxist Leninist ideology for regime legitimation towards a more market-oriented economy and nationalistic political vocabulary. The regime became more determined in its pursuit of lost territories, the People's Liberation Army seemed to achieve greater influence in resource allocation politics, and economic growth was given even greater attention and indeed accelerated.

The PRC is clearly, so far, a frustrated aspirant for the status of a regional dominant power (Ji 1999). The evidence for this is not to be found in its Cold War behaviour under the previous communist leadership, nor in its statements about its peaceful intentions, nor in the signs of the modernisation of its political and economic system. Rather, it has been modernising its military forces in such a way as to give it the capacity to project power into the regional order. In the realist methodology there is nothing anti-PRC in this conclusion. All states behave like this, including the US as just described. Under Clinton, the US described its pursuit of national interest in terms of liberal ideology. In the case of the PRC, whereas previously it used the rhetoric of socialist and even revolutionary ideology, it now utilises Chinese nationalist terminology and sometimes irredentism, particularly with respect to Taiwan and the South China Sea.

Chinese military forces are being improved with the objective of giving them the capacity to project power. During the 1970s and 1980s PRC military forces were moved away from a pro-Soviet posture to one designed to defend the country against Soviet attack. In the last ten years they have been re-jigged to provide the PRC with an augmented power projection capacity. Alongside this the PLA is trying to develop a rudimentary capacity to fight the US in the event of military conflict and to deter the US from using its vastly superior nuclear arsenal. Important in this respect are the stated purposes of achieving a naval blue water projection capacity; an air strike capability based on the 300 plus SU 27 Flankers acquired from Russia; modernising its nuclear arsenal with a view to being able to strike more distant targets (including the US mainland); a presence in space which might deliver some capacity to disable US space stations for detection, surveillance and targeting; and participation in the so-called Revolution in Military Affairs which could enable a rapid catch-up on US technology by leaping a technological generation. Few of these objectives are likely to be achieved in the near future, particularly while the military embargoes by the US and allied powers stay in place. This explains severe US reactions to transfers of military technology to the PRC by Israel or espionage activities.

The PRC has a long way to go to match the US in military, economic or political terms. Its military capacity does not enable it to project power against the Republic of China (ROC) merely 100 miles across the Taiwan Strait. Its economy is between 10 and 20 per cent of the size of the US economy. Its political system and nationalist/military ideology has the attraction of that of the Burmese dictatorship to anyone who is not ethnic Chinese and for many who are.

Periodically, the PRC attempts to make up for these weaknesses by seeking to establish allies against the dominance of the US. So far it has been unable to form a coalition by the traditional Balance of Power behaviour which realist theory would anticipate. It has purchased military equipment from the Russian Federation and has on several occasions achieved joint declarations that have, among other things, taken a sideswipe at American power. But no lasting and durable anti-American partnership has been possible with either Yeltsin or Putin. It has had more success in forging an anti-US posture with Myanmar, a pariah for other reasons, but this adds little to PRC power. It has won a few friends in the Middle East by weapons and other diplomacy, but these are assets of questionable utility. Similarly, the provision of arms to Pakistan has been of limited diplomatic value, particularly when it has continued to alienate India. The qualified support of Serbia during the Kosovo War yielded limited gains, almost all of which were lost with the fall of Milosevic.

Part of the problem for the PRC involves its inability to offer rewards as great as the US can in the form of access to the processes and institutions of globalisation. Part of the problem is that the PRC claims are nationalist and attract little support from other states which have no interest in whether the PRC controls Taiwan and the South China Sea – or more often are against it. Of course, being both Chinese and (ostensibly, anyway) Marxist, the PRC regime may just be taking a longer term perspective on the matter in looking for outcomes closer to, say, 2050 than this paper intends to allow for. After all, after nearly 50 years the PRC got Hong Kong and Macao back; it may take another mere 30 to do the same for the ROC and the South China Sea. By then the US will have worked its way through at least another four administrations of quite unpredictable complexion.

Japan

The Japanese state was touted as recently as in the 1980s as a potential rival to the power of the US as the Soviet Union declined. Japan has, in the last 50 years, achieved the most rapid rise to over-maturity (Mulgan 2000; and compare with the more optimistic Helweg 2000). The model of political management of a capitalist economy which appeared for 30 years to be more effective than the *laissez faire* practices of the Anglo-Saxons or the welfare statist behaviour of the western Europeans, now looks too ossified to accommodate new technological requirements or commercial organisations. The Japanese economy has been effectively stagnant now for a decade, during which time it has progressively expanded its state sector by continuing but ineffective fiscal stimulations and contracted its foreign trade surpluses. The combination of a sclerotic domestic economy and hollowed out manufacturing sector, exacerbated by sociological trends in demography, immigration and cultural aspirations, has retarded its economy.

This economic stagnation has only worsened the geo-political ambivalence of the political elite. It was already undertaking strategic objectives only at the behest of the Americans. By the late 1980s, however, some politicians were urging an expansion of its strategic responsibility under the US alliance. Some statements had been made to this effect and Japan contributed modestly to some UN peacekeeping operations. In the later 1990s this expanding role was progressively abandoned as a series of administrations came and went, losing further authority with each change of political leadership and the corresponding capacity to lead an expansion of Japan's power projection. By the time of the revision of the responsibilities under the US-Japan Security Treaty in 1998, the Japanese armed forces' role – and indeed that of its territory – had been reduced almost entirely to one subordinate to that of regional US forces.

By 2001 Japan had a lame duck Prime Minister in Mr. Mori, whose authority was further eroded by a renewed deceleration of economic growth and maladroit handling of the collision between a US navy submarine and a Japanese vessel. This account of recent Japanese developments demonstrates the triumph of political will over economic competence. Japan has a limited but real capacity for military power projection; it lacks almost entirely the will to use it.

SITES OF GREAT POWER CONTESTATION

The US, then, is the most powerful nation in the world. For the most part it seeks its objectives in the East Asia region with only limited opposition from the other major powers, which for reasons just described are hamstrung in their capacities.

This is not to say that there are not substantial regional problems involving conflicting claims between important states. Indeed there are several, and every so often they break out into crises, which often have both regional and wider dimensions. The three that are of greatest significance are, in part, remaining legacies of the Cold War. They are, in declining order of short-term importance, the Koreas, Taiwan and the South China Sea.

The Koreas

The total power of a united Korean state of 70 million and a large economy with advanced technological capabilities and strong military forces would be considerable. It is unlikely, however, that it would have the aspiration to project such power substantially, since the focus of both Korean states has been on the peninsula. Since one very costly war and half a century of strategic competition between these two states has involved all major regional powers and the deployment of forces from another 50, there is considerable interest in a peaceful resolution of this issue.

The developments of the last year have been among the most promising of the last 50 years. The lurch towards unification has been occasioned by the economic crisis in North Korea; the regime modification there; the democratisation in the South under a President deeply committed to national unification; and the interests of all great powers involved in a peaceful resolution to the dispute. The end of the Cold War has, albeit belatedly, brought a relaxation of the tensions attendant on the problems of the division of the Korean nation into two hostile states.

The end of the Cold War itself has stimulated these positive developments by weakening the capacity of the North Korean state to sustain its revolutionary character, and by liberalising the South Korean regime and unleashing thereby nationalist sentiments which were previously subsumed by Cold War ideology.

Taiwan

Taiwan remains the most important single site of direct conflict between US and PRC interests. In 1996 it was the occasion for the most public display of force by the US against the PRC since the end of the Cold War. Since then the issue has been hosed down substantially by an apparently unlikely series of events, including the election of a non-KMT ROC President on the island state with an apparent commitment to developing an independent state. Nonetheless, President Chen Shui-bian did not bring with him an eight decade long history of hostility with ideological, personal, family and financial dimensions.

The democratisation of the ROC has provided the impetus for an acceleration of the process of cross-strait dialogue. This contains the possibility of a negotiation of terms for the long-term settlement of the sovereignty dispute which has prolonged a Cold War conflict for more than a decade beyond its use-by date. As in Korea, the possibility of a resolution or more stable accommodation of this seemingly intractable issue arose only a decade after the Cold War itself was resolved. Again, the diminution of Cold War ideological imperatives on both sides of the Taiwan Strait has enabled a more realistic posture of accommodation to emerge in both of the previously competing political regimes.

The South China (and East China) Sea

The South China Sea is claimed in its entirety by the PRC (Catley and Keliat 1997). This is not, however, strictly a Cold War issue and arguably worsened after that strategic conflict ended with the increasingly nationalist direction of the PRC regime. If this claim were successful and complemented by its claims in the East China Sea, it would add a territory of about 50 per cent of the existing PRC state territory. It would also add some territory which is presently claimed by Malaysia, Indonesia, Brunei, the Philippines, Taiwan, Japan and the Koreas.

This claim is a continuing but, at present, fairly low order irritant to PRC relations with many neighbouring states. If it were to be prosecuted successfully and lead to the PRC control of the strategic Sea Lanes of Communication contained within the claimed waters, further complications would arise within PRC relations with users of these SLOCs including the US, Japan, Korea and Russia, not to mention other more distant powers with similar interests in the EU, Australia and the oil exporting countries of the Middle East.

These PRC claims are a continuing and distressing indication of what PRC regional hegemony might bring for other neighbouring states. Nonetheless, since the Taiwan Strait crisis of 1996, the PRC claim has been pursued with less vigour. Some of this declining enthusiasm may be attributed to that demonstration of superior US power, but some also to the continuing dialogues about the South China Sea held under Indonesian auspices throughout the 1990s. These processes made the PRC aware of both its military deficiencies and the diplomatic costs of pursuing this ambitious territorial claim.

LESSER POWERS: ASEAN

ASEAN

The history of ASEAN has gone through three main phases: accelerating success 1967-97; regional financial crisis, during which it was largely impotent, 1997-99; and a modest recovery 1999-2001. The ASEAN states each now have their own individual concerns which are related to the maintenance of regime stability and the remaining consequences of the financial meltdown. In the foreign policy arena they also have some collective problems involving the ambitions of the PRC, US pressures for the acceleration of globalisation and, in several countries, regional disputes with neighbours. The problems for twenty-first century ASEAN are multi-layered, multi-fissured and multi-dimensional. They are no longer able to be defined in simple Cold War terms, nor indeed within the competing agendas of the regional Great Powers. They deserve careful and individual consideration and regional mechanisms to address them.

Within that context each of the ASEAN states has had mixed fortunes.

Indonesia, the largest of the ASEAN states, is presently going through a process of deep restructuring, the precise dimensions and consequences of which are impossible to predict. It now has an unstable political structure, a resentful armed forces, several actually or potentially rebellious provinces, and a mass population deeply divided along a number of fissures. While its economy has shown some sign of recovery, it is far from recovering the Tiger status that it almost acquired in the mid-1990s. These multi-dimensional pressures could, of course, lead to the disintegration of Indonesia as a post-colonial state, although most observers discount this possibility (Emmerson 2000).[1] By March 2001 the Indonesian Armed Forces were appealing to the US for more assistance to fulfil their task of maintaining national unity. This responsibility would be more appropriately addressed by regional states – if necessary with the support of the US.

The Vietnamese state has clearly long since abandoned its external aspirations for the projection of revolutionary impulses. But its leadership has been unable to agree on an appropriate strategy for dealing with the opportunities and dangers of the processes of globalisation (Nathan 1999). It seems to be almost permanently "twixt reform and retreat". It has, however, abandoned the militaristic impulses that the success of its war against the US generated a quarter century ago. The synonym for strategic theories of the mid-twentieth century, Vietnam in the twenty-first is unlikely to conjure much more than notions of stagnation, irresolution and isolationism. Again, effective regional economic organisations might assist the Vietnamese leadership in its search for an appropriate resolution to these problems. In this effort, US resources would be an invaluable combination with regional states' enabling activities.

Myanmar/Burma, under the continuous although changing rule of its military forces for the last four decades, was unable to access the East Asian Miracle. During the last decade its military has enforced harsher repression assisted by PRC military equipment. While this has brought a higher degree of national unification with the defeat or accommodation of most of the secessionist and revolutionary movements within its territory, it has not brought substantial economic growth. Burma/Myanmar remains one of the region's least developed countries but with a powerful state apparatus nonetheless. The legitimacy of the ruling elite's hold on power has been continually questioned by the National League for Democracy (NLD) led by Aung San Suu Kyi, of course. The only opportunity to assess this occurred in the elections of 1990 when four fifths of the population voted against the government, which ignored the verdict. Recent negotiations with the NLD have raised some optimism for a negotiated settlement. It is too early to tell whether these may succeed, or indeed whether they are genuine. Despite the efforts of the PRC to recruit the military regime to its anti-US cause in the early 1990s, however, Myanmar still stands aside from the regional strategic balance.

Thailand enjoyed its economic hyper-growth for three decades when administrations changed frequently. But the power of the military was a continuing political factor, only exacerbated by the Cold War and continuing competition with Vietnam. In 1997 it was the first country to be hit by the Asian financial meltdown. Thailand has revived somewhat from the 1997 financial crisis. It had a change in government in November 1997 and the new administration subsequently undertook notable but, as elsewhere in the region, limited reforms. Although the results of the 2001 election are still being disputed at the time of writing, it can be said that the influence of the military has been reduced.

On 6 January 2001 Thailand voted in an election that was expected to produce not only a new parliament but also several months of political and constitutional uncertainty. Dozens of winners in the five hundred seat parliament might be disqualified by an aggressive new election commission for vote buying and other irregularities. The apparent victor is Prime Minister, Thaksin Shinawatra, of the Thai Rak (Loves) Thai, who is under indictment and could be removed from office if he fails in an appeal.

The focus now is on Thailand's renewed campaign, under a new constitution, against corruption. Again, this may involve an attack by the regime on itself. This has led to fears of political instability and economic stagnation after the economic crisis of 1997. The former Prime Minister, Chuan Leekpai, came to office during that crisis, in November 1997 when the economy was contracting by 10 per cent a year and the International Monetary Fund (IMF) was administering a $17 billion rescue package. Chuan stabilised the economy and restored growth to 5 per cent a year, but the IMF package caused widespread pain.

Thaksin, a telecommunications tycoon who became one of Thailand's richest men during the decade-long boom that preceded the crash, formed his own party two years ago. Thaksin's own image as a new-style politician was badly damaged when the National Counter Corruption Commission, a centre-piece of the reformist constitution passed three years ago, found he had hidden assets. The military, so powerful in Thai politics since the 1930s, is now apparently on the sidelines. It remains politically influential, although it has said there would be no coup. Since 1997 Thailand has wound back its previously quite ambitious arms procurement policy as it has tried to re-ignite economic growth.

Malaysia has been one of the success stories of East Asia in the last several decades. Its regime has been successful in securing a surprising level of stability among geographically and ethnically distinct political elites. It has used the resulting New Economic Policy to sustain a rapid rate of economic development and to spread widely (if nepotistically) the growing resources thereby generated. It has been among the leading advocates of a regional grouping which excludes external powers, including the US and Australia. Mahathir was a stand out from taking IMF advice in 1997-98, and following the recent admissions from the IMF about mistakes it made in the 1997 crisis, Mahathir's standing is further enhanced. Malaysia has done well, and its government won an election victory on that basis in 1999. It is of course a small if noisy player in the strategic environment. In addition its recent record has exhibited a slowdown in its success. The economy is slowing and the several high prestige one-off projects – including the twin high rise towers, new airport and high technology corridor – are looking less successful.

Malaysia's pursuit of an exclusivist regional grouping, while understandable, is not conducive to regional stability. There is and can be no regional counterweight to the PRC. Without a US presence in East Asia, presently aligned with Australia, South Korea and Japan, PRC dominance will be assured. Given PRC claims and historic aspirations, which includes claims against Malaysian administered territory in the South China Sea, this would not provide a healthy long term strategic balance.

Singapore has been showing more alarm as ripples from the financial crisis of 1997 has spread more widely geographically and into the political sphere. Singapore's assured and rapid ascent to the ranks of High Income Economies and developed countries has depended on regional stability, growing trade and an inflow of capital. All these factors have been at risk since 1997. The Indonesian regime was an early casualty, but the stability of Thailand and the Philippines has not been spared entirely.

Since the dictatorship of Marcos the Philippines has had trouble in joining the East Asian economic miracle. It had a weak economy during the dictatorship and did not become a new Tiger economy after Marcos, especially with a continuing potential political legitimacy crisis. During the period of President Aquino nationalist sentiment and resentment against the perceived US relationship with Marcos led to the eviction of the US military bases but no corresponding buildup of domestic military strength. The result was some panic when the extent of PRC ambitions on adjacent islands became clearer in the mid-1990s. While President Ramos was able to generate economic growth, it was always fragile and seemed vulnerable to his departure. Estrada's populist base in Philippines mass commercial culture at the cost of substantial policy confirmed these fears.

The removal of the populist Estrada and his replacement by the more cerebral new Philippine President Gloria Macapagal Arroyo in January may be a good development. But the country still has not developed a major economy either in bulk or growth rate. It is a small power, with very limited military force projection capacity and may remain politically unstable for a while.

The larger states of ASEAN have become generally more problematic, less self-confident and more self-centred since the onset of the 1997 crisis. Arguably, their regimes are more responsive but also more fragile. The stability of the region is more unpredictable than during the Cold War, and this may be politically healthier. But it also makes the need for a more coherent regional security architecture more pressing, in order that a now more likely domestic disturbance does not readily become a regional crisis.

Southeast Asia: The Lesser States

Southeast Asia also contains some smaller states with lesser power.

Cambodia and Laos

Cambodia and Laos were previously peculiar communist powers. The Cambodian regime was viciously introverted and much of its personnel survive in the present authoritarian and incompetent administration. Laos has been little more than a Vietnamese protectorate for a generation. It is unlikely to change much in the foreseeable future. Both these countries weigh lightly in the strategic balance and are more likely to be sites of contestation than sources of power projection.

Brunei

Brunei is an oil rich Muslim dictatorship, aka a Sultanate, important only for its dominant resource. Its independent existence is a result of the policies of the British colonial administration and oil diplomacy in the 1960s. It is unlikely to survive independently forever but the precise nature of its demise is impossible to predict.

East Timor

East Timor is the newest of the states of the region and will only assume its full sovereignty in late 2001. It must be questioned whether that sovereign status will ever be any more than imaginary. East Timor was birthed by the unusual combination of a temporarily determined Australian government and a vacillating regime in Jakarta. Neither may have wanted an independent East Timor state had they been directly polled. They have nonetheless got one. It is unlikely it can survive with any degree of sovereignty without Australian tutelage and, probably, Indonesian benevolence. How long these two strategic characteristics will survive is problematic.

It is often observed that Southeast Asia is in transition from a region of relative success to relative failure. There has been a cyclical recovery in ASEAN countries, but the bulk of structural economic reform still lies ahead. Corporations are weak; and banks have not restored their balance sheets. As a result, ASEAN's share of investment into Asia has fallen dramatically. The World Bank and International Monetary Fund have warned of its vulnerability to a further external shock. ASEAN as a regional group has been drifting since 1997.

THE SOUTHWEST PACIFIC

Australia

The only country of the Southwest Pacific with any substantial power projection capability and strategic importance is Australia. Australia is a global middle power and a dominant regional power in the Southwest Pacific (just). Its capacity is levered up by its alliance with its major US ally. But it is, on its own, not a substantial power to its north, where it is unable to wield power alone in contested circumstances. Its power projection capacity is limited to 'the arc of instability' (or, more accurately, weakness).

Australia is in danger of being excluded by East Asia. Australia's new opponents in Southeast Asia are Malaysia and Indonesia. For 50 years Australia has been a close security partner of the US through the ANZUS treaty. The Howard Government is prepared to become a close economic partner of the US for the first time. This has been widely criticised in Australia as reversing the Asian direction of the last decades. Nonetheless it has substantial economic, financial, cultural and strategic advantages.

The Australia-Indonesian security agreement is finished and the Canberra-Jakarta shared vision (Catley and Dugis 1998) for the region has evaporated. Canberra and Jakarta now struggle to retain a civil relationship, whereas previously they cooperated to shape the strategic architecture of the region. Indonesia has undergone a hugely destabilising transformation. The move to democracy has been coupled with Islamic assertion, virulent nationalism, religious tension and the risk of fragmentation. A democratic Indonesia will be a challenge for Australia and harder than arranging things with Suharto. Indonesia is increasingly a regional opponent of Australia. The dispute over Irian Jaya involves Australia's churches, non-government organisations, media and trade unions supporting self-determination. Australia may be treated in Jakarta as an enemy seeking the dismemberment of the Indonesian nation, as it may yet do.

New Zealand

Australia's other major ally is New Zealand under the 1944 Canberra Pact and a plethora of subsequent agreements. New Zealand is economically in steep decline and has been, for a decade or so, the worst performing of the developed or OECD economies. This has substantially reduced its capacity to contribute to either the global or regional strategic configuration because it lacks the finances to upgrade continually the technology of its armed forces. It also now lacks the will. The Labour/Alliance coalition government is filled with politically good intentions, but it has shown no economic calculations. Partly as a result, the economic decline continues. It is not punching above its weight except where the US permits, for example in the UN. This is paradoxical since the governing Labour Party has taken an anti-US position since the nuclear ships controversy of the 1980s, when the Lange Government refused to support the US in its final and decisive confrontation with the Soviets.

The Nationals Government led by Jenny Shipley in 1998-99 had plans to revive the relationship with the US and took an option on maintaining some air power capacity by leasing/purchasing 28 F-16s. This deal was dropped by the present coalition/Labour government last year. It has also been accused of intending to drop its air strike capability altogether and has, indeed, publicly canvassed this option.

New Zealand will, however, maintain some existing but limited naval capacity to intervene in strategic problems in the South Pacific region. It has already done so in conjunction with Australia in Papua New Guinea (Bougainville), East Timor and the Solomon Islands. How determined it will be in pursuit of such activities in the longer term is questionable in view of the cost and political will which would be required (Catley 2001).

'Australia now finds itself surrounded by states that are either unviable (several states of the South Pacific and possibly East Timor), unstable (Papua New Guinea and Indonesia) or useless (New Zealand)', one participant in an Australian defence seminar was recently quoted as saying.

Arc of Instability

Elsewhere in the region of the South Pacific it is widely feared that an 'arc of instability' may be emerging. This is not entirely fanciful, but for the most part is limited to Melanesia.

In Fiji 2000 witnessed the third coup against the rise of ethnic Indian organised political power. Although both Australia and New Zealand applied sanctions against the new regime – Australia under the Liberals ironically to a greater extent than New Zealand under a more moralistic Leftish government – it is unlikely that Melanesians will permit Indian political rule on the islands and political instability will continue.

In Fiji, Papua New Guinea, and other Melanesian states it may be that recent political upheavals should be viewed as the victory of the pre-colonial over the post-colonial. As in a number of other countries, the Fijian political order is once more decisively in indigenous hands. In West Papua a series of demonstrations have been held against Indonesian rule, which have escalated the 1980s independence movement from a fringe organisation into something to be taken seriously in its secessionist aspirations – as it has already been by sections of the Australian political community.

In Papua New Guinea central government control over the entire country appears to have become progressively more tenuous as regional political aspirations combine with a general economic and administrative retreat to produce the possibility of a fracture in the state apparatus (Standish 1999). This is likely to be exacerbated by the possibility of a military revolt that re-emerged in March 2001.

Ethnic and linguistic tensions have been long endemic in Vanuatu – although they have been more recently contained. In the Solomon Islands a more extensive conflict has broken out over the last few years with quite substantial casualties and the need for an Australia-New

Zealand evacuation program. Most of these problems may be seen as the triumph of the pre-colonial over the post-colonial political structures.

In Polynesia, on the other hand, where the post-colonial states have more or less coincided with the pre-colonial authority and loyalty patterns, there is a greater degree of stability in evidence. In Samoa, Tuvalu and Tonga, pre-colonial political structures have largely re-emerged with some modification into the twenty-first century; in the Cook Island, Niue, Hawaii and New Zealand indigenous political societies have been absorbed into the politics of a larger nation state with resulting greater stability. Micronesia contains no state of sufficient size or geopolitical weight to count for much in this survey.

OPTIONS FOR THE BUSH ADMINISTRATION

The strategic architecture of the Asia Pacific region is still in transition from that of the Cold War. The chief faultline between the major powers still runs along the border between US and PRC power, that is to say, through the Koreas, the Taiwan Strait and between much of ASEAN and the PRC. Unlike during the Cold War, however, discernable progress is being made in the resolution of these disputes along that fissure, notably in the cases of Korean reunification, easing relations between the PRC and ROC, and the PRC's regaining lost territory in Hong Kong and Macao. The PRC pursuit of its claims to adjacent seas has been wound down in recent years.

As the ideological dimension of this great power confrontation eases, however, the regional system of international politics looks more classical and less ordered. For regimes, problems of development, democratisation, identity, and statehood are replacing those of ideology and geo-politics. The region may become less predictable as a result. What is required for the pursuit of regional stability is no longer the strategic architecture of the Cold War and the containment of PRC or Soviet power along the faultline of the rim of mainland East Asia, but a structure of institutions which enable interstate regional solidarity and provide a set of mechanisms to resolve the now more likely problems of regime stability, national cohesion and inter-state dispute.

Post-Cold War US interests coincide with these objectives. The main threat to US objectives is no longer communist aggression, but rather a series of inter-layered social, economic and political issues that break out from a variety of sources with unpredictable regularity. Cold War alliance patterns will not deal with them. Nor will direct US intervention in pursuit of clearly defined US interests always provide an appropriate policy, still less one that is acceptable to regional powers.

If there were one direction in which US policymakers might probe during the next few years to enhance the prospects for stability in the region, it might be a firmer foundation for a regional security architecture along the lines that have been constructed in Europe. The viability for such a project will lie largely with the policies of and relations between the PRC and the US. If President Bush had not been too determined in his unilateral pursuit of US national interests and Beijing more accommodating in its determination to restore China's regional power, this may have been a task within reach. In fact it moved in the other direction.

THE BUSH ADMINISTRATION'S TAIWAN POLICY 2001

Asia has become more of a focus for the foreign policy of USA during the Bush administration. This is largely because the other major area of geo-political power, Europe, presents fewer problems which require urgent attention at the onset of the twenty-first century. The third area of major geo-political contestation, the Middle East, has been designated for low key US diplomacy by a Republican administration less eager to pursue and support Israeli interests. In East Asia, the opportunities and risks are greater, largely because it is the location of the only serious potential rival to US power – the PRC. The Republicans have also long espoused a policy that shows stronger support for the integrity of the Taiwanese state. As the ROC has developed economically, democratised, and then, in the elections of 2000, thrown off the KMT, so support for a more overtly pro-ROC policy has spread. Since support for such a policy has long been strong in both the Congress and the Republican Party, it is hardly surprising that it has seen some expression in the foreign policy of George W. Bush.

During the 1990s, especially during the period of President Clinton's second term, the US administration clearly paid considerable attention to its relationship with the PRC. Broadly, it tried to establish a 'strategic partnership' after the rifts which emerged after the Taiwan Strait crisis of 1996 and, later, the US bombing of the PRC Embassy in Belgrade in 1999. This policy not only put the ROC in an unfavourable position, but also neglected the most important ally of the US in East Asia – Japan. Therefore, many conservative Congressmen, and particularly Republicans, frequently made strong criticisms of the Democratic administration's seemingly pro-PRC stance. It was matched by frequent and appropriate warnings about the considerable military buildup being undertaken by the PLA and the fact that this was most commonly directed at strengthening the PRC capacity to deal with the United States, should the need arise.

During the campaign for the year 2000 US Presidential election, the Republican camp, including its candidate George W. Bush and most of his aides, had clearly shown their own taste for a tougher stance toward the PRC. After their victory, US policy toward the Taiwan Strait certainly became a noteworthy issue for checking any policy movement. The previous pro-PRC policy was indeed adjusted, and this impacted on the US-ROC-PRC triangular relationship. Central to the Clinton policy had been the 'strategic ambiguity' posture, which did not unequivocally commit the US to defend Taiwan against the PRC, thereby limiting Taiwan's room for manoeuvre while – it hoped – leaving sufficient deterrence against a PRC attack on the island state.

In early 2001 the new administration seemed to abandon the doctrine of 'Strategic Ambiguity'. On 25 April 2001, President Bush released what was claimed by critics to be a statement of an 'ambiguous strategic ambiguity' policy[2] towards the Taiwan Strait. He expressed his resolve to defend the ROC against the PRC, while supporting the 'one China' policy at the same time. On the program 'Good Morning America' on the ABC, on the morning of 25 April, Bush replied to an interviewer that the US had an 'obligation' to defend the Taiwanese and 'the Chinese must understand that'. When asked whether that would be 'With the full force of American military?', Bush responded, 'What ever it took to help Taiwan' (*Washington Post* 2001a).

Bush's declaration on the ABC show immediately raised a new controversy over America's Taiwan policy. Many US China experts, such as Kenneth Leiberthal and David M. Lampton, said that Bush's initial comments on the ABC went beyond previous American commitments and would have serious implications for the US-PRC relationship (Babington and Milbank 2001). 'This clearly does go beyond what any previous administration has indicated either orally or in writing', said Leiberthal, previously Director of Asian Affairs at the Clinton administration's National Security Council. He said Bush even went beyond the US commitment under the 1955 US-ROC defence pact, which was abrogated as one of the preconditions to establishing the formal US-PRC relationship in 1979 (Mufson 2001).

At hearings before the House Subcommittee for Asian and Pacific Affairs, Professor David Shambaugh commented that President Bush might have been misunderstood and would probably correct himself later (*China Times* 2001b). Senator Joseph R. Biden Jr (Democratic, Delaware) also criticised Bush's comments, which he said infringed the 1979 Taiwan Relations Act, as the TRA had not promised Taiwan defence from the US against the PRC (Biden 2001).

Several hours later, in a CNN interview, Bush stressed that 'the Chinese must hear' that his administration 'is willing to uphold the spirit of the Taiwan relation law, the Taiwan Relations Act'. He also said, 'Nothing has really changed in policy, as far as I'm concerned. This is what other presidents have said, and I will continue to say so'. Nevertheless, he did not again say he would 'defend Taiwan'; instead, he repeatedly stressed his resolve to 'help Taiwan to defend herself'. Besides, he also said that 'at the same time, we support the one-China policy, and we expect the dispute to be resolved peacefully'. When asked by the interviewer, 'What if Taiwan declared independence first?', Bush replied, 'First, I have said that I will do what it takes to help Taiwan defend herself, and the Chinese must understand. Secondly, I certainly hope Taiwan adheres to the "one China" policy. And a declaration of independence is not the "one China" policy, and we will work with Taiwan to make sure that that doesn't happen. We need a peaceful resolution of this issue' (*Washington Post* 2001a).

Bush's remarks on CNN seemed a retreat from what he had said on the ABC. The main point, however, was whether the US under Bush would change or had changed its Taiwan policy. Although Bush himself and his National Security Advisor, Condoleezza Rice, have both said that they did not change the long-standing US Taiwan policy, they indeed had changed their policy. The Bush administration had abandoned the ambiguous policy concerning Taiwan's security, and most of its ranking officials, including Vice-President Cheney, Defense Secretary Rumsfeld, and Rice herself, stressed a few days later that Bush's remarks meant 'we are very serious about defending Taiwan' (*Agence France Presse* 2001; *China Times* 2001d). Cheney also stressed that the Bush administration is 'less ambiguous around the world', with a style that differs from that of former President Bill Clinton. 'What we have now is a straight-talking president from Texas who says exactly what he thinks, people around the world will get used to that', added Cheney (*Agence France Presse* 2001).

To some extent, this was actually merely an adjustment of US Taiwan Policy. At the very least, the Bush administration had clearly expressed its resolve of upholding the TRA and helping Taiwan defend herself, which the Clinton administration had never done. In fact, before the US 2000 Presidential election, George W. Bush had on many occasions shown his tough stance toward the PRC and his resolve to adjust Clinton's apparently pro-PRC policy. On 6 December 1999 and 2 March 2000, he remarked at Republican Presidential nominee debates that if the PRC got aggressive with the Taiwanese, he would help Taiwan defend itself (*Washington Post* 1999; 2000a). On 21 November, he also said that, 'to Taiwan, I think it's important for us to have a viable anti-ballistic missile system that'll help keep the peace' (*Washington Post* 2000b). In addition to these statements, he also said that he supported the Taiwan Security Enhancement Act, which was overwhelmingly passed by the House of Representatives in 2000.

During the campaign for the 2000 US Presidential election, under Paul Wolfowitz's guidance, the Republicans strongly criticised Clinton for his supposedly pro-PRC policy. With respect to the 'one China' policy, the Republicans just 'acknowledged' its existence without endorsing it. The Republican platform reads, 'America has acknowledged the view that there is one China. Our policy is based on the principle that there must be no use of force by China against Taiwan'. Bruce Jackson, Chairman of the Republican platform subcommittee on foreign policy, further rejected the 'one China' policy as the basis of their foreign policy toward Asia. Instead, he stressed that 'our policy in Asia is based on freedom, democracy and the peaceful resolution of disputes'. As for the policy of 'strategic ambiguity' toward Taiwan's security, the Republicans also eroded it by stating in the platform that if the PRC attacked the ROC, 'America will help Taiwan defend itself'. Jackson also said, 'What we said is that it should be resolved peacefully. We are correcting the imprecision that has been creeping in' (Mufson 2000).

These developments set the stage for changing the US Taiwan policy by the new administration. In fact, most of the Bush administration's ranking officials, including Vice-President Cheney, National Security Adviser, Condoleezza Rice, Secretary of Defense, Donald H. Rumsfeld, and Deputy Secretary of Defense, Paul D. Wolfowitz, have been regarded as hard-line, anti-PRC conservatives. Some of the other senior officials, such as Deputy Secretary of State, Richard L. Armitage, had also explicitly advocated the scrapping of 'strategic ambiguity' in the past (Mufson 2001). For example, a report was published by the US *Business Week* in May 2001, which said that during a visit to Beijing in 1999, the now Defense Secretary Rumsfeld found that Jiang Ze-min was dubbed the 'unifier' on the archway of a museum, and a mural inside the museum showing Chinese military attacking Taiwan with massive missiles, ships, submarines, and tanks. Rumsfeld was jolted and believed that the Clinton administration's pro-PRC position had made the PRC doubt US resolve to risk its soldiers and commercial interests to fight for Taiwan. Wolfowitz delivered a speech in Washington in November 1999, saying that previous US policies of ambiguity had elsewhere been misunderstood and led to the 1950 Korean War and the 1990-91 Persian Gulf War. He feared that the PRC would doubt that the use of force against the ROC would be met with strong American response in the future. He also emphasised, 'If we leave any ambiguity about that, all we are doing is encouraging Chinese actions that could get both of us in trouble' (*Business Week Online* 2001).

In addition to Bush's strong remarks about defending Taiwan against military threats from the PRC, there were other signs that demonstrated the Bush administration's Taiwan policy was different from that of the Clinton administration. These included an increase in US arms sales to Taiwan. Since the 1982 US-PRC Communiqué, US arms sales to the ROC have been a controversial issue between the US and the PRC and a larger indicator of the US-ROC relationship. In recent years, as the PRC modernised its military forces and it deployed about 300 short- and medium-range missiles in its southeastern coast opposite the ROC, the balance of military force across the Taiwan Strait gradually shifted, to the detriment of the ROC. On 26 February 1999, the Pentagon sent a report to the US Congress concluding that, by 2005, the PLA would 'possess the capability to attack Taiwan with air and missile strikes, which would degrade key military facilities and damage the island's economic infrastructure' (US Department of Defense 1999). This caused deep Congressional concern over Taiwan's security. The Clinton administration, however, refused to sell many advanced weapons which had been requested by the ROC. In 2000, in spite of the prompting of many pro-ROC Congressmen, the Clinton administration deferred selling to the ROC the sophisticated Aegis destroyer, which could effectively reduce the threat of a PRC missile attack and was strongly opposed by the PRC.

In 2001, before the annual US-ROC military meeting about the arms sales, due in April, the issue drew broad domestic and external attention, and was viewed as an indicator of the Bush administration's Taiwan Strait policy. Many pro-ROC congressmen urged the new administration to carry out the TRA and provide Taiwan with more sophisticated arms. In order to try to block the arms sale, the PRC announced it would dispatch its Vice-Premier, Qien Qi-chen, and some previous PRC Ambassadors to the US to visit President Bush, his father, Henry Kissinger, and some of former President Bush's influential aides in March, before the scheduled US-ROC arms sales meeting.

In response, on 8 March, Secretary of State, Colin Powell, answered a question from Senator Jesse Helms, Chairman of the US Senate's Foreign Relations Committee, by saying that the US would observe the 1982 'Six Assurances' and would not consult with anyone from the PRC regarding arms sales to the ROC (*Taiwan Headlines* 2001). During the hearing, it was also noteworthy that Powell twice used the term 'Republic of China', which was taboo during the Clinton administration.

On 23 April, just two days before Bush pledged to help the ROC to defend itself, the US approved the sale to Taiwan of a weaponry package estimated at more than $US4 billion, which included four Kidd-class destroyers, eight diesel-powered submarines, a dozen P-3 Orion surveillance aircraft, known as submarine-hunters, and some submarine-launched Harpoon anti-ship missiles. This was the largest US arms sale to the ROC since 1992, when under the previous Republican administration the US sold the ROC 150 F-16 fighters.

According to the US Defense Department, because Taiwan's military was not up to speed, it would take eight or ten years to build, develop, sell and deliver the Aegis missile systems. Therefore, the Bush administration decided against unnecessarily irritating the PRC by selling the Aegis system to Taiwan (CNN 2001). The Kidd-class destroyers, which are less sophisticated than the Aegis destroyers but could be delivered to the ROC within two years, provided the best and most effective substitute. In addition, Bush administration officials assured some influential conservative congressmen, who demanded a more muscular arms package to Taiwan, that the President was open to a later sale of the more high-tech weapons, if the PRC continued to deploy short and intermediate range missiles targeting the ROC (CNN 2001). The US had kept the 'one China' policy, even though it was gradually being eroded.

Although the ROC did not get the Aegis destroyers this year, most other items on its shopping list were approved. The most significant was the sale of submarines and anti-submarine forces, because 'Underwater defense is the most fragile front in Taiwan's efforts to modernize its forces', according to Yang Chih-heng, deputy director of the Taiwan-based Division of Strategic and International Studies (*China Times* 2001a). The Pentagon's 2000 *Annual Report on Military Power of the PRC* agreed, saying, 'Chinese numerical superiority in submarines constitute a threat to the Taiwan Navy…the Taiwan Navy probably would have an extremely difficult time opposing a naval blockade with its existing resources' (US Department of Defense 2000a). The ROC had tried to buy submarines for many years but had failed to acquire them even from US allies keen for sales, such as Australia. Fearing submarines would be considered as offensive weapons by the PRC, previous US Presidents had declined to sell submarines to the ROC. Nevertheless, Bush was convinced that the ROC needed a more up-to-date submarine capability to defend itself against PRC attack and/or economic blockade (*New York Times* 2001b). Furthermore, with the P-3's range of 2,500 km, the ROC could expand its anti-submarine capabilities from the Taiwan Strait to as far as the South China Sea or the Pacific (*Taipei Times* 2001a). The Bush administration decided on the arms sales to the ROC in spite of diplomatic warnings and strong opposition from the PRC. The deal won praise from the US Congress. Senate Chairman of Foreign Relations Committee, Jesse Helms, praised President Bush for his 'courageous' decision, and said that 'the US, at long last, has an administration that is taking the critical matter of Taiwan's defense seriously' (*Taipei Times* 2001a).

On 25 April, in an interview with the US-based *Time* magazine, Bush defended this decision saying that upholding the TRA was his obligation, although the US-PRC relationship would be more complicated in the future (*China Times* 2001c). Bush's decision seemed to signify that the ROC had come out of the shadow of the 1982 US-PRC Communiqué, which had seriously restrained US arms sales to the ROC.

Two other developments demonstrate the new US determination over Taiwan's security. On 27 April, the *Washington Post* reported there was a secret US plan for military operations toward the Taiwan Strait stored in the headquarters of the US military forces in the Pacific (*Washington Post* 2001b). And in early May, the ROC military confirmed that Admiral Blair, Commander of US forces in the Pacific, had made an extremely rare and secret visit to Taiwan on 1 April. He had then quickly returned to Hawaii to attend to the incident of a collision between a US surveillance plane and a harassing PRC fighter jet (*Taipei Times* 2001b). Of course, this incident exacerbated the other dimensions of increasing strain between Washington and Beijing. Admiral Blair's staff stayed in Taiwan to assess the ROC Army's defensive capabilities and to discuss with the ROC military plans for establishing a 'safe corridor' in the Taiwan Strait for US aircrafts and ships, should the US need to come to Taiwan's aid (*China Times* 2001e).

Clearly, the Bush administration was more strongly determined to help the ROC to defend itself against the PRC than was its Democratic predecessor. In fact, this more hard-line position had been expressed since 1999, when the US 2000 Presidential election was effectively launched. The Pentagon Report on Implementation of the TRA, released on 19 December 2000, would merely have strengthened Bush's determination. It says, 'The US takes its obligation to assist Taiwan in maintaining a self-defense capability very seriously...This is not only because it is mandated by US law in the TRA, but also because it is in our own national interest' (US Department of Defense 2000b).

In addition to Bush's remarks about assisting Taiwan to defend itself and the US-ROC arms sales, there were other messages showing that the long-standing US 'one China' policy was being gradually eroded. In late April 2001, the Bush administration approved a visa for the ROC President, Chen Shui-bian, for two stopovers during his visit to and from Latin America in the next May. Chen was, of course, elected to the Presidency in early 2000, was the first non-KMT leader of ROC/Taiwan, and had long been associated with popular and DPP agitation for Taiwan to become an independent state. This stopover was a breakthrough in US-ROC diplomatic history, as Chen became the first incumbent Taiwan President to visit New York since the ROC retreated from the Chinese mainland in 1949. Besides, the US accorded President Chen considerable freedom, including permitting his meeting with over 20 Congressmen in New York. It was a sharp contrast to his previous stopover in August 2000, when the Clinton administration set strict conditions for a brief layover that kept him in political quarantine. In 2001, the Bush administration explicitly announced that meetings between the US Congressmen and a foreign President would 'advance US interests'. The Department of State also assured Chen in advance that his stopovers should be 'convenient, comfortable, and safe'. The Bush administration's treatment of President Chen was widely regarded by many as being a 'visit' of almost official status.

Although the US Republican camp expressed a tougher stance toward the PRC during the 2000 Presidential campaign, some observers believed that Bush would, like previous US Presidents, including Reagan and Clinton, criticise the PRC at the beginning of their tenure and change afterwards. But the current international situation is different. In Reagan's era, the US was continuing to play the 'China card', which Kissinger and Carter had dealt, to contain the USSR; in Clinton's era, the US was eager to 'comprehensively engage' the PRC to deal with other international issues. Both these administrations had to cooperate with the PRC to pursue their other strategic goals.

The situation in 2001, however, is different. The PRC is regarded by the Bush administration as the only existing serious competitor to US hegemony and its probable rival in the future for regional dominance and systemic superiority. In such circumstances, geo-political competition may well replace strategic partnership. The more determined US policy towards the protection of the ROC state may well be the early signs of this evolution and harbinger of a new relationship.

CONCLUSION

Unlike in the European/Atlantic sphere, no regional security or economic architecture has been constructed in post-Cold War Asia to enable multilateral resolution to major issues and disputes. In the late stages of the Clinton administration the opportunity for creating such an environment appeared to exist. The ASEAN initiative, the AFR had extensive contacts with 'dialogue partners' and APEC had survived the Asian financial meltdown, even with its reputation degraded. The reduced regime confidence in many of the regional states reduced economic growth, and renewed apprehension about PRC aspirations, combined to present the opportunity for the US-PRC strategic partnership to initiate a new round of regional and multilateral institutional building.

The record of most of the personnel in the new Republican administration gave little cause for believing this opportunity would be seized. By mid-2001, indeed, the opportunity appeared to be lost. In the relationship between the two dominant powers in Asia, the US and the PRC were once again becoming more like competitors than partners.

REFERENCES

Agence France Presse (2001) 30 April.

Babington, Charles, and Dana Milbank (2001) 'Bush Advisers to Limit Damage'. *Washington Post* April 27.

Biden Jr., Joseph R. (2001) 'Not So Deft on Taiwan'. *Washington Post* May 2.

Business Week Online (2001) 'Sea Change on China: The Bush Team Takes a Hard Line'. May 21.

Buzo, A. (1999) *The Guerilla Dynasty: Politics and Leadership in North Korea*. Boulder, Colorado: Westview Press.

Catley, B. (1999) 'The Arrogance of Power'. *Contemporary Southeast Asia* August.

—— (2001) *Waltzing with Matilda; Should New Zealand Join Au*stralia? Wellington: Dark Horse Publishing.

Catley, B., and Makmur Keliat (1997) *Spratlys, The Crisis in the South China Sea*. UK: Ashgate.

Catley, B., and V. Dugis (1998) *Australian Indonesian Relations Since 1945*. UK: Ashgate.

China Times (2001a) April 25.

—— (2001b) April 27.

—— (2001c) April 29.

—— (2001d) May 7.

—— (2001e) May 14.

CNN (2001) April 24.

Emmerson, D. (2000) 'Will Indonesia Survive?' *Foreign Affairs* May-June.

Helweg, M.D. (2000) 'Japan: A Rising Sun?' *Foreign Affairs* July-August.

Ji, You (1999) *The Armed Forces of China*. Sydney: Allen and Unwin.

Lloyd, Grayson (2000) 'Indonesia's Future Prospects: Separatism, Decentralisation and the Survival of the Unitary State'. *Australian Commonwealth Parliamentary Library*, Current Issues Brief 17 1999-2000, Foreign Affairs, Defence and Trade Group, 27 June.

Mosler, D., and B. Catley (2000) *Global America: Imposing Liberalism on a Recalcitrant World*. New York: Praeger.

Mufson, Steven (2000) 'In GOP, a Simmering Struggle on China Policy'. *Washington Post* August 22.

—— (2001) 'President Pledges Defense of Taiwan'. *Washington Post* April 26.

Mulgan, A.G. (2000) 'Japan: A Setting Sun?' *Foreign Affairs* July-August.

Nathan, Melina (1999) 'Vietnam: Is Globalisation a Friend or a Foe?' *Southeast Asian Affairs*. Singapore: ISEAS.

New York Times (2000) 'Man in the News: A Pentagon Veteran – Donald Henry Rumsfeld'. December 29.

New York Times (2001a) January 21.

New York Times (2001b) April 24.

Standish, Dr. Bill (1999) Parliament of Australia, Parliamentary Library, Research Paper 4 1999-2000, 'Papua New Guinea 1999: Crisis of Governance', Foreign Affairs, Defence and Trade Group, September 21.

Rice, C. (2000) 'Promoting the National Interest'. *Foreign Affairs* January-February.

Taipei Times (2001a) April 25.

—— (2001b) May 2.

Taiwan Headlines (2001) March 9.

US Department of Defense (1999) *The Security Situation in the Taiwan Strait.* Report to Congress, February 26. http://usinfo.org/usia/usinfo.state.gov/regional/ea/uschina/twnst.htm

—— (2000a) *Annual Report on Military Power of People's Republic of China.* Report to Congress, June 22. http://usinfo.org/usia/usinfo.state.gov/regional/ea/uschina/dodrpt00.htm

—— (2000b) *Report to Congress on Implementation of Taiwan Relations Act*, December 19. http://usinfo.org/usia/usinfo.state.gov/regional/ea/uschina/taisec.htm

Washington Post (1999) December 6.

—— (2000a) March 2.

—— (2000b) November 21.

—— (2001a) April 25.

—— (2001b) April 27.

Weeks, S.B., and C.A. Meconis (1999) *The Armed Forces of the USA in the Asia-Pacific Region.* Sydney: Allen and Unwin.

ENDNOTES

1 See Emmerson 2000; and Lloyd 2000, which concludes similarly, 'the Indonesian nation state is unlikely to disintegrate at the moment'.

2 US Senator Joseph R. Biden Jr criticised Bush's remarks as a policy of 'ambiguous strategic ambiguity'. See Biden 2001.

Chapter 4

THE DIFFERENTIAL IMPACT OF THE ECONOMIC CRISIS ON THAILAND, INDONESIA AND SOUTH KOREA

Chung Sang-Hwa
Institute of East and West Studies
Yonsei University
Korea

INTRODUCTION

Korea began the process of industrialisation in the late 1960s, followed by Thailand and Indonesia in the mid-1970s. Despite variations in resource endowments, all three countries had recorded such impressive records of industrialisation[1] that international society loudly applauded their economic successes. In the late 1990s, however, the Asian economic crisis had entered a totally new phase, spawned by the July 1997 foreign currency crisis in Thailand. 'Currency crisis', defined as a large drop in the value of currency in a short period of time, had spread to Southeast Asia, and eventually reached Korea. Among the victims, Thailand, Indonesia and South Korea (hereafter Korea) asked the International Monetary Fund (IMF) for rescue loans, but Malaysia, which also had been hard hit by the crisis, closed its foreign exchange market instead of requesting the IMF for help.

The three Greater East Asian countries had several characteristics in common when they encountered economic crisis: they relied on trade in the process of economic development; enjoyed high levels of liquidity; had recently introduced financial liberalisation; and had opaque corporate and banking systems.[2] After they accepted the IMF stabilisation programs, they also faced such problems together as the precipitate decline of currency value, the instability of financial sectors, market contractions, decreases in investment, and increases in unemployment. As of early 2001, the economic crisis appears to be contained in Korea, but it still scratches Indonesia with its fingernails, and Thailand is located somewhere between the two.

Although there has been much research on the Asian economic crises, many issues still remain unclear and unanswered. Were the crises unavoidable? What was the decisive cause(s) of the foreign exchange crises? Were the IMF interventions adequate? What were the political and economic consequences of the crises? Should and can Asian countries reform their political and economic management styles? Which international political economy approach, for example, the interdependence school, neomercantilism, or structuralism, more adequately explains the crises?

This analysis examines the economic crises of Indonesia, Thailand and Korea in order to understand better their causes, processes and consequences. A comparative study has an advantage in that it clarifies the issue by contrasting similarities and differences. In the next section, the pre-crisis political and economic developments are compared. The following section explores the causes of the three countries' economic crises. Then, IMF programs and each country's reform efforts, and the consequences of the economic crises, are surveyed. The last section critically assesses the nature of the Asian economic crises based on the discussions of the previous parts, and presents theoretical and policy implications.

BEFORE THE ECONOMIC CRISES

1. Politics and Economics

Thailand had recorded spectacular economic growth rates since it implemented export-led industrialisation policies in the mid-1970s. Annual growth rates had been over 8 per cent and new buildings had changed the skyline of Bangkok (Table 1). In the early 1990s, the Anand and the first Chuan Governments had pushed on deregulation and liberalisation in order to attract more foreign investment. In 1996, however, an economic slowdown was expected and the Bank of Thailand revised its estimation of GDP growth rates from 8 per cent at the end of 1995 to 6.7 per cent. Exports were inactive and the current deficit was rising (Table 2). The Banharn Government in 1995 and the new Chavalit Government in 1996 could not handle the situation appropriately. Deregulation and financial liberalisation, along with political reforms, had weakened these governments' discretion and power. The fixed exchange rate system could not respond swiftly to the fast-growing trade deficit.

The Thai economy started to show signs of fading in 1996, and by early 1997 GDP growth rates were not as robust as previously. The GDP growth was sluggish in the third quarter of 1996, and recorded a minus growth rate in the first quarter of 1997. While inflation had been modest (between 4.2 per cent and 7.4 per cent) (www.nso.go.kr/cgi-bin/sws_999.cgi 2001),[3] external debt reached at the end of 1996 was US$108.7 billion (about 60 per cent of GDP) where short-term debts accounted for US$47.7 billion (43.9 per cent of the total external debt) (www.bot.or.th/bothomepage/databank/EconData 2001). In 1997, Thai external debt increased further, and so did the proportion of private debt. The government and the central bank failed to control the excessive borrowings of private financial institutions (Punyaratabandhu 1998, 162).[4] In July, the Thai government adopted a floating exchange system, but foreign investors competed to withdraw their money from the Thai market. The popularity of the Chavalit Government had dropped considerably. In the same month the cornered government asked for a Stand-by Credit Arrangement from IMF.

Table 1 Gross Domestic Product, Q1 1996 - Q3 2000

Year and Quarter	Thailand (mil. of baht)	Indonesia (bil. of Rp)	S. Korea (bil. of won)
1996			
Q1	1,120,089	122,530	94,533
Q2	1,151,915	128,846	102,169
Q3	1,154,597	136,940	104,870
Q4	1,196,231	144,253	116,907
1997			
Q1	1,159,123	145,801	101,061
Q2	1,168,765	149,406	110,337
Q3	1,181,739	163,252	113,227
Q4	1,230,622	169,252	112,865
1998			
Q1	1,211,955	217,654	107,674
Q2	1,118,301	232,387	107,992
Q3	1,112,595	273,463	108,357
Q4	1,185,580	266,108	120,344
1999			
Q1	1,162,112	281,052	107,797
Q2	1,095,676	279,712	116,412
Q3	1,144,423	277,583	121,847
Q4	1,213,177	281,095	137,722
2000			
Q1	1,229,472	301,929	121,240
Q2	1,197,668	317,604	126,123
Q3	1,226,205	329,279	130,426

Data: Indonesia - www.bi.go.id/bank_indonesia2 (2001);
Thailand – www.bot.or.th /bothomepage/databank/EconData (2001);
S. Korea – www.nso.go.kr/cgi-bin/sws_999.cgi (2001).

Until mid-1997, Indonesia under Suharto had healthier macroeconomic indicators than Thailand and Korea. GDP had grown steadily (Table 1) and inflation had been contained under 10 per cent (www.nso.go.kr/cgi-bin/sws_999.cgi 2001). Although current account was in deficit, the trade balance was positive (Table 2). Also, Indonesian external debt had been slightly decreasing in 1996 and in early 1997, from US$64 billion to US$56 billion (about 25 per cent of GDP) (www.bi.go.id/bank_indonesia2 2001). However, the New Order had been eroding the soundness of the Indonesian economy. Mostly Chinese private banks had been spawned by the 1988 deregulation, and many of them had connections with Suharto's family and friends. Foreign investments were wasted in support of prestige national projects such as the construction of a bridge to Malaysia and the tallest building in Jakarta (Bird 1998, 172).

Before the crisis, Bank Indonesia had set the rupiah's exchange rates to be depreciated 4-5 per cent annually. This 'managed' floating foreign exchange system was doomed to collapse when international funds massively flowed out, as occurred in Thailand, and the rupiah was depreciated by 9 per cent in August. The government further eased the 49 per cent limitation of foreign investors' stakes in corporations for holding foreign capital, but even this could not compensate for the short-term borrowings amounting to US$33 billion. In November, the Indonesian government and the IMF agreed on a US$38 billion package loan.

Table 2 National Account Balance / Trade Balance (millions of US$), Q1 1996 - Q2 2000

Year/Quarter	Thailand	Indonesia	S. Korea
1996			
Q1	-3,420 / -2,741	-2,034 / 1,166	-4,358 / -2,383
Q2	-4,888 / -3,032	-2,564 / 910	-5,127 / -3,125
Q3	-3,628 / -2,154	-2,111 / 1,343	-7,249 / -5,528
Q4	-2,756 / -1,561	-954 / 2,529	-6,272 / -3,931
1997			
Q1	-2,098 / -1,492	-2,192 / 1,438	-7,353 / -5,402
Q2	-3,134 / -1,413	-1,103 / 3,482	-2,723 / -806
Q3	-696 / 705	-1,393 / 2,176	-2,053 / -27
Q4	2,907 / 3,773	-201 / 2,979	3,962 / 3,055
1998			
Q1	4,183 / 4,100	1,001 / 4,821	10,712 / 9,717
Q2	2,799 / 3,633	669 / 4,971	11,007 / 11,458
Q3	3,406 / 4,148	1,682 / 5,100	9,745 / 10,596
Q4	3,854 / 4,357	744 / 3,537	8,901 / 9,856
1999			
Q1	3,954 / 3,671	1,512 / 4,039	6,057 / 6,770
Q2	2,220 / 3,274	852 / 4,457	6,146 / 7,902
Q3	3,003 / 3,597	1,886 / 6,344	6,597 / 6,923
Q4	3,251 / 3,471	1,535 / 5,804	5,676 / 6,776
2000			
Q1	3,188 / 3,350	1,898 / 6,264	-
Q2	1,484 / 2,408	-	-

Data: www.nso.go.kr/cgi-bin/sws_999.cgi (2001).

Korea was economically different from Indonesia and Thailand.[5] It was a member of the OECD and the eleventh largest economy in the world, and its per capita income was US$13,269 in 1995.[6] The history of Korea's economic development also had been considerably more seasoned than those of Thailand and Indonesia. Moreover, the country's development was mainly owing to the internal savings gained from export, although foreign capital had had its share. Korean GDP growth was set back in early 1997 (Table 1), but not many seriously worried about it because macroeconomic indicators such as inflation, the unemployment rate, and fiscal balance appeared to be sound.[7] The foreign currency market had maintained stability until October 1997, despite the Southeast Asian countries' foreign currency crises.

However, several interrelated factors had eroded the robustness of the Korean economy. First of all, trade had been under continuous stress in the 1990s. The US, suspecting Korea to be another Japan, had pressed heavily on the Korean government to reduce its trade surplus. In 1992, Korea started to record a trade deficit with the US.[8] Meanwhile, other East Asian countries, notably China, had emerged as competitors in international markets. Thanks to the democratisation in the latter half of the 1980s, labour unions and strikes had appeared, and wages had increased at unprecedented levels. In the presence of deteriorating businesses, Korean corporate owners tried in 1996 to trim their sizes by legalising lay-offs. However, the relevant bill could not pass the legislature because of strong opposition from both the unions and the opposition party. Korean companies were obliged to rely on borrowing to cope with decreasing profits.[9] Taking advantage of the recently introduced liberalisation and deregulation,[10] financial institutions, especially the newly established secondary (non-bank) financial institutions, competitively invited short-term loans from foreign financial institutions.[11] The result was growing national debt; external debt had increased from US$127.5 billion in 1995 to US$163.5 billion (about 32 per cent of GDP) in 1996.

Making things worse, the ratio of short-term borrowing in total foreign debt had been increasing and rose to 59 per cent at the end of 1997, while the foreign exchange reserves usable during this period had been reduced to approximately US$33 billion (www.nso.go.kr/cgi-bin/sws_999.cgi 2001). In addition to this, business accounts of major firms and banks were deteriorating due both to the bankruptcies of some big companies like Hanbo and to the foreign exchange crises in Southeast Asian countries.[12] Foreign creditors refused to roll over their loans, and the lame duck of the Kim Young Sam Government prevented Korea from steering clear of economic instability. In December 1997, the won slumped and foreign currency reserves dropped from US$22.5 billion in October to the value of US$3.9 billion. The Korean government, afraid of a moratorium, urgently requested help from the IMF, and a relief loan of US$55 billion was agreed between the IMF and Korean government on 3 December.

To summarise, macroeconomic statistics reveal that the Thai economy was the worst among the three countries before their crises. Its production looked worse than that of Korea, and, above all, its debt was too heavy compared to its GDP. If we look at just macroeconomic data, it is not easy to understand why Indonesia had fallen into an economic crisis.[13] Above all, the political leaderships of Indonesia and Korea had been without serious threats, although Thai governments had been short-term as usual. However, all three countries' governments could not effectively control their economies because of recent deregulation and liberalisation.

2. International Perspectives

It is not difficult to explain an event after it took place; more illuminating is an examination of what the international society had in mind when the crisis was in progress. The IMF claimed that it had given the Thai government continuous warnings for the 18 months preceding the foreign exchange crisis. However, according to Gohama (1999, 128), it was nothing but an *ex post facto* excuse. Although the Thai financial industry had shown signs of unhealthiness, there is little evidence indicating that the IMF as well as individual governments did in fact realise the formidable seriousness of the problem. On the contrary, the IMF and the World Bank reports continuously praised Thailand as a model country of sound macroeconomic management and open economy. Even foreign debt, the lion's share of which belonged in private hands instead of being the direct responsibility of the government, was regarded as a sign of Thailand's favorable business environment for foreign investors

(Focus on the Global South and CAFOD 1998, 12-16). Thailand's 1996 economic inactivity was regarded by the other East Asian governments and international institutions as a sign of tuning up its overheated growth (*Joongang Ilbo* 1997). It is not surprising that Thai governments and financial institutions failed to respond accordingly. Like Thailand, Indonesia was also praised by international financial institutions as a country of successful macroeconomic management, deregulation and liberalisation, as was Korea. Korean president Kim Young Sam argued just several days before his country's asking for rescue that Korea was different from Southeast Asian countries.

In short, it would be reasonable to say that Asian countries and international agents, with the exception of speculative investors, did not take the situation seriously before the crises became apparent.

Causes of the Economic Crises

There are many analyses that address the causes of the Asian crises (see Goldstein 1998; Delhaise 1998, 11-32; Yoo and Moon 1999; Warne 1998; Demetriades and Fattough 1999). The causes presented range widely from a simple liquidity bottleneck, a US conspiracy, and so on, to the defects of Confucian state and corporate governances.[14] Now there seems a general agreement that all of these factors are interwoven.

1. Internal Factors

Among the explanations focusing on internal factors, the negativity (or out-of-datedness) of the East Asian development model or Confucian capitalism are prominent. The so-called East Asian development model[15] is characterised by the close formal and informal relationship between government, business and finance sectors. It sometimes means the patriarchal character of governmental leadership and the protection of domestic industries, and, in an extreme expression, crony capitalism where human networks play a much more important role than institutional provisions. Of the three countries, Korea seems to fit the first type, and Suharto's Indonesia can be labelled as the last type. Thailand is located somewhere between the two.

According to critics, the East Asian model of development has produced moral hazards and market inefficiency, and eventually hurt the soundness of the market economy, resulting in the crises (Delhaise 1998, 33-35). The crony relations among governments, banks and corporations have developed weaknesses in financial institutions and inadequacies in bank regulation and supervision (Fischer 1998). Large corporations had relied on lending to fuel their expansions. It is also true that capital for investments had been inefficiently used in real estate and money games leading to bubble economies (Corsetti, et al. 1999; Bird and Milne 1999). However, there is evidence that modifies this argument. First, it is not clear why the problem bulged out at that time. The government-led development strategy had been long embedded in East Asia, and many developmentalists had praised it when the regional economy looked good.[16] Also, the argument *per se* cannot explain why China, where the government was heavily involved in economic management, was immune from crisis when the others were not.

It is not clear, moreover, what proportion of bankers' and businessmen's moral hazards can be explained by the East Asian development model. Their moral hazards may simply be the result of protracted economic growth and generous investment. East Asian business and financial actors with limited experience could be too optimistic about their futures to respect risks. In fact, most East Asian countries except Hong Kong and, controversially, Singapore, have adopted state-led developmental strategies, and the countries devastated by the crises were ironically the model students of deregulation and liberalisation.[17] As we will see later, especially in the case of Indonesia, the negativity of politico-economic coalitions is prominent in the process of coping with the crises, not in the introductory phase of the crises.

Another explanation focusing on internal factors is the argument of governmental failure. It cannot be denied that Thailand, Indonesia and Korea had liberalised and deregulated their financial industries without adequate provision of supervisory and auditing institutions.[18] Although contemporary international financial transactions are very speedy and grow at rates well over those of objective economies, the governments can not avoid being blamed for their negligence. However, as mentioned before, the exchange rate crises and the economic crises should be distinguished from each other. Governmental agents were surely responsible for the occurrences of the exchange rate crises, but the ensuing economic crises included many other factors beyond that.

2. International Factors

If we turn to the explanations focusing on external causes, a series of factors can be named. Firstly, the conspiracy hypothesis claims that the crises were intended by Western economic powers that were feeling threats from the rising Asian economies. According to this argument, the Western interests concerned had agreed to discipline Asian countries to follow 'international' market principles. It is true that the essence of the so-called Washington consensus in the early 1990s was liberalisation and deregulation. Accordingly, one of the major objectives of IMF programs is the realisation of transparent and freer business activities. It is in a sense a compulsory program for making recipient countries assimilate into the US-led global market system. Although this argument seems persuasive, it might be implying a more complicated reasoning than is actually the case.

According to Sachs (1998, 17), the IMF's imposing of conditionality on troubled economies had made the international financial market aware of the looming crises. The IMF had encouraged rather than subdued the crises in East Asia. To normalise the foreign exchange crisis, investors' confidence needed to be restored as soon as possible. However, the investors equipped with electronic transaction instruments respected uncertainty above other indicators. Hedge funds and credit rating companies have also been blamed for contributing to the situation. Although hedge funds did not account for great volumes, they could have played the role of pilot in the international financial market. In Thailand, hedge funds sold baht in May and strengthened the confidence of those concerned about the Thai economic crisis (*Economist* 1998a). In a similar vein, the downgrading of country and corporation credits by such international credit rating companies as Moody's Investor's Service and Standard and Poor had driven foreign investors to retreat from risky businesses. Although the empirical causality between the prophecy effect and the economic crisis is not easy to trace, this argument seems logically robust.

Thirdly, some argue that the Asian crises were rooted in the changed international politico-business environment. In the post-Cold War era the US was not sufficiently concerned with protecting its strategic partners. Its hegemony had more interest in maintaining system-level stability than in helping individual needs. When the shocks shattered Asian economies, the victims were individual countries, not the international financial system itself.[19] Since the 1980s, China, with plenty of cheap labour, has risen as a competitor of the other Asian countries in export markets. The growth rates of Chinese exports of goods and services in GDP were 17.5 per cent in 1990 and 24.0 per cent in 1995 respectively, while its GDP growth rates during the equivalent years were each 4.0 per cent and 10.5 per cent (World Bank 2001). What these statistics show is that Chinese exports had grown at a very fast rate. Behind this development lay the 40 per cent depreciation of Chinese currency in 1994. Thai and Indonesian goods, therefore, lost their competitiveness in the presence of cheap Chinese products. Moreover, wages in manufacturing had risen rapidly in Thailand and Indonesia because of an insufficient pool of experienced workers.

The Japanese economic slump has been also blamed. When real estate and stock prices fell after the bursting of the bubble, Japanese financial institutions began to look for new international markets. They had increased their investments in Southeast Asia to a great degree; in 1994, Japan's investment in that region was US$40 billion, but by 1996 it was US$260 billion (*Businesshankyung* 1998, 52). The massive inflow of capital into Southeast Asian countries had raised real estate prices, encouraging speculative investment in real estate that eventually led to the bubble economies. Moreover, the low yen since the mid-1990s had weakened the competitive powers of the other East Asian countries, especially Korea, which had entered a technological upgrading process.[20] In addition to this, the Japanese trade surplus could not efficiently provide liquidity to East Asian countries because of the troubles and backwardness of its own financial institutions. Most trade surplus had been either kept inside Japan or invested in US Treasury bonds.

The boom of the US economy has also been named as a cause of the Asian economic crises. When the exchange rate crises took place, opportunistic international investors were not obliged to remain on risky East Asian capital markets. They regarded the US capital market that had prospered for nearly 10 years as a safe refuge. The economic boom of the US in the latter 1990s has sucked in considerable foreign direct investment (FDI), providing a shelter for the capital flowing from Asia. The total amount of the world FDI had been US$320.4 billion in 1995, and increased to US$884.5 billion in 1999, but during this period the FDI flowing into the US amounted to US$57.8 billion and US$275.5 billion, respectively (World Bank 2001). While the world FDI grew 2.8 times, the US equivalent increased 4.8 times, accounting for 31.1 per cent of the total world FDI in 1999. These international factors can partially, although not completely, explain the occurrence of the crises.

Lastly, the 'contagion effect' needs to be mentioned. When the Thai crisis had become apparent, international investors suspected the soundness of the other East Asian countries' economies. A country's vulnerability to the contagion of economic crisis is conditioned by both the visible similarities of economic behaviour and the proximity of geographical location between the country under crisis and the other countries (Pavan 2000). The strategic behaviour of foreign investors is understandable in two senses. One is rooted in the nature of money games. When selling is the common strategy of players, the faster player is less damaged in stock markets. Even banks competitively collect their lendings to make sure they receive their money back. The other driving factor is uncertainty and risk. If a country's business operations lack transparency, foreign investors cannot secure sufficient information in making decisions and generally choose safety over risk (as was claimed to be the case in East Asia). However, this argument refers to a catalyst factor and cannot explain the crises *per se*.

In brief, there were numerous factors in the Asian economic crises. If we concentrate on actors for the convenience of discussion, three groups seem prominent. The first is the group of international investors who made speculative or strategic choices of withdrawal. The second is the IMF that amplified the exchange crises. The third is the group of Asian governmental officials who neglected their roles in supervising dangerous financial games, and businessmen who engage in them. It was possible to cope with some changes in the international business environment in advance, but not all. The crisis-hit countries could have prepared for the intensification of international competition, but a shock like the sudden depreciation of the Chinese currency was purely, at least in the short run, external. Above all, it is noteworthy that the contemporary international financial market is not a perfect market in that, while demand exists everywhere, supply rests with the limited number of wealthy countries' financial institutions and funds (see Radelet and Sachs 1998, 70-71). This oligopolistic supplier market can be unstable in the short run and the occasional instability can hurt individual economies seriously, although it may seek an equilibrium in the long run.

Coping with the Economic Crises

1. IMF Conditionalities

IMF conditionality prescribes in general fiscal balance, price stability, restructuring of corporate governance, and free trade and capital/foreign exchange transactions. While these neoliberal prescriptions have positive effects in augmenting the transparency of economic activities and market efficiency, they may bring about unemployment, tax increases, and high interest rates (Choi 1999). However, the recipient countries that desperately need IMF money usually cannot make their own voices heard in arranging the loan conditions.

In Thailand, the Chavalit Government was replaced in early November 1997 by the Chuan-led coalition government on the excuse of its failure to handle economic disturbances. Although the new cabinet was not a cohesive body, Thai economic ministers could devote themselves to implementing IMF-recommended programs. Indonesia under Suharto admitted the IMF's assistance reluctantly, unlike Thailand and Korea. To this old dictator, Indonesia was a regional hegemony and a big country in terms of population and natural resources. The conflict between the IMF and Suharto, however, had caused enormous pain to the Indonesian people. Post-IMF Indonesia had fallen into confusion; Suharto's health was in doubt; his family and ministers had continued their old-style practices; and the IMF was embarrassed in the presence of the discrepancies between governmental announcements and actions. Later on, Indonesia had to negotiate with the IMF twice to gain the relief loans.

Although President Kim Dae Jung's party was not the first major party in the National Assembly, he could concentrate on rebuilding Korea's economy thanks to his coalition with the third party. The opposition party, the former government party responsible for the economic crisis, could not influence the new government at its disposal. Kim, who was elected just before the occurrence of the crisis, managed to implement the IMF package consistently.

The total amount of the rescue loans agreed to be given to Thailand was US$17.2 billion, and the equivalents to Indonesia and Korea were US$42.3 and US$58.4 billion, respectively (Gohama 1999, 122). Although the IMF was the main donor, the World Bank, the Asian Development Bank, and individual countries also contributed to these funds. Despite the IMF's announcements of rescue, there had been a continuous exodus of foreign investment from all three countries. As the Fund later painfully admitted, Thai, Indonesian and Korean markets failed to regain foreign investors' confidence.

It has been said that the IMF committed some critical mistakes in the early phase of the crises (Madrick 1998). The first was tight monetary policy, that is, maintaining high interest rates in the framework of a floating exchange system. In the three countries, the sharp increases in interest rates were associated with the flight, not holding or invitation, of foreign investments. Investors suspected that higher levels of interest rates would bring about the bankruptcy of companies. As a result, risk levels in these countries had increased, and speculative investors had turned their faces away (Basurto and Ghosh 2000).[21] Moreover, even if interest rates were set at high levels, they could not invite foreign investments if the levels were not high enough to compensate the decrease in exchange rate.[22]

It is conventionally believed that an external impact or shock is absorbed in the exchange rate regime under a floating exchange system. However, it did not happen in any of these three countries.[23] The depreciation of their currencies had failed not only to restore market confidence, but also to boost exports. The economies of the three countries, especially Thailand and Korea, are heavily dependent on their exports (about 30 per cent). In the presence of the contracted domestic markets, exports should have led their economic recoveries. Exports, however, were sluggish, at least in the early phase of the crises. The Thai baht, Indonesian rupiah, and Korean won dropped by about half their value after the crises, but these countries' exports had recorded only one digit rates of increase, unlike that of Mexico in the mid-1990s that recorded over 30 per cent. The currency values of the other competing exporters also dropped, while the prices of imported raw materials and parts increased. Moreover, following the IMF guidelines, the banks of these countries sharply raised interest rates (about 20-30 per cent) and became more prudent in their lending activities in order to meet the international Bank for International Settlements (BIS) standard.[24] One of the main outcomes was a kind of liquidity trap and severe credit crunch. The three Asian countries could not secure the raw materials and parts necessary for their exports because of their foreign currency shortage and domestic credit crunch. What made things worse was that the Asian market had shrunk[25] because of the member countries' tight fiscal policies and high interest rates, and Japan's economic stagnation. The IMF's prescription for recovering trade balance worked in the end, but it owed more to import contraction than to export growth, and above all it led to the costly extension of the economic disaster.

The IMF also made strong requests for the restructuring of corporate governance and bank activities. Many of the Thai, Indonesian and Korean business and financial sectors had high levels of moral hazard from their long associations with the financial and business conglomerates, *chaebols*,[26] which had dominated markets. As mentioned earlier, the IMF imposed the BIS capital ratio on banks, and, in order to maintain their reserve and capital adequacy ratios, banks were very prudential in their lending. As governments guaranteed deposits and investors did not have other viable alternatives, banks could accumulate deposits. However, the high interest rates resulted in a credit crunch, which in turn led to the contraction of business and to the increase in non-performing loans. Although the IMF programs have positively contributed to the transparency of business activities and to the decrease in moral hazards, they had led to business contraction and a tightening of liquidity. After this early post-IMF period, the East Asian governments lowered interest rates but their economies already had deep scars.

What were urgently needed in troubled Thailand, Indonesia and Korea were not austerity programs but agreeable expansionist policies that would have made up for the decreases in foreign investment. The government finances of the three countries had been healthy before the crises. The tight fiscal policies 'recommended' by the IMF in the early stage of the foreign exchange crises had driven these countries near to a state of economic depression. The fiscal adjustment requested by the IMF was 3 per cent of GDP for Thailand, 1 per cent for Indonesia, and 1.5 per cent for Korea, reflecting the sizes of their current account deficits (Fischer 1998). The IMF later agreed to ease the tightness of the targets but they had badly hurt the economies already.

2. Post-IMF Intervention Development

Since the first half of 1999 the three East Asian countries have shown healthier economic indicators than right after the crises. However, the improvements of these indicators are mainly due to such Keynesian credit creations as the expansion of fiscal expenditure, generous monetary policies, and international rescue funds. Their real economies have not recovered fully to the pre-crises level. Although the trade balances of the three countries have been positive (Table 2), such surpluses were, as previously mentioned, owed more to the decrease in imports than to the increases in export.

The Thai GDP has recovered since the latter half of 1999 (Table 1). Inflation also has been reduced from the mid-1998 double digits to lower one-digit levels since early 1999. The exchange rate, which plunged by 77 per cent in December 1997, has become stable in the range of around Bt40 per US$1 since the latter half of 1998. As the Thai economy has become healthy, so has its stock market. The Stock Market Exchange of Thailand (SET) increased by 29.8 per cent in mid-June 1999 (*Hanguk Ilbo* 1999). In 1999, the Bank of Thailand, the Ministry of Finance, the National Economic and Social Development Board, and international agencies such as the World Bank and the IMF agreed that the Thai economy has recovered steadily, although slowly (Bowornwathana 2000, 88-89). Although Thai businesses have shown clear signs of recovery since the latter half of 1999, thanks to the improvements in consumption, manufacturing output, export (cars and electronics), and construction, the country still has a huge sum of bad loans. The ratio of non-performing loans to the total bank loans was over 46 per cent in the first half of 1999 (*Far Eastern Economic Review* 1999, 63). Thus, the clearance of bank debts has become an urgent agenda for the Thai government.

Unlike the situation in Thailand, the Indonesian economy has taken a jagged way. It was only since late 1999 that Indonesia has shown signs of the restoration of economic stability. Indonesia was hit worse by the crisis than Korea or Thailand. Right after the crisis of 1997, the Indonesian rupiah plunged to Rp5,000 per US$1; the stock market index dropped from

734 to 335; inflation recorded double digits; and numerous small companies in Java closed their doors (Bird 1998, 175). In November 1997, Indonesia closed 16 private banks by the direction of the IMF,[27] but the closure of banks made people rush to withdraw their deposits, and Chinese capital started flying out to Singapore and Hong Kong looking for safe refuge. The Indonesian financial crisis had deepened, and the internal and international confidence in the Indonesian economy had weakened. Thus, in January 1998, the value of the rupiah dropped further to Rp11,200 per US$1. Of the 282 companies listed in the stock market, 260 were put into a state of default. The inconsistent attitudes of Suharto towards reform had made things worse. Sometimes he cooperated with, but sometimes resisted, the IMF. The Fund detailed the dismantling of the cartel, monopoly, and preferential treatment, and the cancellation of national projects where Suharto and his family had their vested interests (*Economist* 1998b).

In early 1998, unlike its Thai and Korean equivalents, the Indonesian financial system had not yet restored stability. As living expenses went up (inflation had increased by 250-500 per cent since July 1997),[28] attacks on ethnic Chinese and other social disturbances proliferated. In May, riots and violent demonstrations by not only students, but also by the middle class, took place. The sudden rise in food prices further led to the paralysis of food trading because many decided to secure foodstuffs at home. Importers could not fulfil their jobs because foreign banks refused to issue letters of credit, and the prices of importing goods were doubled or trebled. The exchange rate plunged beyond Rp10,000 per US$1, even lower than that of the foreign exchange crisis period in 1997. The central bank raised interest rates by 58 per cent making it impossible for many borrowers to pay back their interest. The number of unemployed reached around 8 million in May. Eventually the government dispatched soldiers to control the social disturbances. The then president Habibi and the IMF, realising the seriousness of the Indonesian economic situation, agreed with the third revision of the original IMF program. As a result, fiscal tightness was eased and macroeconomic targets were rearranged.[29]

The Indonesian GDP has shown signs of recovery since the end of 1999 (Table 1). From that time on, official inflation also declined considerably to less than 2 per cent, but it has increased again to more than 5 per cent since August 2000 (www.nso.go.kr/cgi-bin/sws_999.cgi 2001). The exchange rate had become stable since October 1998 at less than Rp9,000 per US$1, but has slightly increased again since May 2000 (www.nso.go.kr/cgi-bin/sws-999.cgi 2001). Also, the Indonesian composite stock price index rebounded in the latter half of 1999 but has dropped again since May 2000 (www.bi.go.id/bank_indonesia2 2001). Indonesian macroeconomic indicators such as inflation, exchange rate, and stock index, have deteriorated since the latter half of 2000, albeit not as seriously as before. The leadership crisis of Wahid is named as one of the main reasons.[30]

The recovery of the Korean economy has been relatively smooth compared to those of Thailand and Indonesia. The foreign currency reserve increased to US$30 billion in May 1998, US$64.3 billion in October 1999, and to over US$90 billion in 2000. International investors have started to reinvest in Korea since 1998. Exchange rates have been stable from the end of 1998 at under 1,300 won per US$1. GDP, National Account and the Balance of Trade all have shown robust signs of improvement (Tables 1 and 2). In 1999, some even worried about the possibility of business overheating. The recovery was owed largely to the increase in exports, thanks to the robust US economy and to the government's pump-priming policies. Consumption and major internal businesses like construction, however, were not yet so active. In 1999, the investments in manufacturing machines and equipment reached only 77 per cent of the pre-crisis level. Korea then encountered, in the latter half of 2000, another, although less serious, economic setback when the stock market deteriorated and the Daewoo, the then third greatest *chaebol*, became insolvent. As a result, the exchange rate increased to about 1,300 won per US$1 in early 2001 but there have been no apparent signs of serious economic setback.

Although Thailand and Korea have suffered from the crises, Indonesia has been most damaged of the three. In Indonesia, politics and economics have amplified each other's negativities. Political leadership has been unstable, and Indonesian business activities, which have long been explained by human networks rather than market principles, have been in turmoil. The Indonesian government also traditionally has been involved in the country's resource allocation to a greater degree than Thai and Korean governments. Indonesian society experienced much greater social disintegration than the other two countries. These factors together have aggravated the country's efforts to restore economic stability, and distorted the effects of reform programs (*Far Eastern Economic Review* 1999).

Consequences of the Economic Crises

1. Political Aspects

Thai, Indonesian and Korean governments all launched campaigns against corruption, clientism and cronyism in order to enhance efficiency and invite foreign investment. It has been said that their crises in part had stemmed from the opaque relationship between political and business sectors. As a byproduct of the economic crises, these countries could in some degree promote political development.

However, behind this façade, the political developments of individual countries show divergent paths. While the Korean political situation has been relatively stable compared to Thailand and Indonesia, the latter two countries' political situations have not settled down. The Thai general election of 6 January 2001, the first small-district election in Thai history, and the re-election of 26 January (held because 109 of those elected were nullified on the accusation of dishonest campaigns by the newly established Election Commission), showed enormous evidence of electoral irregularities, as did the 1998 Senate election. Apparent vote-buying and even bloody shootings contaminated the elections. The leader of the Thai Rak Thai (TRT, Thai Love Thai) party and a telecommunications tycoon, Thaksin Shinawatra, could secure the support of more than half of the 500-member Lower House. However, Thaksin himself is still under the investigation of the National Anti-Corruption Commission because of his intentional omission of millions of US dollars worth of stocks when he was inaugurated as deputy Prime Minister in 1997. His commitment to writing off farmers' and banks' debts would also be a political burden in the future. Further, one major reason for the defeat of the Chuan-led Democratic Party was the popular criticism of his government's selling-off of national banks and companies to foreigners. In order to perform economic reform successfully, Thaksin needs to convert the Thai people's nationalism to positive means of economic recovery. If he fails to handle it (and returns to protectionism), Thailand may invite further trouble.

Indonesia has experienced political instability ever since the crisis. Because of this political, and thus social, instability, Indonesia could not attract its previous levels of tourism, despite its depreciation of currency, although traditionally it has been a famous sightseeing country. In 1997, the number of tourists to Indonesia was 5.2 million, but it dropped to 4.6 million in 1998 and to 4.7 million in 1999 (www.bps.go.is/statbysector/tourism 2001). Suharto, whose 32 years' dictatorship[31] had been blamed for the economic crisis, stepped down on 21 May 1998, leaving his country near a state of default. Habibi, the then Vice-President, replaced Suharto, but gave his position to Wahid in October 1999. Wahid's democratisation programs (such as the legalisation of the communist party) have provoked internal disputes in his government. As a coalition, Wahid's government could not exert its power effectively, and, as a byproduct of democratisation, some Indonesian provinces have asked for their independence. Moreover, Wahid himself has been suspected of embezzlement, and the powerful military and students still have strong voices in Indonesian politics. In early 2001, street demonstrations both for and against Wahid have covered the front pages of the press, and Wahid's cabinet has continued to experience internal disputes.

Korea has been under the leadership of President Kim Dae Jung from the crisis until now. Although there was a general election in 2000, the political landscape of Korea has changed little. What has been lucky for Korea is its relative political stability compared to the other two countries after their crises.

In brief, the crisis has changed government in Thailand, and a more nationalistic and, in a sense, populist Thaksin and his party replaced the old coalition government. Indonesian politics has been beleaguered by government change and instability, troubling its economics and shaking its role as the leader of ASEAN. The present Korean government that took its power right after the crisis has managed to get along with economic difficulty.

2. Economic Aspects

The three countries have partially trimmed their economies. In Thailand, 56 of the total of 89 financial companies closed permanently because of bad loans. In Indonesia and Korea, 16 and 5 commercial banks were closed, respectively. In Thailand and Korea, corporate restructuring has proceeded in some degree, and parts of non-core businesses have been sold off through asset auctions aimed at lowering debt. Also, many Chinese family business networks in Thailand have disintegrated.

In Korea, many *chaebols*, such as Daewoo, Kia, Donga and Hanla, have disappeared. Although some bigger *chaebols* regarded their groups as too big (and thus too important to the economy) to be discarded, the Daewoo Group, the then third biggest conglomerate, could not continue its existence. The Daewoo case appeared to show that, if *chaebols* refuse to change their old-style business practices, they would, without exception, be restructured.[32] In August 1999 President Kim reconfirmed his government's will to reform corporate governance in order to enhance transparency. Regulations imposed on *chaebols* include the prohibition of cross-share holding, unfair internal transactions, and mutual assurance of payment. Mandatory framing of combined (consolidated) balance sheets has been codified also. As a result, the transparency of business has been enhanced considerably, and the financial soundness of the *chaebols* has become robust at the level of an approximately 200 per cent debt-equity ratio. However, this record of Korean restructuring should not be exaggerated. Many corporations had been marginal before their bankruptcy, and restructuring has been more successful in promise than in action.

The ratio of short-term loans in the total debt has significantly fallen in all three countries. In Thailand, it dropped from US$44.1 billion in 1995 to US$23.4 billion in 1999 (World Bank 2001). The equivalent figures for Indonesia and Korea are each from US$26.0 billion to US$20.0 billion, and from US$46.6 billion to US$34.7 billion (World Bank 2001). All countries have introduced safeguard systems and early warning systems. For example, in Korea, the Fair Trade Commission and the Financial Supervisory Service were established in 1999 for the supervision, examination and enforcement of the business activities of financial institutions.

Among the three East Asian countries, the Thai FDI had fallen from US$2.4 billion in 1990 to US$2.1 billion in 1995, but recovered to US$6.2 billion in 1999 (World Bank 2001). Korea has shown a continuous increase in inviting FDI after its foreign exchange crisis; from US$0.8 billion in 1990, to US$1.8 billion in 1995, and to US$9.3 billion in 1999 (World Bank 2001). Unlike these two countries, Indonesian FDI has dropped from US$4.3 billion in 1995 to US$2.8 billion in 1999 (World Bank 2001). This difference in inviting FDI is the reflection of the country's difference in economic recovery.

Certainly there have been negative effects of the crises. Public debt has increased in the East Asian countries because their governments have pursued expansionist fiscal policies during the last two or so years for the purpose of stimulating their economies. While tax collection, which may contract business again, cannot be activated, governmental expenditures either for bailing out troubled major corporations (Korea) or for supporting public corporations and activities (Thailand and Indonesia) have increased considerably.

In addition to this, the Thai external debt recorded in 1999 was US$94.3 billion, and it still cast a murky prospect on Thai economic recovery considering its GDP (US$124.4 billion in 1999) (World Bank 2001). The external debt is also too great considering its GDP. As of 1999, the external debt is US$149.7 billion, whereas that of GDP is US$142.5 billion (World Bank 2001). Korean external debt in 1999 was US$124.3 billion, a little over one fourth of its GDP (US$406.9 billion) (World Bank 2001). This external debt is a considerable amount, even if it indicates a much better performance than exists in Thailand and Indonesia, and the country can avoid foreign exchange crisis thanks to its provision of over US$90 billion foreign reserve.

There have been growing numbers of foreign investors in the economies of these countries, especially in their stock markets. After the crises foreign investors could increase their shares in many business and financial institutions when entry restrictions were lifted. Foreign hands took over some of the major banking and finance industries.[33] Also, much real estate has been sold to foreign investors.

The ratios of trade in national production have increased in all three countries, helping the recovery of their economies (World Bank 2001). The world averages of the trade ratio to GDP have been 19.4 per cent in 1990, 21.4 per cent in 1995, and 26.0 per cent in 1999 (World Bank 2001). However, the equivalent ratios of Thailand's trade are 37.9 per cent in 1990, 45.2 per cent in 1995, and 51.1 per cent in 1999, and those of Korea, 29.7 per cent in 1990, 31.0 per cent in 1995, and 38.7 per cent in 1999, respectively (World Bank 2001). Indonesian trade ratios in GDP have shown relatively sluggish growth rates (24.5 per cent in 1990, 27.0 per cent in 1995, and 30.9 per cent in 1999) compared to those of Thailand and Korea, reflecting its economic instability. Although trade *per se* can not be assumed to have negative effects on the economy, and it is true that trade growth is an international phenomenon, these figures imply that the three countries' economies have become increasingly sensitive to outside influences, and other outer shocks could interfere with policy efforts to revive their troubled economies. For firm economic restoration, domestic consumption needs to be revived.

There have been resistances and delays in reforming as well.[34] In Thailand, where many cabinet members are former businessmen, politicians and other vested interests have slowed the pace of restructuring (*Far Eastern Economic Review* 2000, 76-79). One typical example is Siam Cement, the largest Thai business group which is also partially owned by the royal family. The company was funded in the early crisis period by international investors who believed the announcement of restructuring. Many believed that the group could play a role as the model for Thailand's corporate restructuring. However, the group's selling-off of non-core branch companies and slashing of debt seem to have failed to show any progress (*Far Eastern Economic Review* 2000, 81). According to a foreign entrepreneur in Bangkok, Thai companies do not yet quite understand why they should change their managerial practices, which traditionally have stressed total assets and gross outputs, into those emphasising net assets and profits (*Far Eastern Economic Review* 2000, 82). Lack of legal provisions, as well as political interventions, mean that punishment of economic criminals has not been very visible. Moreover, the estimated non-performing loans as of July 1999 are still 46.1 per cent of the total loans (Limskull 2000).

In Indonesia, financial scandals have been more frequent than restructuring stories. The Bank Indonesia, the Ministry of Finance, and even the Indonesian Bank Restructuring Agency (IBRA), which was established after the 1998 banking collapse to assume the function of financial restructuring, have been riddled with scandals (Liddle 2000, 40-41). Also, populist styles of policy have continued, for example, bus fares were frozen and the rice and sugar industries have been protected. Politicians have resumed their interventions in market functioning, too. President Wahid claimed that four large, but financially troubled, Indonesian business groups, the Texmaco Group, Barito Pacific, the Gajah Tungal Group, and the Slaim Group, must be saved in order to keep up their exports (*Far Eastern Economic Review* 2000, 76).[35] Many major companies are still under the influence of a small group of Chinese families who have intimate relationships with politicians. Moreover, Indonesian restructuring has been focused on debt-to-equity swaps, loan extensions, and debt discounts rather than the introduction of new accounting and management systems and corporate culture. In Indonesia corporate restructuring has failed to show visible outcomes.

In Korea, lay-off has turned out to be the first and highest hurdle in the restructuring process. While the cosmetic accounting practice of corporations is finally being wiped out thanks to strengthened auditing, many public corporations are still believed to have excess labour (*Digital Chosunilbo* 2001). The resistance of workers and labour unions against layoff have intensified also. As the term of President Kim Dae Jung will end in 2002, the government will encounter increasingly difficult obstacles.

In brief, the signs of economic recovery vary across countries. While Korea has shown the most robust outcomes of recovery, Indonesia has fared worst, reflecting its political and social instability. What the restructuring efforts in the three countries have revealed in common is that old practices stubbornly remain in place. Moreover, as economic liberalisation proceeds, governments are losing their policy leverages *vis-à-vis* private financial institutions and corporations. Restructuring has a trade-off nature; while the benefit may be given to the society in general, the immediate cost is likely to be borne by certain social groups, especially workers and small investors; and the government enthusiasm for driving restructuring may hurt either democratic or market values. Although restructuring is a worthy pursuit, its structural complexity requires strenuous policy efforts and time.

3. Social Aspects

The crises have yielded enormous impacts on Thai, Indonesian and Korean societies. Because of restructuring and bankruptcy many people had fallen into a state of poverty. In all three countries a considerable proportion of the middle classes has disappeared. In the absence of social safety nets for the unemployed, and of flexible labour markets, lay-offs have brought serious social problems.[36]

The unemployment rates of these countries, however, have shown different patterns. In Thailand, the official unemployment rate at one time reached 10 per cent (3 million), and many unemployed had to go to the countryside where the situation was by no means better than in the cities. However, the unemployment rate has fallen from 4.6 per cent in February 1998 to 3.7 per cent in November 2000 (www.bot.or.th/bothomepage/databank/EconData 2001). In Indonesia, the unemployment rate increased to 10 per cent (20 million) and over 40 per cent of 220 million had been put into a state of absolute poverty (*Chosun Ilbo* 1998a). Even after the initial stage of the crisis, the situation has not improved significantly; even the official data reveals the rise of unemployment from 4.7 per cent in 1997, 5.5 per cent in 1998, to 6.4 per cent in 1999 (www.bps.go.id/statbysector/employ 2001). Thailand and Indonesia have numerous unofficial and provisional labourers, and the official statistics may not represent adequately their abject situations.

In Korea, the income of the middle class (those between the upper 20 per cent and lower 20 per cent) decreased on average by 5.5-5.8 per cent in 1998, and, as of June 1998, 64.9 per cent of Koreans thought they belonged to the lower class while only 34.8 per cent responded that they belong to the middle class (*Chosun Ilbo* 1998b).[37] A year ago those figures were 44.5 per cent and 53.1 per cent, respectively. The unemployment rate reached 6.8 per cent in 1998, and, moreover, among the unemployed, the ratio of the structural unemployed had increased to 20 per cent. In 1998, the real wage considering inflation dropped by 9.3 per cent, while the upper 10 per cent of urban households raised their annual income by 4 per cent thanks to their increased banking and portfolio incomes. But, in the same year, the lower 20 per cent, mainly relying on wage income, had experienced a 17.2 per cent decrease in their incomes.[38] However, the recent data shows an improvement; the unemployment rate has dropped to 6.3 per cent in 1999 and to 4.1 per cent in 2000 (www.nso.go.kr/eindex 2001).

The resistance of the workers in these three countries has been stronger and more effective than before thanks to the rise of their union powers and activities. Korean trade unions, which have developed through the democratisation movements in the 1980s, seem to be much stronger than their Thai and Indonesian counterparts. In Thailand two factors have suppressed labour union movements; one is the segregation of labour by region, gender, age, skill, and the like, and the other, submissive attitudes owing to the Buddhist culture (Yoon 1997, 83-84). Thai civil organisations have initiated many protests and demonstrations for the poor, and union strikes also have increased since the crisis. In Indonesia, thanks to the democratisation pursued by Wahid, trade unions have been spawned and labour movements have expanded since early 1998. Before that, Indonesian trade union movements had been heavily suppressed by the strong authoritarian state. According to a foreign businessman in Indonesia, the lack of experience with labour movements has encouraged the unorganised labour campaigns by workers (*Digital Chosunilbo* 1998b).

Another social issue stemming from the crises is racial conflict. Although Chinese hold economic power both in Thailand and Indonesia, Thai Chinese have had good relationships with the indigenous Thai. Their immigration history can be traced farther than that of Indonesian Chinese, and many of them have been incorporated into the Thai nation. In Indonesia, however, the indigenous Indonesians often have attacked Chinese in the presence of economic difficulties.

Since the economic crises, all three countries have curtailed expenditure on health, education, social development and welfare. Social vices gain secondary consideration in relation to economic recovery in these countries. Poverty, disease, crime and child abuse, all of which have long-term negative effects, have increased enormously. The neglect of these issues may cost them dearly in the future.

4. International Aspects

The East Asian crises reminded the international society of the predominance of the US in the region. Although Japan contributed significant funds to help the three Asian countries, its role has not been so conspicuous.[39] The United States sponsored, either directly or via international organisations, the post-crisis economic management.

While the crises have proceeded, the need for regional cooperation has gained attention. The Asian Monetary Fund (AMF) was proposed by Japan at the annual meeting of the IMF, in September 1997, to prevent another crisis and to enhance the region's financial stability.[40] At first the US and China, afraid of lowering their voices and concerned by the rise of Japan's influence,[41] opposed the proposal; later, at the APEC Conference in November 1998, they indicated positive attitudes towards its institutionalisation. In a separate arrangement, Korea, China, Japan and ten ASEAN countries agreed in May 1998 to establish a collective foreign exchange swap system. Already Korea-Japan and Japan-Malaysia had organised reciprocal foreign currency swap systems after the crises.

CONCLUSIONS - SUMMARY AND POLICY IMPLICATIONS

The East Asian crises, originating in Thailand, spread quickly to other countries. Not many predicted the occurrence of the crises. Among those countries affected by the crises, Thailand, Indonesia and Korea requested IMF rescue loans. These countries had open economic systems heavily reliant on export and foreign investment, and all three countries had weak, underdeveloped financial sectors. Numerous factors, which are to some degree or another inter-related, explain the crises. Although the three countries' foreign exchange crises are unlikely to be repeated (except, perhaps, in Indonesia), the economic crises are not over yet, especially if one considers consumption, investment, and the normalisation of the banking system.

From a theoretical perspective, the development of the Asian crises strongly supports the argument of structuralism rather than liberal or realism traditions. US hegemony fails to provide regional stability, or, at best, it could contain the spread of economic instability beyond the region. Mutual transactions between Western investors and East Asian countries turn out to be structured for the interests of the former. The deeply vulnerable position of the borrowers casts doubt on the universal application of the interdependence thesis. The economic philosophy of neoliberalism and its practical program of globalism appear to downplay the difference in size and strength of transaction partners. Moreover, the beneficiaries of the crises have not been national entities, as the argument of neomercantilism would have it. Although the US Treasury and the IMF have initiated the post-crisis treatments, capital interests, not the states in general, have benefited most. Such structural approaches as Wallerstein's world-system argument (Wallerstein 1974; 1989) and Galtung's international structuralism (Galtung 1971) provide robust explanations of the Asian economic crises.[42] While Western investors, who had long enjoyed lucrative businesses in Asia, were exempted from paying the cost, the socially disadvantaged in the victim countries encountered most of the backwash. Foreign investors could successfully collect their shares from the crises, while many East Asian citizens paid the prices and donor countries' citizens contributed to the funds through their taxes.[43]

The conditionality of the IMF propelled the damaged economies into a vicious chain reaction of economic troubles that eventually led to economic contraction. In order to be flexible, the IMF should consider both the particular conditions of individual countries and the long-term stability of the regional economy. Thanks to the effects of the crises themselves as well as the policy prescriptions of the IMF, the three countries could somehow or other tune up their economies to varying degrees. However, the old practices have strongly resisted reform. The crises have had great impact on political and social fields, too. While democratisation has been enhanced to some extent, social problems have been generated by the crises. The most conspicuous costs of reform and restructuring have been the sharp increase in the number of the unemployed and the poor, and the contraction of the middle class. Along with economic difficulties, both class and ethnic conflicts have intensified. The shadow of the crises will long linger in the three countries.

The policy prescriptions of the IMF have centred on securing investment and institutionalising neoliberal economic order, rather than promoting healthy and smooth economic development. The general feature of the Asian economic crises clearly shows that the present international financial system is of advantage to investors rather than to investment recipients.

International financial institutions should take responsibility for their imprudent investments. The amount of international money transacted overnight is known to be more than US$1 trillion. If financial big hands play a game of 'casino' capitalism, small open countries are easily exposed to economic turmoil. Although individual investors and traders are rational, the contemporary international economic system is neither perfect nor rational in nature, considering both the imbalance of power between participants and the high mobility of information and transaction. Foreign exchange crisis can take place in any weak economy, especially in fast developing countries where capital is short, generating serious negative externalities that are very likely to develop into serious financial and economic crises. In order to prevent this inhumane misfortune, both national and international safeguarding arrangements should be introduced.

REFERENCES

Basurto, Gabriela and Atish Ghosh (2000) 'The Interest Rate-Exchange Rate Nexus in the Asian Crisis Countries'. *IMF Working Paper WP/00/19.*

Bird, Judith (1998) 'Indonesia in 1997: The Tinderbox Year'. *Asian Survey* 38: 2.

Bird, Graham and Alistair Milne (1999) 'Miracle to Meltdown: A Pathology of the East Asian Financial Crisis'. *Third World Quarterly* 20: 2.

Bowornwathana, Bidhya (2000) 'Thailand in 1999: A Royal Jubilee, Economic Recovery, and Political Reform'. *Asian Survey* 40: 1.

Businesshankyung (1998) 'Special Report: Asian Economic Crisis (Korean)'. March 3.

Chosun Ilbo (Korean Newspaper) (1998a) August 14.

—— (1998b) September 26.

Choi, Kwang (1999) 'Korean Financial Crisis and Fiscal Policy'. *International Area Review* 2: 2.

Chun, Jin-Hwan (2000) 'East Asian Economic Development and Confucian Tradition'. A Paper at the 8th International Regional Cooperation in Northeast Asia, Cheju, Korea.

Corsetti, Giancarlo, Paolo Pesenti and Nouriel Roubini (1999) 'Paper Tigers? A Model of the Asian Crisis'. *European Economic Review* 43.

Delhaise, Philippe F. (1998) *Asia in Crisis: The Implication of the Banking and Finance Systems*. Singapore: John Wiley and Sons.

Demetriades, O. Panicos, and Bassam A. Fattough (1999) 'The Korean Financial Crisis: Competing Explanations and Policy Lessons for Financial Liberalization'. *International Affairs* 75: 4.

Digital Chosunilbo (Korean Newspaper) (1997) October 1.

—— (1998a) April 3.

—— (1998b) April 10.

—— (2001) March 6.

Economist (1998a) June 13-19. 'A Hitchhiker's Guide to Hedge Funds'.

—— (1998b) January 17-23. 'And Now the Political Fall Out'.

—— (1999) August 21-27. 'On their Feet Again?'

*Far Eastern Economic Review (*1998) October 15.

—— (1999) August 19.

—— (2000) October 19.

Feng, Zhu and Jaewoo Choo (1998) 'Asian Financial Crisis and East Asian Economic Cooperation: A Chinese View'. *Global Economic Review* 27: 4.

Fischer, Stanley (1998) 'The Asian Crisis, the IMF, and the Japanese Economy'. *www.imf.org/external/np/speeches/1998/040898.htm*. April 8.

Focus on the Global South and CAFOD (1998) *IMF's Taming of Asian Tigers: The Economic Crises of Korea, Thailand, and Indonesia* (Korean). Seoul: Munhwagwagaksa.

Galtung, Johan (1971) 'A Structural Theory of Imperialism'. *Journal of Peace Research* 8: 1.

Gohama, Hirohisa (1999) 'The East Asian Economic Crises and Japan's Cooperation (Korean)'. *Wolganataejiyukdinghyang* 88.

Goldstein, Morris (1998) *International Policy Brief.* Washington, D.C.: Institute for International Economics.

Hanguk Ilbo (Korean Newspaper) (1999) June 9.

Joongang Ilbo (Korean Newspaper) (1997) March 10.

Kim, Gyu-ryun (1998) 'Financial Crises and Asian International Relations (Korean)'. *Sinasea* 5: 1.

Ko, Woo-sung (1998) 'The Influence of Southeast Asian Politico-Economic Instability on Korea (Korean)'. *Ataefocus* 9.

Kumar, Manmohan S., Paul Masson and Marcus Miller (2000) 'Global Financial Crises: Institutions and Incentives'. *IMF Working Paper WP/00/105*.

Lee, Kyung-Sook (1998) 'The Three Countries' Exports are Less Lively than Expected (Korean)'. *KIET Silmukyngje*.

Liddle, R. William (2000) 'Indonesia: Democracy Restored'. *Asian Survey* 40: 1.

Limskull, Kitti (2000) 'The Financial and Economic Crisis in Thailand: Dynamics of the Crisis-Root and Process'. *Economic Crisis in Southeast Asia and Korea: Its Economic, Social, Political and Cultural Impacts*. Seoul: Tradition and Modernity.

Madrick, Jeff (1998) 'The IMF Approach: The Half-Learned Lessons of History'. *World Policy Journal* 15: 3.

Park, Dae-Geun (2000) 'Looking for the Indicators of Overestimated Exchange Rate during the Asian Foreign Exchange Crisis (Korean)'. *Daedoekyungjejongchaekyongu* 4: 1.

Pavan, Ahluwalia (2000) 'Discriminating Contagion: An Alternative Explanation of Contagious Currency Crisis in Emerging Markets'. *IMF Working Paper WP/00/14*.

Punyaratabandhu, Suchitra (1998) 'Thailand in 1997: Financial Crisis and Constitutional Reform'. *Asian Survey* 38: 2.

Radelet, Steven and Jeffrey D. Sachs (1998) 'The East Asian Financial Crisis: Diagnosis, Remedies, Prospects'. *Brookings Papers on Economic Activity* 1.

Rosenstein-Rodan, Paul N. (1989) 'External Economies and Industrialization'. In Gerald M. Meier, ed., *Leading Issues in Economic Development*. New York: Oxford University Press.

Sachs, Jeffrey (1998) 'The IMF and the Asian Flu'. *The American Prospect* March-April.

Sikorski, Douglas (1999) 'The Financial Crisis in Southeast Asia and Korea: Issues of Political Economy. *Global Economic Review* 28: 1.

Wallerstein, Immanuel M. (1974) *The Modern World System I: Capitalist Agriculture and the Origin of the European World-Economy in the Sixteenth Century*. New York: Academy Press.

—— (1989) *The Modern World System III: The Second Era of Great Expansion of the Capitalist World-Economy, 1730-1840s*. New York: Academy Press.

Warne, W. Robert (1998) 'Washington's Perceptions on Korea's Financial Crisis'. *Korea Observer* 29: 3.

Wesley, Michael (1999) 'The Asian Crisis and the Adequacy of Regional Institutions'. *Contemporary Southeast Asia* 21: 1.

World Bank (2001) May 3. 'Country Data'. *www.worldbank.org/data/countrydata*.

Yoo, Jang-Hee and Chul Woo Moon. 'Korean Financial Crisis during the 1997-1998: Causes and Challenges'. *Journal of Asian Economics* 10: 2.

Yoon, Jin-ho (1998) 'IMF Regime and the Unemployment Crisis'. *Korea Focus* 6: 2.

Yoon, Jin-Pyo (1997) 'Changing State-Market Relations: The Case of Thailand (Korean)'. *Dongnamasiayongu* 5.

www.bi.go.id/bank_indonesia2 (2001) February 4.

www.bot.or.th/bothomepage/databank/EconData (2001) Feburuary 4.

www.bps.go.id/statbysector/employ (2001) May 3.
www.bps.go.is/statbysector/tourism (2001) May 3.
www.nso.go.kr/cgi-bin/sws_999.cgi (2001) February 7.
www.nso.go.kr/eindex (2001) May 5.
www.standardand poors.com/ratings/sovereigns/index.htm (2001) January 25.

ENDNOTES

1 Korea had poor natural resources, but it could develop its economy thanks to skilled manpower and the effective governmental policies of the time. Indonesia and Thailand had rich natural endowments and could invite generous foreign investments to encourage speedy industrialisation.

2 However, it is also true that each country had its own political and economic specificities as will be discussed later in detail.

3 Developing economies usually have higher rates of inflation than those in developed economies.

4 The Bangkok International Banking Facility, established in 1993 by the central bank, played an intermediary role between foreign lenders and private Thai corporations (Punyaratabandhu 1998, 163).

5 Korea was a creditor and an investor in Southeast Asia.

6 When the IMF prepared the draft of its conditionality, the IMF, the US Treasury, Wall Street and major European bankers, as well as the American Chamber of Commerce in Korea, acted in coordination. The IMF introduced a new loan system for Korea, the Supplemental Reserve Facility, in order to circumvent the quarter option. Korea received a rescue loan that was 20-fold larger than its quarter (Focus on the Global South and CAFOD 1998, 54-56).

7 The issue of currencies seems tricky because there is no agreed standard for judging a currency's overvaluation. According to Park (2000), exchange rates of the three countries before the crises were not seriously overvalued if the currency value is analysed based on the evaluation of their purchasing powers. However, if the currency value is tested based on the equilibrium of real exchange rates considered in terms of trade, the difference of productivity between domestic and international industries, capital accounts, and the ratios of governmental expenditure on national product, all three countries had had considerably overvalued currencies for one or two years before the crises.

8 The US asked for voluntary restrictions on exports such as cars and steel, and strongly protested along with the EU at the Korean government's boycott campaigns against importation of luxury goods.

9 In early 1997, chaebols like Hanbo, Sammi, and Kia were on the verge of bankruptcy. It is also true that chaebols, the long-served engines of Korean economic development, had sunk into moral hazards; they had neglected efforts in R&D when their businesses were doing well. Many of them, instead, sought to make profits in real estate and portfolio investments.

10 Korea was not prepared for the opening of its financial market. Without appropriate regulatory, supervisory, and legal provisions, Korea hastily permitted financial liberalisation in order to acquire OECD membership, which was encouraged by the US Treasury Department, on the basis that Korean financial liberalisation would serve US financial interests (*Joongang Ilbo* 1997).

11 Korean financial institutions played a dangerous game; they borrowed short-term loans for long-term lending.

12 In 1997 Korea had lent a total of US$173 million to Thailand, and 34 per cent of export was destined to Southeast Asian countries (*Digital Chosunilbo* 1997; 1998b).

13 However, this judgement should be weighed against the consideration that there are no clear or agreed standards to judge a country's economic conditions based on statistical figures.

14 If we talk about the cause of the 'exchange rate' crises, this can be understood simply as the combined force of the withdrawal of foreign funds and the shortages of an individual country's liquidity. According to a report of the McKinsey consulting company, the Thai exchange rate crisis was initiated by the loan collecting of Japanese, French, and German banks, not by either stock or foreign exchange withdrawing (*Digital Chosunilbo* 1998a). However, when we say the Asian 'economic' crises, we comprehend them in a broader conceptual framework comprising major macroeconomic instabilities.

15 For discussion of the Asian model, see Chun (2000).

[16] Many developmentalists recommend developing countries appropriate governmental interventions for their economic development. They argue that it is necessary in the presence of, among other elements, capital shortage (Rosenstein-Rodan 1989).

[17] Some may argue that the East Asian developmental state is out of date because corporations now can access the global capital market. However, the Asian crises have shown that states still can exert their wills to tame corporations. Moreover, the crises had stemmed from the lack of governmental regulation, not from regulation. Thus, East Asian states require changes in regulation not the removal of regulation itself.

[18] In Korea the policy confusion had been partly due to the reorganisation of government. In December 1994 the Korean government had merged the Economic Planning Board and the Ministry of Finance into the Board of Finance and Economy, which later in February 1998 changed its name to the Department of Finance and Economy, transferring some rights to other governmental agencies.

[19] The socially disadvantaged in the victim countries were hurt most and the international capital investors fared best.

[20] Some argue that Japan should increase its imports from the troubled countries; the US already has trade deficits with East Asian countries, and Europe is busy both preparing for further economic integration and supporting former communist neighbours. Thus Japan, which has close production networks with Southeast Asia, should play a leading role as export market. However, we have to admit that Japan's economy itself has long been in recess.

[21] Although there were other factors that conditioned country risk, it cannot be said that this tight monetary policy was irrelevant to the decreasing country risk ratings of Thailand and Indonesia. The Thai foreign currency rating could not recover until early 1999, and that of Indonesia, in late 2000 (www.standardandpoors.com/ratings/sovereigns/index.htm 2001). Korea, however, has increased its equivalent rating ever since the occurrence of the foreign exchange crisis.

[22] If an interest rate increases by 10 per cent and an exchange rate decreases by 10 per cent, there are no offsetting effects from which foreign investors benefit.

[23] Indonesia and Korea had had floating foreign exchange systems before their crises, although the former had 'managed' the system. Thailand changed its foreign exchange system just before the crisis from a managed floating to a floating system.

[24] The Bank of International Settlements is located in Switzerland. Established after the First World War to take care of German reparation, the bank now mainly deals with European central banks' foreign currency exchanges. The bank proposed in 1988 an international standard of banks' capital ratio (the BIS standard) in order to cope with risk.

[25] The Asian market explains about 30-40 per cent of the total exports of Indonesia, Thailand and Korea (Lee 1998).

[26] The US and other developed countries worried about the Korean chaebols' aggressive building of semi-conductors, steel, and car producing facilities.

[27] Also, four national banks were merged into one.

[28] The IMF asked for the dismantling of the *Bulog*, a monopolistic importing organisation aided by the government and responsible for providing food such as rice, sugar, cooking oil, and the like at lower prices than international levels. This led to an abrupt rise in cost of basic necessities.

[29] They agreed to lower their expectations as follows: GDP growth rate, from -5 per cent to over -10 per cent; inflation, from 45 per cent to 80 per cent; and the end-year exchange rate, from Rp6,000 to Rp10,000 per US$1 (Ko 1998, 119).

[30] On Wahid's announcement in spring 2000 of the legalisation of the communist party, Islamic parties threatened to leave the coalition government. In spring, Indonesia also suffered from the independence movements of Sulawesi and Aceh.

[31] Suharto had made political parties powerless by the forcible merging of opposite parties and by organising a de facto ruling party, *Golkar* (a coalition of vocational representatives). Moreover, all parties had to adopt *Pancasila* (nationalism, democracy, internationalism, socialism, and monotheism) as their party ideology.

[32] However, the relief of the near bankrupt Hyundai construction company in spring 2001 shows that there can be an exception.

[33] For the Thai case, see Bowornwathana (2000, 18).

[34] For detail, see Sikorski (1999); *Economist* (1999).

[35] These groups have accounted about 41.6 per cent of the total amount owed to the Indonesian Bank Restructuring Agency (IBRA). Of major concern, however, is that, rather than being punished, the owners are still controlling their groups without inviting new management partners.

[36] Thailand and Indonesia still have traditional sectors. Fortunately, the effects of the crises in the modern sector did not reach into the more remote areas, which consequently avoided significant economic hardship.

[37] For the detailed discussion of the Korean unemployment issue, see Yoon (1998).

[38] Although the Korean job market recently has been generous, many of the jobs offered are part-time. It is not surprising that many workers, who have witnessed their discharged colleagues' tragedies, stubbornly resist being dismissed.

[39] Japan provided US$44 billion to help the three troubled Asian countries (Gohama 1999). Kim (1998) argues that Japan's role has been neither enough nor appropriate. Because of its lack of initiative, Japan seemed to fail to gain international respect. However, considering that the total amount given to the three countries was US$117.9 billion, Japan's monetary contribution should be appreciated.

[40] For a discussion of new international rescue systems, see Wesley (1999); Kumar *et al.* (2000).

[41] See Feng and Choo (1998).

[42] Although both macrohistoric approaches pay attention to the inequality of international and internal structures, Wallerstein emphasises the exchange structure, while Galtung stresses the actors.

[43] Unlike Latin American foreign currency crises in the early 1980s, foreign investors were exempted from accountability in the East Asian crises.

Chapter 5

THE EAST ASIAN CRISIS AND THE BRETTON WOODS INSTITUTIONS: THE DEMISE OF THE 'WASHINGTON CONSENSUS'?[1]

Iyanatul Islam

School of International Business and Asian Studies,
Griffith University
Australia

INTRODUCTION

The East Asian crisis has wreaked havoc on the lives of millions of people in the region; it has also caused unprecedented turmoil in current thinking on development policy. Should the fact that a prevailing paradigm is in disarray be the source of concern or a cause for celebration?

It should be the latter, according to Joseph Stiglitz, former chief economist of the World Bank.[2] In a series of speeches and papers, Stiglitz has led the way in pronouncing the demise of the conventional wisdom, or the 'Washington consensus' as he prefers to call it, in the domain of development policy.[3] It reflected the intellectual imprint of Washington-based institutions – the US Treasury, the IMF and the World Bank. The emphasis was on a constellation of virtues – free markets, free flow of trade and capital across the globe, macroeconomic management characterised by sound money, fiscal prudence and limited governments – that were regarded to be the source of sustained economic prosperity for both poor and rich nations. It was an important set of ideas. It was operationally powerful because of its simplicity. However, the East Asian crisis has exposed its limitations and has demonstrated that, in important respects, it is also misguided.

The stage is now set, argues Stiglitz, for the forging of a 'post-Washington consensus'. Such a consensus pertains to the need to be cautious and circumspect about globalisation both as a concept and as a strategy. It means the need to reform global capitalism. It calls for a renewal of the trust in Keynesian demand management policies as a cornerstone of macroeconomic stabilisation, and it urges the need to broaden policy goals to reflect emerging social concerns pertaining to democratic governance, social equity and sustainable development more fully than has occurred in the past.[4] These should be the salient responses of the international community to the East Asian crisis.

The notion of a paradigm shift in the domain of development studies is an apt theme for the post-crisis era. The core elements of what could become the 'post-Washington consensus' among the international development community are briefly highlighted in this chapter, but there is a cruel irony: the threat to the emergence of a post-Washington consensus may well be Washington itself! Hence, the transition to a new paradigm in the post-crisis era is likely to face considerable challenges.

THE LIMITS OF THE WASHINGTON CONSENSUS

An appreciation of the post-Washington consensus requires a brief digression into an evaluation of its predecessor, the 'Washington consensus'. The contrasting experiences of debt-ridden Latin America in the 1980s and the historically unprecedented growth of East Asia over the same period provide the empirical context against which the Washington consensus evolved. The failure of key Latin American economies – high inflation, outright recession and slow growth, failure to make any major progress in poverty alleviation, unsustainable fiscal deficits and money creation, the inefficient, protectionist policy of import substituting industrialisation – provided a sharp contrast to East Asia – low inflation, fiscal prudence, outward-oriented industrialisation, robust growth, and sustained declines in poverty. Furthermore, the dismantling of the Soviet Union and East Europe's general embracing of the ethos of a market economy reinforced the ideological supremacy of neoclassical economics over its *dirigiste* counterparts. It was in such an atmosphere that the 'so-called "Washington consensus" of U.S. economic officials, the International Monetary Fund (IMF) and the World bank was formed…'.[5] It made sense to talk of sound money and fiscal prudence as the pillars of macroeconomic policy, to argue the case for privatisation and limited governments and to extol the virtues of globalisation that were epitomised by free trade and unrestricted capital movements.

Despite its global influence, the Washington consensus could not satisfactorily explain growth in pre-crisis Asia and could not satisfactorily explain why such economies were, almost overnight, thrust into a crisis of such stark magnitude. After all, these economies were paragons of macroeconomic stability and embraced the cause of globalisation as a centrepiece of their economic strategy. Even in Latin America, countries such as Argentina and Brazil successfully pursued stabilisation, but the returns – in terms of sustainable and equitable growth – have been disappointing.[6] The answer to these puzzles, it now seems, lies in an undue faith in the virtues of globalisation championed by the Washington-based Bretton Woods institutions. Indeed, some observers have claimed that the last two decades have been conspicuous for a dramatic slowdown in economic growth (relative to the 1960s and 1970s) for most of the developing world, largely because the IMF-World Bank orthodoxy discouraged the pursuit of country-specific growth and development by national governments (Weisbrot *et al.* 2000). The construction of a post-Washington consensus thus has to grow out of an awareness of the inherent limits of its predecessor.

THE CORE ELEMENTS OF A 'POST-WASHINGTON CONSENSUS'

As Stiglitz (1998a, 6) notes, the ideas embedded in a post-Washington consensus are 'unfortunately not simple. They are not easy to articulate as dogma nor to implement as policy'. Nevertheless, they must be articulated and the central relevance of these ideas in engineering a sustainable recovery in post-crisis East Asia must be demonstrated. One way of embarking on this challenging task is to couch the complex ideas in a set of core propositions. Here is an attempt to state such propositions:[7]

1. At the core of the East Asian crisis lies the failure to appreciate the fatal risks of globalisation in a context of weak domestic institutions, particularly in the financial and corporate sector, and inadequacies in international capital markets. The appropriate response is neither 'de-globalisation' nor the speedy sequencing of economic liberalisation. Given that it takes time to build up institutions, the appropriate response is selective globalisation. This entails an approach that steers an economy away from the addiction of domestic enterpreneurs to 'hot money' or short-term capital flows, but that maintains the trust in free trade and the virtues of direct foreign investment.
2. The East Asian crisis has shown that it is far too costly – in terms of lost output and blighted lives – to try and play the 'confidence game'. Macroeconomic policy has become hostage to winning the confidence of speculators and purveyors of 'hot money'. Developing economies must be allowed to renew the trust in the 'Keynesian compact', that is the notion that it is the legitimate role of governments to engage in countercyclical policies to fight recessions that can follow from an externally driven financial crisis.
3. The reform of global capitalism should entail the reform of the Bretton Woods institutions (IMF and the World Bank). They bear the inordinate influence of the US Treasury and Wall Street and have probably become a burden on the capacity of the development policy community to articulate genuine alternatives to the Washington consensus.
4. The East Asian policymakers must also take the blame for being so vulnerable – after decades of such wonderful and equitable growth – to an externally driven financial crisis. One must now invest efforts in developing an inclusive social model that fully recognises the weaknesses of the past without jettisoning the strengths. This entails a greater commitment to democratic governance, issues in social equity and sustainable development. Institutional development along these lines may well provide an enabling environment for the East Asian economies to respond to the challenges of the twenty-first century.

A fully-fledged discussion of all the issues entailed in the above propositions is beyond the scope of this chapter. The focus is therefore on proposition number 3.

The Bretton Woods Institutions and the Reform of Global Capitalism

It is banal, but true, to make the point that the agenda of reform in post-crisis Asia must proceed from a clear appreciation of the causes of the 1997 financial catastrophe. In the early stages of the crisis, many pundits, who were prepared to heap praise on East Asia for their miraculous economic and social achievements, rushed to explain their fall from grace from the perspective of inappropriate domestic policies and imperfect institutions. 'Crony capitalism' became an epitaph for the death of the East Asian tigers.

Gradually, professional opinion has shifted towards the view that imperfections in the international financial architecture also have a prominent role to play in understanding the tragedy of East Asia. This has inevitably led to the realisation that there are few effective mechanisms in place that can prevent international financial panics in emerging economies. The industrialised countries have developed a range of mechanisms – such as lender of last resort, tough banking supervision and regulation, deposit insurance and bankruptcy laws – that have enabled them to gain resilience against financial crises. There are no international counterparts to these national regulatory mechanisms. Not surprisingly, a core element of the reform of the international financial architecture has entailed the need to upgrade the financial system of the developing countries to industrial country norms.[8] Thus harmonisation of financial systems will provide the enabling environment for all countries – rich and poor – to reap the rewards of globalisation.

Harmonising Financial Systems across Countries

The harmonisation of financial systems across countries at disparate levels of development can be pursued in two ways. First, reform of financial systems can be regarded as purely national agendas, left to domestic policymakers and the domestic political process. This route, as experience suggests, will be painfully slow, and will entrench the dichotomy of laggards and leaders in the domain of financial sector reform. Second, the reform process can be 'internationalised'. This seems to be reflected in the conditionality instruments that the International Monetary Fund has applied to the crisis-affected economies in East Asia. But once the crisis management phase is over, there may be a case for formalising the harmonisation agenda through the IMF as a long-term strategy. Under one such scheme, originally proposed by Calomiris (1998), countries will have to satisfy a set of strict conditions – robust financial systems aligned with international norms, macroeconomic prudence, low incidence of short-term foreign debt, etc. – in order to retain membership of the IMF.

A variation of this proposal entails a two-tiered membership of the IMF: a top-tier of members with special privileges and a standard tier without those privileges. Those who satisfy the strict conditions will have automatic entitlements to a new facility that will activate financing in the event of a crisis without the need to go through a protracted phase of negotiations as currently happens in the case of IMF interventions.[9] The alleged advantage of the two-tiered system is that it may provide an incentive for all members to aspire to reach the top tier. In this way, the agenda of harmonisation may be achieved that will collectively raise the resilience of all nations against financial crises.

There are a number of problems with these proposals. It tries to persuade economies into a 'one-size-fits-all' category and may be seen as an attempt to salvage the Washington consensus and adapt it to the circumstances of the new millennium. The view espoused by this paper is that the principle of selective globalisation and the need to align the goals of macroeconomic policy with the interests of domestic constituencies, rather than the interests of global investors, should guide the reform agenda in post-crisis Asia. This in turn suggests the persistence of disparate systems of macroeconomic governance across the world, some operating with varying degrees of capital controls, others without. Financial sector reform should primarily be a national agenda. Such reforms generate benefits that are ends in themselves (greater diversity and efficiency of financial services delivered to domestic clients, reduced probability of banking crises) and need not be justified solely on the basis of their capacity for national economies to have fully open capital accounts. Indeed, the original architects of financial liberalisation in developing economies justified their case by arguing that it was necessary to drive domestic industrialisation, not to serve as a mechanism for nourishing short-term capital mobility.

The Need to Reform the Bretton Woods Institutions as Part of the Reform of Global Capitalism

Perhaps the fundamental political economy objection to an IMF-led reform of global capitalism is that the legitimacy of the Bretton Woods institutions has been seriously undermined by the experiences of the East Asian crisis. These institutions have always been the object of criticism by left-wing scholars and dissidents, but what is perhaps quite novel is the chorus of dissenting voices that emanates from eminent professional economists against the Bretton Woods institutions, in particular the IMF. When Sachs (1998, 3) pronounces that '[t]he IMF and World Bank have behaved with stunning arrogance in developing countries', he is presumably not doing so as a cheap grand-standing exercise. To him – and others like him – the development policy agenda is in very serious danger of being derailed, because it is seen to lack legitimacy and ownership by the emerging economies.[10]

The thesis of impaired legitimacy of the Bretton Woods institutions – precipitated by the East Asian crisis – is not really about the competence or motives of the professionals who form the core analytical capacity of the IMF and the World Bank – although one could argue that '[i]n reality, the IMF has been seeking a new permanent role ever since the demise of the Bretton Woods system it was designed to oversee' (Obstfeld 1998, 27). Nevertheless, it is necessary to make the point that these institutions are endowed with highly professional, compassionate and honest analysts and managers – and to make malicious inferences about their analytical capacity or integrity is a travesty of the truth.

The fundamental problem is that the Bretton Woods institutions lack organisational independence from their dominant 'shareholders' (the 'G7' nations) and can thus become captive to their agenda. This point has been made by a number of authors – see Corden (1999), Feldstein (1998), Kapur (1999) and Bhagwati (1998). As Corden (1999, 52) notes: 'One has to remember that the IMF is governed by its Executive Board, not by its staff. The governments are the owners of the IMF, and the largest owner is the United States'.

Feldstein (1998), for example, suggests that the IMF interventions in East Asia have been compromised because of the need to reflect the trade and investment agenda of the creditor nations. This is often reflected in a long and meticulously detailed list of fundamental changes in economic and institutional structures as a condition for receiving IMF funds. He regards this as a fundamental departure from traditional practice when the IMF focused primarily on dealing with short-term measures for rectifying macroeconomic imbalances.[11]

Kapur (1999, 31) characterises the Fund as the 'credit community's enforcer' and draws attention to numerous examples of political pressures that undermined the IMF's institutional effectiveness. He highlights the case of the Francophone African countries that were advised against devaluation under pressure from France, the 'soft' treatment of Egypt and Russia under pressure from the United States and a 'long history of failed programmes to the Mobutu regime in Zaire' in order to accommodate the interests of Belgium, France, Germany and the United States.

Among mainstream economists, Bhagwati (1998, 5) has perhaps gone the furthest in propounding the view that US interests have usurped the development policy agenda. This is reflected in his thesis of the 'Wall Street-Treasury complex'. As he puts it:

> Wall Street has exceptional clout with Washington for the simple reason that...there is a definite networking of like-minded luminaries among the powerful institutions – Wall Street, the Treasury Department, the State Department, the IMF and the World Bank...This powerful network which may be aptly, if loosely called the Wall Street-Treasury complex, is unable to look much beyond the interests of Wall Street, which it equates with the good of the world.

The thesis of impaired legitimacy of the Bretton Woods institutions mean that the vision of reconstructing a new East Asia out of the current crisis is unlikely to be enthusiastically embraced by domestic stakeholders. There will certainly be sullen acceptance of this vision by the crisis-affected economies under IMF tutelage, but there will also be lingering resentment that a reform agenda is being externally driven. As Chalmers Johnson (1999) observes:

> With the end of the Cold War, the United States decided it had to launch a rollback operation in East Asia if it was to maintain its global hegemony. The high-growth economies of East Asia had been the main challengers to American power in the region, and it was time they were brought to heel.[12]

Reinventing the Bretton Woods Institutions: The Response from the IMF and the World Bank

How have the Bretton Woods institutions responded to the growing allegations of 'impaired legitimacy'? It seems plausible to speculate that Stiglitz has taken on the mantle of leading a 'post-Washington consensus' largely because he wanted to differentiate the World Bank from the much-maligned IMF and reposition the Bank as a warm, caring institution. The fruits of his intellectual endeavours appear to be reflected in the adoption of the 'Comprehensive Development Framework' (CDF) by the World Bank. In essence, the CDF – which is currently being field-tested in 13 countries – is built on a number of principles:[13]

1. Ownership by the country, *in the sense that the country, not external actors, determines the goals, the phasing, timing, and sequencing of the country's development programs.*
2. Partnership *with government, civil society, assistance agencies, and the private sector in defining development needs and implementing programs.*
3. A long-term vision of needs and solutions, *formed on the basis of national consultations, which can engender nation-wide support.*
4. Structural and social concerns *need to receive the same priority as macroeconomic and financial concerns.*

It is widely seen as an attempt by the Bank – as a premier International Financial Institution (IFI) – to enhance its acceptability with its client countries, particularly given the relative ineffectiveness of development assistance by IFIs that uses conditionality to initiate comprehensive, Washington consensus-based policy reform in developing countries.[14]

While the CDF is a laudable move, it may not be enough. Critics are quick to point out that the idea is by no means novel and has been around in the development assistance agenda for some time – see OECD (1996). More importantly, critics wonder whether

> the IFIs can overcome their bias towards a particular, 'neo-liberal' socio-economic model – a model that is approximated, if not fully replicated, in the real world by the United States...Even if the IFIs could shed their preference in favor of the neo-liberal model, there would remain an organizational bias towards providing similar, if not identical advice, to client governments. It would be difficult for institutions like the World Bank and IMF to adopt a 'let a hundred flowers bloom' strategy...The result is likely to be at best unfriendly to institutional experimentation on the part of client governments. (Rodrik 1999, 33-34)

Others approach the reform of the World Bank from a somewhat different perspective. Sachs (1998, 4) points out that the World Bank should disengage itself from the banking business, where it is little needed, and move into the knowledge business where it could 'truly serve the world'. This would mean privatising a large part of its operations, since a large part of infrastructure aid can be privately financed with long-term capital. This will provide the World Bank with the scope and incentive to emerge as the 'pre-eminent international institution to mobilize the knowledge to address the problems of the developing world' (Sachs 1998, 4).

What about the reform of the IMF? The thesis of the impaired legitimacy of the IMF has prompted some practitioners to make the IMF operations more transparent. Stanley Fischer (1998, 5), the Deputy Managing Director of the IMF, has responded to this suggestion by maintaining that much progress has been achieved in recent years. He also maintains that 'if more details of IMF operations were published, there would be more room for appraisal by outsiders – which would be to the good'.

Horst Koehler, the current Managing Director of the IMF, has acknowledged that 'most fundamentally, the IMF needs to refocus' to its core mission of offering assistance to member countries in the domain of macroeconomic and financial policies (Koehler 2000, 5). But he is unlikely, or unable, to respond to the suggestion that a restructuring of the powers and procedures of the IMF and its voting rights is necessary so that the inordinate influence of creditor nations on the development agenda can be lessened.

There is also the suggestion that the monopoly of the Fund as an institution dealing with macroeconomic imbalances in emerging markets ought to be counter-balanced with a regional institution – a sort of 'Asian IMF'. A US-led lobby argued that such an institution would cause confusion about the domain of responsibility of the IMF and cause debt-ridden economies to seek a soft option. Thus, the idea was promptly shot down, but it seems to have resurfaced. For example, the ADB-sponsored Asia Policy Forum (2000, 10) recommends that:

> Asian economies may consider establishing a new regional financial arrangement (RFA) that would provide a lender of last resort facility together with the implementation of an effective surveillance system over Asian economies. The RFA should complement the activities of the IMF through close collaboration with each other.

Dealing with the Bretton Woods Duo: The Meltzer Report[15]

Perhaps a prominent example of current thinking on the reform of the Bretton Woods institutions is represented by the Meltzer report (see the Economist, 'Slimming the Bretton Woods Duo', May 18-24, 2000, 88). This report – encapsulating the collective fruits of eleven members – was sponsored by the US Congress and led by Allan Meltzer of Carnegie-Mellon University. Not all members agreed with the final version of the recommendations that form the basis of the reform of the Bretton Woods institutions. The majority (eight) did. It also bears the imprint of Jeffrey Sachs of Harvard University, whose views on the Bretton Woods institutions have been discussed in this chapter at previous junctures.

In essence, the Meltzer report recommends sharp cutbacks in the lending operations of both the Fund and the Bank. The commission majority argued that the World Bank should focus on grants rather than loans, and fully disengage from countries who have investment-grade bond ratings (and hence are able to attract private capital) or per capita incomes exceeding US$4,000. Countries with incomes above US$2,500 would qualify for only limited World Bank assistance. The Bank's efforts should focus on 80 of the world's poorest countries.

These recommendations were moulded by the evidence that, in the past, some 70 per cent of non-concessional lending by the World Bank has gone to 11 countries (such as China, Argentina, Mexico and Brazil) that had access to capital markets. This is contrary to the commission's notion of core principles that should guide development assistance. Thus, such assistance should provide international public goods (such as research into the treatment of tropical diseases) and should be a mechanism for transferring resources to alleviate poverty in the very poorest countries that do not have access to private capital.

As far as the Fund is concerned, the aim of the commission clearly is to refocus the institution to one primary market failure: financial panics in which solvent economies cannot borrow. The Fund is recommended to stop 'policy conditionalities', that is the standard practice of making financial bailouts contingent on the acceptance of wide-ranging structural reforms.

The Meltzer report makes it clear that countries would have to pre-qualify for IMF assistance by reforming their banking systems and taking other steps that are likely to reduce their vulnerability to financial crises. Even then emergency loans to countries that pre-qualify would be short-term (eight months) and would be lent at penal rates. Only in cases of systemic crises would non-eligible countries receive Fund bailouts.

How has the international community reacted to these proposals? Critics of the Meltzer report worry that it would be politicised by conservative Republicans in the US congress who are against any US support to multilateral institutions. More importantly, a reduction in the Bretton Woods institutions envisaged in the report would have to be matched by a dramatic increase in foreign aid to the poorest countries of the world. However, there is the risk that the shareholders of the Bretton Woods institutions may use the report to reduce their own foreign-aid budgets even more than the prevailing inadequate levels. In that case, the entire *raison d'etre* of the Meltzer commission would be seriously undermined.

Other critics of the Meltzer commission raise the fundamental point that the reform agenda leaves untouched the issue of 'ownership' of the Bretton Woods institutions – in particular the IMF – by ignoring the influence of creditor nations on their agenda. Oxfam (2000), for example, argues that the G7 countries account for 57 per cent of the votes in the Executive Board of the Fund, although they account for 14 per cent of the world's population. It goes on to suggest that the vote of any single country should be limited to 10 per cent, thus limiting the influence of the creditor nations' agenda in the Fund.

Will such radical ideas – or even the reform proposals of the Meltzer commission – have a chance of being tested? Unfortunately, the prospects are not particularly good. The US, under the guidance of the Treasury Secretary Lawrence Summers, is 'scrambling' to propose its own versions of reform that will dilute the thrust of the Meltzer report (*Asian Wall Street Journal* 2000, 5). Policy conditionality imposed by the Bretton Woods institutions on debtor nations, so often the source of intense controversy, will apparently continue.

Ironically, signs that the recession in East Asia has bottomed out and that in some cases – as in South Korea – one sees persuasive evidence of a recovery, mean that the pressure to dismantle the Washington consensus will abate. If growth indeed consolidates itself across the region, and if Japan does indeed recover from its dire straits, the pain and trauma of the past two years will recede from collective memory. Washington and the Bretton Woods institutions will be seen as the saviours of East Asia. For example, in a recent assessment, Rudi Dornbusch (1999, 28) observes, 'So what are the lessons from the past two years? It's that the IMF...has been right about the remedies for these crises....So in the end, three cheers for the IMF'. In such an atmosphere, the mistakes and mismanagement by the IMF pertaining to the crisis will probably be forgotten. Instead, one could see an even greater effort to improve governance in East Asia, thus justifying the view that the crisis after all was a virulent home-grown product.

Concluding Remarks

The East Asian crisis and its aftermath have set the stage for the forging of a 'post-Washington consensus' among the international development community. Such a consensus should build on the principle of selective globalisation as a medium-term goal. It should build on the notion that macroeconomic policy should not become hostage to the interests of the international investor community. It should build on the idea that improved governance in East Asia ought to entail a focus on democratisation of institutions, the construction of a viable social protection policy and a renewed emphasis on sustainable development.

How broad is the support for such a 'post-Washington consensus', both within East Asia and outside? Here, one can detect some troubling trends. On the one hand, the ethos and language of the 'post-Washington consensus' – democracy, social equity, sustainability of the environment – are powerful enough to elicit a wide following both within the development policy community, the extant regimes and emerging political forces within East Asia. On the other hand, the vision of a 'post-Washington consensus' led by the Bretton Woods institutions will not find ready acceptance among key stakeholders in East Asia. Both policymakers and civil society in the region – humbled and hobbled by the crisis – are likely to interpret any systemic reform agenda directed at strengthening East Asian domestic institutions as an ill-intentioned ploy led by the creditor nations that dominate the global development policy community. As Stiglitz (1998e, 33) warns, 'whatever the new consensus is, it cannot be based on Washington'.

To make matters worse, the current 'bottoming out' of the recession in the region – and evidence of pretty robust recovery in some cases – will breed a sense of vindication among key players of the 'Wall Street-Treasury complex'. The pain and trauma of the 1997 financial crisis will fade from collective memory. The rest of the world will regard the Bretton Woods institutions as the saviours of East Asia. But a fundamental question will remain unresolved: will the East Asian economies become safe from the scourge of another externally driven crisis as a result of all the painful reforms that they are going through?

REFERENCES

Asian Policy Forum (2000) 'Recommendations for Preventing Another Capital Account Crisis'. Mimeo, July 7, Tokyo: Asian Development Bank Institute (website version).

Asian Wall Street Journal (2000) 'Summers to Propose Limited Reforms for World Bank'. March 21.

Bhagwati, J. (1998) 'The Capital Myth: The Difference Between Trade in Widgets and Dollars'. *Foreign Affairs*, May/June (website version).

Calomiris, C. (1998) 'Blueprints for a New Global Financial Architecture'. Mimeo, September.

Corden, M. (1999) *The Asian Crisis: Is There a Way Out?* Singapore: Institute of Southeast Asian Studies.

Cummings, B. (1999) 'The Asian Crisis, Democracy and the End of "Late" Development'. In T.J. Pempel, ed., *The Politics of the Asian Crisis*. Ithaca and London: Cornell University Press.

Dornbusch, R. (1999) 'The IMF Didn't Fail'. *Far Eastern Economic Review*, December 2.

Economist (1999) April 24.

—— (2000) '*Slimming the Bretton Woods Duo*'. May 18-24.

Eichengreen, B. (1999) *Towards a New International Financial Architecture: A Practical Post-Asia Agenda*. Washington DC: Institute for International Economics.

Feldstein, M. (1998) 'Refocusing the IMF'. *Foreign Affairs*, March/April (website version).

Fischer, S. (1998) 'Reforming World Finance: Lessons from a Crisis'. *Economist*, October 3-9 (website version).

—— (2000) 'Strengthening Crisis Prevention: The Role of Contingent Credit Lines'. Speech given at the Banco de Mexico, Mexico City, November 15 (website version).

Goldstein, M. (2000a) 'Strengthening the International Financial Architecture: Where Do We Stand'. *Working Paper* 00-8, Institute for International Economics, Washington (website version).

—— (2000b) 'IMF Structural Programs'. Paper prepared for NBER Conference, Woodstock, Vermont October 19-21 (website version).

Griffith-Jones, S. (1998) 'How To Protect Developing Countries From Volatility of Capital Flows'. Institute of Development Studies, Sussex University, Paper prepared for the Commonwealth Secretariat for the Expert Group Meeting, London, June 15-17.

Islam I., and A. Chowdhury (2001) *The Political Economy of East Asia: Post-Crisis Debates.* Melbourne and Oxford: Oxford University Press.

Johnson, Chalmers (1999) 'Revisiting Asia's Crony Capitalism'. *Indonesian Observer* June 30 (original article in *Los Angeles Times*).

Koehler, H. (2000) 'In Search of Stability and Broadly-Shared Prosperity: Reform of the International Monetary System'. Address given at a meeting with EU Parliamentary Committees, Brussels, November 7 (website version).

Kapur, D. (1999) 'The International Monetary Fund: A Cure or a Curse'? *Cooperation South* 1, June (Reprinted from *Foreign Policy*, Summer, 1998).

Kolodko, G.W. (1999) 'Ten Years of Post-Socialist Transition: Lessons for Policy Reform'. *Policy Research Working Paper 2095*, April. Washington DC: The World Bank.

Krueger, A. (2000) 'IMF Stabilization Programs'. Mimeo, National Bureau of Economic Research (NBER).

Krugman, P. (1998) 'The Eternal Triangle'. Mimeo (website version).

—— (1999) *The Return of Depression Economics*. New York and London: W.W. Norton.

Obstfeld, M. (1998) 'The Global Capital Market: Benefactor or Menace'? *The Journal of Economic Perspectives* 12: 4.

OECD (1996) *Shaping the 21st Century: The Role of Development Cooperation*. Paris: OECD.

Oxfam (2000) *Submission to Jubilee 2000: Fifty Years is Enough.* United Kingdom: Oxfam International.

Polackova, H. (1999) 'Contingent Government Liabilities: A Hidden Fiscal Risk'. *Finance and Development* 36: 1 (website version).

Pritchett, L. and D. Dollar (1998) *Assessing Aid: What Works, What Doesn't and Why.* A World Bank Policy Research Report. New York: Oxford University Press.

Radelet, S. and J. Sachs (1998) 'The East Asian Financial Crisis: Diagnosis, Remedies, Prospect'. Mimeo, Harvard Institute for International Development, April 20.

—— (1999) 'What Have We Learned, So Far, from the Asian Financial Crisis?' Mimeo, Harvard Institute for International Development, January.

Rodrik, D. (1999) 'Institutions for High Quality Growth; What are They and How to Acquire Them'. Harvard University, Paper for the International Monetary Fund Conference on Second-Generation Reforms, Washington DC, November 8-9.

Sachs, J. (1998) 'Global Capitalism: Making it Work'. *Economist* (website version) September 23.

Stiglitz, J. (1997) 'An Agenda for Development in the 21st Century'. Keynote Address to the Ninth Annual Bank Conference on Development Economics, Washington DC, April 30.

Stiglitz, J. (1998a) 'More Instruments and Broader Goals: Moving Towards the Post-Washington Consensus'. *The 1998 WIDER Annual Lecture*, Helsinki, Finland.

—— (1998b) 'Responding to Economic Crises: Policy Alternatives for Equitable Recovery and Development'. *North-South Institute Seminar*, Ottawa, Canada, September 29.

—— (1998c) 'Redefining the Role of the State: What Should it Do? How Should It Do It? And How Should These Decisions be Made?' Paper Presented on the 10th Anniversary of MITI Research Institute, Tokyo, Japan March 17 (website version).

—— (1998d) 'Participation and Development: Perspectives From the Comprehensive Development Paradigm'. Mimeo, Seoul, Korea (website version). February 27.

—— (1999) 'Whither Reform? Ten Years of the Transition'. Mimeo, Washington DC: World Bank (website version).

United Nations Committee on Economic and Social Affairs (1999) 'Towards a New International Financial Architecture'. *Cooperation South* 1, June.

Weeks, J. (2000) 'Latin America and the "High Performing Asian Economies": Growth and Debt'. Mimeo, School of Oriental & African Studies, forthcoming in *Journal of International Development.*

Weisbrot, M, D. Baker, R. Naiman and G. Neta (2000) 'Growth May be Good for the Poor – But are IMF and World Bank Policies Good for the Poor'. Center for Economic and Policy Research. Mimeo, August 7 (website version).

Williamson, J. (1990) 'What Washington Means by Policy Reform'. In John Williamson, ed., *Latin American Adjustment: How Much Has Happened?* Washington DC: Institute for International Economics.

—— (2000) 'The Role of the IMF; A Guide to the Reports'. International Economics Policy Briefs, *Working Paper* No 00-5, May, Institute for International Economics.

—— ed. (1994) *The Political Economy of Policy Reform*. Washington DC: Institute for International Economics.

Wolfensohn, J.D. (1999) 'A Proposal for a Comprehensive Development Framework'. *A Discussion Draft, January 21*, Washington DC: World Bank (website version).

World Bank (1998) 'Partnership for Development: Proposed Actions for the World Bank'. *A Discussion Paper, May 20*. Washington DC: World Bank.

ENDNOTES

1 This paper was written when the author was attached to the ILO Area office, Jakarta as Senior Employment and Labour Market Specialist (31 January 2000 to 31 January 2001). The chapter draws on Islam and Chowdhury (2001).

2 Stiglitz announced his resignation from the World Bank on 26 November 1999. His term was due to end at the end of February 2000.

3 The clearest expression of this view can be found in Stiglitz (1998a). Other highly pertinent contributions include Stiglitz (1997; 1998b; 1998c). The term 'Washington consensus' was coined by Williamson (1990). See also Williamson (1994). The issues discussed in this paper also bear the influence of Sachs (1998), Radelet and Sachs (1998; 1999), Krugman (1998; 1999) and Bhagwati (1998).

4 Some authors, including Stiglitz, now argue that the dismal experience of the ex-Soviet Union and a large number of economies of the East European communist bloc in making the transition to a market economy has also reinforced the critique against the 'Washington Consensus'. See Stiglitz (1998d, 1999). Rodrik (1999, 2) refers to the 'dismal failure in Russia of price reform and privatization in the absence of supportive legal, regulatory, and political apparatus'. Kolodko (1999) argues that the dismantling of the communist states in East Europe was not accompanied by appropriate institutional arrangements. This

caused an institutional vacuum and fatally undermined the capacity of the ex-communist states in the region to make an effective transition to a market economy.

5 Stiglitz (1998a, 4) actually emphasises the key influence of the Latin American experience, but does not explicitly refer to East Asia in shaping the Washington consensus. One could argue that orthodoxy is strengthened if it is able to show that poor economic performance occurs when its basic tenets are not followed (allegedly as in Latin America), but that stunning economic success occurs when its basic tenets are embraced (allegedly as in East Asia).

6 Weeks (2000) maintains that the 'Washington consensus' policies actually led to a demand compression in Latin America in order to generate resources to service the debt burden. The result was predictably poor economic growth in Latin America *vis-à-vis* East Asia.

7 It must be emphasised that Stiglitz will not agree with all the propositions that are being subsumed under the 'post-Washington consensus'. The reform of the Bretton Woods institutions is the most controversial proposition. As will be argued later, prominent voices outside these institutions have put forward a fundamental reform agenda. Others do not make this point explicit, but it is implicit in their analyses.

8 For an exhaustive review of proposed reforms of the international financial architecture, see the United Nations Executive Committee on Economic and Social Affairs (1999). See also Griffith-Jones (1998) and Eichengreen (1999).

9 This proposal, and the one by Calomiris (1998), is discussed in Radelet and Sachs (1999, 18). *The Economist* (1999, 80) reported that the IMF 'is about to introduce a new "Credit Contingency Line (CCL)"...designed to help healthy emerging economies to ward off financial collapse, by giving them access to substantial amounts of cash when they are threatened by "contagion" from other markets'. Stanley Fischer (2000, 10) states that 'countries so far have chosen not to take up the CCL (because)...the original design had serious flaws'.

10 One exception is Anne Krueger (2000) who offers a sympathetic evaluation of the role of the IMF in managing the Asian crisis. See also Dornbusch (1999).

11 Goldstein (2000a, 13-15), an ex-IMF staff member, also expresses concern about 'mission creep' in the Fund programs, and suggests a range of factors that could have led to this undesirable outcome. These include: (a) the break-up of the Soviet Union and the rise of democracy in Eastern Europe that engendered huge demand for structural reform; (b) 'political' demands from creditor nations for 'structural and institutional reforms', either from interest groups and social activists with such nations or governments themselves; (c) 'political' demands from reformers within countries under an IMF program; (d) from Fund staff themselves who may be keen to protect their 'turf' from competing international financial institutions (IFIs). See also Goldstein (2000b).

12 Cummings (1999) makes the point that the United States tolerated the emergence of the East Asian model of state-led development under the Cold War era because these polities were seen as bulwarks against communism. With the demise of the Cold War, the benign hegemony of the Unites States has given way to a much greater assertiveness in which countries in the region are expected to emulate American-style capitalism.

13 The World Bank has released an 'Update' on the CDF on 13 September 1999 (see www.worldbank.org/cdf). Pertinent discussion papers include Wolfensohn (1999) and a paper released by the Bank on 20 May 1998.

14 The most recent critique of the ineffectiveness of conditionality in engendering policy reform in developing countries is understandably that by Stiglitz. Others include Paul Collier and Jan Willem Gunning. Both the observations of Stiglitz and Collier/Gunning are covered in the *Financial Times* (29 November 1999, 'World Bank Aid Strategy Flawed') based on the November 1999 issue of the *Economic Journal*. The World Bank, in a report released in 1998 and authored by Lant Pritchett and David Dollar, also emphasised that 'conditionality is unlikely to bring about lasting reform if there is no strong domestic movement for change' (Pritchett and Dollar 1998, 18).

15 There has, in fact, been a raft of proposals on reforming the Bretton Woods institutions. The Meltzer report is a representative, prominent example of such proposals. See Williamson (2000) who reviews six proposals to reform the IMF.

PART II.

POLITICAL AND STRATEGIC PERSPECTIVES: THE NATURE AND RESPONSES TO ASIAN CRISES

Chapter 6

DOMESTIC AND REGIONAL RESPONSES TO THE ASIAN CRISIS IN SOUTHEAST ASIA

N. Ganesan

National University of Singapore
Singapore

This chapter documents the representational responses of four Southeast Asian countries (Indonesia, Malaysia, Singapore and Thailand) to the Asian financial crisis. Additionally, it identifies the spillover effects of the crisis on these states, their political leadership and their societies. These observations will comprise the first and immediately following section of the chapter. The next section examines some of the impacts of the crisis on inter-state relations and ASEAN. The following section examines how the crisis has altered regional perceptions of extra-regional powers. The final section identifies future areas of difficulty for the region unleashed by the crisis. It may be worth noting at this juncture that institutional and leadership responses of Southeast Asian countries are interactive and typically determined by the latter, both in terms of scope and latitude. There are, however, some attempts in the aftermath of the crisis to evolve independent institutions with greater latitude to perform an overseer function, especially in the financial and public sectors.

DOMESTIC DEVELOPMENTS AND RESPONSES

The Asian financial crisis clearly ruptured social cohesion and challenged incumbent governments.[1] Fissures in social cohesion were brought about by widespread socio-economic displacement as the effects of the crisis slowly filtered into society. Such displacements and resulting deprivation and violence were most visible in the metropolitan areas, which were home to a disproportionately large workforce and benefited from the previous decade of economic boom. The displacement, which coincided with shrinking employment and skyrocketing inflation, was significantly exaggerated by policy mistakes during the early stages of the crisis. In Indonesia, for example, IMF-mandated subsidy removal on essential household items like cooking oil and kerosene led to the violent outbreak of food riots in May 1998 that eventually led to the collapse of the Suharto Government.

In the Indonesian case, the tensions and resulting violence spilled over into a number of other areas. Inter-ethnic violence that led to the loss of hundreds of lives was precipitated partly by anger and envy against ethnic Chinese and non-natives as a result of the country's transmigration policies (see Djalal 2000, 56-60). The violence between the native Dayaks and transmigrated Madurese in Kalimantan is a case in point. Occasionally, the violence had a religious twist and flared into fighting between Muslims and Christians, as was the case in Maluku. In a sense, Indonesia's breakdown of its social fabric was brought on as much by the difficulties of the crisis as the poor assimilationist policies of the state and, perhaps most importantly, *agents provocateurs* despatched by the disgraced elite of the New Order Government.[2]

Apart from challenges to the social fabric of individual countries, there were also challenges to state sovereignty and to elite legitimacy. The disturbances in Indonesia that unseated Suharto and led to the installation of the Habibie Government were short-lived before democratic elections, held after a three-decade hiatus, unleashed new socio-political forces. Charges of corruption and cronyism also led to the unseating of the Thai Prime Minister Chaovalit Yongchaiyudh in November 1997, the latter being replaced by Democrat Chuan Leekpai. Likewise, in Malaysia, Mahathir's removal, trial and detention of his deputy Anwar Ibrahim in 1998 unleashed widespread support for the political opposition and widespread cynicism over the leadership of the United Malays National Organization (UMNO) – the predominant party in the country's Barisan Nasional (BN) coalition government. The Indonesian situation was exaggerated by the state's inability to hold its diverse territories together. East Timor, after a referendum under UN-sponsored supervision spearheaded by Australia, and Aceh continue to agitate for political independence. The poor and unrestrained record of *Angkatan Bersenjata Republik Indonesia* (ABRI – Indonesian Armed Forces) in both these territories provided significant inspiration for secessionist tendencies. The latest entrant into this arena is the territory of West Irian, which was annexed by Indonesia in 1963.

Of the new forces that have been unleashed as a result of the crisis, ethnicity and religion (or an admixture of the two) continue to be the most potent, as evidenced by developments in Indonesia and Malaysia. Indonesia has seen a greater reassertion of *pribumi* interests, particularly in relation to Chinese economic dominance and the mutually beneficial relations between the leading Chinese business elite and the Indonesian State and its enforcement agencies.[3] Similarly, Islam, which was exiled as a political force by Sukarno in 1959 but enjoyed brief prominence in the 1990s under the Suharto Government, has returned with some force. The Indonesian Democratic Party, which made the most spectacular electoral gains in the 1999 general election, was forced to play a supportive role when the Islam-inspired middle axis nominated Abdurrahman Wahid for the presidency and Amien Rais for Speaker of Parliament. Although Indonesian Islam is generally syncretic, infused as it is with Javanese mysticism and not homogeneous, the largest socio-political organisations in the country, *Nahdlatul Ulama* and *Muhammadiyah* with a membership of some 30 million each and which form the support base of Wahid and Amien Rais, could not be ignored.[4]

Islam is also the inspiration and political platform of the *Parti Islam Se-Malaysia* (PAS) which secured the states of Kelantan and Terengganu in peninsular Malaysia's east coast.[5] The *Parti Keadilan* (PK – Justice Party), which was formed in support of Mahathir's deputy

Anwar Ibrahim and led by his wife Wan Azizah, was also able to splinter the secular Malay vote after having metamorphosed from a social movement. In fact, there is overwhelming evidence that the BN's electoral victory in 1999 was the result of Chinese rather than Malay support.[6] To drive home the point, PK just secured a state assembly seat in Lunas, Kedah in a by-election that deprived the Prime Minister of a two-third majority in his home state (Jayasankaran 2000). Hence, judging by the revival of Islam in Malaysia and Indonesia as a force to fight against corruption and cronyism, it can be argued that religion will become more politicised over time. Non-Government Organisations (NGOs) and human rights groups have also become more articulate and visible in criticising state policies perceived to be unfair or unjust (Lizée 2000).

Domestic political and structural responses in Indonesia and Thailand were primarily aimed at the institutionalisation of democratic practices on the one hand, and the simultaneous withdrawal of government from involvement in economic matters on the other. Democratic governance and the enhancement of the private sector were obtained from agreements to institutionalise reforms as demanded by the IMF and from domestic political pressures that converged to produce a similar outcome. Thailand took to the path of political reform before Indonesia did, and the headstart made the task there more manageable than the situation in Indonesia.

In Thailand, the National Assembly, which is democratically empowered to amend the Constitution, endorsed a Constitution Drafting Assembly (CDA) in 1996. In order to encompass the most informed and yet democratic mandate, the 99-member CDA comprised 76 members representing the provinces and the remaining 23 drawn from 'political scientists, legal scholars, and former public officials' (Bunbongkarn 1999). The new Constitution, which was eventually passed in October 1997, introduced extensive amendments to previous practices, including a mixed electoral system for the election of 500 MPs to the Legislative Assembly and direct elections of non-party candidates to the Senate limited to a single six-year term of office. It also brought in the requirement for MPs to resign from the Assembly if appointed to the Cabinet, set up a new National Counter Corruption Commission (NCCC) empowered to impeach politicians and high-ranking civil servants, and provided administrative autonomy for local government. Among the 'softer' features were guarantees of press freedom, civil and political rights, 'including the right of the people to protect the natural resources and the cultural heritage of their communities' (Bunbongkarn 1999, 60).

The privatisation of State-Owned Enterprises (SOEs) is part of the package of structural reforms to which the Thai government has committed itself (Funston 2000b). They are meant to complement democratic political reforms and introduce greater transparency and accountability in the system. Alongside debt restructuring initiatives, the Chuan Government introduced a Public Sector Management Reform Plan in 1999. The plan broadly committed itself, among other things, to consumer protection, labour reform and privatisation. The plan also has provisions to increase the local government share of national revenue from the original 9 per cent to 20 per cent by 2001, and 35 per cent by 2006.

The privatisation plan specifically identified electricity plants, aviation, telecommunications, broadcasting and the tobacco monopoly for restructuring. Of the areas identified, telecommunications has been given priority. The National Telecoms Commission, which recently selected candidates after closed-door meetings, has been accused of choosing candidates connected with either the bureaucracy or private telecoms businesses (*Far Eastern Economic Review* 2000, 10). If the telecommunications industry is anything to go by, then, the evidence seems to reflect a return to involving the same vested interests that the reforms were meant to dislodge.

Over and above these developments, Thailand has undertaken a series of political and administrative reforms aimed at weakening the military that had in the past contributed to opaque authoritarian practices. The shift of power from the Senate to the Legislative Assembly is one such reform. Previously, up to two-thirds of the Senate was made up of active and retired military officers and the Speaker of Parliament was often drawn from the Senate. The new constitution has prevented the military from exercising such discretionary privilege. The appointment of senior military officers to lucrative directorships in state agencies has also been discontinued. For example, in the past, leading officers from the Royal Thai Air Force were automatically appointed to the board of the country's civilian air carrier Thai International.

Other areas where the military has lost control has been in the area of defence policy, budget allocation, arms procurement and senior military appointments. Defence policy is now under civilian control and budget allocations that previously included a secret budget are now subject to civilian audit. Additionally, the military had in the past benefited from lucrative kickbacks through defence procurements. This source of revenue has been significantly weakened and procurements are subject to greater scrutiny and severe reductions. The Asian financial crisis has actually led to a number of purchases (including those of F-18 fighter aircraft, submarines and air-to-air missiles) being delayed indefinitely (Bunbongkarn 1999, 66-67).[7] Finally, civilian governments, especially those led by the Democratic Party from 1992 to 1995 and 1997 onwards, have been actively involved in the appointment of senior military commanders. Concurrently, the most recent of such appointees have vowed to professionalise the military and refrain from involvement in domestic politics. The current armed forces commander General Surayud Cholanont and his predecessor General Cheta Thanajaro have publicly pronounced such commitments.

Compared to Thailand, the situation in Indonesia is different in that the existing constitution, drafted in the immediate post-independence period, established the *Dewan Perwakilan Rakyat* (DPR) as well as the *Majelis Permusyawaratan Rakyat* (MPR), the equivalent of an electoral college. Similarly, the state ideology of *Pancasila* is sufficiently accommodative to absorb and cope with diverse interests while maintaining the integrity of the state.[8] As a result, the post-crisis/authoritarian transition has been characterised by the implementation of proper procedures that were previously subverted by Suharto.

Habibie's interim presidency was replaced by the Wahid Government after national elections were called in June 1999. The tenure of the present government is the result of a meeting held in Ciganjur, Jakarta, at Wahid's home, in September 1999. The meeting established the *poros tengah* (or middle axis) with the explicit aim of denying pro-Suharto forces, including Habibie himself, the possibility of retaining political power. The axis is a loose coalition of Islamic reformist political parties (PAN, PKB, PPP and PDI-P) and represents a convergence of Islamic and democratic values, at least in so far as it is aimed at denying pro-Suharto forces the chance to form the government.[9] The willingness of Megawati Sukarnoputri, leader of the Indonesian Democratic Party-Struggle (PDI-P), to accede to this arrangement despite having secured the single largest share of the total votes cast is in deference to emerging Islamic forces and their following in the *Muhammadiyah* and *Nahdlatul Ulama*. It is also meant to prevent widespread political unrest and to unite with emerging forces in a common struggle against the Suharto regime. Finally, it is designed to placate sentiment in her disfavour as the 'Hindu' leader of a predominantly Muslim country.

Given this background, it is to be assumed that forces allied with Suharto do not have a natural interest in the survival of the coalition. The disturbances and violence associated with the elections and the ongoing ethno-religious conflict that continued well beyond these, are often attributed to 'dark forces', which is invariably a reference to the manoeuvres of pro-Suharto elements or disenchantment within the ranks of the military.[10] However, the coalition itself is an unstable one and not expected to survive in the long term (Kadir 1999, 38). The reasons for this include the mercurial character of Wahid himself, the tainting of his image by a number of scandals including a US$4 million bank loan to his masseur, and the abrupt dismissal of a number of ministers, including Laksamana Sukardi who is well regarded for his honesty and known to be closely identified with Megawati, and his seeming disregard for democratic protocol and transparency in a number of decisions that led to his public censure by parliament, including threats of impeachment.

Fundamental liberties have been restored by post-Suharto governments. Large numbers of political detainees, some imprisoned since June 1967 when Suharto's New Order Government came to power, have been released and the restrictions imposed on freedom of speech and association have been lifted. Publications which were banned in the early 1990s are back in circulation and NGOs have begun to establish a greater presence.[11] The National Commission on Human Rights and the Attorney General's Office are now important organisations to curtail corruption and restrain extra-judicial processes. The socio-economic impact of the Asian financial crisis, however, continues to linger and the difficulties deriving from structural economic adjustments have denied Indonesia the stability that democratic governance obtains.

In the area of economic reforms, the most important and sensitive are those pertaining to the restructuring and recapitalisation of banks undertaken by the International Bank Restructuring Agency (IBRA). It may be remembered how the zealousness of the previous government in meeting IMF-mandated structural reforms led to the closure of 18 banks and the removal of subsidies on basic necessities, which in turn contributed to the outbreak of food riots in May 1998. The recent recapitalisation of three banks to the tune of US$3.3 billion is being closely monitored by the international financial community. There remain significant fears of a leakage of external funds. The second area pertains to the treatment of non-performing loans (NPLs) – loans that have not been serviced for more than three months. Many of these NPLs were pledged as collateral by banks in the process of recapitalisation. While the value of these pledges has gone into steady decline, the more important fear is that they may be sold off at knock-down prices to crony interests. The third and final area pertains to transparent decision making owing to the enormous powers wielded by Suharto, proper transactional procedures, debt-equity ratio and liquidity requirements that were not adhered to by the Indonesian banking sector. As a result, high level corruption involving large sums of money are being exposed on a regular basis, like the Bank Bali scandal, which implicated and led to the detention of the Central Bank governor (Dhune 2000, 22).

As in the case of Thailand, although perhaps even more so, a number of legislative and administrative procedures have been implemented to weaken the military in Indonesia.[12] Suharto's initial attempts to weaken the military's political role included the evolution of certain latitude away from the military and increased support for the Islamic constituency, evidenced by Suharto's performance of the *haj* to Mecca and the establishment of ICMI

(*Ikatan Cendiakawan Muslim se-Indonesia* – Indonesian Muslim Intellectuals' Association) with Habibie as its patron.[13] The appointment of a civilian head in Harmoko for ABRI's functional political party GOLKAR (*Golongan Karya*) was another such initiative. Similarly, ABRI's representation in the DPR was reduced from 100 to 75 seats before the 1998 elections. Finally, Suharto allowed Habibie, as the Minister for Science and Technology, to make major decisions on defence procurements, including the acquisition and upgrading of the entire ex-East German navy. Heavy state expenditure on the manufacture of a domestic passenger aircraft through IPTN (*Industri Pesawat Terbangan Nusantara* – Indonesian National Aeronautical Industry) was headed by Habibie and also irked ABRI.

Within the short span of two years since the downfall of the Suharto Government, a number of other measures have been taken to weaken significantly the political status of ABRI/TNI. Included in these measures is the separation of the National Police Force from TNI in April 1999. This separation meant that matters pertaining to internal security would henceforth be dealt with by the police rather than the military. This measure, apart from depriving the military of control over domestic issues, was also meant to reduce the possibility of an intensification of political violence during difficult times or utilising such situations for strategic political gain.

The TNI's role and representation in domestic politics has also been reduced significantly. In January 1999, TNI's representation in the DPR was further halved to 38 seats with plans for an eventual phasing out of its presence in the DPR altogether. TNI's share of seats in the provincial legislatures has also been reduced from 20 to 10 per cent. Additionally, TNI announced a policy of neutrality during the 1999 elections and did not endorse GOLKAR as its party of choice. Earlier on, the TNI faction within the MPR had even agreed eventually to phase out its dual-function role, although no specific timetable for this pronouncement was offered.[14] The Wahid Government has also broken the army's control over the PANG TNI (Commander of the Armed Forces) appointment through the initial appointment of Widodo as the replacement for Wiranto. Likewise MENHANKAM (Minister of Defence and Security) was, until recently, a civilian appointee in Juwono Sudarsono (Shiraishi, 1999).

Further reductions to the TNI's political role include the removal of DOM (*Daerah Operasi Militer* – Military Operations Area) status from Aceh, which has been wracked by separatist violence in the last decade.[15] ABRI's previous policy of armed suppression of GAM (*Gerakkan Aceh Merdeka* – Free Aceh Movement) had led to widespread abuse of power in the form of extra-judicial killings, rape and torture. The negative publicity associated with ABRI activities in Aceh came at a time when widespread reports were made of the evidence of ABRI collusion in arming and training the pro-integration militias in East Timor who were involved in atrocities against ethnic Timorese before and after the independence referendum in August 1999. The removal of Aceh's DOM status was meant to indicate the Indonesian government's willingness to negotiate with GAM and arrive at an acceptable political settlement.[16] The highly publicised trials of soldiers implicated in military brutality in Aceh and the powers granted to the National Human Rights Commission headed by the outspoken reformist Marzuki Darusman has also helped to restore faith in the government. However, secessionist and ethno-religious riots have broken out with such rapidity and intensity in Kalimantan, Maluku and Sulawesi that restoring civilian control over such areas will take a good measure of time and negotiations. Such governance is meant to be part of the broader plan for administrative decentralisation and relative financial autonomy.

Compared to Thailand and Indonesia, the Malaysian response to the crisis was to opt for introversion and economic closure, albeit there was significant resistance to this prescription. At the outset of the crisis in 1997, the Malaysian economy was severely affected – there was a massive outflow of short-term capital, the stock market and property sector collapsed, and the currency was considerably devalued. The situation, however, did not reach the same level of crisis as in Thailand and Indonesia, since the country was not saddled with large external debts and had respectable reserves to ward off predatory attacks on its financial infrastructure. At the same time, there was no consensus within the elite on how to respond to the situation.

The imposition of capital controls in Malaysia was preceded by a political fallout between Dr. Mahathir and his deputy, Anwar Ibrahim. The latter, who had widespread political support among urban Malays, was also viewed as honest and capable of introducing domestic political and economic reforms that were by this time viewed as necessary to stave off the contagion effect. Additionally, Anwar Ibrahim favoured the international institutionalist prescriptions of the IMF to restore equilibrium. Dr. Mahathir, on the other hand, was not enthused about this prescription and continuously lamblasted Western capitalists, whom he accused of triggering the crisis in the desire to reimpose some sort of neocolonial subjugation of successful Asian countries. Jewish financier George Soros bore the brunt of Mahathir's conspiracy theory.

By the time the Malaysian government decided to impose capital controls, the political fallout between Mahathir and Anwar had resulted in the latter being detained for a series of charges including corruption, abuse of power and sodomy. The detention, resulting trials and conviction in turn left the country's dominant Malay community deeply divided and led to the formation of a social reform movement (*Reformasi*) led by Anwar's wife that eventually metamorphosed into a political party (*Keadilan*), which competed against the dominant Malay political party (UMNO) in the 1999 general election. A number of senior appointees in the Central Bank, who were regarded as supportive of Anwar's position, were replaced, as were the editors of leading local newspapers that were viewed as sympathetic to Anwar and his cause.

The measures introduced by the Malaysian government included, among others, an immediate freeze on the repatriation of funds from the sale of shares in the stock market, progressive levels of taxation on the repatriation of profits from share sales, the suspension of offshore trading of Malaysian shares in Singapore, the forced repatriation of all offshore Malaysian currency deposits, and limits on the local currency that could be carried in and out of the country by individuals. Over and above these measures, the government created national funds which were subsequently utilised to recapitalise the stock market and large ailing state concerns. These funds drew on public savings and pension funds as well as government reserves. The Malaysian government was also fortunate in being able to access loans and funds from East Asia, in particular Japan and Taiwan. The 'Look East' policy of Dr. Mahathir over the last two decades had led to good bilateral relations between Malaysia and Japan in particular, where Japanese Official Development Assistance (ODA) towards Malaysia has been rather generous. Taiwan, for example, paid for gas and petroleum purchases from Malaysia ahead of delivery. All of these measures allowed for Malaysia to be spared the worst effects of the crisis, although Dr. Mahathir's unorthodox prescription was not well received by the international financial community (Khoo 2000). Additionally, the government's treatment of his deputy Anwar led to protracted criticisms from the West as well as regional political leaders from Indonesia, the Philippines, and Thailand.[17]

Singapore's response was, as mentioned at the outset, totally at odds with the response of the other countries. However, it must be noted that, in relative terms, Singapore was the least affected of all countries. The country's response essentially involved economic restructuring that led to lower production costs for its manufacturing sector, the liberalisation of its financial sector, the identification of core skill requirements for the future, the aggressive use of information technology for education and training, and the creation of independent economic linkages with a number of industrialised countries to further enhance trade.

Among the cost-cutting measures, the most significant was a 50 per cent reduction in the contribution of employers towards a compulsory national savings plan.[18] The government, which leases out industrial land and buildings, introduced significant reductions to rental charges and miscellaneous fees to remain competitive in the wake of devalued regional currencies. As for the financial sector, the government provided generous tax incentives for fund managers to locate their operations in Singapore;[19] this measure was introduced to give greater depth and capitalisation to the stock market as well as to allow Singapore to evolve into a major financial centre for the region.

As part of the master plan for its new economy, the Singapore government has identified a number of core skill areas where there is a domestic shortage of skilled labour. They are engineering, information technology and financial management. In order to make up for this shortfall, it has begun aggressive recruitment of foreign talent with generous benefits. It has also unveiled a S$2 billion master plan to invest in the life sciences and significantly boost expenditure in research and development. Retraining programs to educate a segment of its unskilled workforce that is subjected to displacement by a shift to high value-added niche manufacturing have also been introduced. Finally, in order to increase the proficiency of its workforce in computer-related skills, the government has spent liberally to upgrade the information technology infrastructure of its national education system (*Agence France Presse* 2001).

The economic crisis also took a toll on regional initiatives for the further enhancement of free trade. This development is of tremendous importance to Singapore, since it is not only the largest port in the world, but also because the value of its trade is three times that of its entire domestic production. As a result, Singapore has aggressively undertaken the signing of bilateral free trade arrangements with major trading partners. The most recent initiatives in this regard pertain to the ongoing negotiations to conclude such arrangements with the US and the EU (Saywell 2000).

Regional Responses and Impact on Inter-State Relations

Regionally, the outbreak of the Asian financial crisis coincided with the outward expansion of ASEAN to include all the countries of Southeast Asia. The entry of Myanmar and Laos into ASEAN in July 1997 literally overlapped with the devaluation of the Thai baht, which is generally perceived to be one of the catalysts for the crisis. Whereas the entry of Laos was a non-event, the inclusion of Myanmar led to ASEAN's exaggerated tensions with the West. Notably, the EU cancelled joint ASEAN-EU meetings from 1997 onwards, calling on the Myanmar junta to open political dialogue with the leader of the political opposition, Aung San Su Kyi.[20] Similarly, the US imposed a diplomatic embargo on Myanmar that was renewed and expanded annually. The resulting fallout impacted severely on the Asia-Europe Meetings (ASEM), a Singapore-led initiative.

Within ASEAN, there was a chorus of voices calling for constructive and flexible intervention. After Myanmar's inclusion in 1997, it dawned on Thailand, the leading advocate of constructive engagement – the previous policy pursued towards Myanmar – that the military junta in power was unprepared to allow for external involvement in its domestic politics. Indonesia, Malaysia and Singapore upheld this principle of non-interference while ASEAN Secretary General Rodolpho Severino and Thai Foreign Minister Surin Phitsuwan lobbied for a change in ASEAN's institutional culture.[21] The situation was eventually resolved in favour of a Troika proposal that brings together the previous, current and next chairmen of ASEAN to consult and act if necessary in the event of untoward developments in member countries.

The second thorn in ASEAN's side was the issue of East Timorese independence – an outcome that was the result of the Habibie Government's decision to call for a UN-sponsored referendum in East Timor. The implementation of independence was marked by widespread violence perpetrated by pro-Indonesia militia groups that were tacitly supported by the TNI, which viewed the development as a precursor to the fragmentation of the country, especially in provinces with active separatist movements, such as Aceh and West Irian. At the regional level, there was unwillingness on the part of ASEAN countries to lead a mission to oversee Timorese independence for fear of offending Indonesian sensibilities and risking casualties, even though the effort had an explicit UN-endorsed mandate. As a result, Australia led the mission, with assistance from ASEAN, mostly in the form of support personnel. Australian leadership of UNTAET in turn frayed Australia-Indonesia bilateral relations, which have yet to be fully restored.[22]

Regional initiatives that were undertaken before the onset of the crisis also suffered considerably. In terms of economic initiatives, the ASEAN Free Trade Area (AFTA) that committed the member countries of ASEAN to reduce existing tariffs between 0.5 per cent to 5 per cent floundered. ASEAN was traditionally weak on economic cooperation owing to member countries being at different stages of development, relying on tariffs to fuel public expenditure and protect home industries, and competition arising from exporting similar products to the same destinations in the West and Japan. However, beginning in 1993, when AFTA was first mooted with a 15-year time frame to come into fruition, robust growth and an evolving sense of regional identity and the desire to enhance intra-ASEAN trade propelled the Association progressively to prune the timetable for the implementation of AFTA to 2002.[23] The financial crisis forced member countries to become inward looking and expand the exclusion list for AFTA's implementation. The fate that befell AFTA also befell APEC, which also had a staggered timetable for a similar plan taking into account the different levels of development for countries in the Asia-Pacific region (Ravenhill 2000). Owing to the lurking suspicion among politicians and academics over the intentions of the US-inspired grouping, APEC was even more seriously affected.[24]

Economic initiatives were not the only ones affected in the wake of the crisis. The same could be said for nascent security regimes, such as the ASEAN Regional Forum (ARF). At the time when it was first convened in Bangkok in July 1994, the ARF was received with much enthusiasm as the only multilateral security regime that involved all countries of the Asia Pacific.[25] Although the US quickly expressed scepticism over a process that did not have the necessary structures to support a multilateral security initiative, it tolerated the 'ASEAN way' that tended to emphasise process over outcome.[26] However, ASEAN's collective disarray confirmed the worst fears of the cynics: that the ARF's well-being was contingent on a process that had no compliance or enforcement mechanisms. Accordingly, what little progress the forum had achieved in the few years after its formation dissipated very rapidly.

To add to the difficulty of maintaining a multilateral security regime during turbulent economic times, the level of bilateral tensions between ASEAN member countries increased significantly (Ganesan 1999; Tan 2000). The most exaggerated of these tensions appeared at the very core of ASEAN, in the Malay Archipelago. Malaysia's imposition of financial controls in September 1998 came against the background of deteriorated bilateral relations with Singapore that began in 1996 and added on to resolved differences over a number of outstanding issues.[27] The suspension of the Central Limit Order Book (CLOB) that traded Malaysian shares from Singapore, the forced repatriation of some 25 billion Malaysian Ringgit from Singapore, including state reserves, and allegations of Singapore-engineered attempts to weaken the Malaysian financial system were all related to capital controls. Over and above these issues, Malaysia imposed a unilateral ban on flight overspace for Singapore military aircraft without notice and withdrew from Five Power Defence Arrangement (FPDA) exercises.

Malaysia also had its own set of problems with Indonesia. The most serious of these was the presence in the form of some one million Indonesian illegal immigrants, who became displaced as a result of the crisis. Forced deportations of Indonesians often frayed bilateral relations between the two countries and some Indonesian domestic political problems also spilled over to Malaysia.[28] Similarly, the 'haze' from the indiscreet burning of forests to make way for plantation agriculture in Sumatra and Kalimantan also led to poor visibility and pollution, which in turn impacted on national health, communications and tourism. At its worst, in 1997, the state of Sarawak in East Malaysia recorded a Pollution Standards Index (PSI) reading of 800 (that is, at the 'extremely hazardous' end of the scale) and the entire state was forced to shut down for a period of ten days.

Singapore had its own set of problems with Indonesia. A US$5 billion credit facility extended to Indonesia for trade credit was little drawn on since many borrowers were unable to fulfil the criteria required by the facility. President Habibie who replaced Suharto publicly noted his unhappiness with Singapore.[29] His successor, President Abdurrahman Wahid, also made known his ire with Singapore over allegations of the short-selling of the rupiah, and that Indonesia and Malaysia should perhaps control Singapore's water supply to bring the island's actions in line.[30] Hence, ASEAN not only suffered from lethargy over its multilateral initiatives, but also encountered serious problems among its core member states as a result of developments related to the financial crisis.

Southeast Asia's relations with the major powers also underwent some significant changes (Lam 2000; Ganesan 2000). The country that benefited the most from the crisis was clearly China. It did not devalue the renmimbi to make its exports competitive even though regional currencies had weakened substantially. Instead, it offered financial assistance to Thailand within its limited means. Similarly, it exercised restraint and refrained from criticising the Indonesian government for its failure to prevent political violence directed against ethnic Chinese. Japan, despite offering increased aid and assistance to countries in the region, missed a valuable opportunity to play a regional leadership role when it withdrew its support for an Asian Monetary Fund (AMF) with an initial capital outlay of US$100 billion. Similarly, the US had its image dented for insisting on structural reforms through the IMF and for vetoing the idea of the AMF. The US political and policy elite openly criticised Malaysia over the Anwar affair and for opting for economic closure.[31] The US push for democratic reforms also helped to unseat Suharto in Indonesia. For all these reasons, the image of the IMF and the US were badly affected.

Countries worst affected by the crisis became gradually wary of the US and IMF-led liberal economic reforms and structural changes – there were widespread street protests in Indonesia and Thailand against the IMF-mandated removal of subsidies on essential consumer items. However, ASEAN responses to Northeast Asia, notwithstanding US pressure on Japan to withdraw the AMF proposal, were more positive. The crisis has in fact led to the crystallisation of structural linkages between Northeast and Southeast Asia in the 'ASEAN Plus Three' grouping. Whereas Malaysia had lobbied for an arrangement in the early 1990s in which ASEAN could embrace China, South Korea and Japan to deal with emerging blocs in the EU and NAFTA, the proposal finally put forward was APEC. However, with recent developments arising from the crisis, APEC's leadership and credentials too have become rather suspect. As a result, there is now far greater enthusiasm between the countries of both regions for closer cooperation. This embryonic grouping has the potential to emerge as an enlarged ASEAN without Western membership and direction. Recent developments, in particular the meeting of the grouping's finance ministers in Kuala Lumpur, and the agreement to institutionalise a currency swap plan to assist member countries in protecting their currencies, indicates strategic convergence between the two regions.

FUTURE DIFFICULTIES AND DIRECTIONS

Arising from this survey of regional responses to the Asian financial crisis, a number of observations can be made regarding future developments. In the area of domestic governance, countries like Indonesia, Malaysia and Thailand have been left with the task of carrying out structural political and economic reforms. Since corruption and nepotism have become associated with the factors responsible for the crisis, there will be domestic pressures for competent and transparent economic and political management in these countries. However, the reform processes will take time and continue to be impeded by remnants of previous regimes, especially those in Indonesia. Such attempts may lead to widespread sectarian violence that threatens the social compact and integrity of the state. The compact will also be threatened by the severe economic dislocation associated with the crisis.

The crisis has also severely undermined the legitimacy of the state and related institutions, ranging from the financial sector to the enforcement agencies. As a result, there is widespread cynicism expressed concerning governments and their ability to restore the situation to the pre-crisis state. Weakened legitimacy also makes it more difficult for governments to undertake structural reforms, since the two issues are interrelated. Cynicism also extends to the role of Western countries and institutions, both in precipitating the crisis and perpetuating it. Even pro-Western governments now acknowledge the need to introduce controls over the rapid inflow and outflow of short-term speculative capital and the free trade of currencies. By way of regional soul-searching, it may be noted that the Asian model of development has also come under intense scrutiny (Weiss 2000). Notwithstanding such debates, there is likely to be a greater strategic convergence between Northeast and Southeast Asia, especially for consumer markets, investment capital and technology transfer.

REFERENCES

Acharya, A. (1997) 'Ideas, Identity and Institution-building: From the "ASEAN Way" to the "Asia-Pacific Way"?' *Pacific Review* 10: 3.

Agence France Presse (2001) April 26.

Arndt, H.W. and Hal Hill, eds (1999) *Southeast Asia's Economic Crisis: Origins, Lessons, and the Way Forward.* Singapore: Institute of Southeast Asian Studies.

Bertrant, J. (1996) 'False Starts, Succession Crisis, and Regime Transition: Flirting with Openness in Indonesia'. *Pacific Affairs* 69: 3.

Bunbongkarn, S. (1999) 'Thailand's Successful Reforms'. *Journal of Democracy* 10: 4.

Cheeseman, G. (1999) 'Asian-Pacific Security Discourse in the Wake of the Asian Economic Crisis'. *Pacific Review* 12: 3.

Dhune, S. (2000) 'Bank Battles'. *Far Eastern Economic Review* 163: 51, December 21.

Djalal, D. (2000) 'Strangers in Our Own Land'. *Far Eastern Economic Review* 164: 2, January 18.

Far Eastern Economic Review (2000) 163: 42, October 19.

Funston, J. (1980) *Malay Politics in Malaysia: A Study of UMNO and PAS.* Singapore: Heinemann.

—— (2000a) 'Malaysia's Tenth Election: Status Quo, Reformasi or Islamization?' *Contemporary Southeast Asia* 22: 1.

—— (2000b) 'Political Reform in Thailand: Real or Imagined?' *Asian Journal of Political Science* 8: 2.

Ganesan, N. (1998a) 'Singapore: Entrenching of a City-State's Dominant Party System'. *Southeast Asian Affairs.*

—— (1998b) 'Malaysia-Singapore Relations: Some Recent Developments' *Asian Affairs* 25: 1.

—— (1999) *Bilateral Tensions in Post-Cold War ASEAN.* Singapore: Institute of Southeast Asian Studies.

—— (2000) 'ASEAN and its Relations with Major External Powers'. *Contemporary Southeast Asia* 22: 2.

Geertz, Clifford (1968) *Islam Observed: Religious Development in Morocco and Indonesia.* New Haven: Yale University Press.

Jackson, Karl D., ed. (1999) *Asian Contagion: The Causes and Consequences of a Financial Crisis.* Boulder, CO: Westview Press.

Jayasankaran, S. (2000) 'Rude Wake-Up for Mahathir'. *Far Eastern Economic Review* 163: 50.

Kadir, Suzaina (1999) 'The Islamic Factor in Indonesia's Political Transition'. *Asian Journal of Political Science* 7: 2.

Khoo, Boo Teik (2000) 'Economic Nationalism and Its Discontents'. In R. Robison *et al.*, eds, *Politics and Markets in the Wake of the Asian Crisis.* London: Routledge.

Kivimaki, T. (2000) 'U.S.-Indonesian Relations During the Economic Crisis: Where Has Indonesia's Bargaining Power Gone'. *Contemporary Southeast Asia* 22: 3.

Knell, T. (1995) *The Roots of Acehnese Rebellion, 1989-1992.* Ithaca: Cornell University Press.

Lam, Peng Er (2000) 'The Asian Financial Crisis and Its Impact on Regional Order: Opening Pandora's Box'. *Journal of Pacific Asia* 6.

Leifer, M. (1996) *The ASEAN Regional Forum.* London: International Institute for Strategic Studies.

Lizée, P.P. (2000) 'Civil Society and Regional Security: Tensions and Potentials in Post-Crisis Southeast Asia'. *Contemporary Southeast Asia* 22: 3.

McBeth, J., *et al.* (1999). 'Worse to Come'. *Far Eastern Economic Review* 163: 30, July 29.

Nesadurai, Helen E.S. (1996) 'APEC: A Tool for U.S. Regional Domination?' *Pacific Review* 9: 1.

—— (2000) 'In Defence of National Economic Autonomy? Malaysia's Response to the Financial Crisis'. *Pacific Review* 13: 1.

Pempel, T.J., ed. (1999) *The Politics of the Asian Economic Crisis.* Ithaca: Cornell University Press.

Ravenhill, J. (2000) 'Apec Adrift: Implications for Economic Regionalism in Asia and the Pacific'. *Pacific Review* 13: 2.

Robison, R. *et al.*, eds. (2000) *Politics and Markets in the Wake of the Asian Crisis.* London: Routledge.

Saywell, Trish (2000) 'Going It Alone'. *Far Eastern Economic Review* 163: 49.

Schwarz, A. (1999) *A Nation in Waiting: Indonesia's Search for Stability.* 2nd Ed. Sydney: Allen and Unwin.

Shiraishi, T. (1999) 'Indonesian Politics: Current Situation, Future Outlook'. *Asia Pacific Review* 6: 1.

Smith, M. (2000) *Strategic Centrality: Indonesia's Changing Role in ASEAN.* Singapore: Institute of Southeast Asian Studies.

Straits Times (2000) November 27.

Tan, A. (2000) *Intra-ASEAN Tensions.* London: Royal Institute of International Affairs.

Weiss, L. (2000) 'Developmental States in Transition: Adapting, Dismantling, Innovating, Not "Normalizing"'. *Pacific Review* 13: 1.

ENDNOTES

[1] The crisis and the responses to it have been widely studied by scholars. For a sampling of the literature see Arndt and Hill (1999), Jackson (1999), Pempel (1999) and Robison (2000).

[2] Indonesian politics during the post-Second World War period is typically divided into a number of phases or periods. The period from 1945 to 1949, when pro-independence nationalists fought and negotiated with the Dutch, is referred to as the revolutionary period. From 1950 to 1957, the country underwent a democratic period before the outbreak of regional uprisings in Sumatra and Sulawesi, which were eventually subdued by 1959. Following this transitional period, Sukarno disbanded parliament and ruled by presidential decree, inaugurating guided democracy until his fall in September 1965, owing to an abortive coup attempt attributed to the Indonesian Communist Party. A two-year period of violence followed before the establishment of Suharto's New Order Government that spanned the period from 1967 to 1998.

[3] Wealthy ethnic Chinese businessmen (*cukongs*) were utilised by the New Order Government for developmental purposes. However, the *cukongs* were also known for unfair business practices, which

included monopolies and access to state credit and resources. At the time of the crisis, it was estimated that the 3 per cent strong Chinese community in Indonesia controlled some 70 per cent of economic resources and businesses. The Salim Group is usually thought to epitomise such business practices.

4 The major study of Indonesian Islam is Geertz (1968). For a discussion of the emergence of Islam in Indonesian politics, see Kadir (1999).

5 The classic study of Malay politics is Funston (1980).

6 For an appraisal of the 1999 Malaysian general election see Funston (2000a).

7 Where the military continues to retain economic interests is in radio and television transmissions, timber interests in areas bordering Myanmar and Laos, and banking, through the Thai Military Bank.

8 *Pancasila,* or five principles of state, was utilised by the Sukarno and Suharto Governments for both prescriptive and proscriptive action. The first belief is in the unity and omnipotence of God, which extended protection to religions recognised by the state (these included Buddhism, Catholicism, Christianity, Hinduism and Islam). The four other principles are justice and civility, unity, democracy and social justice.

9 For a breakdown of the election results and the background leading to the formation of the Wahid Government see Kadir (1999).

10 Indonesian politics is sometimes characterised as *wayang kulit* (shadow play). A popular cultural art form, the *wayang* involves the movement of cut-out dark silhouettes of personalities from the Hindu epic *Ramayana* behind a white cloth screen. Spectators decipher the drama on the basis of voices accompanying the movements. The puppet master or *dalang* is central to the cultural understanding of Indonesian, and in particular Javanese, politics. Hence, when sporadic violence breaks out for no apparent reason, locals often speak of conspiracies and puppet masters.

11 In order to placate popular opinion in favour of democratic governance, Suharto instituted a policy of openness (*keterbukaan*) in the early 1990s. Three magazines – *Detik*, *Tempo* and *Editor* – which took advantage of the policy and reported on political dealings and intrigues were subsequently banned. See, for example, Bertrant (1996).

12 The Indonesian military was traditionally known by its acronym ABRI (*Angkatan Bersenjata Republik Indonesia*). Owing to the political violence involving ABRI associated with the downfall of Suharto's government, ABRI opted for a name change to TNI – *Tentera Nasional Indonesia* in October 1998.

13 Beginning from the late 1980s, and coinciding with the ascendancy of former ABRI Commander Benny Murdani, Suharto began to weaken the power of ABRI and simultaneously strengthen that of an independent presidency.

14 The *dwifungsi* or dual function role of ABRI is a reference to its preservation of territorial integrity and sovereignty as well as its involvement in domestic politics as a representational functional group. The second function was coordinated through the political party GOLKAR (Schwarz 1999, 375).

15 On the origins of Acehnese separatism, see Knell (1995). A recent appraisal of the situation can be found in McBeth (1999).

16 Negotiations between GAM and the Indonesian government were being held in Switzerland at the time when the paper was being written. A previous six-month truce has just now been extended by another month.

17 Regional elite who criticised Mahathir's treatment of Anwar included the then Presidents Habibie of Indonesia, Joseph Estrada of the Philippines, and Thai Foreign Minister Surin Phitsuwan.

18 The Central Provident Fund (CPF) required a mandatory contribution of 20 per cent of a worker's salary with a matching contribution by the employer. In 1998, the employer's contribution was halved to 10 per cent to be restored gradually over time.

19 For a discussion of some of these measures see Ganesan (1998b).

20 The EU's most recent initiatives in this regard was the poor attendance at the December 2000 ASEAN-EU Summit in Vientiane which was attended by only three EU ministers. Additionally, in November 2000 the EU also lobbied the International Labour Organization (ILO) to call on its member countries to consider imposing sanctions on Myanmar for using forced labour. The ILO's decision is generally viewed as a precursor for an expansion of the existing regime of sanctions.

21 The pressure from Thailand for Myanmar to mend its ways increased significantly following the election of the Democratic Party's minority coalition government that replaced the elected government of Chaovalit Yongchaiyudh. The demonstration effect of democratic developments in Indonesia, Thailand and the Philippines provided the additional backdrop for the pressures. The ongoing changes and domestic

political turbulence left Indonesia ill-prepared to articulate its traditional leadership role in ASEAN. See Smith (2000).

[22] Australian involvement in East Timor dates to the time of the Indonesian occupation in 1975. The murder of a number of journalists and the existence of a large Timorese migrant community, including leaders of a government-in-exile, kept the Timor issue alive in Australia. Some measure of reconciliation was achieved in 1989 when both Indonesia and Australia signed the Timor Gap Agreement, a reconciliation that was fortified by a Mutual Defence Agreement in 1995. The strategic convergence of interests is often attributed to the Australian Strategic Defence Review of 1993, which identified China as the source of long-term regional threat.

[23] The initial 15 year gestation period for the scheme was reduced to 10 years for full implementation in 2003 (and subsequently this was reduced by another year to 2002).

[24] For a cynical view of APEC see for example Nesadurai (1996; 2000).

[25] For a discussion of the ARF see Leifer (1996).

[26] See, for example, Acharya (1997) and Cheeseman (1999).

[27] These issues included unresolved differences over Malaysia's continued ownership of some 200 hectares of land adjacent to railway lines in Singapore, disagreements over Malaysia's continued access to Customs, Immigration and Quarantine (CIQ) facilities in Singapore, Singapore's retention of the CPF savings of Malaysian workers till the age of 55, and disagreements over the terms for Singapore's continued supply of potable water from Malaysia. See Ganesan (1998b).

[28] For example, an outbreak of violence at the Semenyih Detention Centre in Selangor was related to fears among Acehnese immigrants that their deportation would lead to persecution in their home country.

[29] The ostensible reason for Habibie's unhappiness was Singapore Senior Minister Lee Kuan Yew's comments that Habibie was perhaps an inappropriate choice for Suharto's deputy in 1998. Habibie also announced that the Singapore government had been late in congratulating him on his appointment as President and went on to note that he did not get 'friendly feelings' in his interactions with Singapore.

[30] It was reported that Wahid was unhappy that Singapore did not respond positively to his proposal for the latter's membership in a West Pacific Forum that would include Australia, Indonesia, the Philippines and Timor (*Straits Times* 27 November 2000).

[31] The most notable exchanges between US Vice-President Albert Gore and Dr Mahathir and US Secretary of State Madeleine Albright and Rafidah Aziz, Malaysia's Trade and Industry Minister, took place when Malaysia hosted the APEC Summit in 1998.

Chapter 7

'BULOGGATE' AND 'BRUNEIGATE' SCANDALS AND POLITICAL CRISIS IN INDONESIA

Ikrar Nusa Bhakti
Indonesian Institute of Sciences
Jakarta

Indonesia faced a new political crisis after the House of Representatives censured President Abdurrahman Wahid (Gus Dur) on 1 February 2001 for his alleged involvement in two financial scandals and agreed to issue a memorandum, which could be a precursor to an impeachment process against the embattled President. Following a late night plenary session, the House found the President guilty of violating both his oath of office, as under Article 9 of the 1945 Constitution, and People's Consultative Assembly Decree No. XI/1998 on the execution of a clean government, free of corruption, collusion and nepotism. The House also recommended that legal proceedings be conducted to follow up suspicions of legal violations in relation to the State Logistics Agency (Bulog) and Brunei Scandals. However, it is still unclear how legal proceedings would commence, since there has been no precedent in Indonesia of an active President being taken to court. After receiving memorandum 1, Gus Dur had a three month period to take an initiative, either to answer the Parliament, or to implement the content of the memorandum. If the Parliament sent its second memorandum to the President, the latter would have had another one month period to answer Parliament. If it was rejected again, the Parliament had the right to ask the People's Consultative Assembly (MPR) to hold a special session to impeach the President.

The House decision was taken after it voted overwhelmingly (by a vote of 393 to 4) to accept the Special Committee's report on the two scandals allegedly involving the President. Those who accepted the report were Indonesian Democratic Party of Struggle (*Partai Demokrasi Indonesia Perjuangan*) faction (133), Golkar Party faction (108), United Development Party (*Partai Persatuan Pembangunan*) faction (50), Reform faction (National Mandate Party and Justice Party factions) (40), Military and Police (TNI/Polri) faction (38), Star and Moon Party faction (12), Indonesian National Unity (*Kesatuan Kebangsaan Indonesia*) faction (2), Ummat Mandate Party (*Partai Daulat Ummat*) faction (9) and non-faction (1). The 4 registered rejections in the vote came from the Love the Nation Democratic

Party (*Partai Demokrasi Kasih Bangsa*) faction, while 48 members of the National Awakening Party (*Partai Kebangkitan Bangsa*) faction, the President's party, walked out (*Jakarta Post* 2001c).

Three days before, in a plenary session on 29 January 2001, the House received the 34-page report of the Special House Committee's investigation of the two financial scandals, popularly known as Buloggate and Bruneigate. The report was handed over to the House leadership by the chairman of the Special Committee Bachtiar Chamsyah in a closed-door session. According to the report, President Abdurrahman Wahid allegedly had a role in the withdrawal and disbursement of the Rp35 billion (US$3.9 million) funds from the foundation of the State Logistics Agency (Bulog). The Committee also considered that the President had been inconsistent in giving explanations to the public on the $2 million donation from the Sultan of Brunei (*Jakarta Post* 2001a).

Meanwhile, thousands of students across the country took to the streets on Monday (29 January 2001), with divided calls but a unified claim to uphold the reform movement. The students' demonstration divided into three groups. The first group conducted the biggest rally since 1998 (when students undertook a huge rally to topple former President Suharto), where over 5000 students from some 40 universities across Java and Sumatra marched from the University of Indonesia (UI) campus on Jalan Salemba, Central Jakarta, to the House of Representatives to express their full support for the House Special Committee investigating two financial scandals allegedly involving President Wahid. The supporters of the Committee came mostly from UI, Bandung Institute of Technology (ITB), State Academy of Islamic Studies (IAIN), Bogor Institute of Agriculture (IPB), students of private Trisakti University, and other universities from Centra Java and Yogyakarta.

The second group, hundreds of Gus Dur supporters, expressed their demands to maintain the leadership of President Abdurrahman Wahid and Vice-President Megawati Sukarnoputri against the House Committee. The third group of protesters, which came from various groups such as the People's Democratic Party (*Partai Rakyat Demokratik*-PRD), Student Action Front for Reform and Democracy (Famred) and Students' League for Democracy (*Liga Mahasiswa Nasional untuk Demokrasi*-LMND), arrived in the afternoon to demand the dissolution of Golkar as the symbol of the New Order Regime and to uphold the reform movement (*Jakarta Post* 2001b). By late February 2001, street demonstrations were still conducted by the supporters of Gus Dur and by those who demanded Gus Dur step down.

Just after the DPR sent a memorandum to the President, Gus Dur followers in East Java burned Golkar regional offices in Surabaya, Mojokerto and Malang. The politics of fear and violence were used by Gus Dur supporters to push the DPR to withdraw its memorandum to him and to maintain Gus Dur as the President.

This discussion will describe and analyse the political crisis in Indonesia in early 2001. It begins with the description of the end of the 'honeymoon' relationship between Gus Dur and his former supporters in the Parliament, followed by an analysis of political events in that period, and it concludes with the projections of these into the broader political realm.

THE END OF THE HONEYMOON RELATIONSHIP

The result of the June 1999 general election shows that no single political party won the majority in the Parliament. From 500 seats allocated in the People's Representative Council (*Dewan Perwakilan Rakyat*-DPR), PDI-P won 153 seats. Second winner, *Partai Golongan Karya* (Golkar) won 120 seats, followed by United Development Party (PPP), 58; National Awakening Party (PKB), 51; National Mandate Party plus Justice Party which formed the Reform faction, 41; TNI/Polri which received 38 seats without running in the election; Star and Moon Party, 13 seats; coalition of small nationalist party (KKI), 12; Ummat Mandate Party (PDU), 9; and Love the Nation Democratic Party, 5.

The People's Consultative Assembly (MPR) comprises 500 members of the DPR and 200 members of Regional and Functional Groups Representatives (*Fraksi Utusan Golongan* and *Fraksi Utusan Daerah*). According to the Indonesian political system, the President and Vice-President were elected by the MPR, which represents the sovereignty of the people.

During the MPR plenary session on 20 October 1999, Abdurrahman Wahid was elected as the fourth President of the Republic of Indonesia in a dramatic election. Gus Dur was nominated by Amien Rais from the National Mandate Party (PAN) and supported by the Central Axis Force (*Poros Tengah*), Golkar, and more than half of the PKB members. Gus Dur received 373 votes, 60 votes more than Megawati Sukarnoputri, the candidate from PDI-P. Megawati, nominated by PKB and supported by PDI-P and other nationalist and Islamic political parties, was elected as Vice-President, and defeated Hamzah Has from PPP.[1]

After the election of the President and Vice-President, Abdurrahman Wahid established 'the Rainbow Cabinet', consisting of almost all big and small political parties plus four ministers from the TNI (active and retired military generals). It was believed at the time that the 'Rainbow Cabinet' reflected national reconciliation. It was also a reflection of a 'honeymoon' between Gus Dur and the Axis Force (a coalition of Islamic modernist political parties), Golkar (representing the New Order regime, Traditional Islam, Modernist Islam, Nationalist Secular and the *priayi*), PDI-P (representing the Nationalists secular), and the military.

However, the honeymoon between Gus Dur and his former supporters did not last long. On 18 November 1999, Hamzah Haz (Chairman of the PPP) was fired by the President, the reason given being the latter's involvement in Corruption, Collusion and Nepotism (KKN) activities. PPP was the biggest party in the Central Axis Force. It was the beginning of the end of the honeymoon relationship between Gus Dur and the Axis force. Relations between Gus Dur and Parliament became worse when Gus Dur abolished the Department of Social Affairs and Department of Information. During the DPR plenary session, which questioned Gus Dur's policy on the abolition of the two departments, the President made a cynical statement that 'there is no clear difference between DPR and Kindergarten'. After receiving criticism from some members of the DPR, Gus Dur withdrew his unparliamentary statement.

Gus Dur's relations with major political parties became worse again when, on 24 April 2000, the President fired the State Minister of Investment, Laksamana Sukardi (from PDI-P) and Minister of Trade and Industry, Jusuf Kalla (from Golkar). Both Sukardi and Kalla were fired by Gus Dur, again because of allegations of KKN activities. Criticism of Gus Dur not only came from PDI-P and Golkar, but also from Axis Force and the South Sulawesi region, the place of origin of Jusuf Kalla and former President B.J. Habibie.

On 1 May 2000 Jusuf Kalla made a statement that people close to the President in the palace received money to a total of Rp35 billion from the Bulog Foundation. Acting State Secretary, Bondan Gunawan, one of Gus Dur's most trusted men, resigned from his position as a result of these allegations.

On 26 May 2000, about 278 members of the DPR proposed interpellation towards the President regarding the dismissal of Sukardi and Kalla. In early August 2000, there was a threat from the young members of the DPR to change the annual session of the MPR to a special session which could topple the President. In order to maintain his power, President Wahid agreed to write Presidential Decree No. 121/2000, which provided the Vice-President with more power to run half of the day-to-day presidential activities, particularly on economic matters. However, on 23 August 2000, President Wahid informed Parliament of a cabinet reshuffle and fired Coordinating Minister of Economic Affairs, Kwik Kian Gie (from PDI-P), and Minister of Finance, Bambang Sudibyo (PAN), from their positions. As revenge, on 5 September 2000 the DPR plenary session agreed to establish a Special Committee to investigate the Buloggate and Bruneigate financial scandals.

There were some other political events that escalated political tension between the Parliament and the President. The President rejected DPR's proposal that either Prof. Muladi or Prof. Bagir Manan be appointed to the chairmanship of the Supreme Court. According to Gus Dur, both Muladi and Manan were part of the New Order regime. Akbar Tanjung, chairman of the DPR and Golkar, replied that Gus Dur was also part of the New Order regime, since he was once a member of the MPR from the Golkar faction.

If we analyse the political tension between the majority of the DPR members and the President, it becomes clear that it was not the Buloggate and Bruneigate scandals which were the sole problem. These two scandals emerged as a means to achieve the political ends of the majority of members of the DPR, namely, the replacement of the President, or the making of a new political deal between the Parliament and the President. Although President Wahid lost his legitimacy in the Parliament as a result of his actions, the President could not be toppled by the Parliament, because of the presidential system and the equal power between President and Parliament. In accordance with the Indonesian political system, President Wahid was not able to abolish the Parliament. It therefore then depended on whether the MPR held an early special session to replace the President or arranged a new political deal with the President. It was never going to be easy for the Parliament and the President to negotiate this, owing to distrust among political elites, and particularly between the leaders of major political parties and the President.

Gus Dur made many political manoeuvres to maintain his power, such as stating that the military and Megawati were still supporting him, that many people are still behind him, and offered political positions to members of Golkar or PDI-P. However, both Golkar and PDI-P rejected Gus Dur's offers because they could no longer trust him. Megawati distrusted Gus Dur because of his rumour-mongering about her private life. Further, the division of labour for day-to-day governing through Presidential Decree No. 121/2000 did not last long. It was effective for only a week; after that Gus Dur began to intervene in Megawati's job. The military refused to support Gus Dur in the DPR plenary session, believing that he was in error on two financial scandals. The military, particularly the army through Army Chief of Staff (General Endiartono Sutarto), also rejected Gus Dur's proposal to claim an emergency situation in Jakarta during the plenary session. The Axis Force grew angry with Gus Dur because of his proposal to abolish the MPRS Decree No. 25/MPRS/1966 to ban the

Indonesian Communist Party and the circulation of teaching on Marxism/Leninism. Golkar could not trust Gus Dur because of the latter's propaganda aimed at dissolving Golkar, and for allowing his own supporters to burn Golkar regional offices in the East Java province.

Directions that Events Could have Taken as a Result of these Developments

While it became quite difficult to come to any conclusion as to whether Gus Dur would stay in power or fall from his presidency, there were nonetheless five possible scenarios on political developments in Indonesia as a result of the Buloggate and Bruneigate financial scandals.

First scenario: Gus Dur would resign because of political pressures from his opponents and the ineffectiveness of his presidency. His position would be replaced by Vice-President Megawati. It was at all times quite unlikely that Gus Dur would resign, because it is not part of the culture of *Kyai* (traditional Islamic Preacher). It is also believed that President Wahid and his supporters had been of the opinion that if Gus Dur had resigned from his presidency, it would mean that the President has lost the battle before going to war. However, Gus Dur would resign if Vice-President Megawati took a political initiative openly to withdraw her support from Gus Dur.

Second scenario: Gus Dur would give a satisfactory reply to the first memorandum in order to maintain his power. If this was accepted by the DPR, Gus Dur would stay in power. However, it was nonetheless highly likely that this had to be followed by a new political deal between Gus Dur and other political elites.

Third scenario: Gus Dur's continued political manoeuvring using his supporters to suppress the DPR and threats to take the Special Committee to court. If this had been successful, Gus Dur would stay in power, but political tension would continue. If Gus Dur failed, he would face the second memorandum, followed by a special MPR session. The result would have been that Gus Dur would fall from his presidency, but Megawati would not automatically replace him because article 8 of the 1945 constitution does not state that if the President is toppled, his/her position will be taken by the Vice-President. In line with Islamic belief, the Axis force was likely to play their political game again to reject a woman as President.

Fourth scenario: Gus Dur would offer to establish a coalition with PDI-P and the military. If such an offer had been accepted, he would stay in power, but it would have increased opposition from Golkar and the Axis force.

Fifth scenario: he would accept an offer to become Head of State and Megawati would become the Head of Government. It would, however, be difficult for Megawati to run the government because Gus Dur would have continued to intervene as he had done before.

The most likely of these permutations, however, remained Gus Dur being forced from office (or resigning), leading to his replacement by Megawati, his Vice-President. This, indeed, transpired in late July 2001.

THE FIRST STEPS TOWARD THE RESOLUTION OF THE SITUATION

During the plenary session of 30 April 2001, the DPR sent a second memorandum to the President after the former was dissatisfied with President Wahid's reply to the first memorandum. The memorandum was supported by 363 DPR members. In this session, all members of the military and police faction in the DPR abstained in order to demonstrate to the people that the military and the police placed the same distance between the DPR and the President.

A month later, during the DPR plenary session of 30 May 2001, the majority of the DPR members agreed to call for a special session of the MPR (People's Consultative Assembly) to be held on 1 August 2001. On Friday 25 May 2001, President Wahid proposed to hand over 'constitutional duties' to Megawati Sukarnoputri. However, impeachment proceedings against him began, and President Wahid threatened to impose a state of national emergency. However, Vice-President Megawati did not respond to the President's proposition (*Jakarta Post* 2001d). Two days before the DPR plenary session, President Wahid issued an executive order instructing Coordinating Minister for Political, Social and Security Affairs, Susilo Bambang Yudhoyono, to take steps to prevent the disorder likely to follow from the unstable political climate. This executive order was issued after the military, the police and quite a number of his senior ministers rejected President Wahid's idea of imposing a state of civil emergency and a Presidential Decree to dissolve the DPR (*Jakarta Post* 2001e; *Kompas* 2001). Although Susilo Bambang Yudhoyono played a positive role during a critical situation during the end of May, he was replaced in a sudden cabinet reshuffle on 1 June 2001. President Wahid installed Retired General Agum Gumelar as the new Coordinating Minister for Political, Social and Security Affairs. However, this caused the President-legislature row to escalate (*Jakarta Post* 2001f). Vice-President Megawati Sukarnoputri did not attend the ceremony, which installed new ministers and a new Police Deputy Chief. This meant that she did not take part in the decision to replace some ministers and was therefore not responsible for the cabinet reshuffle.

It appears that for President Wahid, 'a thousand enemies are not enough, one friend is too many'. After he could not get the support from the chiefs of the army and the police to impose a state of national emergency, nor a presidential decree to dissolve the Parliament, President Wahid demanded that Chief of National Police General Surojo Bimantoro resign and threatened to replace the Army Chief of Staff. This replacement could not proceed when the army resisted and retired generals rejected presidential intervention in the internal affairs of the army. However, President Wahid was successful in his intervention in Police internal affairs. When Police Chief General Bimantoro refused to resign, President Wahid installed Comander General Chaeruddin Ismail as the new National Police Deputy Chief, replaced Comander General Pandji Atmasudirdja and deactivated General Bimantoro (*Jakarta Post* 2001g). Comander General Chaeruddin Ismail used to be the West Java Police Chief and Chief of Police Staff and Leadership College in Lembang, West Java. The deactivation of a National Police Chief is unlawful because, according to the MPR Decree No. 7/2000, the House of Representatives (DPR) must approve the dismissal of the Chief of the National Police. However, General Bimantoro was appointed to the post last year to replace Rusdihardjo in a move that never received the House's approval.

It seems that President Wahid wanted to use the police as a tool in his bid to retain power, because he could not use the army. However, to President Wahid's surprise, there was a consolidation between the army and the police, because the two institutions saw a common destiny at this point. This consolidation became apparent when the army and police both joined the parade in Jakarta on 5 June 2001, which was held at the National Monument (opposite the Merdeka Palace) and presided over by Jakarta Police Chief Inspector General Sofjan Yacob.

In early June 2001, President Wahid made another threat to impose a presidential decree to dissolve Parliament on Saturday 9 June 2001, should impeachment proceedings against him begin. If President Wahid had been successful in getting the support from the police to impose a state of national emergency and to dissolve Parliament, it would have brought the nation to a new crisis. This would not only have created a damaging competition between the police and the military in dealing with security affairs, but also it could have ended the democratisation process in Indonesia and opened the gates for the military to assume government.

It could be concluded, therefore, that no compromise could be attained between President Wahid and his Vice-President, nor between the President and the legislature. Compromise between the President and other political elites would have prolonged political uncertainty. The only way the recent political crisis could have been resolved was through a special session of the MPR, either to give a new mandate to President Wahid, or to replace him with Vice-President Megawati.

If the President had imposed a state of emergency and successfully introduced a presidential decree to dissolve Parliament, and the Parliament disregarded that presidential decree and called the MPR to an early special session, a constitutional crisis would have resulted. If this had happened, it was likely that the people would have interpreted this to mean that civilian politicians could not deal with the crisis, and consequently ask the military to handle the situation. If this had been the case, Indonesia would fail in its transition to democracy, and it would have shifted into a new 'vicious circle', descending from democracy to an authoritarian regime.

REFERENCES

Jakarta Post (2001a) 'House Gets Report on Scandals'. January 30.
—— (2001b) 'Thousand Rally with Divided Calls'. January 30.
—— (2001c) 'Gus Dur Censured over Scandals'. February 2.
—— (2001d) 'Deal Offered as Emergency Looms'. May 26.
—— (2001e) 'Order Issued to Restore Security'. May 29.
—— (2001f) June 2.
—— (2001g) 'Relations Between Gus Dur and Police Deteriorate'. June 3.
Kompas (2001) May 29.
Tempo (2001) 7 January.

ENDNOTES

[1] These paragraphs were mostly taken from *Tempo*, 7 January 2001, 42-43.

Chapter 8

CRISES IN CHINA AND POTENTIAL DANGERS FOR ASIA

Gerry Groot
Centre for Asian Studies
Adelaide University
Australia

INTRODUCTION

A number of events in the late 1990s and in early 2001 highlighted the possibility that an increasingly wealthy China, a rising China, might indeed become the threat to Asian and world peace and security postulated by some American observers (Bernstein and Munro 1997).[1] The Hainan spy-plane incident of April 2001 allowed the 'China threat' notion to be re-invigorated and followed belligerent Chinese demands and threats towards Taiwan a few years earlier. For a time it seemed possible that China might well drag her neighbours into conflict through the escalation of an international incident into a crisis with a third party or over threats or attempts to take Taiwan by force. This chapter, however, shows that the risk to Asia from China's behaviour in international affairs, even during crises, is low. An examination of China's crisis management of international and Taiwan-related incidents shows that Beijing has clear limits on its actions. While possible, it is unlikely that such crises would be allowed to escalate to the extent that they come to threaten the rest of Asia.

The most likely threat to Asia from China has mundane origins and springs from the Chinese Communist Party's (CCP) inability to address effectively many domestically generated problems. This threat is despite the CCP's constant work since the death of Mao Zedong in 1976 to improve its ability to manage various sorts of crises. The examination of China's responses to natural disaster crises reflects these improvements in management. It also highlights that such disasters are sometimes created and often exacerbated by the Party's inability to solve basic problems, such as corruption. This failure to stamp out corruption reflects the CCP's declining legitimacy and uncertain grip on power in parts of China. The result is a growing public order problem held in check by boosting the forces of state coercion. This failure leaves a reliance on force, nationalism and high rates of growth to assuage the discontent left festering by basic deficiencies of governance. Yet even economic success has had the unintended consequence of further complicating the CCP's problems, while increasing the ability of the discontented to communicate with each other, and to organise and articulate their concerns, thereby further undermining CCP legitimacy.

Chinese Management of International Incidents

On 1 April 2001, an American navy EP3 surveillance plane was flying along the Chinese coast, monitoring Chinese radio transmissions, when it was struck accidentally by one of two Chinese F8 fighters sent to intercept it and discourage such activity. The Chinese plane suffered extensive damage and crashed into the sea, killing its pilot, Wang Wei. The American plane suffered severe damage but its crew managed an emergency landing on the Lingshui military airfield on the Chinese island of Hainan. The Chinese airforce seized the aircraft and confined the crew to a guesthouse. This 'Hainan spy-plane incident' was widely described as a major crisis between the two countries. The Chinese government demanded an end to American spy flights along the Chinese coast, an apology and full acceptance of responsibility. This was despite the incident occurring in international airspace and before the circumstances had been established. The consequences of an American refusal to comply were unclear. However, any ensuing Sino-American armed conflict could conceivably have drawn in Japan, Korea, Taiwan and other Asian nations with military alliance obligations to America.

Reflecting the diplomatic sensitivity surrounding the incident, Asian countries (with the exception of Singapore) were conspicuous by their muted responses and lack of overt support for America (Galen-Carpenter 2001). This silence had a basis in self-interest. China's grievances against the United States, if upheld, had serious implications for many Asian countries. These alleged 'offences' – that America had violated China's (internationally unrecognised) 200 kilometre maritime Special Economic Zone; affronts to China's territorial sovereignty; violation of Chinese airspace and landing without permission – could all easily have been replicated by China's neighbours. Many of these neighbours also have outstanding territorial and other disputes with China, disputes which could escalate if China's claims against the Americans were upheld. In particular, the serious implications for trade of any inhibiting of the free movement of shipping were underlined by the Chinese navy's subsequent interception of Australian naval ships in the Strait of Taiwan. This action brought into question the freedom of passage through this crucial waterway. Any restrictions of this freedom had serious implications for the shipment of Asian exports and international trade generally.

In China, anti-American nationalism that had lain largely dormant since the Belgrade Embassy bombing of May 1999, was re-ignited by the Hainan incident. Internet chatrooms buzzed with young Chinese citizens' expressions of indignation and demands for strong government action. Many foreign observers saw these calls as increasing the political pressure on China's leaders (*South China Morning Post* 9 April 2001; AFP 6 April 2001). Not surprisingly, considering the potential ramifications of any rash actions, it took some days before the Chinese leadership began to canvass in public some of the issues raised by the incident. Many foreign commentators saw this delay as being an indication that China's central leadership was weak and torn by factionalism (AFP 10 April 2001). Others saw the delay as revealing a government under pressure from both outraged citizens and military interests; the latter seeking to use the incident to demonstrate their own importance and justify a greater influence in decision-making (Sisci 2001a). If accurate, such a volatile mix could easily have resulted in this incident escalating into a major confrontation. However, by 11 April, after intense haggling over the wording of an apology acceptable to both parties, the incident was largely defused.

As became clear, the Chinese leadership was confident and well able to handle the spy-plane incident. This confidence was indicated by the fact that President Jiang Zemin felt secure enough to depart for an extensive tour of Latin America soon after it began. It is improbable that Jiang was seeking to distance himself from other members of the Chinese leadership in case anything went wrong, as some speculated (Sisci 2001b). Rather, Jiang could travel safe in the knowledge that those left in Beijing could be trusted, the parameters for action were clear and he could be contacted easily if required.

Jiang's confidence was based on several factors. The most important of these was that the lines of command were clear and issues involved were clearly the responsibility of the Beijing leadership because they involved the centrally-controlled armed forces, state-to-state relations and international law. Jiang himself embodied the relevant responsibilities as chairman of the Central Military Commission and the head of the Leading Group on Foreign Affairs, the CCP's highest decision-making body for diplomatic matters. On 1 April 2001 Jiang reportedly set precise criteria for the handling of the incident.[2] If military interests wished to use the incident for their own ends, they could do so only from the position allowed them.

The ability of Jiang and the CCP leadership to make informed decisions to manage the incident may well have been boosted by its new dedicated international incident crisis management group. Reportedly similar to America's National Security Council, this body was established by Beijing in late 2000 after the Belgrade Embassy bombing. In April 2001 this body was reported to have had its brief extended to include military, political and diplomatic crises at the national level (Future China 1999; *Asahi Shimbun* 10 April 2001).

Another crucial reason the spy-plane incident did not escalate further was the Chinese government's very clear priorities for the conduct of its foreign relations, namely:

> to control the periphery and ward off threats to the regime; preserve domestic order and well being in the face of different forms of social strife; and to attain or maintain the geo-political influence of a major, or even primary state. (Swaine and Tellis 2000)

These priorities and objectives are integral to the maintenance of Chinese state power but predate the CCP. They are embodied in operating principles: to ensure regime stability; and to maintain a peaceful economic international environment. These tenets are intended to preserve conditions conducive to China's economic development and eventual reunification with Taiwan (Wang 1999, 19). The viability of these principles and the leadership's objectives would have been jeopardised if the spy-plane incident had developed into a more serious crisis. Further escalation would have dramatically increased fear of China in Taiwan, resulting in the international diplomatic isolation of China, and possibly economic boycotts; curtailed Chinese access to foreign export markets; and stymied its search for foreign capital. It was apposite then, that the end of the spy-plane incident was announced by the Finance Minister Xiang Huaicheng, at a meeting of the Asian Development Bank in Honolulu on 11 May 2001 (*South China Morning Post* 12 May 2001).

The Question of Taiwan

Taiwan, the Republic of China, is the orphan of China's national revolution of the first half of the twentieth century. It became the refuge of the Nationalist Guomindang after the Nationalists were defeated on the Mainland by the CCP in 1949. The CCP has asserted its claim to the island ever since and, as noted above, national reunification is a key goal of the Party.

While the CCP is committed to a policy of 'peaceful reunification' under the concept of 'one country-two systems', this promise is tempered by the proviso that: 'any sovereign state is entitled to use...any means it deems necessary, including military ones, to uphold its sovereignty and territorial integrity' (Taiwan Affairs Office and Information Office 1993). In 2000, the CCP set out explicitly the three conditions under which it was likely to use force to resolve the 'Taiwan problem':

- if a grave turn of events occurs, leading to the separation of Taiwan from China;
- if Taiwan is invaded and occupied by foreign countries;
- if the Taiwan authorities refuse *sine die* the peaceful settlement of cross-Strait reunification through negotiations, then the Chinese government will have no choice but to adopt all drastic measures possible, including the use of force, to safeguard China's sovereignty and territorial integrity, and achieve the great cause of reunification. (*White Paper on China's National Defense* 2000, 16)

The Chinese government has created an extensive network of government, CCP united front organisations and semi-official bodies to monitor, oversee and control relations between itself and Taiwan. Despite their diffuse nature, these organisations are all under the direction of Beijing and all work to prevent the worst-case scenario from becoming a reality, while encouraging peaceful reunification.

It is the United States and its support for Taiwan that so complicates Beijing's deliberations over how unification should occur. The Chinese government has repeatedly exhibited high levels of hostility with regard to Taiwan-related issues. This has included overt preparations for invasion and more recently in 1995-96, attempts to influence Taiwanese politics by launching missiles in the general direction of the island's major harbour (Chai 1999). This bellicosity followed American approval for Taiwan's President Lee Teng-hui to visit America, and while serious, seems to have served only to increase support for Taiwan's pro-independence elements both within Taiwan and internationally. It also resulted in the first passage through the Taiwan Strait in 17 years by an American aircraft carrier group (Lee 1999, 47). In this case the 'crisis' was induced by China itself and had all the hallmarks of a 'one-sided crisis'. Fortunately, these rarely escalate to violence (Hewitt and Wilkenfeld 1999).

Yet there are good reasons to believe that a China-Taiwan war with American involvement is unlikely. Many of these relate to the CCP's goals and operating principles listed earlier. While the CCP sees national reunification as its third key goal, this is unlikely to involve actions which would undermine or destroy the first two, namely maintaining domestic stability and promoting economic growth. Furthermore, a Chinese invasion of Taiwan is very likely to involve China in a war with the United States, and the potential costs would therefore be extremely high. On 22 April 2001, President George W. Bush declared that America would do 'whatever it takes' to protect Taiwan from Mainland aggression. Bush thereby removed the deliberate ambiguity which had clouded the issue of US support for Taiwan and made the likely costs of war even clearer. China's already constrained policies are thus further limited by American attitudes. These considerations increase the difficulty of decision-making considerably, even if Beijing feels forced to act by any moves towards independence by Taiwan or is pressured to be aggressive by domestic forces. Further, in any war China is likely to sustain considerable damage to its industrial infrastructure, lose its key American market (and probably those of the West in general), and see its sources of crucial foreign investment drying up.

However, if China shows patience over Taiwan, then time is on its side. Continuing high rates of economic growth mean that China is growing in economic (and hence military) strength *vis-à-vis* Taiwan (White 1998). Furthermore, and as a part of China's three-pronged strategy (which also includes isolating Taiwan internationally while containing its pro-independence forces), Taiwan's economic integration with the Mainland is proceeding at an escalating pace (Hu 1997, 377). China has been the chief beneficiary of Taiwanese investment since 1993 (Tung 1999, 220). Taiwanese investment in mainland China over the first 10 months of 2000 totaled US$2.01 billion for 648 projects, 98 per cent higher than in the same period for 1999 (*China Economic Review* 2000). In addition, despite Taiwanese government attempts to slow a rush to invest in China, an economic downturn and political uncertainty affecting the island in 2001 actually encouraged many businesses to speed up investment on the Mainland (Dwyer 2001, 52; Bowering 2001). Taipei fears that Beijing's winning the right to stage the 2008 Olympics will exacerbate this trend (*South China Morning Post* 19 July 2001). By mid-August 2001, the economic pressure on Taiwan was even forcing the government of Chen Shuibian to contemplate abolishing the 56 year-old policy ban on direct trade links with the Mainland. Taiwanese independence activists who gain too much influence in Beijing's eyes would not only run the risk of a CCP backlash, but they would also hurt the basic economic self-interests of a growing number of disproportionately influential fellow Taiwanese (White 1998).

While it retains the threat of force, China is likely to 'exhibit rigidity in official public relations, but flexibility in unofficial matters, such as economic trade, and cultural ties' (Zhao 1996, 72). Beijing is also trying to build better relations with Taiwan through the use of symbolic gestures. In one notable example in September 1999, for example, it offered sympathy and help after a major earthquake.

NATURAL DISASTER CRISIS MANAGEMENT

The response of Chinese governments to natural disasters (droughts, earthquakes and particularly floods) has long been highly politicised. This fact is embodied in the expression, 'whoever governs the country must first govern floods' (Zhou 1998). At its heart, this politicisation reflects the 'mandate of heaven'. This mandate holds that emperors (or governments) rule subject to the condition that they ensure the basic welfare of the people, an idea that has been a key part of the ideology of Chinese states for centuries (Creel 1972, 42). Preventing or mitigating disasters such as floods was integral to the mandate as China's agricultural base has always relied on intensive and extensive control of water. Should rulers fail in their duties, rebels could legitimately overthrow and replace them. Crisis management of such disasters often consists of rapid after-the-fact organisation of relief efforts in order to prevent unrest and damage to the government's legitimacy.

In the recent past, many natural disasters have been concealed from the Chinese public precisely to spare the CCP any opprobrium and damage to its mandate. In 1970, for example, an earthquake in Yunnan Province killed 15,000 people but received no publicity. Even worse, 'when news reached authorities at the time, the People's Liberation Army was dispatched to the area, and there it distributed not relief supplies but copies of *The Thoughts of Chairman Mao*' (Becker 2000, 369). The Tangshan earthquake of July 1976 registered 7.8 on the Richter Scale and was China's greatest ever. Official figures allowed for 240,000 deaths in Tangshan and a further 100,000 in surrounding areas, including Tianjin and Beijing. Despite its location near the national centre of communications and power, it took several days to organise rescue efforts and for the army to provide emergency aid and begin restoring services. Many survivors subsequently spent years living in huts and tents erected on the streets (Salisbury 1992, 365).

These examples reflect the inefficiency and inappropriate responses to such disasters in the Maoist era. The main reasons that these failings did not undermine the Party's reputation was that public knowledge of such shortcomings was severely restricted by the state's almost total control over the means of communication. At its worst (best) this control allowed the complete suppression of the news of the deaths of an estimated 20-30 million rural inhabitants as a result of the largely policy induced famine of 1959-61 that accompanied Mao's 'Great Leap Forward' (Becker 1996).

Since the late Maoist period, however, the CCP's ability to prevent and respond to disasters has improved markedly. In the case of earthquakes, much progress appears to have been made since Tangshan. By 1996 the State Seismological Bureau even allowed visiting foreigners an insight into its workings and methods for the first time (Li and Mervis 1996, 1484). Moreover, in early 1995 the central government promulgated the *Emergency Responses Act for Destructive Earthquakes*, a law designed to 'reduce losses, and safeguard state and private property as well as the lives of citizens' (Li 1995, 6). As part of the nation-wide *Seismic Disaster Prevention and Reduction Plan 1998-2010*, local and provincial governments are now integrating disaster reduction plans into their planning processes (He 1998).

Planning for responses to flood disasters has also come a long way since the devastating floods of 1931 and 1954. In 1998, the United Nations awarded a prize for natural disaster reduction to China (Xinhua News Agency 27 June 2000). After at least a decade of work encouraged by the United Nations' 'Decade of Disaster Reduction (1990-99)', China claims to have established a multi-faceted disaster relief system for disasters in general, and for floods in particular (Xinhua News Agency 13 December 2000). Related initiatives, such as the *Flood Control Law of the Peoples' Republic of China*, also seem to have paid off. Although the major floods of 1998 caused great harm, affecting over 81 million hectares, killing about 3,000 people, damaging almost 5 million houses and causing 167 billion *Renminbi* in losses, even such stark figures pale in comparison with the floods of 1931 (Dai 1998). This improvement is almost certainly at least in part due to China's Flood Control and Drought Relief Headquarters. This body can coordinate numerous bodies, including government departments (such as the Ministry of Health, the Ministry of Water Resources and the Ministry of Civil Affairs) and the People's Liberation Army via the army's General

Political Department. In contrast to the Maoist era, such initiatives are now even openly discussed in international forums including the United Nations (Yang *et al.* 1998), and have even involved foreign Rotary Clubs (Rotary 2000).

Yet even with planning for major disasters improving, China has been repeatedly shocked by relatively small scale disasters. Mine floods and explosions, building collapses and fires killed 47,000 people in the first half of 2001. In 64 accidents, 1,211 people were killed, alarming Beijing (*South China Morning Post* 21 July 2001). The sensitivity of many of these accidents is enough to have local officials, including provincial governors, sacked for failing to ensure public safety.

The involvement of the army's General Propaganda Department in emergencies again reflects the political importance of disaster mitigation in China. Scenes of soldiers bravely fighting the raging floodwaters of 1998 were beamed around the world. Significantly, this image of the armed forces' heroic contribution was in part to help them rebuild their credibility after numerous corruption scandals involving firms owned or operated by the armed forces or their officers. This need reflects a more pressing problem eating away the CCP's mandate of heaven: the need to reassert order, root out corruption and institute a believable system of rule by or of law.

China's Public Order Problems

On 2 April 2001, just as the Hainan incident was unfolding but before President Jiang Zemin travelled to South America, Jiang and all five members of the Central Committee Standing Committee, effectively China's highest ruling body, attended a very important two-day National Public Order Meeting. The topic was China's deteriorating law and order situation (Mitchell 2001; Lam 2001). This meeting was followed by the launch of another *Strikehard!* anti-crime campaign targeting those behind a 50 per cent rise in reported crimes for 1999 (*People's Daily Online* 6 April 2001). Reflecting the connection between political unrest and crime, the *Strikehard!* crusade was intended to strike fear into:

> the hearts of 'rabble-rousers' such as wild-cat trade unionists and underground political activists who might take advantage of unemployment and other social woes to stir up trouble for the leadership. (Lam 4 April 2001)

The public order problem was further highlighted in June 2001 with the publication of a book revealing 'a spreading pattern of collective protest and group incidents arising from economic, ethnic and religious conflicts'. Worse still, the book describes both increasing conflict and rising tension between Party officials and ordinary citizens, tensions which are particularly acute in rural areas (Eckholm 2001b).

It is clear that the law and order situation, particularly in the countryside, has worsened since a survey was conducted on the issue in the early 1990s, when it was already a great concern to Beijing. In 1993, for example, 6,230 rural disturbances were reported, 21 of which involved more than 5,000 people. Almost 80 incidents involved several counties or towns and more than 1,000 people (Austin 1995, 9). In 1997 some 500,000 farmers were involved in mass protests or clashes with police and the paramilitary People's Armed Police (PAP) (Li 1997). In 1998 there were 5,000 serious collective protests throughout China (Pei 1999). By the year 2000, there were incidents involving up to 20,000 farmers each (Lam 24 January 2001). These tensions were emphasised in April 2001 when some 600 police and the PAP subdued protesting farmers in rural Jiangxi Province, killing at least two people (*New York Times* 20 April 2001).

The Chinese government's willingness to use force to quell dissent is well known. The images of the violent suppression of students in Beijing in June 1989 flew around the world via satellite link-ups. Between mid-April and 4 June 1989, thousands of students took part in demonstrations throughout China, most notably in Tiananmen Square. Originally seizing the death of Party leader Hu Yaobang as a pretext, and using the protection afforded by the imminent arrival of the Soviet leader Mikhail Gorbachev, students marched to demand better conditions, jobs and an end to corruption. As the movement developed, public support for the students grew. An unusually high concentration of the world's media was in Beijing to cover Gorbachev's visit and the students used the opportunity to gain extensive international press and television coverage. Even large sections of the Chinese press, emboldened by the students' actions, came out in support of them. The students also made good use of the increasing availability of telephones and fax machines to publicise their cause, highlight their demands and raise funds, particularly amongst overseas Chinese communities and Chinese students studying abroad.

As China's leaders debated how best to diffuse the movement, the students' demands escalated to include an ill-defined 'democracy', subsequently symbolised by a statue of the 'Goddess of Democracy' modeled on America's Statue of Liberty. On 26 April the CCP leadership issued an editorial in the *People's Daily* describing the movement as a conspiracy aimed at overthrowing the government, a move which served only to inflame public opinion.

Believing that the movement posed a real threat to their regime and their leadership, Party hard-liners sidelined Party moderates sympathetic to the students, declared martial law on 20 May, and sent troops to clear the square on 4 June. In subsequent shooting an unknown number of civilians and soldiers were killed. A recent account from an alleged government insider sticks close to the official figure of several hundred public, student, police and troop casualties (Zhang 2000). Other estimates went as high as 3,000, while the Red Cross estimated some 2,600 deaths (Brook 1998, 155). What is clear is that the Chinese government deliberately set about making it as difficult as possible to establish the real death toll (Brook 1998, 164).

Following the shootings, student leaders and those who supported them were pursued vigorously. Those who did not flee overseas were arrested and jailed. The actions of the troops resulted in the army being renamed by some as the 'People's Liquidation Army'. The Party elders, headed by Deng Xiaoping, dismissed Premier Zhao Ziyang for his support of the students and installed Jiang Zemin in his stead. The costs to China included international revulsion and isolation, a drop in foreign investment, calls for boycotts and a loss of prestige for the army and of legitimacy for the Party. The Chinese leadership considered that these costs and the violence were acceptable because the alternative seemed to be the loss of their power.

In 1999 the world again saw images of Chinese police arresting, often with gratuitous violence, members of the so-called meditation movement, Falun Gong. These arrests began on 25 April 1999 after an estimated 10,000 followers of the movement silently surrounded Zhongnanhai (the home of the Chinese leadership). They were demanding legal recognition for Falun Gong and an end to criticism of their movement and its leader, Li Hongzhi. That so many people could successfully assemble in such a sensitive area without the knowledge of the security apparatus came as a great shock to the leaders in Zhongnanhai. The government responded to this peaceful demonstration by outlawing the group and ordering its suppression. By the end of 1999, some 35,000 people had been arrested for attending subsequent demonstrations in support of Falun Gong (Vermander 2001).

Justifying its actions, the government blamed Falun Gong for the deaths of more than 1,600 people. It denounced Falun Gong as an heretical 'evil cult' and condemned it for being in league with unnamed foreign powers, thus implying an intent by Li Hongzhi to overthrow the government. Chinese police continue to detain Falun Gong followers, to try them, to subject them to intense 're-education', and to demand they recant any belief in Li and his teachings. Those who persist in maintaining their faith are sent to 're-education through labour camps'. As part of the campaign, '[l]egislation was used retroactively to convict alleged leaders of the Falun Gong on politically driven charges and new regulations were introduced to further restrict fundamental freedoms' (Amnesty 2001). At least 93 adherents are believed to have died in police custody between 1999 and the end of 2000 as a result of suicides, injuries from forced feeding and/or torture (Amnesty 2001). In August 2001, Falun Gong websites claimed that 263 had died in custody (Falun Data Information Center, 20 August 2001). The violence and scale of this suppression convinced many foreign groups to lobby their governments and Olympic Committees to deny Beijing the right to host the Olympics in 2008, although this eventually failed.

Falun Gong was notable for a number of features which made it seem extremely threatening to the CCP. Despite avowing any claim to be a religion, Falun Gong has an extensive theology in the form of two books written by Li Hongzhi which explain the cause of the world's problems and maintains that Li's teachings and practices are a cure (*Zhuan Falun* and *Falun Gong*). These and many other Falun Gong materials were available free of charge over the Internet. Falun Gong had very wide appeal throughout Chinese society, based in large part on its claims to help overcome or prevent illness and allow the development of supernatural powers. This appeal extended to members of the CCP, the armed forces and police and, beyond these, to many segments of society. Despite claiming it had no organisation, the movement could organise thousands of members at short notice using a cell structure and modern means of communication including faxes, pagers, mobile phones, text messaging, email and foreign websites. Li himself used mobile phones from the safety of the international transit lounge of Beijing airport to organise the surrounding of Zhongnanhai before returning to the safety of the United States. While the Falun Gong claim of 100 million practitioners is not credible, even the Chinese official estimate of 10 million followers made it a potentially formidable political force. The group became political once it withdrew from the official *qi gong* monitoring organisation and began to agitate for special legal recognition and the right to censure its critics. Since being outlawed, Falun Gong has continued to use email and the Internet very effectively to highlight what it claims are human rights abuses against its practitioners in China and to spread the words of Li Hongzhi internationally.

The sudden rise of Falun Gong and its appearance *en masse* in Beijing was an example of the CCP's worst fears about its diminishing control over Chinese society. Yet Chinese authorities have learnt something about how to suppress potentially hostile mass movements, even if the ordinary police forces have yet to adjust to post-reform social changes (Dutton 2000). In the wake of the Falun Gong protests an intermediary force is being created. Chinese cities have been ordered to create or bolster specialist riot squads. Major cities are to ensure they have permanent forces of at least 300 men while provincial cities must have at least 200-man units. Their objective: to support the paramount goal of 'social stability' (*HKiMail* 22 January 2001). It was indeed remarkable that the central authorities did not have a reliable, well-trained anti-riot force in 1989, as this may have solved the government's problem without attracting international condemnation.

To protect the reputation of the army and ensure it has forces capable of dealing with violent situations, Beijing has also greatly developed and expanded the People's Armed Police since 1989 under the direct control of President Jiang. In 1995 the PAP had 696,000 men (Cheung 1996, 531) and in 1999 was aiming for 1,000,000 by 2000 (Blasko 1999, 327). This expansion was achieved by integrating divisions of demobilised soldiers and absorbing army conscripts. The PAP in Beijing had not performed well in 1989 and the force was re-organised. The 'quelling of "sudden incidents" became the PAP's primary mission and the development of rapid response mobile units became the top priority in its force modernisation programme' (Cheung 1996, 527). The PAP has extensive contingency plans for various crises and has been stepping up the intensity of its training. It also has its own intelligence gathering capacity. Fighting Triad organised crime is another major PAP task. Although it was developing its anti-riot capacity throughout the 1990s, it relied mainly on the use or threat of lethal force. The PAP is also often used for disaster relief and work such as fire fighting. That the PAP is regularly involved in dangerous situations is reflected by the 76 fatalities it sustained between 1996 and 1999 (Xinhua News Agency 6 September 1999). Still, the PAP, despite its importance to CCP power, has long been under-resourced relative to the tasks demanded of it and it has been prone to poor discipline and corruption (Cheung 1996, 527).

More significant than the expansion of official forces of coercion to control protests is the fact that the three types of mass protests discussed have been effectively suppressed. The ideals promoted by the students and the example of their protests in 1989 have not resulted in a substantial active underground movement nor in any indications of any common desire for one. The student movement's legacy within China therefore seems minimal. Falun Gong's challenge to the Party and the government's authority was much more substantial in that numerous acts of protest were carried out into early 2001, some two years after it was banned. Yet by mid-2001, despite its claims of having 100 million practitioners, Falun Gong's protests had declined to a handful of desperate low-level acts by scattered individuals and isolated small groups. The police have arrested most activists and apparently successfully dissuaded the overwhelming majority of practitioners from maintaining their interest in the movement. Falun Gong also seems to have been successfully discredited in the eyes of the public. The attempted group self-immolation by followers in Tiananmen Square on 23 January 2001, seems to have seriously undermined the movement's credibility by supporting the official claims that the seemingly innocuous movement is actually a dangerous cult. In the present circumstances, the few hardened and desperate followers hiding underground do not pose any real threat to the state. Likewise, the extensive rural unrest is persistent and increasing but to date the numerous outbreaks have shown remarkably little tendency to link up and organise into a coherent movement. The state continues to suppress each outbreak relatively easily using the overwhelming force of the PAP mobile units and other means.

Suppressing Symptoms

The CCP has obviously increased its capacity to suppress unrest with force. The problem is that it is unable to address effectively the issues giving rise to this repeated unrest. An element common to the student movement, the rise of Falun Gong and rural unrest is deep unhappiness about the CCP failing to deal effectively and convincingly with various issues, especially corruption. This failure reflects the Party's declining ability to enforce its writ down to the village level and the inherent contradictions between the remnant socialist state and the developing market economy. This weakness undermines the CCP's ability to ensure the rule by law and public order, to secure public welfare and to raise standards of living for all. The result is the declining legitimacy of the Party-state.

The root causes of China's problem lie in the transitional nature of the Chinese economy, politics and society. Under the predominantly centrally-planned economy style of socialism developed under Mao, Beijing had overwhelming moral/ideological authority as a result of its commitment to socialism and having won the revolutionary struggle. It exercised control over the provinces by its disbursement of authority, funds and resources. Private business was nationalised and urban residents were employed by the state in work units (*danwei*). These units exercised tight control over their members by authority over their household registration, personal files, and allocation of jobs, housing, education and welfare services. This system allowed close supervision of all and reduced the opportunities for crime. In the countryside peasants were controlled by their mandatory membership of communes. They were prevented from moving to cities by the household registration system that restricted movement unless approved by one's superiors. The means of communication for all people were limited, being both severely restricted in availability and tightly controlled by the state.

To ensure that the correct political line was followed, the apparatus of state was overshadowed by that of the Party. In many cases the members of the nominally separate bodies overlapped and the two became largely indistinguishable. Combined with the complex system of ministries used to implement central planning, this overlap created a very complex, convoluted mix of horizontal and vertical linkages which the Party always dominated. This picture was further complicated by the fact that, despite power nominally being vested in the Party and government congresses, real power was, and remains, in the hands of small committees. Systems of informal politics, not formal institutions, decided state policy (Fewsmith 1996). This situation further reduces the transparency of the decision-making process then as now, answering the need, even at the highest levels, for outward conformity once decisions are made, and, in line with the nominal upholding of Marxism-Leninism-Mao Zedong thought, an ideological justification for every policy initiative (Kluver 2001). This already complex decision-making structure was then duplicated at the lower levels.

The unintended consequence of this complex and *ad hoc* system was, and remains, inefficiency and a 'fragmentation of power' (Lieberthal 1995, 169). The result is that problems left unresolved at the lower levels of the system can be passed up the hierarchy until someone both willing and able to take responsibility is found (Lieberthal 1995, 169). The famine resulting from the Great Leap Forward and the successful suppression of any news of it was ample proof both of the system's failures as well as its ability to control information (Wu 1999, 286-87).

Maoism and the socialist central planning system did deliver economic growth, but often did so very inefficiently and at the cost of millions of lives (Meyers 1980, 225-37). The post-Mao reforms encouraged faster economic growth to raise living standards and prevent China being left behind by rapidly industrialising neighbours like South Korea and Singapore, Taiwan and Hong Kong. These reforms included:

- returning control of farming to those on the land: peasants returned to being farmers;
- allowing the re-emergence of private business;
- emergence of family and village-based industries in the countryside;
- opening up to outside world by encouraging foreign direct investment, allowing in foreign expertise and emphasising exports;
- decentralisation of power over many economic matters to provincial and local levels;
- encouraging the emergence of a consumer-based economy and culture.

The countryside benefited most from the reforms initially. Peasants, with increased control over production and some ownership rights, became farmers again. Agricultural productivity and prices increased, raising living standards until the late 1980s. Today, however, the negative facets of the increased efficiency are overproduction, falling prices and stagnant or falling living standards for many. Tens of millions of ex-farm workers have therefore migrated. Some 128 million workers have moved to work in township and village enterprises, and some 80 million have moved to the cities looking for work in factories and on construction sites. When they fail to find work, significant numbers of these migrants resort to crime and in July 2001 became the special target of an intensification of the *Strikehard!* Campaign (AFP 21 July 2001). Yet an estimated 160 million workers remain under-employed in the countryside (Miller 2001). Absolute poverty remains at about 11 per cent, in concentrated pockets of China (*South China Morning Post* 14 September 2000). Furthermore, despite the hardship facing many, those in the villages must often confront corrupt village officials imposing fees which, despite having been declared illegal by Beijing, are used to cover the cost of employing officials' friends and relatives, or to cover their own extravagant lifestyles (Loussourarn 2001, 34).[3] It is resistance to this corruption which explains many incidents of rural violence suppressed by the PAP's mobile units such as in Jiangxi in April 2001.

Unrest is also increasing in some urban areas. The State-Owned Enterprises (SOEs), once so important, now account for only a 30 per cent and declining share of the economy. Private business and businesses owned by the successors of the communes, the township and village enterprises, now predominate (Dean 2000, 76). The initial goal of the reforms was to allow the SOEs to catch up and become more efficient, but the vast majority merely continued to decline and to require repeated injections of state funds to support the extensive 'socialist' welfare requirements imposed by the work unit system. To try to impose 'hard' budget constraints, the state forced the SOEs to apply to banks for commercially-based loans. This initiative failed when the banks, under pressure from local cadres, nevertheless continued to make extensive loans to the SOEs. This has created a massive debt burden for the state and banking system, amounting to as much as one third of gross domestic product (Overholt 2000, 17). The state is attempting to rid itself of the inefficient SOEs by selling them off, or closing them down altogether. As SOEs still dominate urban employment, this situation is creating a new class of urban unemployed (*xiagang gongren*) who once enjoyed the numerous benefits of the old system. Not surprisingly, such closures often meet worker resistance (Rosenthal 2000). Workers often lack faith in how sell-offs and shutdowns are handled, suspecting corruption by management at their expense.

Some 6.57 million workers were laid off from SOEs in 2000, of whom only 36 per cent can expect to find work within a year (*People's Daily* 5 May 2001). The age and skill levels of many workers, as well as their location in what have become rust belts, means many will never work again. Private polling has found that in 11 of China's largest cities, almost a quarter of the workers will remain in long-term unemployment (*South China Morning Post* 31 January 2001). Officially, urban unemployment is estimated to rise from 3 per cent to just under 5 per cent in five years, but even this led the Minister of Labour and Social Security to warn of 'trouble' if the jobless rate rose (*South China Morning Post* 24 March 2001). Notwithstanding substantial doubts about the veracity of official figures (and this is not a normal official gross underestimation), it masks deep-seated problems. Being dismissed from an SOE also deprives workers of ready access to subsidised health care, which may in part explain Falun Gong's appeal.

The growth in the Chinese economy is coming from private business, which is now contributing 27 per cent of gross domestic product (GDP) (Gregory and Tenev 2001, 1). The non-state sector, which includes township and village enterprises as well as fully-funded foreign and joint-venture enterprises, now makes up 61 per cent of GDP and 74 per cent of value-added industrial output (Fan 2001). In 1998, private firms surpassed state firms as employers, with 78 million employees in the latter against 75 million in the former (*South China Morning Post* 3 March 1999). The problem is that expansion of the private sector is hindered by the overwhelming dominance of SOEs in obtaining loans from banks. Private businesses may constitute 27 per cent of the economy, but they receive only 1 per cent of the loans. Local officials are still able to pressure banks to lend money to SOEs by extending explicit guarantees. Banks are also suspicious of private business and reluctant to lend to them (Gregory and Tenev 2001, 2). The most dynamic sector of the economy, and the one most likely to absorb the unemployed and the annual 12 million new entrants to the workforce, is thus forced to rely on investments from owners or retained savings. The disadvantages of being in the non-state sector extend to access to materials. Many SOEs control supplies of important raw materials and can abuse their position knowing they are protected by the state. Private businesses must also often ingratiate themselves with officials to get appropriate licenses and the like. Compounding these fetters is the increasingly common phenomenon of Party cadres going into business where they can trade on their official status and insider knowledge. State enterprises routinely get preferential treatment including monopoly powers, exemptions from *inter alia* regulations and taxes and relative freedom from official interference. Laws were being drafted to extend these benefits to non-state firms only in late 2000 (China Trade World 2000), but subsequent enforcement is another matter.

The new elements of private and other forms of business have arisen in part because Beijing encouraged provinces and regions to compete with each other for investment in order to spur overall development. It devolved responsibility for decision-making downwards and shifted the rewards for cadres from being ideologically-based to based on success in promoting economic growth. This reduction in direct central state influence was compounded when the lower levels successfully promoted growth and so created local tax bases that further boosted their independence. At the same time, competition between regions and localities and the new promotion incentives encourage cadres to compete with each other for business investment. If necessary, they offer firms particular advantages which may not be necessarily in the national interest and often contravene national laws. In these cases the principles of 'the centre has measures, we have counter measures', and 'the emperor is over the mountains and far away' come into play. Not only has the centre lost influence, but these lower level subterfuges have also helped weaken its tax base, further compounding its problems. By 1997, budgetary revenue had decreased to 11.2 per cent of GDP, down from 32 per cent in 1978 (Lin 2000, 477).

The protection of local and personal interests by cadres is possible because the legal system is under-developed. Publicly promulgated laws are often supplemented by secret, ambiguous regulations. The final power of discretion therefore remains in the hands of officials, who often have incentives to protect particular interests. Should conflicting claims get to court, the matters are presided over by a judiciary beholden to the Party (in line with upholding CPP leadership). Local judges therefore usually uphold local interests as decided by the local Party. Some courts do not even uphold the right to interpret the law, but refer this to the National People's Congress while judicial budgets and appointments are directly controlled by governments at all levels (Rose-Ackerman 1999). There is simply no independence in the Chinese judicial system. The state, however, must then often use force to suppress unrest when unresolved or exacerbated local discontent explodes.

Despite the obviousness of its problems, the CCP sees fundamental problems with some of the effective measures it could use to address issues such as corruption so damaging to its legitimacy. Separation of the Party from the government would obviate a basic cause of many conflicts of interest that provide opportunities for corruption. But such a separation would also dramatically reduce the Party's power. The Party is too insecure to allow this. Even though it began to promote such a separation in the early 1990s, this was quietly dropped because it further weakens the Party-state. The separation of the Party from the judiciary runs into the same problem. Increasing transparency in order to address government shortcomings and crime in general by allowing greater freedom of the press has proven to be a double-edged sword for the Party.

The extensive anti-corruption campaign under way since 2000 initially took advantage of press exposure of cases of corruption to highlight how serious the government was about attacking the problem. This exposure was to help overcome the high levels of public scepticism about the Party's sincerity. The biggest fish caught, exposed and punished was Cheng Kejie, a former National People's Congress Vice-Chairman, the highest official executed since 1949. A provincial governor, Hu Changqing, was also executed. However, the longer the campaign has continued, and the more officials caught and exposed, the more it emphasised the extent to which corruption among officials seems the rule rather than the exception.

This process of exposure has even implicated the family of Li Peng (a former Premier and, in 2001, a senior Party elder and Chairman of the Standing Committee of the National People's Congress) (*HkiMail* 17 January 2001). Furthermore, in the biggest corruption scandal ever revealed, the Xiamen smuggling case, one of President Jiang Zemin's own proteges, Jia Tingan, was implicated and even said to have tipped off the kingpin, Lai Changxing (*HkiMail* 16 July 2001). Despite 130,000 'major cases' being handled by November 2000 (*Shenzhen Daily* 2 January 2001), public suspicion about protection being afforded to those with the right connections began to undermine the credibility of the campaign. In spite of these figures, Chinese researcher Hu Angang has calculated that there is only a 6.6 per cent chance of being caught for bribery, so the risk is worthwhile (*South China Morning Post* 24 March 2001).

Hu Angang has also calculated the broader economic cost of corruption to the economy. He estimates that corruption costs the Chinese economy more than 1,000 billion *Renminbi* every year, that is, between 13.2 and 16.8 per cent of annual GDP (*South China Morning Post* 24 March 2001)! To put this statistic into perspective, China's estimated GDP growth for 2001 is a mere 7 per cent.

Other official corruption statistics are also startling. Some 4,000 individuals are suspected of corruption involving public money totalling more than 5 billion *Renminbi* (US$603 million) (*China Daily* 20 January 2001). However, as a result of increasing official discomfort on the part of the central leadership, numerous newspapers have been shut down or censored precisely for exposing ever more high-level forms of corruption involving Party officials since early 2001 (*HKiMail* 22 August 2001).

Crucially, though, changes initiated by the reform process have undermined the Party's attempts to retain maximum control of information. The rise of private business and consumerism now means that China has 2000 TV stations, thousands of new newspapers, and telephones are no longer rare or strictly controlled. At least an estimated 25 million people, just 2 per cent of the population, make use of the Internet. Mobile phones, though, are increasingly common. One leading Chinese communications entrepreneur, Edward Tian of China Netcom, predicts that in 2006 China will have 300 million Internet devices 'of one kind or another: laptop computers, hand-held electronic organizers, mobile phones' (Landler 2001).

It is already impossible to control information effectively in a 1950s manner and the degree of difficulty involved in such policing is increasing as rapidly as technology take-up. Rumours about the involvement of Jia Tingan in the Xiamen case circulated via the Internet even when relevant press announcements were strictly controlled. In another example, in March 2001 a school in Jiangxi blew up, killing numerous students. The poverty stricken school was using children to make fireworks to raise money. Yet in Beijing, Premier Zhu Rongji announced that a madman had perpetrated this outrage. Unfortunately for Zhu, foreign media had already contacted local officials who responded honestly before being told of Beijing's official line (*Taipei Times* 8 and 10 March 2001). Zhu's and the government's line became untenable.

The CCP's solution to its problems is to stress economic growth at almost all costs. The CCP's latest 10-year plan upholds development as 'an absolute principle'. Without this principle,

> the country would not become strong, the people would not get rich, the nation would not be rejuvenated, the superiority of the socialist system would not be brought into full play, and it would be difficult for China to make still greater contribution to the cause of human progress. (*People's Daily*, NPC and CPPCC Sessions 2001)

The subtext is that the CCP's very survival is in doubt without such development. The CCP has become dependent on high rates of economic growth to cover the cracks left by its inability to make the political decisions needed to address problems such as underlying corruption and unemployment. The CCP hopes that continued high rates of growth will keep most people satisfied while buying time to try to overcome China's basic structural problems. This dependency reveals the fundamental weaknesses of the CCP: its lack of any substantial legitimacy other than that based on its promise of delivering growth. It also explains why the Party has been placing increasing stress on its nationalist credentials in an effort to compensate for its declining influence (Zheng 1999).

CONCLUSION: IMPLICATIONS FOR ASIA

China's potential danger to Asia comes in a number of forms but an economic one is most likely. During the Asian financial crisis of 1997-99 China behaved in a way seen as very responsible towards her Asian neighbours. This approach was based on the recognition of the need for stability and long-term access to Asian markets and investors. China's leaders decided to use public funds to support the banks and state-owned enterprises and use capital controls and China's massive foreign exchange reserves to stabilise the economy (Dean 2000, 73-74). Other measures included lowering interest rates to stimulate domestic demand and the issuing of more state bonds. The Chinese economy remained relatively stable, although growth in exports dropped from 20 per cent in 1997 to a mere 0.5 per cent in 1998 (*People's Daily Online* 2000).

Of China's measures, the decision to maintain strict monetary control and not devalue the currency, the *Renminbi*, was very important for the rest of Asia. Devaluation would have resulted in China competing more fiercely with its neighbours and forced their plummeting currencies even lower. A trade war would have meant rapidly diminishing returns for all, as well as much greater political instability.

China's actions were at some cost. Maintaining the value of the *Renminbi* contributed to subsequent domestic deflation (Li 2000, 939). Others have claimed that the long-term cost of China's policies was a 10 per cent reduction in GDP (Lardy 1998 in Dean 2000, 74). Yet China's apparent consideration for its neighbours was welcomed and enhanced its prestige and influence among them (Dibb *et al.* 1998, 5-27). The salience of China's actions to Indonesia, Thailand, Korea, Singapore, Taiwan and Malaysia showed clearly how important China was becoming in Asian and world affairs as a result of its development and increasing integration into the world and regional economies.

Today though, in the face of a serious enough internal crisis, the CCP could decide that considerations of domestic stability override any others and engage in dangerous competition with China's neighbours. This could occur if economic growth falls to levels low enough to give rise to serious popular discontent. This scenario becomes a possibility when China inevitably encounters a sustained recession, especially if this should occur before the CCP has managed to address China's structural flaws. If the expectations of a better life by a critical mass of urban residents are dashed, they are likely to go out on the streets.

The inability to address corruption might conceivably result in a major recession even without the influence of any other possible causes, such as a drop in international demand for Chinese goods. If Hu Angang's calculations are correct and the costs of corruption are running at over 13 per cent of GDP and exceeding the 2001 GDP growth of 7 per cent, some sort of collapse is inevitable. This failure of basic governance, if corruption is perceived as the cause of an economic collapse, could destroy the CCP's credibility entirely and lead to a leadership vacuum.

During a recession, any event which sends people onto the streets could be extremely dangerous. Mass rallies on occasions like funerals of high-profile individuals could easily become broad-based protests, as, indeed, has already often been the case in China's modern history, most notably in 1989. If these are badly handled (for example, if the PAP were to open fire on peaceful demonstrators), such news would spread nationwide and overseas very quickly. The 1989 student movement and Falun Gong have shown the near impossibility of the CCP keeping the news of unrest secret from the outside world and substantial sections of the Chinese public, at least those in urban areas. This makes control much more difficult. It also allows dissidents to internationalise incidents almost immediately and further increases the difficulty of effective suppression with minimum cost to the reputation of the state. In a worst case scenario, the CCP's tendency to ignore domestic causes responsible for serious political manifestations and to blame outsiders and foreign interference could encourage military aggression against any neighbouring state suspected of being behind domestic unrest and linked to it by international communication networks.

Internationalisation has other significant ramifications in this increasingly integrated world. Under Mao, extensive unrest and violence did occur (most notably during the Cultural Revolution), but this had little direct impact elsewhere. Today, any similar unrest could immediately involve the many foreign nationals resident in China, threats to the investments of such foreigners, threats to the growing number of Mainland Chinese investments in Asia and elsewhere, broken or interrupted contracts and supplies of parts and raw materials for companies all around the world, as well as shocks to international stock markets. In such a situation, China would have the potential to trigger another Asian Crash. Should it occur before 2008, it could endanger the holding of the Olympic Games. Mao could never have envisioned such possibilities.

Very significantly, the CCP has to date, either by luck or good management, avoided or prevented the scattered groups of discontented farmers and rural workers merging into a single block of resistance. Being China's poorest sectors, few in these groups yet have ready access to telephones or mobile phones, let alone computers and email. Yet if under intense competition the prices of such services fall far enough, then they too can potentially organise in a manner similar to Falun Gong. If they are encouraged to perceive a common cause and form alliances, then the public order problem in the countryside could degenerate even further. If Falun Gong had had extensive support in the countryside, the potential to link hitherto scattered and isolated unrest into a coherent movement would have had the potential to resemble the Taiping Rebellion of 1851-64. This loosely religiously inspired movement nearly succeeded in overthrowing the Qing Dynasty and resulted in an estimated 20-30 million deaths, either directly or from associated starvation (Spence 1996, I).

The most dangerous threat to the CCP, however, is a rival organisation with a credible view of the nature of China's problems, a program for addressing them, and an organisational structure with support from outside China. For this reason, the CCP is extremely aggressive in suppressing any possible alternatives to itself, which largely explains why it so forcefully suppressed the fledgling China Democracy Party in 1998. Falun Gong came very close to this type of organisation, lacking only a substantial political program. Yet the CCP's attempts to reform itself while also coping with rapid social economic and political change at home and abroad, have to date been incremental and half-hearted. If this situation persists, it is inevitable that the contradiction between China's systemic shortcomings and the Party's ability to address them will result in a major economic and/or political crisis. Any such crisis is likely to be one with which the international system as a whole must deal.

REFERENCES

AFP (2001) 'China Forced to Play Tough by Army, Jingoistic Public Opinion'. *Yahoo! Asia-News*. April 6.

—— (2001) 'Chinese Leaders Juggling Competing Factions in Spy Plane Crisis'. *Yahoo! Asia-News* April 10.

Amnesty International (2001) *Amnesty International Report 2000 China* (January).

Austin, Greg (1995) 'The Strategic Implications of China's Public Order Crisis'. *Survival* 37: 2.

Becker, Jasper (1996) *Hungry Ghosts: China's Secret Famine*. London: John Murray.

—— (2000) *The Chinese*. London: John Murray.

Bernstein, Richard, and Ross H. Munro (1997) '"China" the Coming Conflict with America'. *Foreign Affairs* 76: 2.

Blasko, Dennis J. (1999) *World and I* 114: 10.

Bowering, Philip (2001) 'A Case of China Fever'. *South China Morning Post* June 21.

Brook, Timothy (1998) *Quelling the People: The Military Suppression of the Beijing Democracy Movement.* Stanford: Stanford University Press.

Chai, Wingberg (1999) 'Relations between the Chinese Mainland and Taiwan: Overview and Chronology'. *Asian Affairs: An American Review* 26: 2.

China Economic Review (1998) 'Banking on Change'. 8: 1.

—— (2000) March 9.

China Trade World (2000) (Chinatradeworld.com) 'China to Launch Three Polices [sic] in Support of Non-State-Companies'.

Creel, Herrlee G. (1972) *The Origins of Statecraft in China.* Chicago: University of Chicago Press.

Chen, Guoming and Ringo Ma, eds (forthcoming) *Chinese Conflict Management and Resolution.* Greenwood Publications,.

Cheung, Tai Ming (1996) 'The People's Armed Police: First Line of Defense'. *China Quarterly* 146.

Creel, Herrlee G. (1970) *The Origins of Statecraft in China.* Chicago: University of Chicago Press.

Dai, Xiaohua (1998) 'Situation on Flood Control and Relief'. *Beijing Review* 337, September 4.

Dean, James (2000) 'Can China Avert Crisis?' *Challenge* 43: 2, July-August.

Dibb, Paul, David D. Hale and Peter Prince (1998) 'The Strategic Implications of Asia's Economic Crisis'. *Survival* 40: 2.

Dutton, Michael (2000) 'The End of the (Mass) Line? Chinese Policing in the Era of the Contract'. *Social Justice* 27: 1.

Dwyer, Michael (2001) 'Mainland Fever'. *Australian Financial Review* May 21.

Eckholm, Erick (2001a) 'Chinese Officials Order Cities to Bolster Riot Police Forces'. *New York Times* January 30.

—— (2001b) 'China's Inner Circle Reveals Big Unrest'. *New York Times* June 3.

Falun Data Information Center (2001) Homepage (http://faluninfo.net).

Fan, Gang (2001) 'Promoting Financial Reform through the Development of Non-State Finance'. Chinese Academy of Social Science, National Economic Research Institute (*http//www.iwep.org.cn/wec/English/articles/fangang_1.htm*).

Fewsmith, Joseph (1996) 'Institutions, Informal Politics and Political Transition in China'. *Asian Survey* 36: 3.

Future China (1999) 'Beijing Moves for US-style Security Body'. *Hong Kong Standard* June 9.

Galen-Carpenter, Ted (2001) 'With friends like these'. *Washingtonpost.com* April 19.

Gregory, Neil and Stoyan Tenev (2001) 'The Financing of Private Enterprise in China'. *Finance and Development* (IMF) 38: 1.

Groot, Gerry (1997) *Managing Transitions: The CCP, United Front Work, Hegemony and Corporatism.* PhD Dissertation, Adelaide University.

Halloran, Richard (1998) 'China's Decisive Role in the Asian Financial Crisis'. *Globalbeat Issue Brief* 24, January 27. (beat/pus/ib24.htm)

He, Yongnian (1998) 'Preparedness and Mitigation of Urban Earthquake Disaster in China'. Materials from Chinese Delegation to IDNDR Programme Forum, Geneva, July 5-9 (*http://www.unisdr.org/unisdrforum/yang.htm*)

Hewitt, J. Joseph, and Jonathan Wilkenfeld (1999) 'One-Sided Crises in the International System'. *Journal of Peace Research* 36: 3.

Hu, Qingyun (1999) *Jiefang zhanzheng shiqi de Di er tiao zhanxian* (The Second Battle Front in the War of Liberation). Beijing, Guofang chubanshe.

Hu, Weixing (1997) 'China's Taiwan Policy and East Asian Security'. *Journal of Contemporary Asia* 27: 3.

Information Office of the State Council (2000) *White Paper on China's National Defense 2000*. Beijing, 16 October.

Klintworth, Gary (2000) 'China and Taiwan-From Flashpoint to Redefining One China'. *Parliament of Australia, Parliamentary Library, Research Paper 15 2000-01.*

Kluver, Randy (forthcoming) 'Political Culture and Political Conflict in China'. In Guoming Chen and Ringo Ma, eds, *Chinese Conflict Management and Resolution.* Greenwood Publications.

Kwong, Julia (1988) 'The 1986 Student Demonstrations in China: A Democratic Movement?' *Asian Survey* 28: 9.

Lam, Willy WoLap (2001) 'Bitter Harvest May Await China's Leaders'. *CNN.com./WORLD.* January 24.

—— (2001) 'Eye on China'. April 4.

Landler, Mark (2001) 'US-Trained Telecom Chief Builds a New Hybrid Model'. *New York Times* August 21.

Lardy, Nicholas (1998) *China's Unfinished Revolution.* Washington: Brookings Institution Press.

Lee, Bernice (1999) *The Security Implications of the New Taiwan.* Adelphi Papers 331. London: Oxford University Press.

Li, B. (1995) 'Rules Adopted for Quake Emergencies'. *Beijing Review* April 24-30.

Li, Hui and Jeffrey Mervis (1996) 'China's Campaign to Predict Earthquakes'. *Science* 273: 5281.

Li, Xiaoming (2000) 'China's Macro-Economic Policies following the Asian Financial Crisis'. *Asian Survey* 40: 6.

Li, Zijing (1997) 'Half a Million Peasants Plunge into Rebellion in Four Provinces'. *Cheng Ming* (Hong Kong) 238, August 1.

Lieberthal, Kenneth G. (1995) *Governing China: From Revolution Through Reform*. New York: W.W. Norton.

Lin, Shuanglin (2000) 'The Decline of China's Budgetary Revenue: Reasons and Consequences'. *Contemporary Economic Policy* 18: 4.

Liu, Alan P. (1990) 'Aspects of Beijing's Crisis Management: The Tian'anmen Square Demonstration'. *Asian Survey* 30: 5.

Loussouram, Anne (2001) 'Rage Against the Exodus'. *UNESCO Courier* January.

Mason, T. David (1994) 'Modernization and its Discontents Revisited: The Political Economy of Urban Unrest in the People's Republic of China'. *The Journal of Politics* 56: 2.

Meyers, Ramon H. (1980) *The Chinese Economy Past and Present*. Hoover Institution on War, Revolution and Peace. Stanford University: Wadsworth Inc., Belmon.

—— (1986) 'The Agrarian System'. In John K. Fairbank and Albert Fuerwerk, eds, *The Cambridge History of China*, 13: 2. Cambridge: Cambridge University Press.

Miller, Matthew (2001) 'Writing's on the Wall for Rural China'. *South China Morning Post* May 10.

Mitchell, Tom (2001) 'Police on Their Mettle as Guangdong Strikes Hard'. *SCMP.com* May 12.

Nathan, Andrew J (2001) 'The Tiananmen Papers (Secret Documents on Chinese Reaction to the Student Demonstrations of 1989)'. *Foreign Affairs* 80, January-February.

O'Niell, Mark (2001) 'Anti-US Fervour Pours into Chatrooms'. *SCMP* April 9.

Overholt, William (2000) 'China's Economic Squeeze'. *Orbis* 44: 1.

Pei, Minxin (1999) 'Is China Unstable'. *Wire* 7: 8.

People's Daily (2001), NPC and CPPCC Sessions (english.peoplesdaily.com.ch/features/ lianghui0

People's Daily Online (2000) June 29.

Perkins, Dwight (1998) 'Impact of the Asian Economic Crisis on China'. *Harvard Modern Asia Series*. Fall.

Rose-Ackerman, Susan (1999) 'Governance, Equity and Global Markets'. Paper presented to ABCDE-Europe, Paris, June 21- 23.

Rosenthal, Elizabeth (2000) 'Factory Closings in China Arouse Workers' Fury'. *New York Times* August 31.

Rotary International (1998) 'Rotary International Disaster Relief Provided Funds for a Shanghai "Disaster Preparedness Centre"'.

Salisbury, Harrison (1992) *The New Emperors: Mao and* Deng. Glasgow: Harper Collins.

Sisci, Francesco (2001a) 'Downed Plane Re-Ignites Power Struggle'. *Asia Times*, atimes.com. April 11.

—— (2001b) 'Plane's Fate Revolves Around Face and Military Might'. *Asia Times*, atimes.com. April 19.

Spence, Jonathan D. (1996) *God's Chinese Son*. New York: Norton.

Swaine Michael D. and Ashley J. Tellis (2000) *Interpreting China's Grand Strategy*. Rand Research Brief (http://www.rand.org/publications/RB/RB61).

Taiwan Affairs Office and Information Office, State Council (1993) *The Taiwan Question and Reunification of China*, Beijing, 1993, Part 1: Taiwan - An Inalienable Part of China (english.peopledaily.com.cn).

Taiwan Affairs Office and the Information Office, People's Republic of China (2000) *The One-China Principle and the Taiwan Issue*. Beijing, February. (White Paper).

Tung, Chen-Yuen (1999) 'Trilateral Economic Relations among Taiwan, China and the United States'. *Asian Affairs: An American Review* 225: 4.

Vermander, Benoit (2001) 'Looking at China Through the Mirror of Falun Gong'. *China Perspectives* 35 May-June.

Wang, Fei-ling (1999) 'China's Self Image and Strategic Intentions: National Confidence and Political Insecurity'. Paper presented to conference of 'War and Peace in the Taiwan Strait'. Duke University, February 26-27.

White, Lynn T. (1998) 'Taiwan's China Problem: After a Decade or Two, Can there be Solution?' *SAIS Policy Forum Series*, Report Number Six, Johns Hopkins University.

White Paper on China's National Defense (2000).

Wortzel, Larry M. (2000) 'Challenges As China's Communist Leaders Ride The Tiger Of Liberalization'. *The Heritage Foundation Heritage Lectures* 669.

Wu, Yuanli (1999) 'The Changing Nature of Non-Transparency'. In Eberhard Sandschneider, ed., *The Study of Modern China: A Volume in Honor of Jurgen Domes*. London: Hurst and Co.

Yang, Qinye, Zhiyong Fang and Peijun Shi (1998) 'The Resettlement of Rehabilitation after Flood 1998 in China [sic]'. *Materials from Chinese Delegation to IDNDR Programme Forum*, July 5-9, Geneva (http://www.unisdr.org/unisdrforum/yang.htm).

Zhang, Liang (2000) *The Tiananmen Papers: The Chinese Leadership's Decision to Use Force Against Their Own People – In Their Own Words*. New York: Public Affairs.

Zhao, Suisheng (1999) 'Military Coercion and Peaceful Offence: Beijing's Strategy of National Reunification with Taiwan'. *Pacific Affairs* 72: 4.

Zhao, Quansheng (1996) *Interpreting Chinese Foreign Policy*. Hong Kong: Oxford University Press.

Zheng, Yongnian (1999) *Discovering Chinese Nationalism in China*. New York: Cambridge University Press.

Zhou, Kuiyi (1998) 'Human-Nature-Disaster Ancient Thoughts on Flood Disasters and Socialization of Their Reduction'. *Journal of IWHR* 2: 2.

ENDNOTES

1 There is a very interesting body of this material, for example: Stephen Mosher, *Hegemon: China's Plan to Dominate Asia and the World* (Encounter Books, 2000); Edward Timperlake, *Red Dragon Rising: Communist China's Military Threat to America* (Regnery Publishing, 1999).

2 These criteria were: The Centre (that is, the Central Government in Beijing) must protect itself from popular criticisms of weakness while not allowing nationalist protests to get out of hand; to teach George Bush a lesson early on, and not let the negotiations drag out more than two weeks.

3 This corruption has given rise to a new version of the Four Cardinal Principles for officials. The original principles are: always adhere to the socialist road, uphold the leading role of the CCP, uphold the people's democratic dictatorship and adhere to Marxism-Leninism-Mao Zedong thought. The new version holds

that: in eating, the cardinal principle is for other people to invite you; in wanting things, the cardinal principle is for people to give them to you as gifts; for one's pay, the cardinal principle is not to do any work; as for one's wife, the cardinal principle is who needs her?

Chapter 9

Regional Dimensions of Political Crises in South Asia

Samina Ahmed
Belfer Center for Science and International Affairs
John F. Kennedy School of Government
Harvard University

Political stability continues to elude South Asia in the twenty-first century. Most South Asian states confront violent challenges to their authority, ranging from civil disobedience to all-out civil war. Internal determinants are primarily responsible for the political crises confronting South Asia. Half a century after their independence from colonial rule, the South Asian states have failed, in varying degrees, to provide political or economic security to their citizens. Official neglect or ineptitude perpetuates unequal economic development and poverty and further impairs inadequate administrative infrastructures. Since weak, incompetent or indifferent governments either fail to meet or deliberately ignore the social, economic and political needs of their populace, it is not surprising that the legitimacy of the state and its institutions are increasingly questioned by the citizenry. Domestic discontent in turn threatens both the security of the state and its citizens since it often results in violent internal conflict.

Internal factors, particularly the state's failure to respond adequately to domestic challenges, are primarily responsible for widespread discontent and threats to state authority. However, regional imperatives also play a significant role in shaping the directions of political crises in South Asia. Focusing on inter-ethnic and ethnic-state tensions and conflict, this chapter will examine the linkages between internal and external determinants of crises in South Asia. Examining regional determinants of internal conflict, the study will identify factors that make South Asian states more or less vulnerable to external influence and intervention in political crises. Assessing the impact of regional imperatives on inter-ethnic and ethnic-state tensions and conflict, the study will analyse the interventionist motivations of substate or state-level actors, and weigh the relative impact of domestic and external factors on political stability in South Asia. Finally the chapter will determine the extent to which the political stability of South Asian states is undermined by their interventionist policies.

THE CRISIS OF ETHNICITY IN SOUTH ASIA

Ethnic conflict is endemic in South Asia. Multi-ethnic India's internal stability is threatened by a violent secessionist struggle in Jammu and Kashmir, by ethnic tensions, insurgencies and separatist movements in its Northeastern states, by caste-based conflict, and by periodic outbreaks of violence between its Hindu majority and Muslim and Christian minorities. Dismembered in 1971 following the secession of its majority Bengali population, multi-ethnic Pakistan continues to confront multiple threats to state authority. Disgruntled ethnic minorities, including the Sindhis, Baluch and Pakhtun, resent the political and economic dominance of Pakistan's Punjabi-controlled centre. Pakistan's internal stability is also undermined by violent sectarian and ethnic conflict, particularly in the province of Sindh. A bloody civil war between its majority Sinhala and minority Tamil populations threatens the security of the Sri Lankan state. Even in South Asian states with greater ethnic homogeneity such as Bangladesh, relations between minuscule ethnic minorities and the state periodically degenerate into conflict.

There is a close linkage between internal and regional determinants of ethnic conflict in South Asia. External imperatives, in varying degrees, influence the dynamics of ethnic relations in all South Asian states. Regional factors contribute to ethnic tensions, ethnic conflict and even the outbreak of civil war. Some cases of inter-ethnic and ethnic-state conflict are more vulnerable to external influence and intervention than others. The effectiveness of regional intervention in inter-ethnic crises is determined by a number of factors. These factors can be specifically ethnic in nature. For instance, the ethnic geography, history and policy preferences of the state determine its internal ethnic dynamics and the scope and impact of external intervention.[1] Indirect factors, particularly inter-state competition, tensions and conflict, also play a significant role in motivating regional intervention and determining its effectiveness in shaping the course of internal political crises.

ETHNIC DYNAMICS AND REGIONAL INTERVENTION

Their ethnic history, geography, and policy preferences have made a number of South Asian states vulnerable to regional influence and intervention in their internal crises. Ethnic dynamics in South Asia are shaped by its colonial past as well as by its post-colonial history. The use of ethnic divide-and-rule tactics by colonial rulers enhanced inter-ethnic tensions, which were further aggravated by colonial practices of drawing and redrawing ethnic borders and relocating ethnic communities for political and economic purposes. Independence from colonial rule also transformed South Asia's ethnic landscape. State borders were arbitrarily drawn by departing colonial powers, dividing communities with perceived common ethnic histories and identities. In post-colonial South Asia too, inter-state conflicts and wars redrew territorial borders, dividing ethnic communities. The presence of divided ethnic communities heightens the potential for external influence and intervention in inter-ethnic or ethnic-state conflict. Crossborder ethnic communities can form a support-base for their ethnic kin, and provide states with an opportunity to intervene in the internal crises of their regional rivals.

Since most South Asian states are also incapable of exerting effective control over their territorial borders, they are particularly vulnerable to regional intervention when dissident ethnic communities are located near international borders (Brown 1997, 524). Porous borders enable ethnic dissidents to acquire sanctuary as well as bases for their military operations in neighbouring states. States are also tempted to intervene in the internal conflict of their regional rivals when border controls are weak and when ethnic dissidents are geographically concentrated along international borders. For instance, Chakma tribal rebels in Bangladesh gained sanctuary as well as bases in India for their armed struggle against the Bangladeshi state, supported initially by their Indian tribal kin.[2] India has extended support to ethnic dissidents in the Pakistani border province of Sindh, while Pakistan has supported Sikh militants in the neighbouring Indian state of the Punjab.

Sri Lanka's ethnic dynamics are shaped by its colonial history, its ethnic geography, and the ethnic policies of the state. Competition over access to political power and economic resources between Sri Lanka's Buddhist Sinhala majority and its Hindu Tamil minority has degenerated into an all-out civil war.[3] The roots of the conflict can be found in Sri Lanka's colonial past. To perpetuate their control over Sri Lanka, the British adopted divide-and-rule policies, extending preferential treatment to the minority Tamil community over the majority Sinhala population. The resultant tensions between the Sinhala and the Tamils were further aggravated by colonial practices of shifting ethnic populations for economic purposes, in the Sri Lankan case by Britain's introduction of Tamil plantation labour from India (Gunaratna 1995, 81). In independent Sri Lanka, guided by perceptions that they had the responsibility of undoing colonial wrongs and motivated by inter-ethnic competition, Sinhala political parties and Sinhala-dominated governments subjected the Tamil minority to political, cultural and economic discrimination.

When Tamil dissent assumed a violent form, Tamils became the targets of Sinhala violence and state repression. While their geographic concentration in north and northeast Sri Lanka helped the Tamils to mobilise politically and militarily, external factors came into play due to the presence of a large Tamil population a few miles away across the Palk Straits in India. Sri Lankan Tamil refugees and dissidents sought the support of their ethnic kin in the Indian state of Tamil Nadu, where they were provided sanctuary as well as military support, including arms and bases to conduct their war against the Sri Lankan state (Rose 1987, 13-14). Sri Lanka's inability to control either the movement of its dissidents or the inflow of arms contributed to the violent conflict that followed.

Colonial history and ethnic geography also play a major role in determining the directions of the conflict in Jammu and Kashmir. Kashmir was included in the Indian state by the terms of the partition of Britain's Indian Empire. Since Britain had given the rulers of its princely states the right to accede to either India or Pakistan, the Hindu ruler of Kashmir opted for accession with India, despite Kashmir's Muslim majority population and its territorial contiguity to Muslim-majority Pakistan. Rejecting the legitimacy of the accession from 1948-49, Pakistan fought its first war with India over Kashmir. As a result, Kashmir's population was divided when Pakistan captured one-third of Kashmiri territory (referred to hereafter as Azad 'free' Kashmir), while the rest remained under India's control (referred to hereafter as Jammu and Kashmir). Five decades later, segments of the Kashmiri population continue to reject the authority of the Indian state, sustained in their struggle for self-determination by the presence of their cross-border ethnic kin in Azad Kashmir and the support of the Pakistani state. The porous border dividing both parts of Kashmir enables Kashmiri dissidents from India to acquire sanctuary as well as bases for their military operations in Azad Kashmir. Kashmiri insurgency is also sustained by the flow of arms and the influx of Pakistani-sponsored Kashmiri and non-Kashmiri militants into Jammu and Kashmir.

INTER-STATE COMPETITION AND CONFLICT

Substate ethnic actors are motivated to intervene in cross-border internal conflicts for a number of reasons: for humanitarian reasons; to protect their ethnic kin against perceived threats from the state or from rival ethnic communities; or in response to a desire to strengthen them politically and militarily *vis-à-vis* perceived ethnic rivals or the state. However, the extent to which ethnic communities can influence or intervene in external conflicts and crises largely depends on the policy preferences of their domestic policymakers. Indian Tamils can provide political and military assistance to Sri Lankan Tamils only to the extent that their objectives coincide with the policy preferences of their state government of Tamil Nadu as well as the central government in New Delhi. The extent to which Kashmiris in Azad Kashmir can intervene in the conflict in Jammu and Kashmir also depends on the policies of the Pakistani government.

The response of policymakers to conflict within the borders of another sovereign entity is also dependent on a number of internal and external determinants. Domestic factors can include the influence of ethnic constituencies in shaping official responses to external political crises. Decisionmakers might, for example, be motivated by the desire to obtain the support of important domestic constituencies or to undermine the support-base of their political rivals. Key external variables include the presence or absence of inter-state competition or conflict and relative inter-state capabilities, political, military and economic. While humanitarian considerations can motivate regional intervention in internal conflicts, states are far more likely to intervene to protect or to advance perceived national interests and goals. States can opt for intervention to attain or to enhance their external influence and standing, to undermine the political stability and military security of a rival state, or to promote the interests of chosen external ethnic clients and partners.[4] Very often, regional intervention is motivated by multiple internal and external factors, a case in point being India's role in the secessionist struggle that led to the formation of Bangladesh.

When the British Indian empire was divided into two successor states in 1947, Muslim-majority East Bengal opted for accession with Pakistan. During colonial rule, Bengali loyalty had been questioned by the British. As a result, Bengalis were deliberately excluded from the British Indian army while Punjabis and Pakhtuns were disproportionately represented. Successive Pakistani governments continued the colonial practice of excluding their majority Bengali population from recruitment to the military (Sisson and Rose 1990, 10). After Pakistan's Punjabi-dominated military took over direct control of the state in 1958, the Bengalis of East Pakistan were deprived of all access to political power. Subjected to cultural discrimination and economic exploitation by the centre, their demands for autonomy rejected, Bengalis at first confronted and then altogether rejected the West Pakistani-dominated state.

Regional imperatives played a major role in the civil war that ensued in the East wing in 1971, separated from the rest of Pakistan by a thousand miles of Indian territory. During the civil war, hundreds of thousands of civilians were killed as a result of Pakistani military action. Millions of Bengali refugees were forced to flee across the India-Pakistan border. Pakistani Bengalis took refuge in the neighbouring state of West Bengal. Divided by religion and culture from their linguistic kin, West Bengalis perceived the influx of refugees from East Bengal as a political and economic threat (Ganguly 1986, 118-19). While Indian Bengalis were disinclined to assist Bangladeshi refugees and dissidents, India opted to support the secessionist demand for an independent Bangladesh. India's decision to provide refuge to East Bengali dissidents and to support Bengali secession was motivated in part by humanitarian motives. Concerns about the political and economic ramifications of the continued presence of millions of Bengali refugees on its territory also motivated India to support the demand for an independent Bangladesh (Koithara 1999, 86-87). However, India's decision to train, arm and organise East Pakistani secessionists and subsequently to opt for direct military intervention and an all-out war with Pakistan was primarily dictated by India's desire to undermine its regional rival at a time when Pakistan was most vulnerable (Sisson and Rose 1990, 207-208).

In the Sri Lankan case, when Tamils violently confronted the state, alienated by the rejection of their moderate demands for autonomy and responding to institutionalised socio-economic and political discrimination, the Sinhala-dominated state opted forcibly to repress Tamil dissent. Sinhala violence and the use of military force by the state resulted in Sri Lankan Tamil refugees and militants seeking refuge with their ethnic kin in the Indian state of Tamil Nadu. Indian Tamils pressured their state government as well as New Delhi to protect their Sri Lankan kin against Sinhala repression. Responding to domestic pressures, successive state and central governments in India extended sanctuary as well as military training and arms to Sri Lankan Tamil rebels. Alongside domestic pressures, perceived security interests also motivated India to intervene directly in Sri Lanka's civil war. Thus, India's military and diplomatic intervention was partly a response to Sri Lankan attempts to gain support from extra-regional actors, including the United States, which would have undermined India's regional influence and standing (Phadnis 1989, 222-23; see also Rizvi 1986, 138-39).

Relative political, military and economic capabilities can also dictate regional responses to inter-ethnic and ethnic-state conflict. Indian Gurkhas, fighting for an independent state, Gorkhaland, took refuge in neighbouring Nepal. Although Nepal has a substantial Gurkha population, its military inferiority and its economic dependence on India dictated a cautious official response (Tiwari 1989, 109-10, 136). Nepal was equally disinclined to adopt an aggressive interventionist role to defend the interests of the ethnic Nepali-speaking minority in Bhutan. Although Nepali speakers were subjected to political and cultural discrimination by the Bhutanese state, Nepal's response was dictated by India's virtual political and military suzerainty over Bhutan.

In the Indian state of Assam, internal unrest is rife, fueled by demands for political, economic and cultural autonomy from the centre and Assamese opposition to the presence of a large Bengali population, West Bengalis as well as immigrants from Bangladesh. Perceiving outsiders, both Indian Bengalis and Bangladeshis, as a cultural, social and economic threat, the Assamese have periodically resorted to anti-state and anti-Bengali violence (Ghoshal 1993, 72-73). Although its citizens are subjected to substate violence in Assam, Bangladesh's military asymmetry with India prevents it from adopting an assertive or interventionist role. However, Bangladesh also chooses, as a result of economic imperatives (mainly population pressures on its limited natural resources) deliberately to ignore the cross-border influx of its citizens to India (Ali 1993, 60-61). Hence Bangladesh's seemingly non-interventionist policy contributes to inter-ethnic conflict and political instability in India's northeastern provinces.

INTERNAL AND EXTERNAL DETERMINANTS OF POLITICAL CRISES

While states can be vulnerable to regional influence and intervention in their internal crises, the extent of their vulnerability ultimately depends on domestic imperatives.[5] In the context of ethnic relations, external intervention is only effective when ethnic tensions transform into conflict, undermining the political stability of the target state. The mere presence of a multi-ethnic population or of a significant ethnic minority does not inevitably result in internal conflict. Ethnic communities will use ethnic markers of identity for political mobilisation, to bargain with rival substate actors, and to negotiate with the state for social, political and economic benefits. While bargaining and competition along ethnic lines can contribute to inter-ethnic and ethnic-state tensions, conflict occurs only when ethnic relations are mismanaged by the state.

Should official policies result in the outbreak of internal conflict in a state, external actors are provided with opportunities to intervene in its domestic crises. The effectiveness of external intervention depends in turn on the extent to which domestic actors are alienated from the state. However, inter-ethnic and ethnic-state relations are not static, and their internal dynamics will continue to be shaped by official policies. Should changes in internal policies successfully manage, reduce, or resolve ethnic conflict, external intervention becomes less effective and external actors can even be deprived of an opportunity to intervene.

While this chapter focuses on the external dimensions of internal crises and not on crisis prevention, management or resolution, it is important to identify the conditions under which official policies can promote, contain or resolve internal conflicts. Inter-ethnic and ethnic-state conflict is most likely to occur in states with over-centralised structures of governance and control, where demands by ethnic groups for political, cultural and economic autonomy are rejected, where representative institutions and forums for ethnic bargaining and negotiation are inadequate or absent, and where policymakers manipulate ethnic relations for domestic purposes. The state's ability to prevent, restrain or resolve inter-ethnic and ethnic-state conflict depends, in turn, on accommodative and mediatory strategies instead of coercion and the use of military force (Brown 1997, 270-71). Even when ethnic conflict assumes a violent form, it can be defused if the emphasis of state policies changes from repression to an accommodation of ethnic political, economic and cultural demands and grievances. Conversely, a continued dependence on coercive strategies or ethnic divide-and-rule policies will perpetuate ethnic-state conflict, enhancing the prospects for effective external intervention.

The political crisis in the Indian Punjab demonstrates the relative weight of domestic and regional determinants in influencing the course and the outcome of internal ethnic conflict. Ethnic-state tensions in the Punjab had escalated as the centre resisted Sikh demands for political, economic and religious autonomy, articulated by a regional party, the Akali Dal. Congress governments in New Delhi attempted to assert their control over the Punjab through divide-and-rule tactics, supporting the political rivals of the Akali Dal. When centralised control combined with central government intervention, heightened Sikh alienation assumed a violent form (Bajpai 1997, 72). Rejecting the legitimacy of the Indian state, Sikh extremists supported the formation of an independent Sikh state, Khalistan. The centre's reliance on repression to contain Sikh dissent worsened the crisis in the Punjab. This included a military operation against Sikh insurgents who had taken sanctuary within the holiest of Sikh religious shrines, the Golden Temple in Amritsar in 1984. Instead of re-establishing state control, Operation Blue Star provoked widespread anti-state violence in the Punjab as well as mutinies by some Sikh military personnel.[6]

The conflict in the Indian Punjab provided the Zia regime in Pakistan with an opportunity to undermine India's political stability in a strategically located territory that borders on Pakistan. Pakistan therefore extended covert military and political support to Sikh insurgents and secessionists (Phadnis 1989, 236-37). However, changes in Indian policies towards the conflict in the Punjab were to limit Pakistan's ability to influence the course of the conflict. By the mid-1990s, Sikh violence subsided, as did Sikh support for secession, as the central government combined coercive tactics with mediation. As representative government was restored in the Punjab, ethnic-state tensions eased, undermining Pakistan's ability to destabilise India by exploiting Sikh alienation.

External factors have played a far more significant role in determining the internal dynamics of ethnic conflict in Kashmir, a bone of contention between India and Pakistan. Since India and Pakistan refuse to accept each other's sovereignty over the Kashmiri territory they control, neither side accepts the boundary separating Jammu and Kashmir from Azad Kashmir as an international border. Their bilateral dispute over the territory dictates Indian and Pakistani policies towards the conflict in Jammu and Kashmir. For India, which considers Jammu and Kashmir an integral part of the Indian state and which also asserts a claim over Azad Kashmir, Pakistan has no legitimate role in determining the territory's political future. Indian governments also believe that Pakistani political and military intervention is primarily responsible for the conflict within Jammu and Kashmir. For its part, Pakistan believes that Muslim-majority Kashmir was forcibly prevented from acceding to Pakistan by India (Schofield 2000, 225-26). Hence, Pakistan has the moral right to support Kashmiri demands for self-determination. Their denials notwithstanding, consecutive Pakistani governments have extended both political and military support to anti-Indian Kashmiri dissidents and chosen Kashmiri clients. On several occasions, from 1947-49, in 1965 and in 1999, Pakistan has also intervened directly, through cross-border incursions and military attacks on Indian-administered territory. While Pakistani intervention influences the directions of Kashmiri dissent, the extent of Pakistan's influence is determined by Jammu's and Kashmir's internal dynamics.

Historically, Kashmiri dissent has increased or dissipated in response to Indian policies towards domestic grievances and discord in Jammu and Kashmir. Given the contentious manner in which Kashmir was integrated into the Indian Union, Indian policies initially focused on accommodating Kashmiri grievances to contain Kashmiri dissent and to cajole its population into accepting India's sovereignty. Through special constitutional arrangements safeguarding Jammu's and Kashmir's political and economic autonomy and through preferential economic development, India succeeded in containing anti-Indian sentiment. However, by the 1960s, anti-Indian tensions escalated when India began to erode Kashmir's special constitutional status, although Kashmiri alienation did not transform into widespread support for secession (Koithara 1999, 112). Hence there were limits on Pakistan's influence in Jammu and Kashmir, demonstrated, for instance, by Pakistan's failure to subvert Indian authority through covert military intervention in 1965, since the Kashmiri population did not support the Pakistani raiders (Ganguly 1986, 88).

From the 1970s onwards, the legitimacy of the Indian state and its institutions gradually eroded and India's authority was increasingly questioned by Kashmiris because of central government intervention, including divide-and-rule policies. Elections in Jammu and Kashmir were rigged, elected governments dismissed, and the territory's constitutional autonomy incrementally eroded by the centre (Ganguly 1996, 151-52). As a result, anti-Indian dissent became widespread and violent in Jammu and Kashmir. Since the late 1980s, Indian efforts to forcibly suppress Kashmir dissent have further alienated its populace. As Kashmiri grievances mount and internal conflict becomes endemic, Pakistan is provided with the opportunity to intervene, politically and militarily, in a far more effective manner than in the past.

External Intervention and Internal Security

External intervention in internal conflicts can bear adverse consequences for the political stability and security of an intervening actor even when it is motivated by purely humanitarian reasons. Sanctuary provided to refugees on humanitarian grounds can fuel inter-ethnic and ethnic-state tensions if it changes the ethnic composition of the receiving state. Communities that are strengthened by the presence of their cross-border ethnic kin will attempt to use the transformed ethnic balance to gain domestic advantages. Ethnic communities that are adversely affected by a refugee influx will perceive outsiders as a political, cultural and economic threat. Competition with refugees over limited economic resources and access to employment can also contribute to inter-ethnic and ethnic-state tensions and conflict, destabilising the host state.

When states intervene in external crises for political and strategic reasons, for example, to counter external threats, to undermine the security of an external rival, or to gain or expand their regional influence, they are even more likely to undermine their internal security. Arms provided to external insurgents can flow back across borders, undermining the state's monopoly over the use of force. Inter-ethnic relations in the intervening state can deteriorate when regional intervention involves military and political support for a chosen cross-border ethnic partner or client. Internally, the state can be perceived as a biased ethnic actor, undermining its capacity to mediate inter-ethnic and ethnic-state conflict. Should the state choose to modify or to abandon its interventionist behaviour by, for instance, withdrawing support from a particular external ethnic partner or client, it could provoke a violent domestic or regional backlash. Moreover, external clients gain autonomy over time and can themselves pose a threat to the intervening state. Finally, both the internal and the external security of an interventionist state can be threatened if its interventionist behaviour destabilises its immediate neighbourhood, heightens inter-state hostility, and increases the prospect of war.

India's interventionist policies towards the crisis of ethnicity in Sri Lanka have adversely affected its internal security in a number of ways. Although Sri Lanka's military inferiority prevented it from challenging Indian intervention, Indian interventionist policies in Sri Lanka, including political and military support for Tamil extremists, were to undermine India's security. India's support for the Tamil insurgents and India's pressures on Sri Lanka to accept its policy preferences culminated in the signing of the Indo-Sri Lankan pact of 1987. By the Indo-Lankan accord, Sri Lanka pledged autonomy to the Tamils in return for a cessation of the conflict, while India took upon itself responsibility to monitor the peace. India sent a contingent of its military, the Indian Peacekeeping Force (IPKF), to separate the two warring sides in Sri Lanka and to disarm the Tamil rebels. However, when Tamil militants refused to end the fighting, India was forced to confront its erstwhile Sri Lankan allies. The fighting that ensued between the IPKF and the Tamil rebels resulted in high Indian military casualties (Shastri 1997, 156-57; see also Kodikara 1993, 233-34). India's failed political and military mission in Sri Lanka fueled unrest within its armed forces, threatening to destabilise civil-military relations in India. Moreover, the backlash that resulted from the withdrawal of India's support for Tamil extremists was also responsible for the assassination of Indian Prime Minister Rajiv Gandhi in 1991 by a Tamil suicide-bomber.

Pakistan's involvement in Afghanistan's internal crises also bears serious consequences for its political stability as well as its external security. Pakistan's ethnic geography and the legacy of colonialism form the backdrop of its interventionist policies in Afghanistan. As the heir to the northwestern approaches of the British Indian empire, Pakistan inherited a disputed border with Afghanistan, the Durand Line, established by the Anglo-Afghan treaty of 1893, dividing a common Pakhtun population. Relations with Afghanistan deteriorated since Afghan governments rejected the Durand Line, asserted claims over Pakistan's Pakhtun areas, and supported secessionist demands by Pakistani Pakhtun extremists for an independent state, Pakhtunistan, that would include the Pakhtun majority areas of Pakistan and Afghanistan (Hasan 1993, 274).

Since internal dissent was also rife in Afghanistan as repressive regimes ignored the political, cultural and economic needs of their populace, Pakistan retaliated against Afghan intervention in its internal crises by supporting Afghan dissidents (Ahmed 1996, 25; Phadnis 1989, 231). By the 1980s, Pakistan persuaded powerful extra-regional allies, including the United States, China and Saudi Arabia to back the Afghan opposition against the Soviet-supported government in Kabul. Using the Soviet intervention in Afghanistan and the resultant influx of millions of Afghan refugees and rebels into Pakistani territory to legitimise its intervention, Pakistan provided sanctuary, training, arms and bases to the Afghan insurgents. Although the Soviets withdrew from Afghanistan in the late 1980s, the Afghan civil war continues unabated due to inter-ethnic conflict in Afghanistan and Pakistani political and military intervention.

Although Pakistan's chosen Afghan clients, the predominantly Pakhtun Taliban, control 90 per cent of Afghanistan's territory, their authority is violently disputed by ethnic minorities including the Tajik, Uzbek and Hazara. Political instability and a devastated economy prevent the return of millions of Afghan refugees from the contiguous Pakistani provinces of Baluchistan and the Northwest Frontier Province. While the Afghan refugees are perceived as an economic burden in both provinces, the presence of the predominantly Pakhtun refugees has destabilised the delicate demographic balance between Pakistani Baluch and Pakhtuns in Baluchistan, heightening ethnic tensions. Sophisticated arms provided to Afghan insurgents by Pakistan as well as by a number of extra-regional actors in the 1980s and the drug economy that was used to finance the Afghan resistance have had their own repercussions on Pakistani security (Ahmed 1997, 108-109).

Since Pakistani insurgents have access to arms and drugs from neighbouring Afghanistan, inter-ethnic violence has reached unprecedented heights in Pakistan, particularly in the province of Sindh. Political links between Pakistani and Afghan predominantly Sunni religious extremists contribute to periodic outbreaks of sectarian violence with Pakistan's Shia minority, undermining its internal stability. Pakistan's external security is also threatened since Afghan and Pakistani religious extremists also target powerful extra-regional actors, including the United States, Russia and China. Moreover, Pakistani support for crossborder attacks by Afghan and Pakistani religious extremists in Jammu and Kashmir heightens tensions with India, increasing the prospects for war.

South Asia: The Road Ahead

Ethnic tensions and crises in South Asia continue to provide a conducive environment for regional intervention. In Pakistan, authoritarian rule and centralised structures of governance perpetuate internal conflict, while the denial of minority ethnic demands for political, economic and cultural autonomy heighten alienation against the Punjabi-dominated state. Should ethnic conflict in Pakistan become widespread and violent, political instability in Pakistan could tempt India to escalate its support for Pakistani dissidents, motivated by its hostility to the Pakistani state. In India, efforts are currently underway to reach a peacefully negotiated end to the conflict in Jammu and Kashmir through a dialogue with segments of the Kashmiri leadership. However, the legitimacy of the process is marred by Kashmiri concerns that the state is attempting to divide and weaken Kashmiri resistance. Should the state fail to cajole major Kashmiri factions into abandoning violence, the conflict in Jammu and Kashmir will continue to challenge India's political stability, enabling Pakistan to intervene at will. In Sri Lanka the civil war appears to have acquired its own momentum. Although the Sri Lankan government is attempting to reach a peacefully negotiated settlement with Tamil militants in tandem with the use of force to curb Tamil dissent, the road ahead will not be an easy one. While Tamil extremists have an internal stake in perpetuating conflict, any governmental accord to provide political, cultural and economic autonomy to the Tamils will be opposed by powerful segments of the Sinhala political elite. Should Sri Lanka fail to resolve its ethnic crisis, the state will remain vulnerable to Indian intervention.

Since eternal determinants are clearly secondary to domestic factors in South Asia's internal crises, changes in the priorities and policies of the South Asian states will enhance both their internal and external security. If changed state policies ease domestic tensions, they will also protect the state from regional intervention. Should the South Asian states abandon repression, coercion and divide-and-rule strategies for negotiation and bargaining with ethnic dissidents, if centralised state structures of governance are restructured to accommodate ethnic demands for political, economic and cultural autonomy, if the South Asian states succeed in de-escalating internal tensions and resolving political crises, they will deprive their neighbours of the ability, if not the will, to intervene.

References

Ahmed, Samina (1996) 'The Crisis of State Legitimacy in Afghanistan'. *Regional Studies* 16: 3.

—— (1997) 'Centralization, Authoritarianism and the Mismanagement of Ethnic Relations in Pakistan'. In Brown and Ganguly, *Government and Ethnic Relations*.

Ali, S. Mahmud (1993) *The Fearful State: Power, People and Internal War in South Asia*. London: Zed Books.

Bajpai, Kanti (1997) 'Diversity, Democracy and Devolution in India'. In Brown and Ganguly, *Government and Ethnic Relations*.

Bajpai, Kanti P. and Stephen P. Cohen, eds (1993) *South Asia after the Cold War*. Boulder, CO.: Westview Press.

Brown, Michael E., ed. (1996) *The International Dimensions of Regional Conflict.* Cambridge, MA.: MIT Press.

—— (1996) 'The Causes and Regional Dimensions of Internal Conflict'. In Brown, *International Dimensions of Internal Conflict.*

—— (1997) 'The Impact of Government Policies on Ethnic Relations'. In Brown and Ganguly, *Government and Ethnic Relations*.

Brown, Michael E., and Sumit Ganguly, eds. (1997) *Government and Ethnic Relations in the Asia and the Pacific.* Cambridge, MA: MIT Press.

Buzan, Barry, et al. (1986) *South Asian Insecurity and the Great Powers.* London: MacMillan.

Cohen, Stephen Philip, ed. (1987) *The Security of South Asia: South Asian and American Perspectives*. Chicago: University of Illinois Press.

Ganguly, Sumit (1986) *The Origins of War in South Asia: Indo-Pakistan Conflicts Since 1947.* Boulder, CO: Westview Press.

—— (1996) 'Conflict and Crisis in South and Southwest Asia'. In Brown, *International Dimensions of Regional Conflict.*

Ghoshal, Baladas (1993) 'Internal Sources of Conflict in South Asia'. In Bajpai and Cohen, *South Asia after the Cold War.*

Gunaratna, Rohan (1995) 'The Burden of Ethnicity, Insurgency, and Insecurity in Sri Lanka'. In Weinbaum and Kumar, *South Asia Approaches the Millennium.*

Hasan, Shaukat (1993) 'Problems of Internal Stability in South Asia'. In Kodikara, *External Compulsions*.

Kodikara, Shelton U. (1993) 'Internal Politics and Foreign Policy: Prospects of Indo-Lankan Relations in the Nineties'. In Kodikara, *External Compulsions.*

Kodikara, Shelton U., ed. (1993) *External Compulsions of South Asian Politics.* New Delhi: Sage.

Koithara, Verghese (1999) *Society, State and Security: The Indian Experience.* New Delhi: Sage.

Phadnis, Urmila (1989) *Ethnicity and Nation-Building in South Asia.* New Delhi: Sage.

Rizvi, Gowher (1986) 'The Role of the Smaller States in the South Asian Complex'. In Buzan, *South Asian Insecurity and the Great Powers.*

Rose, Leo E. (1987) 'India's Regional Policy: Nonmilitary Dimensions'. In Cohen, *The Security of South Asia.*

Schofield, Victoria (2000) *Kashmir in Conflict: India, Pakistan and the Unfinished War.* London: I.B. Tauris.

Shastri, Amita (1997) 'Government Conflict and the Ethnic Crisis in Sri Lanka'. In Brown and Ganguly, *Government and Ethnic Relations*.

Sisson, Richard, and Leo E. Rose (1990) *War and Secession: Pakistan, India and the Creation of Bangladesh.* Berkeley: University of California Press.

Tiwari, Chitra K. (1989) *Security in South Asia: Internal and External Dimensions.* Lanham, MD: University Press of America.

Weinbaum, Marvin G., and Chetan Kumar, eds. (1995) *South Asia Approaches the Millennium: Reexamining National Security.* Boulder, CO: Westview Press.

ENDNOTES

1 Michael Brown (1997, 512) analyses ethnic-state dynamics in the context of five factors, 'demographic factors and ethnic geography; pre-colonial and colonial legacies; the histories, fears, and goals of ethnic groups in the country; economic factors and trends; and regional and international influences'.

2 Bangladesh, however, accused the Indian government of supporting the Chakma insurgents.

3 Sinhalas and Tamils comprise 74 per cent and 18 per cent of Sri Lanka's population respectively.

4 Michael Brown (1996, 25-26; 595-96) divides regional interventions into 'comparatively benign interventions', motivated by humanitarian concerns or to restore regional peace; 'defensive interventions', to safeguard national security interests threatened by cross-border conflict; 'protective interventions', to protect threatened ethnic kin; 'opportunistic interventions', aimed at advancing a state's political, military and economic interests'; and 'opportunistic invasions', launched when a rival is weakened by internal conflict.

5 Brown (1996, 582-83) argues that while internal conflicts 'often involve neighbors who jump in once hostilities are under way, they are almost always triggered by internal forces of one kind or another'.

6 One of the domestic repercussions of Operation Blue Star, the military action against the Golden Temple complex, was Prime Minister Indira Gandhi's assassination by two of her Sikh bodyguards on 31 October 1984.

PART III.
TERRITORIAL, SOVEREIGNTY AND NUCLEAR CRISES: ACTUAL AND POTENTIAL CRISES

Chapter 10

POLITICAL CRISES IN NORTHEAST ASIA: AN ANATOMY OF THE TAIWAN AND KOREAN CRISES

Stuart Harris
Research School of Pacific and Asian Studies
Australian National University

To discuss political crises in Northeast Asia we need a conception of what constitutes a political 'crisis'. The term has been used widely and often loosely to cover a range of situations that have occurred recently in Northeast Asia. They include domestic political happenings such as the South Korean economic crisis of 1997-98, the food supply problems of North Korea, more recently the November 2000 no-confidence motion against the Japanese Prime Minister, Mr Mori, and the situation currently surrounding the Chen Shui-bian presidency in Taiwan. Internationally, they include the periods of heightened tensions in Taiwan-China relations, on the Korean Peninsula or between China and Japan over the Senkaku/Diaoyu islands.

This chapter concentrates on two political crises with international dimensions – the 1995-96 missile crisis across the Taiwan Strait and the 1993-94 nuclear/missile crisis in North Korea. These crises are generally regarded as the major political crises in Northeast Asia in recent years and both have the potential to recur. The chapter follows Michael Brecher by taking as the two principal criteria for defining such a political crisis as first, a series of political developments posing a high risk of military conflict and second, a threat to basic values (Brecher 1979, 446-80). In the two cases under review, it was widely believed that the political developments involved posed a high risk of military conflict. They were also seen as threatening the basic values of the countries concerned.[1] Not all crises emerging from external developments meet the criterion of threatening a risk of war. For example, the oil crisis that faced Japan in the early 1970s had no military conflict potential but seemingly posed a threat to Japan's basic values.

While the crises examined here had external dimensions, we accept that in these situations internal politics were crucial, both because particular crisis-initiating actions by one country in each case reflected internal political concerns, and also in terms of the constraints or otherwise on crisis management.[2] In James Richardson's study of great power crises, the sources of each state's crisis behaviour were found in its internal politics (Richardson 1994, 353). As we will see, internal politics were important in the two examples considered here.[3]

Much of the debate in the West about the 1996 Taiwan Strait crisis and the 1993-94 Korean crisis reflected, and reflects, internal differences of view over the international intentions and objectives of China and North Korea. Even though they were ostensibly at greatest risk, Taiwan and South Korea are seen as only part of this question but they play a critical role in shaping Western thinking in the broader context. In return, for China and North Korea, perceptions of the US in particular played a similar role.

In looking at these examples, we will examine the nature of the crisis and its causes. Given that the tensions across the Taiwan Strait and on the Korean Peninsula were a consequence of underlying factors that were present long before, and predisposed the occurrence of, the events in question, one question is why these crises emerged as and when they did. We then look at the mutual understandings of the objectives and intentions of the parties involved, the responses – including any bargaining involved – and the possible lessons.

The 1995-96 Taiwan Strait Crisis

In March 1996, China fired four short range ballistic missiles at targets in the waters off Taiwan, one to the north and three to the south of the island. These missile firings represented a peak in a series of military exercises by China, including missile firings in the vicinity of Taiwan, over the eight-month period between July 1995 and March 1996 (Yang 2000, 1-3). During this time, Taiwan also engaged in military exercises, some with missile firings, in July and September/October 1995, and again early in 1996.

The March 1996 exercises were judged the most serious of China's exercises – with missiles falling closer – and close – to Taiwan's main ports, Kaohsiung in the south and Keelung in the north. While, reportedly, there was no interference with shipping in or out of Taiwan (Ross 2000, fn. 72), Taiwan's exchange rate fell significantly, as did prices on the stock exchange, foreign exchange reserves fell sharply, airline routes were changed and fishermen stayed at home (Mann 1999, 328-29). There were also more intense fears of escalation and of the dangers of errors. In response, the US sent two aircraft carrier battle groups to the area.

The crisis effectively ended when, on 25 March, two days after the election of President Lee with a significant majority, China declared the military exercises ended.

The Background

The crisis had both short-term causes and long-standing structural causes. In 1945, 'Taiwan once more became a province of China' (Lee 1999, 20). The potential for a military confrontation with the mainland arose in 1949, however, when the civil war between the communists and the nationalists ended in a stalemate, the nationalists under Chiang Kai-shek escaping to Taiwan (then Formosa) where they have remained. Both claimed to be the rightful government of a China that included Taiwan as part of China and until the early 1970s Australia, along with the US and most other countries, supported Taiwan's claim.

Taiwan's government had declared its intention to retake militarily the mainland, but although retaking some small offshore islands during the Korean War, ultimately disavowed this intention in 1987. Although its constitution still sees it as part of China, there has been a growing move in Taiwan to regard itself as separate from the PRC. Yet the view from China, that Taiwan is part of China, and that from Taiwan, that it is a largely independent *de facto*, remain the dividing issues. The tensions around this issue, while fluctuating in intensity, have continued over the succeeding years.

Although the tensions were largely between China and Taiwan, the Korean War had brought the US directly into the cross strait issue when, in June 1950, President Truman sent the US Seventh Fleet to block the Taiwan Strait. Subsequently, following China's shelling of the Nationalist-held islands of Quemoy and Matsu in 1954-55, the US signed a defence treaty with Taiwan and the US subsequently helped Chiang to break another artillery blockade of the offshore islands in 1958 (Christensen 1996, 133-37).

The US naval involvement prevented either side from pursuing the civil war for the next two decades. When the US restored relations with the PRC from 1972 onwards, it 'understood' that Taiwan was part of China. Overall, for nearly three decades after 1949, the US was, in practice, Taiwan's patron, its formal defence treaty with Taiwan being discarded only when US relations were restored formally with China in 1979. There was an added understanding, however, subsequently reinforced by the 1979 Taiwan Relations Act (TRA), that any reunification would be peaceful.

It is generally argued that there had been a period of relative stability, even of significant rapprochement, for several years before the Chinese took the actions that led to the 1995-96 crisis. Their reasons and their objectives and intentions remain a matter of some debate, although some elements seem clear.

Given the PRC's overwhelming belief in its sovereignty over Taiwan, hence its overriding interest in reunification in some form with Taiwan, and its longstanding policy that a declaration of independence by Taiwan would lead to war, it had been watching with growing concern two developments that it saw as related. One was a strengthening of the pressure for Taiwanese independence under President Lee Teng-hui. Beijing regarded various actions by Lee as worrying. These included Taiwan's pursuit of UN membership that, if achieved, would constitute international acceptance of Taiwan's independence; Lee's 1994 'golfing' or 'vacation' diplomacy during which he met a number of Southeast Asian leaders; his visit to the US on an ostensibly private visit but in which he made an overtly political speech strongly promoting the ROC as an independent sovereign state; Lee's closer identification with Japan than with China; and Lee's lukewarm April 1995 'six points' response to Jiang Zemin's January 1995 basically conciliatory 'eight points' statement on Beijing-Taipei relations.

The other was a leaning by the US towards Taiwan and away from US commitments under agreements between the two countries. Although the missile firings were a clear statement to Taiwan of resolve by the Chinese, in many respects the message could be seen as more directly meant to warn the US. On top of the 1992 US decision to sell 150 F16 war planes to Taiwan (which was in breach of the US pledge to China on such arms sales), the US decision in 1995 to give a visa to Lee Teng-hui to visit the US that reversed long standing US diplomatic practice was particularly worrying. As Ross notes, starting with the large sale of military aircraft to Taiwan, the visa decision came at the end of three years of an evolving US policy that leant increasingly towards Taiwan (Ross 2000, 87).

Objectives and Signalling

Understanding each other's objectives and information on, and communication of, intentions is crucial in crisis situations if unintended escalation is to be avoided. In the events leading to the March 1996 crisis, communications had been far from good. This was most notable in the underestimation by the US of the breach of its assurance to China that no visa would be given to President Lee, shortly before it was actually granted. It was also reflected in the US response, or the lack of response, to the gradually intensifying rounds of Chinese military exercises that the US understood as Chinese pressure to which it did not need to respond. Scobell's judgement, that Washington was 'asleep at the wheel' (Scobell 2000, 246), may be a little harsh, however, since there was some logic in a US view that China's exercises at least delivered a useful message to Taiwan.

Diplomatic discussions, including a Jiang-Clinton meeting in New York in October 1995, seemed to US officials to have eased the tensions temporarily but this was a misperception by the US (Ross 2000, 100-101). China was not satisfied. Lee, moreover, continued with what China saw as provocative statements and actions and Taiwan publicised the passage of a US carrier battle group through the Taiwan Strait. Although apparently for operational and not political reasons, Chen says the announcement of this passage by Taiwan infuriated the Chinese (Chen 1999, 131). The US also approved transit visas for senior Taiwanese political figures that were seen as further illustrations of the US lean towards Taiwan. Consequently the decision was taken by China to pursue more substantial action.

It is often difficult to be clear on China's intentions, as the US misunderstandings of the earlier Taiwan Strait crisis in the 1950s had indicated. At the time of the March crisis, however, communications on intentions were less evidently a major problem. Periodic discussions had been taking place between the US and Chinese officials on political and defence issues and, on the day the missile firings began, the Director of China's State Council Office of Foreign Affairs, Lui Huaqui, was in Washington for discussions on Taiwan issues. At these meetings, Lui gave details of the time, scale and location of the missile tests and made clear that no invasion or attack on Taiwan was intended. Taiwan intelligence sources were also aware of the limits of the exercises through Chinese military dispositions as was indicated subsequently by Chen Li-an, a presidential candidate and previously defence minister in the KMT government (Ross 2000; Klintworth 2000).

As noted earlier, although China's actions were designed to be coercive in a limited way, it is an open question whether China's primary objective in 1995-96 was to coerce Taiwan or the US. Certainly, with respect to Taiwan, there were two major interlinked objectives. The Lee Teng-hui election campaign was seen as one where independence would be an issue and it wanted to discourage Taiwan's steps towards independence by conveying to Taiwan the major risks involved. Associated with this was a reputational objective, the need to ensure the credibility of its threat of force in the event of an independence declaration.

At the same time, China had failed to reverse diplomatically the US policy slide towards Taiwan, a slide that was encouraging Lee in his wayward ways. This led it to judge that a more forceful approach was necessary to get the US to recognise China's concerns about increasing US arms sales to Taiwan despite the 1982 agreed guidelines and to recognise how seriously China took Taiwan's steps towards independence.

For its part, having warned China not to proceed with its exercises, the objectives of the US in its response were to uphold its credibility and the credibility of its commitment to a peaceful resolution of the Taiwan conflict. Consequently, there appeared to be an irreconcilable face-off between China wanting to change US and Taiwanese policies, and the US opposing China's actions and not prepared to accept coercion. Despite the apparent face-off, however, ultimately both sides achieved their objectives, although as Ross concludes, both China and the US could have achieved those objectives without the costs involved (Ross 2000, 89-90).

Ross notes that the US also had reputational objectives, in that it wanted to indicate to the region its resolve and credibility (Ross 2000, 110). More seems to have been made of that after the event than during it, however. Moreover, the achievement of the objective of sustaining regional credibility was qualified, since the region generally supported China's position on Taiwan and did not favour outside interventions in such situations. Few countries in the region expressed open support for the US action.

The Role of Internal Politics

Although these external factors were important, in all three parties to the crisis, internal politics were also important in raising cross-strait tensions to the point of crisis. In this context, internal politics include the influence of differences over how to deal with coercive or threatening actions; differences that came from perceptions, often ideologically-based, of the other's intentions; and differences about how negotiations should be pursued. It also includes the influence of positions taken for political advantage domestically, or other factors adopted for reasons not related directly to the crisis.

China

The domestic politics of the Taiwan issue are regarded as crucial in Beijing. It is commonly argued that any leader who loses Taiwan will go down in Chinese history as a traitor – and that the regime's legitimacy will be undermined. As a result, the Taiwan issue is clearly embedded in domestic Chinese politics. Moreover, while many analysts believe that China sees the world in realpolitik or balance of power terms, it is also greatly influenced by its national perceptions and historical experiences.

Within China, the role of the US coloured much of its approach to Taiwan. Sino-US relations have consistently been a basis of domestic contention, particularly since the end of the Cold War, with the issue of Taiwan seen as symptomatic of US antagonism. A widely held belief within China is that Taiwan offers one means of implementing a US policy to contain China and to limit its growth in order to remain the hegemon. On this, views differ but there was extensive suspicion in China of ultimate US intentions with respect both to China and Taiwan. On several occasions PLA leaders addressed formal communications to the political leadership complaining about what they saw as weak leadership on Taiwan, targeting particularly the Ministry of Foreign Affairs and its weakness in dealing with US antagonism. A hard line PLA policy may have had other motives beyond Taiwan: advancing the PLA's political role as the guardian of party supremacy; and strengthening their case for resources (see, for example, Gurtov and Hwang 1998, 279). Nevertheless, in discussing the different expectations in China of whether or not there would be a US response to its March 1996 missile exercises, Garver argues that, even for those expecting a US response, forcing the US to act would be useful because it 'would expose the true containment essence of US policy' (Garver 1997, 112).

Copper argues that, at the time of the 1995-96 crisis, China's hostility to Taiwan was closely linked to a leadership struggle in Beijing, given the expected death of Deng Xiaoping, intimately connected to the Taiwan issue (Copper 1999, 42). On this argument, Deng and those associated with him were vulnerable to charges that they were sacrificing the recovery of Taiwan to the cause of better Sino-American ties, a claim made from the opposite perspective at the time by Lee Teng-hui about the US. This view, however, has been challenged. Thus, Chen notes that while some observers believe the timing of Jiang's 'eight point' statement was mainly dictated by the desire to consolidate his power in the political transition, in practice the statement had had a long gestation (Chen 1999, 133). You Ji accepts that Jiang was criticised by his colleagues for what they saw as weakness towards Taiwan that encouraged Lee to be more provocative. He believes it exaggerates, however, the divisiveness of the Taiwan issue in domestic Chinese elite politics. He argues that, on the contrary, Taiwan's provocations helped achieve a common response rather than a division of views among the Chinese leadership (You 1999, 77).

There are understood to be differences among party leaders over the ways of handling the Taiwan issue. There were also communications from leaders in the southern provinces urging caution but we do not know what influence they had. Overall, there is little suggestion that there were significant differences in objectives. Differences may exist in the methods used, but it seems there were few major doubts in 1996 about the need for action such as the missile exercises.

Taiwan

Views within Taiwan differ markedly over relations with China. With the emergence of democratic processes in Taiwan, relations with China moved centrally into Taiwan's domestic politics involving succession, interest group and partisan politics (Chu 1999, 163-95). No consensus existed – the main political divisions favoured support for independence, the status quo (often with ultimate reunification) and reunification, respectively. For the DPP, then the main opposition to the KMT, Taiwanese independence was an important issue of policy principle. Much of the business sector in Taiwan, however, which gave considerable support to the KMT, was in favour of closer links with the mainland, and not all the KMT was solidly behind Lee's seemingly provocative stance towards the Mainland. In 1993, the New Party was formed, mostly from those in the KMT opposed to Lee's leadership generally, but including his cross-strait policies.

As 1993 ended and following the December Legislative Yuan elections, Taiwan was about to enter a presidential campaign with Lee as a candidate. Lee said on several occasions that, when elected, he would pursue high profile diplomacy. He was under pressure from those in the DPP seeking independence, and from the New Party which had done well in the December elections. China's missile exercises in the Strait did not dampen the Lee rhetoric since he knew there was no intention to attack Taiwan. For Lee, moreover, it was not unhelpful to have international events to distract the debate from issues of corruption, environmental pollution and other domestic issues on which his party was politically vulnerable.

The US

US policies on China and Taiwan have been important domestically for various reasons since the end of WWII. Even the Seventh Fleet's location in the Taiwan Strait in 1950 has been argued as motivated (at least partly) by a desire to gain domestic support for Truman's involvement in the Korean War (for background to these events see Christensen 1996; Klintworth 1995, ch.3). Since then, a variety of factors have been important. These include anticommunist ideologies; the gradual emergence of democracy in Taiwan; arguments that China is potentially a threat to the US because of its political system and its hegemonic ambitions; partisan political belabouring of the administration; and defence industry interests – of which the 150 F16s were not the only example. Heavy financial and other lobbying by Taiwan have been important in gaining support in the US for Taiwan's position. This was a factor leading to the heavy congressional pressure that gave rise to the Taiwan Relations Act. The Clinton decision to give a visa to Lee was similarly a consequence of congressional pressure and an expensive Taiwanese lobbying effort to influence US politicians.

US administrations of both political colours have maintained a 'one China' policy. Congressional pressure over Taiwan policy has been applied to US administrations for a mix of genuine and partisan political reasons, but successive administrations have nevertheless attempted to maintain a policy of strategic ambiguity towards the Strait.

In shaping the particular US response to China's missile firings, domestic political factors were important. Congressional pressure was intense on Clinton and the US Administration in the latter part of 1995, with Clinton sensitive to a reelection campaign to come in 1996. It was particularly focused on Secretary of Defense Perry because of concerns that he was close to John W. Lewis of Stanford University, at the time the latest individual to be under attack from congressional conservatives, in this case for being involved in what they claimed were improper US transfers of sensitive technologies to China. Active involvement by the US in the crisis was itself not surprising but the extent of that involvement was perhaps a reflection of those political pressures. The sending of two carrier groups was interpreted as a military and not just a political response, as one would have been. Given that the US knew that Taiwan would not be attacked when it made the decision, many outside China would argue that a political rather than a military response was required. Certainly, the Chinese believed the US response was excessive given that they had kept the US fully informed.

Bargaining

As Schelling argues, most conflict situations are essentially bargaining situations, whether this is made explicit or remains implicit (Schelling 1980, 5). Moreover, bargaining processes are important for determining the scope or otherwise for accommodation. In the case of the Taiwan Strait crisis, little explicit bargaining took place during the crisis. China's aim was to ensure the status quo was not changed against its interests. The US did not seek to negotiate with China over its intentions, merely to deter it from pursuing them. Yet it was indirectly a bargaining crisis in that China sought to use threats to coerce the US and Taiwan against further changes to the status quo and this was successful. The US did seek subsequently to reassure China of its firm commitment to the 'one China' policy and to caution Taiwan against provocation.

Was It a Crisis?

It is possible to argue that the 1995-96 events did not meet the criteria of a crisis as specified earlier. Leaders of both the US and Taiwan knew that the missiles were not targeted at Taiwan, as did Australia, and that war was not intended. Taiwan preferred the status quo and Beijing could accept the status quo provided that was the outcome.

Given acceptance of the arguments of the Chinese as to their intentions, which seem to have been supported by intelligence data, the 1995-96 crisis was largely theatre or, as Gurtov and Hwang put it, a 'phony crisis' (Gurtov and Hwang 1998, 277). Not everyone agrees, however, with the interpretation that the crisis reflected posturing or theatre rather than substance. Certainly, at the time some saw the possibility of war as real.

Moreover, for those outside the small group with access to full information, it certainly appeared to threaten conflict. Moreover, it appears that the Japanese were not in the information loop or, at least, that the information was not passed to Japan's leaders. Also, they were not told of the deployment of the Japan-based Nimitz aircraft carrier, about which they subsequently complained formally to the US. Nor were the respective publics effectively informed and so a sense of crisis was widespread. There were widely held fears that either the missile firings could be ratcheted up to strike targets in Taiwan, could miss the target dangerously, or that a sometimes unpredictable Lee Teng-hui could act recklessly and that, for whatever reason, the US and China could become involved directly in hostilities. Even if this particular crisis was theatre, the situation across the Strait remains one with considerable potential for a crisis with greater consequences.

Lessons

The lessons to be drawn from this crisis include the understanding that, in order to avoid escalation, the need for good, *shared* information is important. Pending this, action and response should be qualified. That will help keep the heat of the crisis related to the reality. In the US, what is apparent is that in the period before the 1995-96 crisis, the substance of US policymaking was often neglected in favour of the 'noise', much of it from the Congress. Hence messages fail to be heard. After the crisis, the US acted postively, starting a process that ended with an exchange of presidential visits and President Clinton's articulation of the 'three noes'.[4] The need for the US and other third parties to be cautious in maintaining a balance between the two sides, and to avoid political adventurism, is clear.

The lesson for Taiwan was less well taken. Lee continued with his provocative diplomacy, and tensions were again high in 1998 and 1999 with the US increasingly articulating its concern at Taiwan's wagging the US-China dog. The question, as Owen Harries put it, was whether 'the United States should cede decisions over whether to go to war' to Taiwan (Harries 1999, 146). Ross similarly says that the US cannot allow Taiwan's domestic politics to determine the politics of war and peace between the US and China (Ross 2000, 123). In the event, Chen Shui-bian saw it as necessary, in order to gain election, to be much more cautious in his 1999 presidential campaign.

One lesson drawn by China from the intervention of the two carrier groups was that the US was more likely to intervene in any conflict across the Strait and, while this has made China more cautious, it has also had a military response. China's purchase of two Sovremeiny destroyers and anti-ship missiles from Russia is designed to increase the risk of US naval deployments in the region, so raising the intensity, and potential danger, of any future crisis.

THE 1993-94 NORTH KOREA CRISIS

In the 1980s and early 1990s, US intelligence came to suspect that the DPRK was developing a nuclear weapons capability. The DPRK had signed the NPT in 1985 at the urging of its then ally, the Soviet Union. Following a series of disputes with the inspectors of the International Atomic Energy Agency (IAEA), however, over the accounting procedures associated with the IAEA's inspections of its reactors and nuclear waste sites under the NPT, North Korea gave notice on 12 March 1993 that it would withdraw from the NPT 90 days later, on 12 June 1993.

Given the growing concern at the potential nuclear threat from North Korea, the US saw this action as pointing to North Korea both deploying nuclear weapons and exporting weapons grade fissile material and, more generally, as undermining the NPT and the global non-proliferation effort. The DPRK said that the problem to which it was reacting could only be resolved through discussions with the US. Although reluctant to accept such discussions, the US finally agreed to enter into them both to satisfy the Chinese in the Security Council that normal diplomatic methods had been exhausted and to use them to convince the DPRK not to withdraw but to meet their NPT obligations. The US threatened, in the absence of success, to press the UN for international economic sanctions against the DPRK, and in May the Security Council indicated it would act if the DPRK withdrew from the NPT. In response, the DPRK said that UN sanctions would be construed as a 'declaration of war'. Ultimately, in the course of a series of meetings, the DPRK suspended its withdrawal notice, and an Agreed Conclusion emerged towards the end of 1993, involving a resumption of IAEA inspections. Tensions remained, however, and this agreement fell through subsequently because of differences over the proposed arrangements for an intra-Korean dialogue.

The second stage of the crisis emerged in May 1994. The IAEA suspected that, for its nuclear weapons program, the DPRK had extracted more plutonium than it had admitted. It wanted to determine whether this was so through a detailed analysis of the fuel rods of the DPRK's reactor. The IAEA was concerned that the unloading be done with their full cooperation, including isotopic analyses of the fuel rods, to enable checks to be made on the history of the DPRK's past extraction of plutonium. The US, in support of the IAEA's position, had set the unloading of fuel rods except under IAEA supervision as a 'line drawn in the sand'. In May, however, North Korea decided to unload fuel rods from its small (5MW) reactor without permitting effective cooperation with the IAEA.

Some senior US officials saw the decision to unload the fuel rods without effective IAEA involvement as designed to hide the history and as a justification for considering a preemptive military action against North Korea (Snyder 1999, 72). Concerned at the mounting tension between the US and North Korea, and the limited knowledge base of the US officials regarding North Korea, ex-President Jimmy Carter offered his good offices and they were accepted by President Clinton. His subsequent meeting with North Korea's leader, Kim Il Sung paved the way for an agreed approach between the two countries. This was ultimately developed into the Agreed Framework, including the establishment of the Korean Peninsula Energy Development Organisation (KEDO). On the basis of phased delivery of benefits, including provision of two light water reactors (LWRs), and supplies of fuel oil in the meantime, the DPRK agreed to the freezing of its nuclear program, and permitted inspections and other measures in accord with international concerns. This effectively ended the 1993-94 crisis.

The Background

The major structural factor in this case, as in the case of Taiwan, was an unfinished civil war, this time between North and South Korea. In this case, too, the US was directly involved following its 1950 entry into the Korean War as leader of a UN coalition. The US-South Korean alliance was a direct consequence. Apart from the North's sustained hostility and competition for legitimacy with the South, there had been unrelenting hostility and mistrust of the US from that time. Indeed, those relations in both cases were crisis oriented. On North Korea's side, apart from its continuing threat of aggression against South Korea, a succession of North Korean terrorist actions occurred over much of the postwar period that stopped only in the late 1980s. On the US side, according to Sigal, the US had threatened North Korea with nuclear weapons on at least seven occasions over the postwar period (Sigal 1998, 33), and the US had based nuclear weapons in South Korea from 1957 to 1991 (Oberdorfer 1997).

With the end of the Cold War, North Korea's international position weakened, as did its negotiating strength. It lost its ally, the Soviet Union, to add to the diminished interest of China as it became more closely integrated into the global economic and political system. Snyder notes that its objectives also changed. The objective of gaining Cold War propaganda value from its activities was replaced, given its increasing economic difficulties, by its need for tangible outcomes, such as access to the international financial institutions, from its dealings with South Korea but more particularly with the West, notably the US (Snyder 1999, 9).

Objectives and Signalling

Given the duration of the crisis and changes in the personnel involved, including a change in the US and South Korean administrations, objectives were not in all respects constant. It was widely believed that the DPRK's objective was to develop a nuclear arms capability, and US intelligence assessments tended to accept this as fact. Given the DPRK's increasingly isolated strategic position, this had its own intrinsic logic. Yet the arguments against this as a priority objective – notably that North Korea had not reprocessed nuclear fuel rods to extract the necessary plutonium since 1991 and had deferred the unloading of fuel rods that would have enabled weapons grade plutonium to be extracted – also seem strong (Sigal 1998, 6). Rather than the development of nuclear arms capability, however, the long-term priority objective of the DPRK was increasingly seen to be the achievement of a direct political and economic relationship with the US, unmediated by South Korea, in part to legitimise its regime and in part for negotiating purposes. As Carter indicated, however, and as had been made evident before, it also wanted security assurances from the US, mainly against South Korea, who also had been pursuing its own plans for nuclear development.

The early US objective was to determine how much plutonium the DPRK had extracted, to ascertain whether the North had nuclear weapons. Subsequently, the prime US aim changed, giving less weight to the past and more to any further uranium reprocessing, and to curbing future bomb-making by the North, initially through adherence to the safeguards agreement under the NPT and then as part of a negotiated deal. As reflected in the text of the Agreed Framework, the US also wanted to achieve a process of normalisation including the DPRK's participation in Four Party (US, China, South Korea and DPRK) talks.

South Korea, while wanting to ensure the North did not produce nuclear weapons, wanted to be in control of the dialogues and, in particular, did not want direct US-North Korean talks or ties, and was prepared to create conditions designed to stop them if necessary. If they were to take place, however, it wanted serious North-South talks in place before the US-DPRK talks.

The IAEA was another player throughout the 1993-94 crisis and was a major, if not the major, player in its initial stages. For its part the IAEA wanted full compliance with the safeguards agreement with North Korea. Most specifically, it wanted to document the history of reprocessing by North Korea and opposed negotiation.

To a considerable degree the objectives of those countering the DPRK were not consistent. The South Korean and US objectives were not fully consistent since the US was prepared to accept direct links with North Korea but South Korea was not comfortable with that. The IAEA wanted a rigidly legal compliance but the North Koreans wanted to bargain over the nature of the inspections and was unwilling to concede without gaining some benefit in return. The IAEA's concern with both detailed compliance and with determining the past history of reprocessing was to be at odds with the US as the US gave priority to the objective of stopping future nuclear development.

Signalling among the major participants was by no means clear, in part because of the nature of the regimes, notably that of the DPRK but also in part because of internal political influences. Misreading the DPRK's intentions accentuated the heat – thus the 90 day notice in the case of the 1993 crisis can be interpreted as a signal for negotiation. It was interpreted as irreversible by the US – and led in consequence to confrontation (Sigal 1998, 50). In the negotiations within the US-DPRK discussions, the DPRK specifically sought two light water reactors in return for giving up its own nuclear development. The DPRK's interest in light water reactors surprised the US, despite this being a repeat of a request made to the IAEA in 1992 and to the Soviet Union in 1985.

Much of the subsequent debate has been about how far the motives and intentions of the North should have been discernible from the history. Snyder argues, as does Sigal, that the North Korean approach to the negotiating process was rational and consistent, as it had been for a long period. Snyder notes that North Korea's negotiators 'used the tactics of crisis diplomacy to gain the attention of the United States' (Snyder 1999, 69). This triggered the announcement by the DPRK of its withdrawal from the NPT and, later, withdrawal of the fuel rods from its reactor.

Snyder, for example, noted that the history of negotiation with North Korea indicated that coercion and compulsion, or what Sigal calls the crime and punishment approach, were unlikely to be successful, but that comprehensive deal making was likely to be achievable. He pointed to the instance of the DPRK's positive response to the withdrawal of nuclear weapons from South Korea by President Bush in 1991. In that response, DPRK signed its nuclear safeguards agreement with the IAEA, halted the reprocessing of spent fuel and delayed removing spent nuclear fuel from its reactor (effectively until May 1994) (Sigal 1998, 32). Yet 'the Bush administration ignored North Korea's efforts at accommodation' (Sigal 1998,

37). Despite such signs of responsiveness, the US rejected further approaches for some time in favour of the coercive approach because of basic perceptions about the DPRK regime and its methods, as well as US domestic political pressures.

A considerable learning process, however, did take place in the course of the bilateral US-DPRK discussions that involved improved signalling or, at least, some dispelling of misperceptions.

Internal Politics

Like China, North Korea's worldview reflects, among other things, its national perceptions and historical experiences. In its case this includes Japanese colonialism and its own virtual destruction in the war with the US and its allies. Differences consequently existed internally over the approach to take to the US during the crisis process. Those in the US arguing for reassurance as a way of persuading the DPRK to give up its nuclear weapons program saw this as reinforcing the position of those in North Korea's leadership favouring engagement with the US. Firm evidence on the details of the domestic North Korean debate is limited. However, as Downs notes, domestic factors included: differences between hard and soft line factions in Pyongyang; DPRK umbrage at its loss of face during previous IAEA inspections; national paranoia; succession politics as Kim Il Sung prepared to hand over power to Kim Jong Il; and anger at the resumption of Team Spirit, a large joint US/South Korea military exercise focused on North Korea (Downs 1999, 227-28).

The increasingly emotionally charged US domestic debate over dealing with the DPRK divided along several lines. That the DPRK was a hard line communist regime with a record of past seemingly irrational hostility to its neighbours and to the US also reinforced the view that normal diplomatic methods were not applicable. There were also genuine differences of view regarding both North Korea's objectives and way to deal with North Korea, which involved senior officials as well as those politically committed. There was a widely-held US view, within the administration, in Congress and in the media, that coercion and compulsion was the way to achieve US objectives. Opposition to any package arrangement that involved accommodation as well as deterrence was also based on the belief that this would help the regime to survive. The belief was widespread that it was not possible to negotiate with the DPRK and that the regime needed to fall. In addition, partisan criticism of the Clinton administration was an important factor in the domestic debate. Domestic opposition provided a constraint (for some time at least) on the approach of the US administration, limiting it basically to a coercive approach. Some of this changed as the tensions rose, but also as the engagement with the DPRK progressed, notably after the Carter visit to Pyongyang. Even so, while the US administration accepted the need for accommodation that Carter had outlined, domestic criticism remained strong.

South Korean domestic politics under Roh Tae Woo and Kim Yong Sam's governments, often encouraged by US hardliners, reflected many of the same positions, including concerns that concessions to the North would enable the North's regime to survive. As already noted, South Korea was anxious not to lose control of the dialogue with the North, seeing that control as undermining its legitimacy *vis-à-vis* the North as well as reducing its own position *vis-à-vis* the US. As the US dialogue went beyond direct nuclear matters to which the South had reluctantly agreed, difficulties were created in the South's relations with the US with public criticisms from President Kim. On one hand, Korean nationalism was strong and this gave rise to beliefs that not only would the division on Korea be perpetuated, but also that this was a US objective to justify maintaining a US troop presence. On the other hand, the military was concerned that rapprochement with the North would reduce its privileged position – and its budget. Consequently, South Korea's attitude towards the US-DPRK dialogue was often difficult. It vacillated between supporting the US when there were problems, and creating obstacles when progress seemed apparent.

Internal politics were also important for the IAEA. It had been slack and error prone in responding to North Korea's accession to the NPT. In addition, its overall effectiveness had been questioned following discoveries of large networks of undeclared nuclear facilities in Iraq. Consequently, it was eager to take the international lead on the DPRK nuclear issue and in 1993 the incoming Clinton administration, in particular, was comfortable with that. Moreover, it requested 'unprecedented and intrusive special inspections in North Korea' (Snyder 1999, 69).

Given the internal US debate among the foreign policy community, the initial dependence of the US upon the IAEA and South Korea left it hostage to their internal politics. Ultimately, however, for a variety of reasons, the influence of domestic politics diminished as a major factor in the ultimate outcome. In particular, the opposition to a negotiation with the DPRK was ultimately not the dominant influence on the administration. What eventuated was a comprehensive package involving accommodation as well as deterrence.

Bargaining

In the Korean case, bargaining was more explicit than in the case of Taiwan. A use of brinkmanship and crisis diplomacy is characteristic of North Korea's negotiating approach, and it appears that the DPRK created a crisis situation consciously in order to gain the attention of, and to bargain with, the US.[5]

The internal divisions within the US over how to deal with the DPRK were important in shaping the US response to the crisis. The mix of beliefs that failure to adhere to international obligations under the NPT should be punished, that offering concessions to persuade adherence was succumbing to blackmail, and that any concessions would enable the DPRK regime to survive provided a solid basis of opposition to anything but a coercive approach. Yet as it became apparent that, short of actually proceeding with armed conflict, the coercive approach to the DPRK was unlikely to work, some form of bargaining became inevitable. In practice, the willingness of the US to enter into discussions with the DPRK involved an element of a bargain, since that was a DPRK legitimising objective in itself. Its strategy was a wider one, however, and that was to bargain with the US unmediated by South Korea. While for some considerable time the US was unwilling to enter into a substantial bargaining process, eventually it changed to a bargaining strategy. As tensions rose in 1994, the US administration was able to overcome the differences with South Korea, the IAEA and its domestic critics to enable a bargaining strategy to work. Perhaps without the intensification of the sense of crisis in May 1994, internal politics may have been more significant.

Voices at a senior level in the US administration had wanted a more responsive US approach earlier – believing that the crisis had been prolonged by not offering 'enticing benefits' earlier and showing North Korea what was in it for them. In other words, they wanted a tit-for-tat strategy, one posited by Axelrod as the most likely to succeed in a bargaining relationship between parties that mistrust each other (Axelrod 1984, esp. ch.9). Others saw it as conceding to blackmail. Yet the final outcome, which was a tit-for-tat approach, achieved the US objective of a shutdown of the DPRK's nuclear program, and the DPRK meeting more fully its obligations under the NPT (including the safeguards agreement preventing reprocessing of the spent fuel and its eventual removal from North Korea). Sigal argues that ultimately it was 'a strategy of cooperative security' that succeeded, while coercion and threats alone proved to be counterproductive.

Was It a Crisis?

Certainly the rhetoric reached intense levels and a sense of a risk of war became palpable. At one dialogue with South Korea in March 1994, a DPRK representative predicted that war would turn Seoul into a 'sea of fire', a term widely reported. Less widely reported was a South Korean defence minister's remark some months earlier about the possibility of using military action to stop North Korea's nuclear program (Oberdorfer 1997, 294).

On the question of how close to war it came, debate continues. On the one hand, war or accommodation is seen as a high risk but logical strategy for North Korea (Downs 1999, 259). On the other, accommodation was achieved by way of an agreement between Carter and Kim Il Sung. It was not evident that the DPRK wanted military conflict or was looking for an excuse to go to war; it would certainly not have prevailed. Although much of the fear was fear of a US military response, no action seems to have been taken by the US military, or by US decision-makers, to move towards implementing an attack on North Korea.

Could it have got out of control? Escalation is not always predictable but we need to think in terms of specific scenarios, most of which would seem improbable. One scenario posited was that offering concessions might have indicated softness by the US, with the DPRK taking advantage of that softness. A more feasible scenario posed that, had the threatened imposition of sanctions towards the end of 1993 resulted, as expected, in a North Korean response and had that been countered, as planned, with precautionary movements of US troops and weapons, the DPRK would almost certainly have mobilised. Even so, in both cases, only those who believed in the irrationality of the DPRK leadership might have judged significant escalation possible. On the US side, in the absence of an irrational DPRK act, escalation was improbable because the limited justification and global consequences would have weighed heavily in the decision-making processes despite the heat of the external debate.

The fear, nevertheless, was real, given a heated public debate to which a breathless media and official comments inadvertently contributed by seeming to imply more than they meant. A comment from President Clinton that 'North Korea cannot be allowed to develop a nuclear bomb' seemed apocalyptic in such a context. A possible US response was not the only question. A *New York Times* editorial cautioned that, since the IAEA was making demands on North Korea beyond those agreed by the US, this could lead to a 'dangerous confrontation' on the Korean Peninsula (*New York Times* 1994).

Developments since 1994 have been mixed. Despite considerable continuing opposition to the Agreed Framework and KEDO, it has continued as the major link between the West and the DPRK. For a long period, an increasing expectation that North Korea would collapse, given its growing economic problems, put the rationale of engagement into question, while partisan US opposition remained intense, as did opposition in elements of South Korean politics. Concerns heightened in Japan and Washington but less so in Seoul (Cossa 1999, 185) with the firing of a long-range missile by the North in 1998, and the DPRK's missile program is now the centre of US attention, as well as a rationalisation for the US NMD program.[6]

The difficulties of meeting the costs of the West's commitments under the Agreed Framework, notably through KEDO (its implementing authority), had been evident to the DPRK. One interpretation of the 1998 missile firing by the North was that it was another use of the North's crisis diplomacy, a consistent, if probably counterproductive, repetition of the DPRK's brinkmanship. Development and likely sale of missiles by North Korea added to the political pressure on President Clinton from critics of the US policy. A commissioned review of that policy by ex-Defense Secretary Perry nevertheless argued the benefits of the Agreed Framework as the verifiable cessation of plutonium production, the basis for international checks on suspect underground sites, and resumption of North-South talks.

There was initially disappointment over the limited movement beyond the Agreed Framework towards normalisation. Despite the difficulties, however, there have been many positive developments, including the summit between the two Presidents, family exchanges, and the agreement to recover US 'missing in action' remains, with a second North-South summit scheduled for 2001 and hopes in the South that 2001 will be 'a year of establishing peace on the Korean peninsula' (*Chungang Ilbo* 2000).

Not all has been positive and not all positive developments came directly from the crisis. Leadership successions in North and South Korea led to changes in policies, particularly the South's 'sunshine' policy towards the North. South Korean caution over a collapse of the North also increased.

Lessons

Ross has noted that the Taiwan crisis tells us 'how easy it is to stumble into a collision' with China (Ross 2000, 123). A similar conclusion can be drawn about North Korea. In considering the lessons of the Korean case, our analysis suggested that problems were magnified by various factors. This included a lack of willingness initially to consider bargaining. Further there was a lack of consensus within the Washington bureaucracy and political system, often based on a lack of knowledge and understanding of North Korea, and an unwillingness to draw on what expert knowledge there was available on North Korea, a 1994 failure that particularly worried Carter. While information gaps were inevitable, more could have been done to reduce the largely ideological nature of the debate. There was also a problem of inconsistent objectives among the parties dealing with North Korea, notably the US, South Korea and the IAEA, that were not addressed fully in the early stages of the crisis.

Many of these problems were addressed implicitly in the Perry report's recommendations. That report endorsed the comprehensive package approach of accommodation and deterrence (although with the requisite denial of responding to 'blackmail'); sought more effective coordination of US policies and efforts to achieve more bipartisanship in Washington; and proposed a mechanism to coordinate more effectively among allies, notably South Korea and Japan. As well as the Trilateral Coordination and

Oversight Group (TCOG), the Four Party talks now help by involving South Korea directly, while KEDO involves both South Korea and Japan. Perry added a further recommendation that related to pressures subsequently experienced in Washington: avoid threatening to abrogate the Agreed Framework in response to any future untoward action by the DPRK outside the Agreed Framework (Perry 1999).

NOTE

While it is important to look at and learn from the lessons of these two crises, since the structural conditions suggest crisis situations could recur in some form in the future, in any crisis there are alternative visions and different lessons will be drawn from those different visions. Nevertheless, the two crises we have discussed, although different in important respects, have important similarities. In both cases it is possible to typify them as bargaining crises. This has a number of implications, among them that the normal bargaining practices are relevant, such as having a higher level authority available to appeal to, the Carter/Kim exchanges in the DPRK case, as part of the bargaining 'game'.[7] In both cases, the overriding motivation of China and North Korea was to attract attention, most notably that of the US. China sought to reverse the US tilt towards Taiwan. For North Korea, the aim was to gain international legitimacy, to improve its security (and that of its regime) and to gain economic benefits without going through the South. It was not to reach an outcome that in actuality posed a major threat to the values of the major participants.

Consequently, in both cases there was a large degree of theatre in the event. In the Taiwan case in particular the elites in the US and Taiwan knew that there was no intention by China actually to attack Taiwan. What starts as theatre, of course, can become substantive, given miscalculation or misperception. Again holding action and responses pending adequate information is desirable.[8]

Although unpredictable events, inevitable given the important role of individuals, and the possibility of accidents, intensified the crisis in both cases, structural factors provided the conditions in which the crises could emerge. Yet, while structural factors include the underlying attitudes within each party, the responses in China and North Korea were basically contingent upon and reactive to the actions of the other parties. Internal politics and circumstances were critical in giving rise to both the conditions for the crises and the responses to those emerging conditions with ideologically-based perceptions being a barrier to rational judgements.

The DPRK case in particular illustrated that emotion and ideology could affect judgements in a way that is hard to manage, leading to discordant public views from supposedly objective officials. Thus CIA Director Woolsey took a political rather than analytical position in public, thereby raising the heat of the public debate.[9] Kim Yong Sam reversed his apparent support for US policy at one stage in the light of his electoral politics of the day.

While international institutions are not participants in the Taiwan situation, in the Korean case, the Security Council and the IAEA had a direct interest in the issue. This raised issues of the at times ambiguous relationship between the US and the Security Council. In part this is because the Security Council has limited intelligence capacity and capability for implementing its decisions. Consequently, it tends to rely heavily on the US. Thus, in the dispute with the US, the Security Council was not seen as a neutral party, although China's involvement helped to qualify such a judgement.

The IAEA's involvement raised different issues. It could be seen as being too close to the US particularly when, following the criticism linked to Iraq, the IAEA was given the right to accept US intelligence, bringing its neutrality into question. This was a view argued by the DPRK and, however defensible the IAEA's objectives in the initial stages, it was seen as pursuing US objectives. US objectives and those of the IAEA subsequently diverged, posing different problems. Bargaining in the crisis meant that the legalisms of the international institution were basically overridden.

The lessons from these experiences are not simple. One lesson is that in relationships that are problematic, careful interpretation of messages, free of ideological or other blanket presuppositions, is critical. Hostile rhetoric may imply hostile intent but it may not, and differentiating between the two can prevent differences emerging as crises. Once a political crisis situation has emerged, it is important to limit action and responses to what is needed for insurance purposes pending adequate clarity as to what is involved.

What is also common with other crises, such as the economic crisis of 1997 onwards, is the need for a clear and comprehensive coordinated strategy based on more detailed and objective knowledge and understanding at the official, political and public levels of the specific structural and political circumstances involved and the long term policy objectives being sought.

REFERENCES

Axelrod, Robert (1984) *The Evolution of Cooperation.* New York: Basic Books.

Brecher, Michael (1979) 'State Behaviour in International Crises'. *Journal of Conflict Resolution* 23: 3.

Chen, Qimao (1999) 'The Taiwan Strait Crisis'. In Suishing Zhao, *Across the Taiwan Strait.*

Christensen, Thomas (1996) *Useful Adversaries: Grand Strategy, Domestic Mobilisation and Conflict 1947-1958.* Princeton: Princeton University Press.

Chu, Yun-Han (1999) 'The Political Economy of Taiwan's Mainland Policy'. In Suishing Zhao, *Across the Taiwan Strait.*

Chungang Ilbo (Seoul) (2000) January 3 (Internet edition).

Copper, John (1999) 'The Origins of Conflict Across the Taiwan Strait'. In Suisheng Zhao, *Across the Taiwan Strait.*

Cossa, Ralph, ed. (1999) *US-Korea-Japan Relations: Building Towards a 'Virtual Alliance'.* Washington: CSIS Press.

Downs, Chuck (1999) *Over the Line: North Korea's Negotiating Strategy.* Washington: American Enterprise Press.

Garver, John (1997) *Face Off: China, the United States and Taiwan's Democratization.* Seattle and London: University of Washington Press.

Gurtov, Mel, and Byong-Moo Hwang (1998) *China's Security: The New Roles of the Military.* Boulder and London: Lynne Reinner.

Harries, Owen (1999) 'A Year of Debating China'. *National Interest* 58.

Hoffman, Stanley (1998) *World Disorders: Troubled Peace in the Post-Cold War Era.* Lanham, Md: Rowman and Littlefield.

Klintworth, Gary (1995) *New Taiwan, New China: Taiwan's Changing Role in the Asia-Pacific Region.* Melbourne and New York: Longman and St Martin's Press.

—— (2000) 'China and Taiwan – From Flashpoint to Redefining One China'. Department of the Parliamentary Library, Research Paper No. 15, November 7.

Lee, Teng-hui (1999) *The Road to Democracy: Taiwan's Pursuit of Identity.* Tokyo: PHP Institute.

Mann, James (1999) *About Face: A History of America's Curious Relationship With China, From Nixon to Clinton.* New York: Alfred Knopf.

New York Times (1994) February 11.

Oberdorfer, Don (1997) *The Two Koreas: A Contemporary History.* Reading, MA; Addison-Wesley.

Perry, William (1999) *Review of the United States Policy Towards North Korea: Findings and Recommendations* (unclassified version). Washington. October 12.

Richardson, James (1994) *Crisis Diplomacy: The Great Powers Since the Mid-Nineteenth Century.* Cambridge: Cambridge University Press.

Ross, Robert (2000) 'The 1995-1996 Taiwan Strait Confrontation: Coercion, Credibility and the Use of Force'. *International Security* 25: 2.

Schelling, Thomas (1980) *The Strategy of Conflict.* Cambridge: Harvard University Press.

Scobell, Andrew (2000) 'Show of Force: Chinese Soldiers, Statesmen and the 1995-1996 Taiwan Strait Crisis'. *Political Science Quarterly* 115: 2.

Sigal, Leon (1998) *Disarming Strangers: Nuclear Diplomacy with North Korea.* Princeton: Princeton University Press.

Snyder, Scott (1999) *Negotiating on the Edge: North Korean Negotiating Behaviour.* Washington: United States Institute for Peace Press.

Yang, Andrew Nien-Dzu (2000) *The 1996 Missile Exercises: China's Political Manipulation and Taiwan's Crisis Management.* CAPS Papers No. 27, China Council of Advanced Policy Studies, Taiwan, March.

You, Ji (1999) 'Changing Leadership Consensus'. In Suishing Zhao, *Across the Taiwan Strait.*

Zhao, Suishing, ed. (1999) *Across the Taiwan Strait: Mainland China, Taiwan and the 1995-1996 Crisis.* New York: Routledge.

ENDNOTES

1 Brecher includes a further criterion – a finite time to respond to the threat to basic values. The time constraint was less central to the Taiwan Strait issue but was important to North Korean crisis behaviour.

2 The importance or otherwise of internal influences on foreign policies is contested among international relations specialists. Neorealists such as Kenneth Waltz do not consider internal factors important; classical realists such as Thucydides, neoliberals such as Robert Keohane and constructivists such as Peter Katzenstein do. For a useful discussion of the realist/liberal divide see Stanley Hoffman 1998, ch.4.

3 We would note, however, that in both prime examples in this paper, precise understanding of the internal politics of a major participant, China in one case and North Korea in the other, is inevitably incomplete and views are contested.

[4] Namely, that the United States would not support Taiwan's independence, the creation of two Chinas or Taiwan's admission to the United Nations. The last of the noes was later extended to no support for membership in organisations that require members to be sovereign states (Mann 1999, 330; 356-58).

[5] The term 'crisis diplomacy' differs here from Richardson's use of the term. He prefers it to mean the management of a crisis once it is in being. For North Korea, it implies the creation of a crisis situation for negotiation purposes.

[6] In August 1998, the DPRK launched a three-stage rocket that passed over Japan. Ostensibly to launch a satellite, and its trajectory was apparently consistent with that, it created intense concern in Japanese security and media circles. It was also significant in demonstrating a North Korean missile capability greater than previously understood.

[7] That was why the early involvement of the US and Chinese Presidents at too detailed a level was unhelpful in the April 2001 US surveillance plane incident over Hainan Island.

[8] Another lesson that would have been helpful for the April 2001 crisis.

[9] Oberdorfer reports that the CIA acknowledged that they overestimated North Korea's likely plutonium availability (Oberdorfer 1997, 306-307). This not only led to exaggerated conclusions about the North's potential for nuclear bombs but also reinforced views of the unreliability of the North's explanations which, they later acknowledged, 'could have been right'.

Chapter 11

TERRITORIAL SOVEREIGNTY AND NUCLEAR CRISIS: NORTHEAST ASIA AND JAPAN'S ROLE

Akiko Fukushima

Keio University

National Institute for Research Advancement

Tokyo, Japan

Looking at the Northeast Asian region as a whole, there are territorial disputes that remain unresolved. Japan and Russia have not signed a World War II peace treaty. Although the San Francisco Peace Treaty celebrated its fiftieth anniversary in September 2001, the Soviet Union never signed it. Russia, which succeeded the Soviet Union, has not signed a bilateral peace treaty with Japan. As such Japan and Russia are still negotiating the sovereignty over the four Northern Islands (namely Habomai, Shikotan, Etorofu and Kunashiri), known as the Northern Territories in Japan and the Southern Kuriles in Russia. For Japan, the conclusion of a peace treaty means, above all, the final resolution of this territorial issue with Russia. Furthermore, the resolution means re-establishing Japan's sovereignty over the Northern Territories. This unresolved problem has marred Russo-Japan relations over the years, spilling into fishing disputes that continue to emerge now and then, even though Japan has provided substantial economic assistance to the Soviet Union and subsequently Russia.

There are other unresolved territorial issues involving Japan, such as the Tokdo/Takeshima dispute between South Korea and Japan, and the Senkaku/Daioyutai dispute between Japan and China; the existence of these territorial issues means that sovereignty matters greatly in Northeast Asia. The geopolitical situation in Northeast Asia, thus, has not allowed a flexible pooling of sovereignty as can be found, say, in the European Union.

One remnant from the Northeast Asian Cold War period is a divided country: the Korean Peninsula, separated into North and South after the Korean War, has yet to experience a genuine thaw after the Cold War. The two Koreas maintain an armistice, awaiting a final settlement, while the absence of a full settlement of the situation remains a seed for potential instability in the region.

Whether the Cold War has ended in Northeast Asia or not, the sub-region clearly suffers from the loose ends of the Second World War and the Cold War. In addition, Northeast Asia faces new challenges like research and development of Theatre Missile Defense (TMD)[1] by the United States and Japan, and reported arms buildup by China and the Democratic People's Republic of Korea (DPRK).

With the perpetuation of these numerous territorial and irredentist challenges in Northeast Asia, the majority of observers do not anticipate a major interstate war to break out in the sub-region. Some, however, argue that if the world should see gunfire again, escalating to a Third World War, it couldn't break out anywhere else but Northeast Asia.

This chapter, therefore, first of all examines one of the territorial issues still lingering in Northeast Asia involving Japan and Russia over the Northern Territories. Second, it reviews some of the security challenges emerging in the sub-region. Third, it attempts to explore Japan's role in reducing actual and potential crisis in Northeast Asia.

CONTENDED VIEWS: THE JAPANESE-RUSSIAN TERRITORIAL DISPUTE

The Japanese-Russian territorial dispute is not likely to escalate to major conflict between the two nations, as it did nearly a century ago with the outbreak of the Russo-Japanese War in 1904. But it has caused strained bilateral relations since the end of World War II. It may further limit the development of bilateral relations, which may in turn impinge on Northeast Asian stability as a whole. This unresolved territorial dispute has major political and psychological implications. It is indeed the main obstacle to normalising relations between Russia and Japan, obstructing the conclusion of a long-overdue peace treaty between them.

For Japan, the conclusion of a peace treaty means the final resolution of the territorial problem with Russia and the re-establishment of Japanese sovereignty over the northern islands. For Russia the same event is interpreted primarily as a loss of territory. But Russia also recognises that both sides need to put their bilateral relationship on a firm basis for a long-term partnership, key elements of which, in the eyes of Russians, are close economic cooperation and closer geopolitical and security relations with Japan.

It is odd that the two countries have not signed a peace treaty in the 55 years since the end of World War II. This situation developed because the then-Soviet Union did not sign the San Francisco Peace Treaty, which Japan signed with other countries. The Soviet Union and Japan did, however, hold negotiations on a peace treaty in the 1950s, culminating in the 1956 Japan-Soviet Joint Declaration.[2] This document stipulated the end of hostilities between Japan and the Soviet Union and resulted in resumption of diplomatic relations. Paragraph 9 of the Joint Declaration specifically mentioned the continuation of negotiations on a peace treaty and the transfer of Habomai and Shikotan to Japan after the signing of a peace treaty. Soon after the announcement of the 1956 Joint Declaration, Japan and the United States signed the revised Security Treaty (in 1960), which led to the Soviet Union reneging on its commitments in the Joint Declaration. In turn, Japan was angered by the Soviet Union's not transferring to Japan the two islands they had agreed to return in 1956, while continuing to ignore the open question of the other two islands, Kunashiri and Etorofu.

Acknowledging Differences

The Soviet Union did not recognise the existence of the territorial disputes in a clear manner until the beginning of the 1990s. Thus, negotiations were held in suspension throughout the 1970s and 1980s, although the foreign ministers of both countries met briefly in New York at the UN General Assembly every year. There was, however, in this period one glimmer of an attempt to move negotiations forward, when, in 1973, Soviet Communist Party General Secretary Brezhnev received Prime Minister Kakuei Tanaka and agreed to include 'unresolved issues after the Second World War' into their Joint Communiqué.

Brezhnev admitted orally that this meant the four islands. It was the first, though only verbal, acknowledgement by the Soviet Union of the four northern islands as being the subject of territorial negotiations. The Soviet Government soon changed its position again, however, tacitly denying the existence of the 'four island issue'. This, in effect, halted any further bilateral negotiations on the territorial dispute.

In 1991, when President Gorbachev visited Japan, the Japanese side argued that the territorial issue covering Habomai and Shikotan was resolved previously in the 1956 Joint Declaration, and the only remaining issue was the status of Kunashiri and Etorofu. Gorbachev, however, argued that he could not uphold the 1956 Joint Declaration due to contextual changes since the 1956 Declaration; specifically, Russia subsuming the Soviet Union. The Joint Statement announced by President Gorbachev and Prime Minister Toshiki Kaifu, in contrast, stated that the two countries had discussed a peace treaty, including in this discussion the issue of the sovereignty of the four islands. Thus, the 'four island issue' came to be recognised in a written form.

Gorbachev's successor, the Russian President Boris Yeltsin, visited Japan and signed the Tokyo Declaration[3] with Prime Minister Morihiro Hosokawa in 1993. This became a cornerstone for the development of bilateral relations, and also formally confirmed the existence of territorial issues between Japan and Russia. The Tokyo Declaration clearly identified the four islands by name. It also clearly described the procedure for normalising relations between the two countries by solving the territorial issue and concluding a peace treaty. During a press conference at the time, President Yeltsin responded 'Yes' to a question as to whether the 1956 Joint Declaration was included among Russia's inherited international commitments.

Efforts at Resolution

New momentum to solve the territorial issue of the four islands emerged again in the spring of 1997, after Yeltsin was returned to power in the Russian presidential election in mid-1996. It led to a series of informal summits between Japan and Russia. In November 1997, President Yeltsin and Prime Minister Ryutaro Hashimoto met in Krasnoyarsk for an informal summit and agreed to exert maximum effort in concluding a peace treaty, and to do so by way of addressing the issue of the northern islands by the year 2000. They met again in April 1998, this time at a retreat called Kawana in Japan. At that meeting, Prime Minister Hashimoto made an informal proposal to draw a line demarcating a Russo-Japanese border between Urup and Etorofu first, and subsequently to discuss the return of administrative rights over the islands as a whole.

However, after the Birmingham G8 Summit in 1998, due to President Yeltsin's failing health and Russia's economic downturn, momentum on the territorial issue waned. When Prime Minister Keizo Obuchi and President Yeltsin met in Moscow in 1998, the Russian side proposed to conclude a treaty of friendship and cooperation (a so-called 'intermediate treaty'), separate from a peace treaty, but including the territorial issue. This was tantamount to shelving the border demarcation issue for future negotiations and, in effect, did nothing more than confirm the two sides' resolve in tackling the issue.

When Yeltsin's successor President Putin paid an official visit to Japan in September 2000, the Russian side declined Japan's proposal for Russia to cede sovereignty of the four islands but retain administrative control during a period of phased return to Japan. Japan, in turn, rejected a friendship and cooperation proposal that left the territorial issue unresolved. President Vladimir Putin, with some surprise to the Japanese side, recognised in a straightforward way that the 1956 Joint Declaration remained valid to this day. With this ambiguous 'hint' from Putin,[4] Japanese and Russian senior negotiators met on four more occasions: twice at the Foreign Ministers' level (in November 2000 and in January 2001); and twice at Prime Ministerial level (in mid-November 2000 at a side-meeting of an APEC Leaders' gathering, and at a separate bilateral meeting in March 2001).

The Irkutsk statement by then-Prime Minister Mori and President Putin[5] set out the documents and agreements to be used by the two countries as a basis for negotiations on a peace treaty, namely: the 1956 Japan-Soviet Joint Declaration; the 1973 Japan-Soviet Joint Communiqué; the 1991 Japan-Soviet Joint Communiqué; the 1993 Tokyo Declaration on Japan-Russia Relations; the Moscow Declaration on Building a Creative Partnership between Japan and the Russian Federation on the Issue of a Peace Treaty; and the 2001 Irkutsk Statement.

In order to build and maintain 'an atmosphere based on mutual understanding, trust and wide-ranging mutually beneficial cooperation for negotiations', Japanese and Russian think-tanks co-organised (in Moscow) the first Japan-Russia Forum on Japan-Russia relations in the Asia-Pacific to discuss geopolitical, economic and cultural issues in May 2001.[6] Keidanren (The Federation of Economic Organizations) also sent a mission comprising 150 members as an official dispatch to Russia in June 2001 to promote cooperation in the economic sector. Although the two nations could not meet the deadline for the conclusion of a peace treaty set by the November 1997 Krasnoyarsk meeting, both Russia and Japan are continuing their efforts to resolve this thorny territorial issue.

Meanwhile, since September 2000 elements of the Japanese press have outlined an approach to the lingering problem, asking for the transfer of the two islands. Some argue, however, that if Japan asks for the return of the islands Habomai and Shikotan first, this will be taken as a waiver for the remaining two islands, Kunashiri and Etorofu. This has subsequently developed into a heated debate, focusing on 'two islands first' or 'four islands as a package' in resolving the Northern Territories issues.[7]

OTHER SECURITY CHALLENGES IN NORTHEAST ASIA?

In the course of the 1990s, the sub-region has encountered a series of events signalling that Northeast Asia is not necessarily free from actual and potential crises. As an illustration, there were large-scale missile exercises by China on the high seas north of Taiwan in July and August 1995, as well as joint exercises by the Chinese army, navy and air force in March 1996 (at the time of the presidential campaign in Taiwan). The test launch of missiles by the DPRK (a Nodong missile in May of 1993 and a Taepodong missile in August of 1998), in addition to unidentified ships slipping into the Japan Sea in March of 1999, also exemplify security concerns. While there are a variety of actual and potential crises that can take place in Northeast Asia, this section focuses on two: one emanating from the division of the Korean Peninsula, and the other stemming from proliferation of nuclear technology.

The Division of DPRK and ROK, and Its Consequences

Although the Korean War ended with the signing of the Military Armistice Agreement on 27 July 1953, North and South Korea are still legally in a state of war and a permanent ceasefire document has yet to be signed. At the 38th parallel, heavily-armed North and South Korean troops (along with UN forces) face each other, thereby implementing the armistice. Over the past 47 years, there have been numerous violations of the Armistice Treaty, small-scale clashes of uniformed soldiers along the De-militarized Zone (DMZ), and even incidents pushing the contending parties to the brink of war.

The DPRK has been suspected for its development of nuclear weapons. In fact the DPRK rejected a request for special inspections by the International Atomic Energy Agency (IAEA) of the DPRK's undeclared facilities, assumed to be storage areas for re-processed plutonium that could be used for making nuclear weapons. In February 1993 it threatened to withdraw from the Nuclear Non-Proliferation Treaty, which shocked the international community's non-proliferation regime. This indeed deepened concern over North Korean intentions in its development of nuclear weapons.

Through difficult negotiations, the General Agreed Framework was signed on 21 October 1994. This was an agreement reached between the US and DPRK 'to freeze and eventually dismantle North Korean nuclear facilities that could be used to manufacture fuel for nuclear weapons, in return for the provision of technologically superior, proliferation-resistant light-water reactors (LWRs), and 500,000 tons per year of heavy fuel oil (HFO) to the DPRK'. The Agreed Framework laid the basis for an eventual resolution of concerns about North Korea's nuclear program and provided a path for the DPRK to rejoin the Nuclear Non-Proliferation Treaty. It also mandated the creation of a new type of international organisation, the Korean Peninsula Energy Development Organization (KEDO), an institution that would implement the provisions of the Agreement, including the supply of heavy fuel oil to the DPRK and construction of the LWRs.[8]

Despite the General Agreed Framework, the DPRK is still suspected of possessing nuclear weapons. It is also reported that it has produced facilities to manufacture chemical and biological weapons. As for ballistic missiles, the DPRK is considered to have produced and deployed Scud B, C and Nodong missiles.[9] Indeed, there is a likelihood that it was a Nodong missile that landed in the Japan Sea in May 1993. Furthermore, the DPRK seems to have been developing longer-range ballistic missiles, the Taepodong I. The DPRK is also reported to be developing a Taepodong II, which uses a two-staged configuration, with a new type of a booster for stage 1 and Nodong at stage 2. This gives it a longer range of 3,500 to 6,000 kilometers. In August 1998 a test launch was conducted, most probably based on the technology developed for the Taepodong I.[10]

Although increased diplomatic activity on the Korean peninsula has reduced tensions, the threat of the DPRK military remains unchanged. The DPRK regime has been strengthening its military, with a view toward adding pressure for unification, as well as improving that state's own military capabilities. The DPRK's current interest in weapons is concentrated on submarines and missiles. Its military, it must be noted, is large, with 1,000,000 personnel, 3,000 tanks, and 600 fighters. However, modernisation has been delayed,[11] although the DPRK is shifting from conventional to nuclear weapons. The military can mobilise special agents and undertake blitzkriegs against adversaries. The psychological use of weapons of mass destruction (WMD) could also be effective in actual battlefield scenarios.[12] In particular, the DPRK's neighbours have not yet come to terms with its missile development program, a fact which remains a security challenge for Japan and, indeed, Northeast Asia as a whole.

Missile development by the DPRK is a source of concern for the international community as a whole, particularly when this is combined with its development of nuclear weapons. It is also reported that the DPRK is exporting its missiles to Iran, Syria and Pakistan, earning around US$1 billion from its exports of weaponry.[13] Missile development has therefore been the key element in US-DPRK and EU-DPRK talks. Regarding negotiations with the DPRK, since concern is shared by the Republic of Korea (ROK) and Japan, a Trilateral Coordination and Oversight Group (TCOG) was created among high level officials from Japan, the US, and the ROK to consult on their policies toward the DPRK.

On a more positive note, however, in June 2000 an important summit meeting between North Korean leader Kim Jong Il and South Korean President Kim Dae Jung was held in Pyongyang; it was the most significant event on the Korean Peninsula, arguably, in half a century. The summit resulted in the 6.15 Declaration and both sides agreed to strive toward the unification of the two Koreas. The summit has eased the sense of confrontation on the peninsula, creating favorable conditions for greater bilateral cooperation. The summit meeting affirmed President Kim Dae Jung's 'Sunshine Policy' or 'engagement policy' in the eyes of the international community. Kim Jong Il's warmth in receiving Kim Dae Jung during their meetings permeated the television screen and invited positive comments from the international press. The summit helped to improve the image of the DPRK's enigmatic leaders, as well as the DPRK itself, in the eyes of the international community, which has regarded the DPRK as a closed, rogue state.

The inter-Korean summit has helped the DPRK to revive its ties with China and Russia, its traditional partners during the Cold War. This was demonstrated by Kim Jong Il's visits to China in 2000 and 2001, as well as the visit of President Putin to Pyongyang in July 2000. The DPRK has also opened diplomatic relations with countries like Italy, Canada and Australia, as well as receiving an EU delegation to Pyongyang in May 2001. Furthermore, the DPRK was allowed to join the ASEAN Regional Forum (ARF) in July 2000.

Immediately after the summit, there was a sense of warming – a post-summit euphoria – in the ROK towards the DPRK, demonstrated by a series of actions by the ROK. After the summit, the ROK sent a variety of items, including additional food aid of 600,000 tons, fertiliser and computers, to the DPRK. A meeting of separated families was allowed by both sides in August 2000. The ROK also initiated construction of fresh links with the Kyongeui Railway on the DMZ, as well as the prevention of floods from the Imjin River and the introduction of the Mt Kungun economic free zone.

However, the euphoria was short lived, and the implementation of the 6.15 Declaration seemed to need more attention and care. DPRK-US relations have also undergone some twists. After the decision of the Clinton Administration to provide heavy fuel oil to the DPRK through KEDO, the DPRK announced that it would discontinue further missile launches, although it did not pledge to roll back its missile development. In October 2000, DPRK Deputy Defense Minister Jo Myong-Rok visited Washington DC. This was followed by the US Secretary of State Madeleine Albright's visit to Pyongyang, bringing with it a hint of a possible visit by President Clinton to Pyongyang before the end of his term in office. However, this visit did not take place, partly because of the presidential election and partly because of the unresolved missile question.

The fifth round of US-DPRK missile talks in 2000 (held in Malaysia) were deadlocked when the DPRK demanded that the US compensate it with US$1 billion in exchange for the DPRK's abandonment of its export of missile parts and technologies. Indeed, the DPRK went so far as to announce through its spokesman that '[t]he US does not have the right to criticise the DPRK's missiles while thousands of its own missiles are still deployed in East Asia'.[14] In renewed US-DPRK talks, the DPRK's missile development will be a key agenda item.

Proliferation Problems: Action and Reaction

While nuclear proliferation is a concern, Northeast Asia was also concerned about the nuclear tests of India and Pakistan in 1998, as well as the August 1999 agreement signed between the United States and Japan to collaborate on missile defense research, the latter generating sharp opposition from China and the DPRK. Ironically, the North Korean test launch of Taepodong I provided a direct impetus for Japan's signing of the 1999 Theater Missile Defense (TMD) Memorandum of Understanding. China rejected the notion that TMD is a 'defensive weapon system', arguing that it could serve offensive purposes if it were used to protect forces launching an attack.

Russia has also aired its concerns about a TMD system, arguing that it is a possible first step towards revising the Anti-Ballistic Missile (ABM) Treaty. Russia and China have argued that practical implementation of TMD plans without regard to the interests of Russia and China might undermine the existing balance of forces in the region, leading to an escalation of international tension and a new spiral in the regional arms race. Although Russian and Chinese leaders repeatedly state that they do not want to forge a formal political or military alliance, they are seeking closer security cooperation, progressing from the level of acquisition by China of relatively simple Russian arms, to the import of the latest Russian weapon systems and transfers of sophisticated military technology. Thus, in addition to the earlier acquisition of Su-27 combat aircraft and anti-submarine warfare (ASW) helicopters, in 1999 China ordered about 40 Su-30 K combat aircraft, the most advanced in the Russian Air Force. In the same year China received the first of two Russian Soveremennyi Class destroyers equipped with modern missile and radar systems, and two Kilo Class submarines (*SIPRI Yearbook* 2000, 352, 387-388). These acquisitions helped modernise the Chinese air and naval forces substantially.

TMD, which is still in the research and design stage, may have a military capacity to counter limited missile attacks, but it has created political instability and alliance in the region, which may, finally, undermine the regional security equation. TMD or Ballistic Missile Defense under George W. Bush's administration may lead to higher political costs, while the missile defense system itself has 'potential military benefits [that] lie far in the future' (Mederios 2001, i). Ballistic Missile Defense (BMD) has been developed as a 'response to military developments in East Asia, including China's missile build-up across the Taiwan Strait and North Korea's efforts to develop nuclear weapons and long range ballistic missiles' (Mederios 2001, 23). BMD research and development alone, not to mention eventual deployment, may destabilise political and security relationships between the US and Northeast Asian countries.

The US and others involved in the conceptualisation of the TMD ought to balance the security contributions of the system and political costs of the development of a ballistic missile system. Moreover, the US announcement to withdraw from the Comprehensive Test Ban Treaty (CTBT) in July 2001[15] does not help the situation. It could fuel another round of nuclear proliferation if not it is not managed well.

What Role Can Japan Play to Reduce Actual and Potential Crisis?

Some have questioned the relevance of the US-Japan alliance that has dominated Japan's security, thereby leading to an argument that the Japan-US alliance was adrift (Kuriyama 1997, 20, 92). Commentators in the US have even argued for the termination of the Japan-US security alliance (Funabashi 2001, 2-3). In Japan, some have argued for continuing the Japan-US Security Treaty, but without providing bases for American troops (Hosokawa 1998).

The events in the 1990s have led Japan to regard the US-Japan security alliance as the basic pillar of its national security. While Article 5 of the US-Japan Security Treaty, which focuses on the defence of Japan, was the main facet of the alliance during the Cold War, Japan and the US towards the end of 1990s have come to emphasise Article 6 of the treaty, which centres on working for the peace and stability of the Far East.

Japan and the United States reaffirmed the importance of the bilateral alliance through the 'Japan-US Joint Declaration on Security – Alliance for the 21st Century' announced by Prime Minister Ryutaro Hashimoto and President Clinton on 17 April 1996.[16] This Declaration confirmed the existing bilateral alliance, and also alluded to regional cooperation 'to achieve a more peaceful and stable security environment in the Asia-Pacific region'. This reference to US-Japan cooperation in the Far East (the so-called Article VI cooperation), in addition to the traditional Article V cooperation on defence of Japan, is further reflected in the Guidelines for Japan-US Defense Cooperation, announced on 23 September 1997. This document has established a basis for Japan-US cooperation in crisis conditions, as well as under normal circumstances. These guidelines include a specific section on Japan-US defense cooperation in surrounding areas. Following the announcement of these guidelines, Japan introduced laws and agreements to ensure their effectiveness; namely the Law Concerning Measures to Ensure the Peace and Security of Japan in Situations in Areas Surrounding Japan. Although China has questioned the geographical scope of the surrounding area, this is generally seen as an attempt by Japan to play a role in the event of a crisis in areas beyond its national territory.

Through these formal agreements and measures, Japan reconfirmed the importance of its alliance with the United States. However, does Japan limit itself to a bilateral alliance, or does it look beyond bilateralism in responding to and preparing for a contingency in Northeast Asia?

Progressive Japanese Security Contributions

Consideration of alternative forms of security orders in Northeast Asia is an underdeveloped area of scholarship. Two options are almost never raised: political integration (including the creation of supranational organisations) and political convergence (the idea that peace can be built on the emergence of democratic regimes throughout the region). This forces one to ask: Are Northeast Asian countries inherently unable to manage their own security affairs? Facing a security challenge from the DPRK, Japan lacks a direct means to prevent crises on the Korean Peninsula. While continuing its diplomatic negotiations with the DPRK to normalise relations, Japan plays a role by moving along a multilateral path. One avenue is through TCOG (mentioned above). The other avenue is through KEDO. Japan currently sends one deputy executive director and other staff members to KEDO meetings, and is generally regarded as playing an important role. Although KEDO's achievement is mixed, it has laid the foundation for increased institutionalised or formalised cooperation among the United States, Japan and South Korea, including providing support for increased trilateral coordination in the areas of contingency planning to respond to the possibility of a North Korean collapse.

It has also led to the meeting of senior officials from the US, South Korea and Japan in April 1999, in addition to a trilateral summit meeting among President Clinton, Prime Minister Obuchi, and President Kim Dae Jung on the sidelines of the APEC Leaders' Meeting in New Zealand in September 1999. Prime Minister Obuchi proposed six party talks that could be a new framework or an extension of the existing 'Four Party Talks'. The latter do not include Japan, but have been convened in Geneva (between the US, the two Koreas and China) to produce a peace regime for the Korean Peninsula. This can be expanded to include other Northeast Asian countries which would be affected by the turn of events on the Peninsula.

Japan's role on the Korean Peninsula would first and foremost be to negotiate normalisation between the two Korean states. Until this takes place, however, Japan will continue to play its role through the multilateral path, namely through its participation and its support of KEDO as well as through TCOG, coordinating its policy in relation to DPRK.

On the matter of ballistic missile defence, Japan should exert an effort not to run up political costs in Northeast Asia. One way is to organise a multilateral forum to discuss ballistic missile defence, perhaps at the track two level to gain transparency to a certain extent. The ballistic missile defence system and its development in Northeast Asia needs to be addressed in the context of its ramifications for the peace and security of the region.

On overall nuclear proliferation, Japan has an obvious role to play because it was the victim of atomic bombing in 1945. Japan, however, should graduate from the emotional argument of 'no more Hiroshima and no more Nagasaki', and promote nuclear disarmament.

Japan has a longstanding policy found in the three non-nuclear principles: Japan will not manufacture, possess, or allow nuclear weapons to be brought into its territory. Also, the 1955 Atomic Energy Basic Law prohibits the military use of atomic energy. Furthermore, in July 1997 Japan ratified the CTBT, becoming the first of the 44 states required to ratify the CTBT before it can be enforced.

Criticism and Contradictions

Despite the difficulties Japan faces in conducting its foreign policy in such complex environments, its position has been subjected to varying degrees of criticism: for example, the apparent contradiction in its policy of appealing for nuclear disarmament while remaining under the protection of the US nuclear deterrence. When Japan criticised India and Pakistan for nuclear testing, their counter-argument was to point to Japan's hypocrisy in remaining under the so-called US nuclear umbrella, while criticising those who try to develop their own arsenal, because they do not benefit from a similar umbrella. The National Defense Program Outline of November 1995 states that 'with respect to the threat from nuclear weapons, Japan will play an active role in making realistic and steadfast international efforts towards nuclear disarmament, aiming at creating a world without nuclear weapons while relying on US nuclear deterrence'.

How can Japan solve this contradiction? If one were to adopt an extreme position, the option for Japan to move away from its intimate relationship with US nuclear deterrence may be a possibility. How, then, it might be asked, would Japan maintain its own security? If Japan were to take the steps to acquire nuclear weapons, this would not contribute to nuclear non-proliferation and disarmament. Demilitarised neutrality might be another option for Japan. Yet this option would be a far-fetched one in the context of its own political realities. One further option available to Japan could be, for example, to request that the United States defend Japan by means of an umbrella of conventional weapons instead of a nuclear umbrella. However desirable such an option would be, it is one that smacks of selfishness, and disregards the fact that as long as Japan is in an alliance with the US, it could not be seen as morally (or even practically) completely removed from beneath the US nuclear umbrella.

Thus, Japan must take a realistic option of acknowledging the current usefulness of the US nuclear deterrence and make efforts gradually to reduce its reliance on this by working to decrease the salience of nuclear weaponry. An opinion survey conducted by the National Institute for Research Advancement (NIRA) in Japan in the fall of 1999 put the question: 'When Japan protested against the nuclear tests conducted by India and Pakistan, Japan was criticized as being hypocritical and self-contradictory for making such protests while being protected under the US nuclear umbrella. How do you view this?' Of the Japanese polled, 47 per cent responded that this was a contradictory position. To a question on whether Japan should continue to advocate nuclear disarmament, 40 per cent responded 'yes' (NIRA 2001, 271-73).

Japan, given these circumstances, should continue to promote nuclear disarmament by working with groups like the New Agenda Coalition when their perspectives coincide, so that schemes like the CTBT, a Fissile Material Cut-off Treaty and other measures can be realised.

Regional Multilateralism

Turning to the question of regional security as a whole, two options are almost never raised: political integration (as mentioned before) and political convergence. This forces one to ask: Are Northeast Asians habitually unable to manage their own security affairs? Must they depend in perpetuity on external actors, no matter how benign, for their security? If inter-Korean relations improve significantly, even if these are short of formal reunification, is there still a compelling argument for American forward deployment?

In a type of 'reconstituted Cold War' scenario, some believe that the stage is set for the resurgence of two blocs, in the form of a US-led, NATO-like arrangement in opposition to a new multilateral alliance centred on China and Russia (the latter a version of peace through multilateral collective defence). At the other end of the spectrum are advocates of a collective security regime to be built up on the basis of multilateral dialogue, diplomacy and arms reduction. Meanwhile, mainstream debates recognise that the future security order in Asia is likely to be a multi-player one, involving elements of unilateral military preparedness, alliance structures, bilateral diplomatic instruments, and new multilateral institutions that range from devices for dialogue and consultation to regional organisations for promoting economic interaction and management of concrete security problems (Nishihara 1999, 102-11).

Japan, struggling with its own difficult historical legacy of its behaviour in countries like Korea and China, finds a multilateral path attractive because it can take initiatives in regional security without generating concerns of new Japanese militarism, or the image of creating a fresh East Asia Co-Prosperity Sphere.

Numerous skeptics of regional multilateralism in Asia argue that little has been produced during the 1990s and that the window for multilateral cooperation is fast closing. Big power relations, after almost a decade of improvement through the vehicle of concerted bilateralism and bilateral summits in 1997, which produced numerous 'partnerships' amongst powers in the region, have appeared to be regressing into confrontation at the start of the twenty-first century. Northeast Asian states seem incapable of overcoming the divisions created by history, historical memory, culture, language, virulent nationalisms and political and economic systems. At a policy level, there is no multilateral alternative; bilateralism, however flawed and imperfect it seems to be, presents itself as the only feasible option (Rozman 2000, 8-13; Kimura 2000, 40-43). On the other hand, some proponents of multilateralism argue that Asian interest in multilateralism has reached the point when the continued adherence to bilateral alliances appears to be based on an assumption that these provide a breathing space for multilateralism to take root and mature. They argue that bilateral pacts such as the Japan-US alliance, the US-South Korea alliance, and the US-Australia alliance form a hub-and-spoke structure in Asia. This is the basis of the 'wheel' of Asia's security structure, and fulfils admirably the function of deterrence (NIRA 2000, 32-37). Recently, in a departure from the Cold War context under which they were born, some of the bilateral security agreements, especially the US-Japan and US-Australia alliances, provided a deterrence mechanism for region-wide peace and stability, which in turn enables a mechanism for dialogue internal to the region itself to emerge. In other words, the coupling of deterrence and security dialogue mechanisms resemble not a single wheel, but the two wheels of a bicycle.

What we have witnessed so far in Northeast Asia is the creation of a complex structure of security dialogue forums, at a variety of levels, to allow a cooperative security approach to emerge. Initiatives to promote region-wide consultations and dialogues, like the ASEAN Regional Forum (ARF) at one level (track one), and the Council for Security Cooperation in Asia-Pacific (CSCAP) at another (track two),[17] have proliferated in the 1990s. Most have appeared in the context of a broader Asia Pacific setting. Japan has been strongly supportive of these processes, with Taro Nakayama, Japan's Foreign Minister at the time, even proposing the creation of an ARF-like institution in June 1991, although the idea was not taken up at that stage. However, this situation changed when the ARF was launched in Bangkok in July 1994 as the product of ASEAN Ministerial and PMC meetings.

At its second meeting in 1995, an ARF concept paper was adopted which described a gradual three-stage evolution from confidence-building to preventive diplomacy, and finally to a body capable, in the longer term, of developing approaches to conflict resolution. The ARF has also agreed to a *modus operandi* of consensus and to 'move at a pace comfortable to all participants'. While the ARF has introduced numerous initiatives in regional confidence-building, ranging from the issuing of defense white papers to dialogues on confidence-building measures such as pronouncements on issues of search and rescue, it has also encountered difficulties in moving to the second stage of its evolution, preventive diplomacy, in terms of defining the concept and principles.

The establishment of the ARF was an event of historic significance in the sense that, for the first time ever, China's participation in a regional dialogue for cooperative security became a reality. Moreover, the participation of North Korea in the 2000 summit further enhanced the inclusiveness of its membership. The current status of the ARF might be far from satisfactory, to the extent that some critics describe the Forum as merely a 'chat-room'. Compared to the time of its establishment in 1994, however, dialogues at the ARF have taken on such delicate issues as the Spratley Islands dispute and nuclear tests by India and Pakistan. Therefore, it can be said that the ARF has contributed in no small measure to confidence-building in the Asian region (Hiramatsu 1999, 102-11).

Another dialogue forum with the possibility of promoting security as an agenda is the ASEAN +3 (Japan, ROK and China). This forum, which first met at the summit level in 1997, has continued to convene at summit level since then, and has also been held at the economic ministers' level since 2000 (discussions in the latter have included the possible creation of a currency-swap mechanism in case of economic emergencies). This, in effect, becomes a web of bilateral agreements to react to the emergencies in the region. The '+3', namely Japan, the ROK and China, have begun to meet separately at breakfast sessions during the annual ASEAN +3 meetings, discussing issues held in common, and instructing their own research institutions to conduct more joint projects.

Non-Governmental Regional Cooperation

Also of note is the emergence of a more functionalist approach towards regional cooperation, whereby we have seen Asian countries form issue-specific coalitions to deal with thorny questions. Examples of this type of cooperation include the pursuit of a Cambodian peace in the early 1990s and the above-mentioned KEDO. Another example is regional cooperation to stem piracy, a measure involving Southeast Asia, and one in which Japan itself is taking the initiative.

Processes at the second level could include those initiated by the private sector, these involving government officials in their private capacities, together with academics, journalists and others. Unfortunately, such initiatives have been few and far between. The Canadian-initiated North Pacific Cooperative Security Dialogue (1990-93) was the first major program to include governmental and non-governmental participants from the region. When this ceased, the University of California's Institute on Global Conflict and Cooperation (IGCC) initiated the Northeast Asia Cooperation Dialogue (NEACD) in October 1993 (Cossa and Fukushima 1998). Participants have come from ministries of foreign affairs, defence establishments, as well as academic institutions in the US, Japan, South Korea, Russia and China, but, as yet, not North Korea. This US-led program appears to show some American willingness to go beyond bilateralism in dealing with Northeast Asia. A third program is the North Pacific Working Group of CSCAP, and this is the most inclusive dialogue process in the region as North Korea also participates.

More than 60 programs of bilateral, trilateral, and quadrilateral track two meetings have linked countries in Northeast Asia and the North Pacific.[18] Examples include the Trilateral Forum on North Pacific Security Problems, launched in early 1994 by three non-governmental think-tanks from Japan, the US and Russia, with the intention being to lower the psychological barrier between Japan and Russia. In the summer of 1998, another level two process, involving Japanese, American, and Chinese non-governmental experts, was launched to develop three sets of bilateral relations in a balanced manner, and to remove any residual misunderstandings or miscalculations. According to media accounts, 'although Japan and the United States wanted to launch this framework as a track one forum, China rejected the idea, insisting it was premature to let government officials participate in such a forum' (Masaki 1998), which might encourage defence exchanges. These are 'mini-lateral' rather than multilateral, with exclusive membership and a specific aim, in contrast to a process like CSCAP.

The regional mechanisms that have emerged in Asia in the 1990s are security dialogues, and far from what one can identify as security mechanisms. While multilateral processes have not taken root in these areas, 'mini-laterals', assembling less than the full complement of the regional states, but with the specific objectives of building confidence and assuaging any misunderstandings among participants, seem to have maintained their steam. Thus, while it remains self-evident that the majority of Japanese academics and officials are keen to maintain the Japan-US Security Treaty, there is also enthusiasm building up in pursuing the creation and maintenance of a variety of track two security dialogues, that, although they fall short of security cooperation, do fill the void of formal Northeast Asian or North Pacific sub-regional security institutions.

Overall, what have these security dialogues produced? Firstly, this must be put into context: despite the ups and downs experienced within key bilateral relationships, there is no diminution of interest in advancing multilateral dialogues and consultation. Moreover, there have been signs of cumulative progress taking place. Most notable among these has been the role of China, which has become, quite surprisingly, a source of support for dialogue activities. It is, as yet, unclear whether this enthusiasm is best explained in strategic terms (as a new way for Chinese leaders to advance old national interests), or in cognitive terms (as a major adjustment in Chinese thinking about regional order). However, Beijing's enthusiasm for the dialogue process can in its own right be considered a victory for engagement strategies, and as a potential harbinger of things to come.

Forums for dialogue have provided venues for regional policymakers and intellectuals to hear and understand the views of others, while stopping short of formally agreeing on their respective security policies. This positive assessment also applies to North Korea, which has come to participate in regional track two processes like CSCAP in the 1990s, and in ARF from July 2000, although it has been reluctant to participate in sub-regional forums such as NEACD. Broadly speaking, the dialogues are slowly creating shared understandings of basic concepts and vocabulary, as well as promoting the habit and custom of consultation.

Second, and a somewhat more sobering context, is the fact that discussions have tended to focus on fairly abstract threat perceptions and confidence-building measures rather than on the management of concrete problems. It remains a major challenge to move the dialogues onto more contentious issues such as territorial disputes, historical memory and emerging problems in arms control. However, even with these intractable problems we are seeing signs of progress, as evidenced in the past six months, where we have seen momentum gathering toward the discussion of non-proliferation of small arms in Asia.

Third, and related to the above problem, these security dialogues, most notably the ARF, have shown that they are not able to intervene proactively and effectively in conflict situations such as East Timor, Fiji, and the latest case of the Solomon Islands.

Fourth, it has proven difficult to transform track two processes into formal governmental ones, with several key countries, including China, showing a reluctance to take this next step.

Fifth, some argue that the 1997 currency crisis in Asia has stalled this process of multilateral cooperation and made the future prospect much dimmer (Morimoto 2000, 337). Others argue, in the context of the Korean Peninsula, for example, that the Asian Financial Crisis has contributed to a greater spirit of cooperation on both sides of the 38th parallel (Cossa and Fukushima 1998, 13).

The multilateralism that has thus far emerged in the region is limited to the above-mentioned security dialogues. The other forms of multilateral security institutions, such as a collective defense institution, collective security, and concert-type multilateral security cooperation, have yet to emerge in Asia. A collective defence institution, which some would refer to as 'Pacific Treaty Organization (PaTO)' (Samuels and Twomey 1999, 9), requires a common threat or a shared enemy by the member states as a group, and this has not appeared as yet. Although a security threat may have been perceived in the form of China and the DPRK, both Japan and the United States in the past decade have tried to engage these rather than exclude them in regional institution-making. Countries in the region have seen a common interest and benefit in including China in regional groupings, thereby encouraging it to share norms and principles of codes of conduct, in the areas of both economy and security. However, with the absence of a common adversary, moving beyond bilateralism in a form of a collective defence agreement is not a realistic option for Asia to embrace. As for a collective security institution, the region does not embrace such an option today because countries do not share sufficiently strong incentives to act together. Each country appears to have its own concerns and threats that are not necessarily shared by the whole region.

The Inter-Korean Summit of June 2000 has generated a hope for solving one security threat in Northeast Asia, one that has existed for the past five decades, but may yet pave the way for the pursuit of confidence-building in the region. The DPRK's widening engagement with the international community, through the establishing of diplomatic relations and joining the ASEAN Regional Forum (ARF) in 2000, will also produce momentum for security cooperation. The ARF, APEC, ASEM and ASEAN +3, on the other hand, despite their limitations, have been venues for regional players to gain a habit of dialogue, enhancing common understanding. Japan has taken initiatives in organising multilateral and mini-lateral dialogues in the sub-region, which is one of its roles in securing peace and stability in Northeast Asia.

REFERENCES

Ball, Desmond and Pauline Kerr (1996) *Presumptive Engagement*. Sydney: Allen and Unwin.

Cossa, Ralph, and Akiko Fukushima (1998) 'Security Multilateralism in Asia: Views from the United States and Japan'. *IGCC Policy Paper*.

Funabashi, Yoichi, ed. (2001) *Domei no Hikaku*. Nihon Hyoronsha, March.

Hiramatsu, Kenji (1999) 'Ajia Taiheiyogata no Anzenhosho kiko wa seiritsu suru no ka'. *Gaiko Forum, Special Issue*.

Hosokawa, Morihiro (1998) 'Are US Troops in Japan Needed?' *Foreign Affairs* July/August.

Kimura, Hiroshi (2000) 'North Pacific Region – Issues Looming Ahead of Stability and Cooperation'. *NIRA Policy Research* 13: 3.

Kuriyama, Takakazu (1997) *Nichibei Domei: hyoryu karano dakkyaku*. Nihon Keizai Shinbunsha.

Masaki, Hisane (1998) 'Trilateral Security Forum Set; Japan, U.S., Russia to discuss Northeast Asian Issues'. *Japan Times* 15 October.

Mederios, Evans S. (2001) *Ballistic Missile Defense and Northeast Asian Security: Views from Washington, Beijing, and Tokyo*. April. The Stanley Foundation and Center for Nonproliferation Studies, Monterey Institute of International Studies.

Morimoto, Satoshi (2000) *Anzenhoshoron*. PHP Kenkyusho.

National Institute for Research Advancement Research Report (NIRA) (2001) *Japan's Proactive Peace and Security Strategies – including the Question of Nuclear Umbrella*. March.

Nishihara, Masashi (1999) 'Hokuto Ajia ni okeru Anzenhosho sisutemu no shoraisei', *Gaiko Forum, Special Issue*.

Rozman, Gilbert (2000) 'Regional Cooperation in the North Pacific – Changing Strategy at the Turn of the Century'. *NIRA Policy Research* 13: 3.

Samuels, Richard J., and Christopher P. Twomey (1999) 'The Eagle Eyes the Pacific: American Foreign Policy Options in East Asia after the Cold War'. In Patrick M. Cronin and Michael J. Green, eds., *The U.S.-Japan Alliance – Past, Present and Future*. A Council on Foreign Relations Book.

SIPRI Yearbook 2000, Armaments, Disarmament and International Security (2000) Oxford: Oxford University Press.

Snyder, Scott (1999) *Negotiating on the Edge: North Korean Negotiating Behaviour*. Washington, DC: United States Institute of Peace Press.

ENDNOTES

[1] President George W. Bush has removed the distinction between National Missile Defense (NMD) and Theatre Missile Defense (TMD), lumping both under the phrase Missile Defense.

[2] For the text of the 1956 Japan-Soviet Joint Declaration, see Diplomatic Bluebook 1957.

[3] For the text of the Tokyo Declaration between President Yeltsin and Prime Minister Hosokawa, see the homepage of Ministry of Foreign Affairs, http://www.mofa.go.jp.

[4] 'Nichiro Mochikoshi, X shi ha kataru', *Sankei Shinbun*, December 27 and December 28, 2000.

[5] The text of the Irkutsk Statement is available onhttp://www.mofa.go.jp/region/europe/russia/pmv0103/state.html.

[6] http://www.mofa.go.jp/mofaj/area/russia/jr_fpri/html.

[7] For example, 'Ni to, yon to yureugoki', *Mainichi Shinbun*, 8 April 2001, 2.

[8] KEDO's mission, according to KEDO's Annual report 1996-97 is:

(1) to contribute to the strengthening of the international non-proliferation regime while improving the prospects for the lasting peace and stability on the Korean Peninsula and beyond;

(2) to assist in implementation of the Agreed Framework between the United States and DPRK, under which the DPRK agreed to freeze and ultimately dismantle its existing nuclear program, by 1) financing and constructing in the DPRK two proliferation-resistant light-water reactors of the Korean Standard Nuclear Power Plant model, and 2) providing the DPRK with an alternative source of energy for heating and electricity production until the first of those reactors is completed, and, in so doing, meet or exceed international standards of nuclear and conventional safety, environmental standards of nuclear and conventional safety, environmental protection, and ethical business practices;

(3) to serve as an example of how a cooperative and targeted international diplomatic effort can lead to the resolution of regional security or political crises, and provide a work environment where a multinational staff, with varied cultural, social and professional backgrounds, can work harmoniously to accomplish organisational, professional and personal goals. As for the details of the negotiation of the General Agreed Framework and KEDO, see Snyder 1999.

[9] North Korea Advisory Group, Report to the Speaker, US House of Representatives, November 1999.

[10] *Boei Hakusho* 2000. http://www.jda.go.jp/j/library/wp/2000/jpnbun/01030200.HTM

[11] Japan Defense Agency, *Boueinenkan* 2000, 68-69.

[12] Shiryochosakai, *Sekai Gunji Josei*, Hara Shobo, 2000, 58-60.

[13] Defense Agency, *Bouei Hakusho.*

[14] *Sankei Shinbun,* 10 October 2000.

[15] *Nihon Keizai Shinbun,* 8 July 2001.

[16] 'Japan-US Joint Declaration on Security – Alliance for the 21st Century', Tokyo, Japan, 17 April 1996, paragraph 7.

[17] CSCAP was established in Kuala Lumpur, in June 1993, as a dialogue of security studies related research institutes in the Asia-Pacific. It also includes governmental officials in their private capacities. See Ball and Kerr 1996, 31.

[18] See Japan Center for International Exchange (JCIE), *Dialogue and Research Monitor,* http://www.jcie.or.jp/drm/index.html.

Chapter 12

THE PEOPLE'S REPUBLIC OF CHINA AND HONG KONG: A CRISIS OF HUMAN RIGHTS OR THE EMERGENCE OF 'DEMOCRATISATION WITH CHINESE CHARACTERISTICS'?

Felix Patrikeeff
Department of Politics
Adelaide University
Australia

An important part of any examination of China in the context of regional crisis is the place of human rights in its worldview. This has been a major source of contention and friction with the West.[1] An important 'litmus test', so to speak, of China's intentions and performance in this area has been its handling of Hong Kong. Despite the fact that the former British colony has managed to maintain a remarkably open social environment in the Chinese context, the relationship between China and Hong Kong has been beset with crises. More recent examples of this have been the sudden departure of the popular Chief Secretary of the Hong Kong Special Administrative Region (SAR), Anson Chan, and, only a few months earlier, the resignation of Cheng Yiu-chung, the much-respected Vice-Chancellor of Hong Kong University, and his Pro Vice-Chancellor, Wong Siu-lun. The reasons? Anson Chan has been regarded as too free thinking for China's taste (she had been dubbed by some observers as 'Hong Kong's conscience'), and the latter pair were seen as tampering with the independence of a researcher, who was consistently showing the levels that Hong Kong's Chief Executive, Tung Chee-hwa, had sunk to in the eyes of Hong Kong's population.[2] The international press has made much of these cases as clear signs of China's increasingly authoritarian direction of the social and political activities in the SAR, and the diminution of human rights there.[3]

This chapter, however, takes a less catholic line on the issue of China, Hong Kong and human rights, arguing from a positive long-term perspective. This is an unusual line because, first of all, there is a great deal of evidence to suggest precisely the contrary,[4] but also because

I have the dubious honour of being one of the first purveyors of 'doom and gloom' on the subject of Hong Kong and its future after resumption of sovereignty by China. In *Mouldering Pearl* (1990), I suggested that the Hong Kong success story was going to end, or all but end, with the territory's transfer to China on 1 July 1997, indicating that the territory might find itself in a 'twilight status...changed from a window on the world to just another Chinese city' (Patrikeeff 1990, 215). This has not been proven entirely wrong.[5] Hong Kong has actually changed a great deal in the long, and often frustrating, haul between 1982 (when thoughts about its future were first put into diplomatic initiatives) and the present, and many would say that the changes have been for the worse.[6] But of course the picture has not been precisely as I, or the other pessimists coming after me, suggested at the time.

One of the reasons for this is that Hong Kong residents' views on rights are often tinged with pragmatism, indeed perhaps even fatalism, coming as they do come from a slightly less clear-cut perspective compared to that often seen in the West. These views are informed more by the need to find personal accommodation with existing political systems that the Hong Kong Chinese have found themselves living in, and seeking practical, earthly freedoms, rather than those of an idealist or juridical sort. In other words, the forms of freedoms that many Hong Kong Chinese looked to had, in important respects, already been achieved under the British colonial rule. And let us not forget for a moment that, while British rule of its colony was broadly benign, and although the closing stage of that rule was marked by much breast-beating on the part of its last British Governor, Chris Patten, it was still an imposed form of government, as it had been throughout the territory's history,[7] complete with a large number of draconian laws, regulations and policies in place.[8]

One of the best examples of this is that of Professor Milton Friedman, Nobel Prize-winning economist and the one-time guru of an economic rationalist ideology, who, in extolling the virtues of freedom and the capitalist way in Hong Kong for a television documentary in the late 1970s, was filmed in front of the 'Star' Ferry Terminal, a well-known tourist spot with the famed Hong Kong Harbour in the background; a sight familiar to millions of visitors to Hong Kong. Unfortunately, the place he chose to wax lyrical on his econo-political beliefs, using Hong Kong as one of their purest, most exciting examples, happened to have been unwittingly filmed at the sparking point for the divisive, ideologically-charged riots of 1966-67. As a result of the riots, colonial laws concerning assembly and freedom of speech and demonstration were tightened further and have been employed time and time again since then. In other words, if he had been preaching a slightly different, perhaps less positive, line regarding Hong Kong's character, he could have been bundled off immediately by authorities, who remained sensitive to the symbolism of that place being used for political opposition and protest. As importantly, the authorities held the political and legal 'high ground' firmly enough to have done so.[9]

Most people in Hong Kong would have been aware of these facts of political life in the colony, but would nonetheless (and perhaps ironically) still have accommodated them in their views of what it meant to exist in relative, acceptable freedom. This has often been explained by commentators, including the author himself, as an indication that the residents of British Hong Kong had either been born into, or fled to, an environment which was, in terms of the political, and especially economic, freedoms it represented, far preferable to those across the border in mainland China. However, this did not disguise the fact that they were not enjoying the same rights and freedoms that they could have in Britain itself, or the many other Western states which advocated political creeds centring on the notion of universal and inalienable political and social rights.[10]

The sanctity of rights and freedoms in the Western context was not, in other words, central to the lives of the general population of pre-1997 Hong Kong.[11] There are other examples of the delicate balance that political rights represented. In a brief article hidden away in the 'local news' section of the *South China Morning Post* some years ago, it was reported that a Trotskyite group had been arrested in an upper floor flat of an anonymous building in one of the inner suburbs of Kowloon. No indication, as I remember the article, was given as to why they had been arrested, except that they had met as a political group. Nothing was said as to how the authorities discovered that they were there in the first place.[12] Instances such as these provided a background to a somewhat different understanding of rights and freedoms in Hong Kong, even under British Rule. The territory, in other words, was nowhere near as free as commentators such as Friedman would have liked us to think.

Despite these anomalies, human rights remain very much the focus for looking at Hong Kong in its relationship with China. In this context, I would like to examine the issue of this relationship in terms of the 'three muddies'. The first of these is to recognise that the struggle for democratisation – broadly viewed as a way of defending the rights and freedoms of Hong Kong – was not fought in the twilight of British rule, notably in Chris Patten's time as Governor. As suggested earlier, the political set piece Patten was playing out was at all times bound by the parameters and logic of colonial governance. But the publicity value of a high-profile, senior British politician and former Chairman of the Conservative Party, doubtless with genuine sympathy for the Chinese population he presided over, tended to obscure the reality of the situation.[13]

The real battles over questions of democratisation took place well before Patten drew the considerable ire of the Chinese authorities by recommending that a somewhat more intense democratic 'flavour' be introduced to the territory on the eve of the transition.[14] Indeed, the most bitter struggles had begun in the early 1980s, at the time serving as a more important political focus than even the drafting and conclusion of the Sino-British Joint Declaration, which was itself being stormily negotiated between Britain and China then.[15] Essentially, the scrap over the forms and degree (if any) of political liberalisation that was to be brought in before the handover of Hong Kong to China was not between a colonial ruler and the ruled, but, rather, it was between Chinese and Chinese (Patrikeeff 1990, 198, 202). The sides in this contest were a fairly broad alliance of Hong Kong's business elite, and a less integrated array of democrats and welfarists; people scathingly dubbed as the 'the free-lunchers'.[16] The latter groups, the elite argued almost as one, would, if they were allowed to gain power through direct elections, press for the introduction of a comprehensive welfare system in Hong Kong. The path to power for these 'free-lunchers' was inevitable if the Hong Kong Government allowed the introduction of any but the most modest forms of reform of the existing political system. With the creation of a comprehensive welfare system, the members of the business establishment concluded, Hong Kong's economy would become less efficient, and the *raison d'etre* for the territory's existence as a discrete entity would fade in the eyes of the Chinese authorities. Why was this the case? Highly efficient economic forms generated in the absence of a welfare state in the past were going to be affected badly, and with that lines of genuine protection for the Hong Kong lifestyle – and rights – would disappear.[17]

The victory of the business elite and their broad alliance was achieved through the dilution and slowing down of any significant forms of political liberalisation in the context of two documents: a Green Paper (*The 1987 Review of Developments in Representative Government*), and its subsequent re-shaping into the White Paper of February 1988 (*The Development of Representative Government: The Way Forward*), which in fact obliterated the grounds for any further discussion of genuine liberalisation of government or the process of elections.[18] Such a conundrum provided Patten, in effect, with the clearest platform from which to launch his governorship in a memorable way.[19] The unfortunate circumstances surrounding the matter resulted in a thorough muddying of the political waters in Hong Kong, deflecting attention from what constituted an effective, practical system of protection of rights and freedoms, to an unhealthy concentration on rarefied universal values (which China was unlikely to accept), accompanied by a highly divisive debate on whether or not Britain would honour its promise to further the cause of direct democracy there. In fact, Britain had never promised the furtherance of direct democracy, but rather that of a more representative government, a point which was largely obscured by the emotion and recriminations of the vociferous debate.[20]

A second 'muddy' that can be seen with respect to the Hong Kong situation is the question of Taiwan. Taiwan has often been described as the 'big fish' which China plans to catch using the 'little fish' of a successful implementation of the concept of 'one country, two systems' in Hong Kong (see, for example, Montaperto 1997, 192). The idea is a relatively simple one: Taiwan will come around to the notion of reunification with China if the latter deals with Hong Kong in an appropriate, sensitive and, most importantly, successful way. This perspective has also, in a significant sense, however, helped to cloud the way in which we look at Hong Kong and the question of its freedom and rights. Such rights, if they are to be based on the recipients starting off as little more than being the 'bait' for a bigger catch, are hardly the proper groundwork for the systematic creation of an enduring politico-moral code. If anything, what we see in such stark relief in the recent past is Taiwan's relative intransigence in the face of increasingly strident demands from China, and, in the course of the 'megaphone diplomacy' being carried out over the Taiwan Strait, significant implications for the health of Hong Kong's own evolution to more democratically representative forms of politics. In other words, the success of the 'fishing' option is very much dependent on the country doing the fishing (the PRC) and the state being fished for (Taiwan) recognising that this is what they are doing, and being willing to continue to ignore full-blown independence as a viable option. If Taiwan should decide to pursue a future that shuts out China entirely, the implications of this for Hong Kong would be dire. Hong Kong, in the meantime, squirms at the end of an artificial line.

The final 'muddy' is Hong Kong's tendency to fall into protracted bouts of political hysteria. This centres on a pathology of political commentary which, in essence, suggests that Hong Kong, Britain and, indeed, the world should constantly scrutinise China's behaviour and its impact on the rights and freedoms exercised by the population of Hong Kong. Such scrutiny, this approach holds, should use as benchmarks affronts against human rights in places such as Xinjiang, Tibet, as well as China's own political and social dissidents. The political senses have been heightened to such an extent because of this that each time there is even a hint of encroachment on political freedoms or potential compromises of rights in Hong Kong, the dubious record that China has in dealing with the myriad problems within its own borders is trotted out as evidence of its dark intent or incapacity to 'live and let live'. This is not to say, of course, that these encroachments and affronts do not actually occur. Of course they do. But such an approach – which depicts Hong Kong as a powerless 'victim' – has resulted in the territory dwelling in a heightened state of insecurity at the best of times, and hysteria at worst. It therefore clouds the way in which we, and Hong Kong itself, look upon the latter's distinctive role and contributions to the evolution of rights and freedoms in the Chinese context today. These contributions are, arguably, significant.

This last point brings me to another possible subtitle for this paper: 'The Evolution of Human Rights and Democratisation with Chinese Characteristics'. So what does this signify in practical terms, and how has the 'victim mentality' inculcated by Hong Kong's press distorted perceptions of the SAR's strengths? It is instructive here to examine some lines from Liu Kin-ming, a Hong Kong journalist (in fact, the Vice-Chairperson of the Hong Kong Journalists' Association and Op-ed Page Editor of the *Hong Kong Economic Times*), who wrote the following lines a few months after Hong Kong had reverted to Chinese sovereignty:

> Since the Chinese takeover of July 1st, the worst scenarios did not materialise. Not a bad start after all, it has been said. So far so good. But from another perspective it can be seen as so far so bad. None of the factors which contributed to our pessimism before the takeover have disappeared. The overall situation has not deteriorated, but it has not improved either. Aren't we supposed to have another fifty years to go under the one country, two systems formula? We will see what happens over the next five hundred and ninety-seven months. (Liu, 1997)

Aside from the guarded, indeed grudging, style (which barely disguises the strong streak of pessimism that the author himself must have harboured in anticipation of the arrival of 1 July 1997), what is interesting is the title of the paper from which the quotation comes: 'The Honeymoon Won't Last Fifty Years'. In using such a title, which seems to be more a conclusion than a heading, the author appears to be suggesting, 'well, we'll have to watch carefully the course of the next five hundred and ninety-seven months in order to see what *actually* happens in the relationship between Hong Kong and China'. Essentially, therefore, Liu is conveying two things: one, a typically long, intrinsically sceptical, view of Hong Kong's long-term relationship with China; and, two, the delicate, highly charged state of the relations between them. Both the approach itself and the view of relations between Hong Kong and China seem to tell us that the author is ready to continue to doubt until the very five hundred and ninety-seventh month that his suspicions are unfounded. In the meantime, of course, Liu and many of his fellow commentators will go on doubting, suspecting and scrutinising. They can therefore be seen either as sentinels in the defence of freedom, or propagators of profound pessimism and alarm.

How else, then, can we see a positive evolution of rights for Hong Kong? The place of the centre has historically been very important in Chinese politics and political philosophy. This includes, of course, the PRC of today. Few in China, including Liu himself, would have any doubt about this. While the author of the article, and many like him, took a highly sceptical view of the role of Beijing with regard to Hong Kong, others, who not for a moment doubted the centre's power over them, took a less aloof, less antagonistic position. For many years the Chinese business elite in Hong Kong built up their relationship with China, while for much of that time making their fortunes in a British Hong Kong. These business people made their pilgrimages to Beijing, where they supplicated to, and consulted with, the leadership of the Communist Party. In key respects this process was simply an extension of the methods that the business people had used in shaping their businesses, fortunes and power under British rule. Ties were created, based on vertical, paternalistic relationships, 'us[ing] all resources available to induce popular deference and subordination; and in return it had to fulfill its moral obligations to the populace by providing public service and representing the community in its dealings with the colonial government' (Tsai 1993, 290). Importantly, it was not only in the period 1982-85, when Hong Kong's future was negotiated and sealed, that contacts were formed and overtures made. This process was initiated somewhat earlier (notably after the 'Open Door' Policy began in 1979), but took a more intense, determined form after it was clear that China was not going to entertain an extension of British control of Hong Kong.[21]

The supplication by the business elite was intriguing in a number of respects, but most notably because the Hong Kong people going to Beijing both deferred to the leadership there, and were valued by it (although perhaps, as indicated by some China scholars, Hong Kong's elite was neither particularly liked nor respected by the Chinese leadership[22]). Essentially, the members of the elite have, on the one hand, been of very great value in building mature capitalism within Hong Kong's own borders and, on the other, expanded it into China too. Their value is therefore one of being both business strategists and investors, and not just within the confines of Hong Kong alone. The contributions from these people have come in physical forms (which have been considerable, transforming Hong Kong's own profile from an essentially manufacturing one to that of a service-based economy), and also in a higher, symbolic sense. Indeed, it is often forgotten that Hong Kong has become one of the few places in China where capitalism has taken a natural evolutionary path, disturbed seriously by neither the political turmoil that plagued China in the first half of the twentieth century, nor cut short by the rise of the PRC and Chinese socialism in the latter half. The political influence exerted by the evolution and spread of this mature capitalism is, I would argue, greatly under-estimated, if not ignored, in the discussion of rights in Hong Kong by those who insist on seeing only Western benchmarks of human rights and democratisation in the context of Hong Kong itself. The growth of capitalism in Hong Kong produced an immense amount of socio-political 'space' for those sufficiently well off to enjoy it. This 'space' has, quite naturally, been highly valued by those who have experienced it, and the latter have done much to extend the practical underpinnings of this asset. Indeed, one of the main spin-offs of building up long-term contacts in Beijing through the many visits paid to that city by Hong Kong business people has been precisely this; it was achieved through, first and foremost, efforts to acquaint Beijing with the intricacies of how economic continuity was to be achieved in Hong Kong.

It is instructive here to remember that Shanghai, the 'centre of world capitalism in China before 1949', slipped quickly in its economic stature, succumbing to 'the triumphant Communists [who] made [it] the target of a destructive, revolutionary class vendetta, which reduced the city to a gray, urban-proletarian mass where any form of entrepreneurial activity was doomed for the following thirty-five years' (van Kemenade 1997, 57). And, equally, that high levels of mistrust were (and indeed *are*) held by the higher echelons of power in China for Hong Kong, which might have suggested a very similar fate for the latter. Van Kemenade in a recent book describes how a secretary to a Politburo member told him that Hong Kong's wealth proffered many benefits to China, but that:

> Beijing could not respect Hong Kong because it had cleverly exploited historical loopholes....Especially during the last fourteen years, Hong Kong had seized opportunities presented by the opening up and reform of the mainland to enrich itself. It

> [had] grabbed the chances offered by the communist party and profited from them at the party's expense....Except for a handful of patriots, Hong Kong [had] never shown any loyalty to the Communist party. Its only goal was to make profits. It doesn't deserve our love....It is simply a concubine... (van Kemenade 1997, 58)

Concubines, it is true, are kept, but, using guile and shaping the required tactical support from the holder of core power, also *keep* and perhaps *expand* their own political position. They at times exercise influence which runs beyond their supposed station in life, employing strategies that guarantee the *de facto* recognition they require and the wherewithal to continue their comfortable existence. Unlike the hated business elite of Shanghai in 1949, the members of its counterpart in Hong Kong have had over 14 years not only to 'enrich themselves', but also to find ways into the confidence, and perhaps even into the hearts, of their keepers.

One could argue, therefore, that while the business elite and the *haute bourgeoisie* of Hong Kong may not espouse democratic principles, and may not be especially vocal in condemning human rights abuses perpetrated by the Chinese government (in fact, that would be an understatement), they have existed and thrived in a remarkably free politico-economic environment, which they themselves have helped to engineer. They have, moreover, employed this economy to steadily build up their spheres of activity, extending these (often with remarkable tact, diplomacy and not just a little guile) into China itself. In so doing, they have influenced not only China's economy, but also – albeit to a much more limited extent – the polity too. Hong Kong's business elite have been people not too proud to bow before the all-important centre of power; in return they have gained for themselves, and by extension the SAR itself, a strong measure of continuity.[23]

One could perhaps extend this line of argument further still: this legion of Hong Kong capitalists is, in fact, helping to restore China's economic development to an evolutionary path which had formerly been distorted not only by internal contradictions, but also by the rude interruption of Western imperialism in the nineteenth century. But in helping to re-establish the place of the centre in Chinese politics, the members of Hong Kong's business elite – although perhaps slowly – are furthering the process of *enbourgeoisiment* that is evident in the higher reaches of Chinese power. The extension of this process further limited practical rights and, above all, the all-important privileges stemming from being left alone. Hong Kong has been most successful in using these privileges to create for itself a comparatively open, and at times outspoken, society. And it is in the exploration of this aspect of rights and freedoms that scholars of the Sino-Hong Kong relationship may find some positive, and possibly novel, perspectives. This must be a highly qualified observation because it is perforce intuitive, based for the most part on circumstantial evidence, as the supplication performed by many Hong Kong entrepreneurs is frustratingly subtle and discreet (indeed, secretive) in its character.

Amongst the many members of the Hong Kong elite I have interviewed in the course of my research on Hong Kong-in-transition, T.S. Lo[24] is very important in vivifying the point being made here. Lo was a member of the Hong Kong political elite who was for all intents and purposes anti-Communist in his early public life. He climbed to the heights of Hong Kong politics, being a member of both Legislative and Executive Councils, until his sudden resignation from these bodies in 1985. Subsequently, he disappeared not only from British political circles, but from public view as a whole. When he re-emerged he was depicted by many as a 'compatriot' of China. As he elaborated to me in the course of our discussions, in the time he had 'disappeared', much of his effort had been devoted to 'coming to know' China, largely through the forging of relationships with senior party officials and their families. He never mentioned who these people were, of course, except to say that they were 'very senior'. This is an important dimension, it could be suggested, in gaining a certain amount of respect – and perhaps even mystique – not only from other members of the Hong Kong elite, but also in China itself, where having the 'ear' of someone senior in the Chinese Communist Party is a very important step in developing one's own sphere of influence. A sign of how influential he had become in the new political order in Hong Kong was the fact that he, even as a Eurasian, was said to be in contention for the post of Chief Executive (although he did not win the post).

Another most important person in this respect is Henry Fok Ying-tung, a billionaire whose activities span a large number of areas of commerce (ranging from his share of the gambling in the former Portuguese colony of Macau, to the building of hotels and sports complexes in China), and yet a tycoon who doesn't even figure in some of the business journals. For example, Fok, in many ways the power behind the Hong Kong 'throne',[25] is absent altogether from *Asia Incorporated*'s February 1997 issue, which presents a short Who's Who of Hong Kong – and this was despite the magazine's claim that it had surveyed the names of the most important people in Hong Kong.

What is suggested here, therefore, is that there is an important transformative power that individuals such as Lo and Fok (and the many others like them) wield, relating to both the quiet influence that they have on holders of power in Beijing (most notably so in terms of how much attention the latter finally pay to Hong Kong affairs), and how amenable they become in allowing these individuals to have independent influence, and perhaps even authority, in the Hong Kong-SAR. Above all in this process, and this is the crucial factor that the Shanghainese business elite did not command in 1949, is the familiarity which has gradually bred a degree of trust.

The importance of this process of 'familiarisation' echoes in a comment I heard from a Hong Kong businessman some years ago, when I was writing *Mouldering Pearl* and asked if he didn't think that China wanted Hong Kong to go on in its current successful form. His response to this was a simple, indeed earthy, one: 'How long do you think the Chinese leadership spends thinking about Hong Kong each day? One hour? Half an hour? Twenty minutes? Ten minutes?' The point was brought home to me emphatically: in the Chinese political system, as in the cruder politics of Court, it is the attention gained that is often as important as paper concessions secured, a point which had been effectively turned on its head during the negotiation process between Britain and China. Of course, the truth in this process is likely to be that Hong Kong business people have been gradually expanding the attention span of the Beijing leadership and, concomitantly, accumulating important levels of credibility in the latter's eyes. What they are creating, therefore, is political 'space' not only for Hong Kong residents, but also, it *could* be argued, either actually or potentially for a broader Chinese public too.

This is not to suggest that this is an especially straightforward path to follow. Indeed, it is a very slow, tortuous one, fraught with myriad uncertainties and potentially treacherous bends. The Hong Kong entrepreneur has had to decide, with scant knowledge of the inner workings of the Chinese political hierarchy, with *whom* to build up the favour, picking up the signs of senior officials who are actually likely to be amenable and, as importantly, reliable. This process and its results are problematic: political leaders come and go; they are at times deposed violently or precipitously. However, it is clear, I think, that the circle of influence has grown apace since Hong Kong people first started to 'take their tribute' and oblique advice to Beijing; extending, most probably, from outer to inner circles of power, arguably making the issue of regime transition a less worrisome one for Hong Kong's future. Again, such a conclusion must, perforce, be intuitive, as neither the Hong Kong entrepreneur nor the officials with whom they cement relations will be known, except by hearsay. The enlarging of circles of contact to incorporate both outer and inner spheres of power is doubtless deepening and widening the attention of the Chinese leadership with respect to Hong Kong's needs and interests. And by extension certain rights, privileges and favour therefore flow through to the broader Hong Kong community itself.

It must be remembered, of course, that the crystallisation of these rights, which may as much be regarded as privileges, is framed within a very awkward context. This is especially well conveyed by two comments made of late, one from Tung Chee Hwa, who at one point was asked about whether or not there might be Tiananmen-style crackdowns in Hong Kong. His response was that 'Demonstration is part of *our* culture', and then added: '*They* will be free to demonstrate as they please' [my emphasis](*Maclean's* 1997, 4). In other words, while embracing the reality of Hong Kong citizens' proclivity to demonstrate, it is nonetheless part of *their* rights and freedoms, and therefore really, although *we* have in our culture the notion of demonstration, it is *they* who practise that form of political agitation (meaning, of course, the democrats).

The other interesting example to bring to bear here is that of the Chinese Foreign Minister, Qian Qichen, who went even further in confusing the issue of rights and how they should be regarded in the Hong Kong context. With an unusually broad sweep, he assured the territory that it would retain an autonomy 'unmatched in the world' (*Maclean's* 1997, 4). What 'unmatched in the world' actually meant when China had originally promised Hong Kong nothing more than 'a high degree of autonomy' is in itself difficult to puzzle out. The fact that it was the Chinese Foreign Minister who was making this pronouncement in a global context allows an interesting perspective on in the Chinese state's understanding of, and adherence to, formally enshrined standards of universal rights and freedoms that is less than inspiring of confidence.

The combination of the Chief Executive's comments, together with the Chinese Foreign Minister's observations on a higher plain, suggests that the protection that universal rights affords the population of Hong Kong is, at very best, not likely to be in either a distinct nor reassuring form.

The conclusion here, therefore, is that the people who are actually negotiating the forms of rights and freedoms are doing so in an oblique, quintessentially Chinese way, and are achieving gains within the context of a characteristically Chinese world. The ultimate result of this process, if it is successful and enduring, will be rights and freedoms in peculiarly Chinese forms, framed by the standards of 'high degrees of autonomy' rather than by any 'unmatched in the world'. These will not be forms, in other words, that will ever be very clear, or necessarily acceptable, to the West.

By extension, what is also concluded from a Hong Kong perspective is that 'one country, two systems', the original formula by which the Hong Kong problem was resolved by China and Britain, has encouraged the appearance of inconsistencies and contradictions in statements of people like Tung and Qian, who have attempted to depict the emerging relationship between Hong Kong and China in overly mechanical, Western forms. But the essence of the formula was long ago taken on board by a cross-section of the Hong Kong business elite. Rather than clamouring for the defence of paper rights, these elements of Hong Kong society have been steadily pushing the Chinese authorities to their limit in opening up spaces and winning over the 'hearts and minds' of amenable officials in China.

The success of such a process will, of course, to some degree depend on the ability of the PRC officials who are won over to last the course. Given that there is neither a democratic nor a politically transparent system in China, this might suggest a somewhat precarious future for the Hong Kong-SAR. But the positive element here is, of course, that both China and Hong Kong see themselves as being in it for the long run, so to speak. Expressed in a slightly different shade of meaning: both take a long view of their mutual history. The entrepreneurs of Hong Kong, after initial bouts of panic and crises of confidence, have seemingly fallen into line with such a view. In changing their perspective, they have sown and nurtured the politics of pragmatism not only on a day-to-day basis, but have shown through long-term investment and commitment to their relationship with China that they are there to cultivate and to develop, to bridge and to bond.

China had originally stated and viewed the concept of 'one country, two systems' as little more than an artificial construct which allowed the bringing together *organically* of the societies of Hong Kong and China along common cultural and economic lines. Thus, what was not intended at any point by China was 'one country, two *political* systems'. Part of the problem in Hong Kong still is that the notion of 'systems' has been broadly interpreted to include the political dimension. This was never the intention on China's part.

The common economic and cultural interests have gradually shaped the broader relationship between China and the Hong Kong-SAR, bringing into existence something that we can refer to in terms of a natural evolution of rights, privileges and freedoms; ephemera that have emerged from a *modus vivendi* forged by key elements of the two parties. As a result of these signs of change and accommodation, it is suggested that Hong Kong should perhaps be more carefully studied, but not in terms of whether or not Hong Kong can be 'saved' from unacceptable acts of authoritarianism perpetrated by the Chinese political system. Rather, of interest are the inroads that Hong Kong itself is making at the moment, beginning to open up the Chinese political system to more moderate, pragmatic business-like attitudes, attitudes which are not a far cry from those that have characterised Hong Kong in its modern history. These attitudes, a Hong Kong *spirit* so to speak, have gradually begun to extend themselves into China itself, consistently fostered by the activities and investments of the Hong Kong tycoons and entrepreneurs.[26] Such influences, as has been pointed out in the course of this chapter, are very difficult to trace, and perhaps even harder to understand at the moment. There is little doubt, however, that it is these signs rather than the tracking and agonising over the 'paper rights' that possibly allow us some room for hope and optimism for China's nature in the coming years.

REFERENCES

Allen, J. (1997) *Seeing Red: China's Uncompromising Takeover of Hong Kong.* Singapore: Butterworth-Heinemann Asia.

Blakstad, Lucy [Producer & Director] (1997) 'January 1997 – Hong Kong'. *Modern Times.* BBC 2 (broadcast in Britain on 17 February 1997).

Cohen, W.I., and Li Zhao, eds (1997) *Hong Kong Under Chinese Rule: The Economic and Political Implications of Reversion.* Cambridge: Cambridge University Press.

Davies, S., and E. Roberts (1990) *Political Dictionary for Hong Kong.* Hong Kong: Macmillan.

The Development of Representative Government: The Way Forward (1988) Hong Kong: The Government Printer.

Dimbleby, J. (1997) *The Last Governor: Chris Patten and the Handover of Hong Kong* London: Little, Brown.

Enright, M.J. *et al.* (1997) *The Hong Kong Advantage.* Hong Kong: Oxford University Press.

Feinerman, J.V. (1997) 'Hong Kong Faces 1997: Legal and Constitutional Issues'. In Cohen and Zhao, *Hong Kong Under Chinese Rule.*

Heald, T. (1997) *Beating Retreat: Hong Kong Under the Last Governor* London: Sinclair-Stevenson.

Joint Standing Committee on Foreign Affairs and Trade (1997) *Hong Kong: The Transfer of Sovereignty,* Canberra.

van Kemenade, W. (1997) *China, Hong Kong, Taiwan, Inc.* Trans. D. Webb. New York: Little, Brown.

Liu, K.M. (1997) 'The Honeymoon Won't Last 50 Years'. *China Rights Forum* http://www.hrichina.org/topics/hongkong.htm.

Maclean's (1997) 'Hong Kong Pledges (China Pledges to Allow Freedom to Demonstrate in Hong Kong)'. 110: 19, May 12.

Montaperto, R.N. (1997) 'Strategic, Military Implications of Hong Kong Reversion'. In Cohen and Zhao, *Hong Kong Under Chinese Rule.*

Patrikeeff, F. (1989) *Mouldering Pearl: Hong Kong at the Crossroads.* London: George Philip.

—— (1990) *Mouldering Pearl: Hong Kong at the Crossroads* London: Hodder and Stoughton.

Scott, I. (1989) *Political Change and the Crisis of Legitimacy in Hong Kong.* Honolulu: University of Hawaii Press.

Tsai, J.F. (1993) *Hong Kong in Chinese History: Community and Social Unrest in the British Colony, 1842-1913.* New York: Columbia University Press.

Yee, A.H. (1992) *A People Misruled: The Chinese Stepping-Stone Syndrome.* Singapore: Heinemann Asia.

ENDNOTES

1 Xigen Li and Charles St Cyr in their 10-year content analysis of *New York Times* coverage of human rights in China conclude that 'human rights in the People's Republic of China is the most controversial issue in U.S.-China relations'. (The Gazette of *The International Journal of Communication Studies* 60: 6 1998, http://www.msu.edu/~lixigen/HR_paper.htm). Visits to China by Robin Cook (the British Foreign Secretary) in January 1998 and Madeleine Albright (US Secretary of State under the Clinton Administration) in February 1999 both highlighted the human rights issue with the Chinese leadership.

2 For a more detailed discussion of the resignations of the academics, see *BBC NEWS* http://news.bbc.co.uk/hi/english/world/asia_pacific/newsid_914000/914417.stm.

[3] *The Economist*, in its print edition of 18 January 2001, headlined Chan's departure as 'China's Man Pushes Out Hong Kong's Woman', and the subtitle, tellingly, continues: 'Anson Chan's Departure Means One Protection Fewer for Hong Kong's Autonomy'.

[4] One of the more recent publications on the subject of Hong Kong after 1997 is that of J. Allen (1997), whose conclusions are best depicted as ones of 'measured pessimism' (see, for example, 277-83). Another, somewhat curious, example of this strain of pessimism regarding Hong Kong's future under Chinese rule is an Australian official report by The Joint Standing Committee on Foreign Affairs and Trade (1997). The report is idiosyncratic in the sense that, despite the broad ambit of the subject, the conclusions reached focus mainly on the failure of democracy to take root in the territory (xxi-xxiv).

[5] On one hand, Hong Kong was unfortunate to have had the transfer of sovereignty coincide with one of the steepest downturns in the economies of the Asia-Pacific region (the so-called 'Asian Meltdown') which began to take its toll on Hong Kong's economy after the handover. On the other hand, one could also argue that the impact of the regional financial crisis was delayed by the pre-handover boom that Hong Kong experienced. Whichever is the case, the SAR's economy has struggled badly, with property and retail indexes going into sharp decline, topped off by a calamitous fall in tourist numbers, which has added pressure to not only the retailing, but also the service sector. The fall in the number of tourists can be explained in part by their fear that the territory was no longer 'Hong Kong', but 'China'; a country which, to my considerable surprise, still instills a degree of fear and suspicion in meeker travellers. As significant in this respect has been the effect of the handover on the outlook of Hong Kong residents themselves. A dark mood has descended on many long-time residents, observing rarely-seen listings of the many companies under official receivership in their morning papers, watching the new SAR government stumble over and over again either through inexperience or ineptitude, and the first Chief Executive, Tung Chee Hwa, performing in a lacklustre way throughout his first 18 months in office. (Allen describes Tung as a 'cautious man' [1997, 182]; over two years into his period of office, many Hong Kong residents would see this description as being too polite).

[6] With over 13 years lead time to the handover, Hong Kong people had ample opportunity to make plans, produce bolt-holes, or simply to seek 'fresh pastures' straight away. For most of that period, the territory underwent an almost continuous political buffeting, beginning with the stormy conduct of the Sino-British negotiations over the evolution of the territory in the transition period, moving on to the tensions over the formulation of the Basic Law (Hong Kong's quasi-constitution), to the deep scars and lingering after-shocks of the Tiananmen Square massacre, to the strife over the proposed new airport, and culminating with the protracted acrimony over the 'Patten reforms' (see below). The major periods of severe political trauma were interlaced by the general mood of fear and suspicion which prevailed regarding whether or not China could, finally, be trusted to keep its word in allowing Hong Kong its promised limited autonomy. In the face of all of this, many of the more positive outlooks have come from scholars of business. A study by M.J. Enright *et al.* (1997) observes that 'Hong Kong is perhaps the best place in the world to see the future of the global economy' (x), and later that the territory 'adds value because it is unique. Maintaining and developing its unique attributes, its "Hong Kong Advantage", will make its future as impressive as its past' (335).

[7] This point is neatly made by Yee (1992, 86). Patten, one suspects more through his own instincts of self-promotion than fact, helped to shape a broadly held view that his governorship was something of a landmark in the advocacy of human rights and principled political behaviour, and that he had fought China every step of the way in his attempts to develop as equitable a society, and as sound a democratic political foundation, as he could for the territory before it was finally handed over (see *inter alia* Heald 1997, 315-19; Dimbleby 1997, chs.13-14). Confirmation of the somewhat transparent nature of Patten's principled stand was made apparent, when, at the height of the Governor's problems with China in 1993, and with epithets such as 'fat prostitute' being used against him, a member of the House of Lords suggested to Patten that he consider holding a referendum over his controversial proposals. If the bulk of the votes went his way, he could speak with renewed strength, with the 'people being behind him', while if they went against him he could accept the 'voice of the people' and beat an honourable retreat. This proposal was roundly rejected in the House of Lords, but then the parliamentarian concerned received a letter from Patten himself, thanking the peer for his intellectual contribution, and adding that a referendum was not desirable because the Canadians (who had held a dramatic referendum over the Quebec question shortly before) had indicated that this device was, in effect, 'too messy'. [From copy of correspondence in possession of the author.]

[8] Perhaps the most sweeping of legislation in this respect was the Public Order Ordinance, which conferred upon the Commissioner of Police the right to prohibit public gatherings in any particular premises on any particular day, if this furthered 'the interests of public order'; the Governor the right to ban all public gatherings for up to three months, in order to prevent 'serious public disorder'; police officers the right to enter and search premises without a warrant; and specified that an unlawful assembly constituted three or more persons (see Davies and Roberts, 1990, 405-406). Elsewhere, the authors put the situation of Hong Kong's residual political freedoms in stark perspective: 'Political rights are minimal, and the future promises only slight improvements' (365).

[9] For an insightful analysis of the riots, see Scott 1989, 81-126. Given the nature of the laws in place in Hong Kong (see fn.7), if Professor Friedman had been with a camera operator and sound person, this alone would have constituted unlawful assembly!

[10] This point was not especially pronounced in the interviews I was collecting throughout the 1980s for my *Mouldering Pearl* (Patrikeeff 1989). However, it certainly appeared in bright relief close to the time of the transfer of Hong Kong sovereignty – many of those interviewed (and not just by me) expressed the view that, while they were not sad to see the end of British rule, they were nonetheless worried about existing under Chinese authority (see, for example, an interview with 'Jo' in Blakstad 1997). Such examples of complex political outlook are born neither from naivety nor 'political immaturity', as has been argued by the many commentators who have suggested that Hong Kong Chinese were 'unused' to or 'ignored' politics under British rule; a rationale often given for why democratic political processes – one of the inalienable rights in the modern Western political canon – were so slow in coming to the territory.

[11] Vincent Lo, a canny Hong Kong property developer who has Beijing's 'ear', put the point regarding the types of rights and freedoms in the following way: 'I don't think we [the Hong Kong Chinese] necessarily associate freedom with democracy, because we believe that economic prosperity is our protector, our guarantee for the future, the assurance of individual rights' (Dimbleby 1997, 89). Such an attitude was very much in place under British rule, too.

[12] Davies and Roberts (1990) define this organisation as being '[t]hat branch of the Royal Hong Kong Police which monitors the behaviour of potentially subversive groups in the territory....The branch consists mainly of expatriates' (463).

[13] A most telling example of this is presented in Jonathan Dimbleby's fascinating documentary *The Last Governor*, filmed with the acquiescence of the colonial government and providing a rare glimpse into its inner workings. In one episode, Patten is caught pacing a workroom in Government House, anxiously awaiting a 'crucial' vote taken by the Legislative Council (which in his time in office developed all the outward signs of being a *bona fide* lower house of parliament, except that it, of course, remained a consultative body to the very end), which would either support or sink his controversial proposals for a democratisation of Hong Kong politics. With genuine elation and relief he congratulates those around him after the vote has 'gone his way'. The spirit of this episode is transcribed for posterity in Dimbleby (1997). (See especially 253-54 for the tension leading up to the vote, and Chapter 14 'Inside I'm Crowing Like Mad [LegCo Votes on Patten's Reforms]' for the wash). Perhaps the only point – and a crucial one – that was omitted from this depiction of a 'political flowering' of Hong Kong was that the enormous scope of the powers of a Governor would have allowed him unilaterally to negate the decision if it had gone against him. Interestingly too, of course, the decision of the 'parliament' in no way reduced the effective power of the Governor himself. The whole logic of the scene seemed to be founded on his will to see a more open political system emerge before he left office, and his sense of goodwill towards the democratic elements of the Hong Kong political spectrum (for a more sobering interpretation of the episode, see the sections dealing with the Governor's powers in the Letters Patent).

[14] Patten himself was quite surprised by the ferocity of China's response to items of legislative change that he himself saw – I believe quite genuinely – as modest ones. Patten's reasoning, it is clear, was an attempt to find some 'elbow room' in the Joint Declaration and Basic Law to allow a broader opening up of Hong Kong's political system, but it is equally clear that he was not intending to undermine their essential tenets (see Dimbleby 1997, 96-97, 110-12). Ironically, the fact that he saw these as being modest was indicative of a certain unwillingness to entertain the notion of genuine, thoroughgoing democratisation for the territory. A comment on the Soviet Union's General Secretary Nikita Khrushchev and his half-hearted attempts to de-Stalinise the Soviet political system after the dictator's death in 1953 was that he was a man attempting to leap across a chasm in two bounds. The notion of a governor wanting to introduce moderate reforms to a colonial political structure without tackling *inter alia* the question of a genuine dilution of his

own immense power is, to the author's mind at least, not greatly removed from Khrushchev's own method of reforming an authoritarian political system.

15 For a full discussion of the underpinnings of the broad debate over political liberalisation, see Patrikeeff 1990, 200-206.

16 In a place that is so geared to the great dream of moving from rags to riches, the image of a person who resorts to welfare ('free lunch') must inevitably become a highly politicised one. The business elite performed consummately well in transforming the person representing welfare interests into a 'free luncher' deserving not only of scorn and derision, but the label of being a wrecker too. (A concise depiction of the reasoning on which this argument is based can be found in Dimbleby 1997, 87.)

17 The argument was in some respects a potent one (especially to the Hong Kong elite), given that it recognised, and played on, the commonly held notion that Hong Kong's only reason for existence as a separate entity from China (or from Britain, for that matter) was that it had been highly successful economically, and could therefore enjoy a measure of independence as a result, presenting no social, political nor economic problem for China to have to deal with; a more radical social system could well have upset the balance created and necessitated intervention from China. Britain's experience with the riots of 1966-67 in Hong Kong had, in some minds, begun to force that state to reconsider the costs and benefits flowing to it from the linkage (see Patrikeeff 1990, 116).

18 The White Paper of 1988 firmly linked the 'aspirations of the Hong Kong community' and 'the framework set out in the Basic Law' with respect to any further development of representative government. Unfortunately, aspirations of a community could change dramatically and are difficult to measure, while the Basic Law was itself tied to the Joint Declaration (almost literally a 'snapshot' of Hong Kong in 1984) and represented an exercise in political negotiation and formal prescription (*The Development of Representative Government: The Way Forward* 1988, 22). With a coupling of such diverse requirements, finding a broadly acceptable 'Way Forward' was tantamount to an impossibility.

19 I am not suggesting here that the process was orchestrated in any way. Although the mechanism resulting in the choice of Patten as Governor is somewhat opaque, his conflicts with the 'Mandarins' in Whitehall (notably Sir Percy Cradock, a former ambassador to China and a key advisor to the Thatcher Government on Hong Kong) indicate that the China desk at the Foreign Office would probably have preferred another, more modest, 'last governor'. And Patten's role? Here one must conclude that the combination of as influential a politician as Patten (the person responsible for a victory against the odds for the Major Government in 1992), together with inexperience in Chinese and Hong Kong affairs, made a potentially explosive mix. Despite indications and warnings to the contrary, Patten constructed what to his mind was a reasonable platform to begin his term as Governor, incorporating a series of 'minor adjustments' to the evolution of representative government before 1 July 1997. Unfortunately, it took China beyond agreed boundaries. It is difficult to imagine that Patten would have realised (given his inexperience in Hong Kong and China affairs), or necessarily accepted (given his formidable position in the British political establishment), that China would move no further than it had already done in arriving at the 'through train' model of political evolution in the territory (for a discussion of the 'through train' principle, see Feinerman 1997, 86-87; for a summary of Patten's limited credentials to take on the job of Governor, see Dimbleby 1997, 11-12).

20 This is a highly contentious area. Those who have wanted to read into the early British parliamentary debates and official pronouncements the notions of 'democracy' or 'democratisation' are mistaken, given that government and parliament alike steered well away from committing Britain to these ideas. Instead, what was promised all along was the development of 'representative government', essentially based on principles of indirect and *limited* direct representation which gradually unfolded after the Cultural Revolution, when the Hong Kong Government was frightened by the lack of contact authorities had with the district centres beyond the immediate city area. Sir Murray (later Lord) MacLehose was instrumental in encouraging the expansion of representation – for the most part to allow for political 'safety valves' to emerge in districts outside the main conurbation (Patrikeeff 1990, 120-21, 148-54). After the Tiananmen outrage in June 1989, the question of adequate political defences for Hong Kong after it was resumed by China reopened, with – again – little if any reference to democratisation on the part of the British authorities (for a discussion of the British Government's response, see Patrikeeff 1990, 224-28). There were, moreover, serious doubts in some quarters as to the appropriateness of a rapid introduction of democratic forms to Hong Kong, and whether seeing the problem in stark, black and white terms was appropriate to a Hong Kong-Chinese context. As Peter Woo, a wealthy Hong Kong entrepreneur, put it:

'Western observers say, "Boom, democracy! You like it, you're a good guy. You don't, you're a bad guy"....I don't think it is as simple as that' (cited in Dimbleby 1997, 89).

21 The importance of the visits by the business elite, I would suggest, was clouded by the fact that once it was clear that Britain was going to negotiate away Hong Kong, a spectrum of groups made their way up to Beijing to confer with the centre as to their roles in a post-British Hong Kong (amongst these were, it is said, Triad organisations, which were seeking reassurance that they would have a future in the territory after 30 June 1997). In some respects, therefore, it appeared that the whole of Chinese Hong Kong was supplicating to Beijing, which took away from the importance of the traditional elite making its way north to discuss the territory's future.

22 I'm grateful to Professor Bill Jenner for his valuable insight on this point.

23 The act of engagement in the right manner is a key element in the Chinese socio-political idiom. It can be regarded as the repeated acts of deference that elicit confidence in the other party and achieve, ultimately, some measure of one's own ends; but this is done within the context of a scrupulous understanding, and acknowledgment, of the power relationship between the two parties. One could argue, in fact, that the practice employed by the members of Hong Kong's business elite was no different from the acts of deference performed by suzerain states under the sway of the Chinese empire.

24 For a biographical sketch of this intriguing, and important, member of the Hong Kong elite, see the entry for Lo Tak-shing in Davies and Roberts 1990, 278.

25 Fok is a person whose credentials are, from all accounts, immaculate with the Chinese authorities. Although he ran away from China soon after the revolution of 1949, he has kept excellent contacts with Beijing via a number of central and regional channels. He has also distanced himself almost entirely from British circles in Hong Kong, never having received any honours from the crown, and (again from accounts of those close to him) never having actively campaigned for these. Indeed, his only visible passions were the accumulation of wealth and the pursuit and development of sport. And yet, behind the scenes, Fok is most influential, having (some have said) arranged Chinese support for Tung Chee Hwa when the latter's shipping firm was running into difficulties, and (not surprisingly) having his own son sitting at the heart of the new political structure in Hong Kong. Despite his importance, this modest man has remained virtually invisible (for a biographical sketch of Fok, see Patrikeeff 1990, 100-104).

26 In 1998, Professor Woo Chia-wei, President of The Hong Kong University of Science and Technology, proposed the formation of a Hong Kong SAR, Shenzhen, Zhuhai and Nansha region, composing a 'Hong Kong Bay area' comparable to San Francisco, Oakland, San Jose and the Silicon Valley area, saying its traits are eminently comparable to those of the San Francisco Bay area. The project, which has at its heart the extension of the 'Hong Kong way', has been 'encouraged and supported' by the Fok Ying Tung Foundation (see 'The President's Progress Report' from the Spring 1998 issue of *The Hong Kong University of Science and Technology Newsletter*).

Chapter 13

Territorial, Sovereignty and Nuclear Crises: The Case of Southern Asia

Brahma Chellaney
Centre for Policy Research
New Delhi

More than a decade after the end of the Cold War and four years after the outbreak of a major financial crisis, Asia remains at the crossroads, the shape of its future security uncertain. Asia's importance, however, continues to rise in economic and political terms. This is not only because more than half of the global population lives there, but also because Asia has the fastest-growing markets, the fastest-rising military expenditures, and the areas with the most serious potential for crisis flare-up.

In the eighteenth and nineteenth centuries, it was Europe's security and aggressive search for colonies that impacted on the rest of the world. Today, of all the continents, it is Asia that impacts the most on international relations and international security. First, all major world players are active in Asia. Second, several areas or inter-state relationships in Asia carry high risk potential. These troubled areas and relationships are spread across the entire continent. They include, among others, the South China Sea, Kashmir, Central Asia and the Korean Peninsula. The disputes in the South China Sea, covering an area of 800,000 square kilometres, alone involve eight nations, with three of them claiming the entire region. The strategic vacuum in the early post-Cold War years led to coastal states asserting their claims on the islands in the South China Sea. One of the most powerful Asian players, Japan, is involved in territorial disputes with two of the other most powerful Asian players – China and Russia.

Asia is very dissimilar from Europe. While Europe has several major middle powers, principally Britain, France, Germany and Italy, Asia has one major rising power at its centre whose growing weight and assertiveness are casting an increasingly large shadow over much of the continent. China's rise has been accentuated by the decline of Russia and Japan's prolonged economic recession. The 15-nation European Union (EU) is the outcome of an equilibrium among the middle powers in Europe. Asia, however, is still far from evolving an equilibrium among its important states. In fact, the present situation in Asia can be characterised as a case of power disequilibrium.

In Asia there is no security architecture of any kind nor are efforts underway to create a structural framework for security. In addition, the regional consultation mechanisms in Asia are non-existent or weak, unable to handle even incidents such as the 1999 Chinese mischief in encroaching on the Mischief Reef island near the Philippines. The Asian financial crisis has exacted a toll on the vitality and dynamism of ASEAN. Its own expansion to incorporate all the ten Southeast Asian states has made it big and unwieldy, with the momentum for further integration stalling. The political crisis in Indonesia has further added to ASEAN's problems and uncertainities. Straddling vital shipping lanes and beset by great-power competition for influence, Southeast Asia has deep internal faultlines, raising the spectre that it could become the 'Balkans of the East' (Parrenas 2001). Because of the region's strategic and economic importance, major Asian powers like China, Japan and perhaps India regard Southeast Asia as an extension of their security perimeters.

Although an extremely useful body, ASEAN is plagued by many problems, which have helped dampen the high expectations that were aroused when the ASEAN Regional Forum (ARF) was formed. It faces a major challenge to restore its credibility and influence, both of which demand a stable, supportive Indonesia.

The ARF has played a useful role in promoting dialogue and understanding. It deserves credit for focusing attention and stimulating dialogue on the tangle of overlapping sovereignty claims in the South China Sea and thereby keeping gunboats quiet. But, lamentably, it remains essentially a 'talk' not an 'action' group.

The arrangements in Asia are highly varied and potentially unpredictable. On the one side are states in Asia that are untied to bilateral or multilateral alliance commitments in either the military or economic sphere, a posture that has ensured for them maximum freedom in terms of options but which also has its drawbacks. A prime example in that category is India. On the other side are states like Japan and South Korea with close military and commercial partnerships with the United States. ASEAN falls in the middle category.

In a world of rapid change, the Asian strategic landscape is also altering fast. A Rand study has suggested that the Bush administration focus is on Asia and the widening of its strategic alliances there, setting up new military bases in vantage locations like Oman and Gaum (Khalilzad *et al.* 2001). The international line-up on US missile-defence plans may be a precursor of things to come – the United States, its traditional allies and India on one side; China and its three militaristic friends, Burma, North Korea and Pakistan, on the other side; and Russia somewhere in the middle. If Washington manages the missile-defence issue well with Moscow, offering it defensive technology and agreeing to deep nuclear cuts, Russia could possibly become part of the West.

The United States will continue to influence heavily the Asian-Pacific scene. The Asian financial crisis helped stem the erosion of US leverage in Asia. In fact, since 1997, the United States has managed to strengthen its influence in Asian affairs. In the ASEAN region, the United States has set up defence arrangements with the Philippines, Thailand and Singapore. However, China continues to test America's resolve, whether by making open threats against Taiwan or by warning of accelerated nuclear and missile expansion if Washington deploys theatre and national missile defences.

Today, the US-China competition is driving security dynamics in Asia. This is no surprise, however. Just as the US-Soviet rivalry shaped global geopolitics in the past 50 years,

US-China competition is likely to influence Asian and maybe global geopolitics in the next 50 years. Exacerbating the Sino-US competition is the fact that China has placed Taiwan – a state with some American security assurances – under a permanent threat of force.

In the web of bilateral strategic alliances that the United States maintains in the Asia-Pacific region, the most vital to American interests is the US-Japan Security Treaty. Despite its strategic significance and outward stability, this alliance between the world's two largest economies seems in trouble, and it will not be easy to reinvigorate despite President Bush's declared intention to do so. The sense of shared strategic interests that once united Japan and the United States appears to have weakened. With economic woes sharpening nationalist rhetoric in Japan, especially from the Right, questions are being raised by the Japanese about whether or not US security commitments are iron-clad and whether the nuclear umbrella protection makes their nation really secure. Aggravating the doubts is the manner in which President Bill Clinton ignored Japan in pursuit of better ties with China. As Condoleezza Rice put it, 'Never again should an American president go to Beijing for nine days and refuse to stop in Tokyo or Seoul' (Rice 2000, 54). Another factor is the growing local resentment in Okinawa over US military presence. All this, however, does not mean the US-Japanese alliance is unsustainable or in imminent danger of unravelling. But it does mean that Japan is rethinking its role and future security.

Broadly, Asia faces two contradictory trends. On one side are the territorial disputes, nuclear rivalries and increased military capabilities that are threatening to imperil security. On the other side is the rising Asian interdependence through communications, trade and investment, technology and tourism. Asia, however, has to cope with resilient nationalism, protectionism and diverse kinds of negative trans-border influences, including terrorism, subversion and illegal migration. As home to several information-technology giants, including India, Japan, China, South Korea, Taiwan and Singapore, Asia is likely to define the future of globalisation.

The Cold War produced two Koreas, two Chinas and two Vietnams. Today, with growing competition among the major Asian players and the rise of regional powers, it is evident that Asia will be the birthplace of a new world order (or disorder).

ASIAN STRATEGIC TRIANGLE

Western analysts, trained in the Cold War deterrence model with its rival and balancing forces, have a natural tendency to extend their analytical framework to conflicts and problems elsewhere in the world, resulting in analyses that present rather too simplistic a picture. Such an analytical straitjacket, when applied to Southern Asia, can only warp understanding of the complex interactions in the region.

No analysis of the issues related to territory, sovereignty and nuclear weaponry in Southern Asia can be complete if seen strictly from an India-Pakistan paradigm. The one-versus-one model is hardly a useful tool in this part of the world. What we see here is a complex, out-of-the-ordinary strategic triangle. By its very nature, a strategic triangle is a more complex affair than a one-against-one competition.

The China-India-Pakistan strategic triangle has several unique features. The main reference point of each of the three players does not match that of the other two. For Pakistan, India is its main reference point, but to India, Pakistan is not the principal point of reference.

To India, in the words of its Parliamentary Standing Committee on Defence report, 'China is, and is likely to remain, the primary security challenge to India in the medium- and long-term' (1995, 5), but Beijing is loath even to see India as its equal. The last thing China wants is a peer competitor in India, and its entire regional strategy has been geared towards keeping India tied down south of the Himalayas.

Even when another country is not viewed by one regional player as its main reference point, the consequences of what it does will extend to that nation, too. What India does in strategic terms has implications for Pakistan, and what China does impinges on Indian interests.

Another feature of the strategic triangle is the long-standing axis between two of the players. In many ways, the triangle pits two (China and Pakistan) against one (India). Another feature of the rivalry is that Pakistan and China in the past quarter-century have sought to rear indirect threats to Indian security as a more cost-effective way of taking on India. While Pakistan has sought to bleed the Indian military through a proxy war in Kashmir, China has tried to contain India through proxy threats mounted by close allies, Pakistan and Burma, both militaristic states located on either side of India. India, however, still maintains a defence posture pivoted on deterring overt aggression.

The July 2001 Indian tour of Pakistan's military dictator Pervez Musharraf, the man India loved to hate, underscored the unpredictable course of events in the region. Short of putting him on trial in absentia, India did everything possible to show Musharraf as a rogue general. He was painted as a war criminal who masterminded an invasion into the Kargil region, a traitor to peace and democracy, the architect of the hijacking of an Indian Airlines flight, and the sponsor of terrorism. Then, without retracting any of those charges, Indian Prime Minister Atal Behari Vajpayee stunned everyone by inviting Musharraf for peace talks, which not surprisingly failed.

The paradox is that despite a collapsing economy, Pakistan has strengthened its only leverage over India – its ability to bleed its rival by sending arms and extremists into Indian Kashmir. The Pakistan military can indefinitely sustain what it calls a 'war of a thousand cuts' against India because it is cheap – consuming a tiny fraction of the defence budget – and so effective that an enmeshed and weakened India does not dare retaliate, as if it masochistically enjoys being bled by its much smaller rival.

While Pakistan's resort to unconventional warfare against India is part of its drive for retribution for the 1971 India-assisted secession of East Pakistan (now Bangladesh), China realised long ago that raising indirect threats to Indian security was a more politically shrewd way to deal with New Delhi. It was China that helped foster insurgency in India's vulnerable northeast by training and arming Naga and other guerrillas. Pakistan, in pursuing its proxy war against India in Kashmir, stole a leaf out of the old Chinese book. China has attempted to hem India in from three sides – Pakistan, Tibet and Burma. Not only is there a Sino-Pakistan and a Sino-Burma nexus, a Pakistan-Burma nexus is also emerging under Chinese patronage.

The complexities of the strategic triangle in Southern Asia have been compounded by the ambitions of the biggest state, China, which sees itself as a global player and not part of any region. After the disintegration of the Soviet Union, China has emerged as the sole country with the political will and a rapidly rising power to compete with the United States, although militarily and economically Beijing remains far behind. China aims to achieve military and economic security in a way that would seek to impose limits on the capabilities of its potential rivals in Asia but that would allow it to be a peer competitor to the United States.

The Chinese drive for supremacy in Asia has cast a growing shadow over India. As Indian Foreign Minister Jaswant Singh has stated in his book:

> in the absence of any social, cultural, political or economic commonality or interdependence, a bland policy of 'improving relations' with China could, over time, convert into an opiate, consequentially persuading us to mortgage the future yet again for illusions about the present. The Chinese strategic culture remains what it has always been: Wedded to domination, not so much through occupation of the (real or potential) adversary's territory as through a psychological subjugation of mind, an emasculation of the adversary's response options. India, therefore, needs to pose to itself some unsettling questions. (Singh 1999, 270)

TERRITORY AND SOVEREIGNTY

At the root of the conflicts and strategic rivalries in Southern Asia are issues relating to territory and sovereignty, and each state links up its territorial integrity with its sovereignty.

The fact, however, is that borders in Southern Asia have changed repeatedly in modern history, although in today's context it is difficult for any player to reshape frontiers through the use of brute force. Since the partitioning of undivided India by the British, the frontiers have changed significantly. The control of Kashmir is now divided among three countries, with India holding 45 per cent, Pakistan 35 per cent and China the remaining 20 per cent of the undivided state. The politics of revenge on the subcontinent is also rooted in the manner the regional political geography was changed by India when it assisted East Pakistan to secede in 1971.

The Han nationalism that the Communists kindled at the grassroots level to capture power in 1949 was also used to expand the frontiers of China. The early (and easy) fall of Tibet, a vast state as large as West Europe, whetted the desire of the Communists to create a China whose geographical extent would epitomise the high point in Han history. China's subsequent capture of tracts of Indian Himalayan territory, on claims of historical linkage with Tibet, were rooted in the same nationalism.

When Chinese troops marched into the Tibetan capital, Lhasa, in October 1950, they eliminated what had been a 2,000-year buffer between the Indian and Chinese civilisations. No single event has so profoundly affected India's security as Tibet's annexation. That brought Chinese forces to India's borders for the first time in history and created a land corridor (and nexus) between China and Pakistan. Tibet was a trigger for many other Chinese actions, and the larger strategic implications of its occupation will continue to reverberate in Asia for decades to come.

The method of Tibet's absorption – aggressive claims presented as facts, steady but quiet encroachment, and creation of new realities – was replicated by China in annexing one-fifth of the original state of Kashmir and is now being tried out in the South China Sea. The Tibetisation of the South China Sea, if it succeeds, will give Beijing a stranglehold over vital sea-lanes.

With 60 per cent of its present territory comprising homelands of ethnic minorities, China has come a long way in history when the Great Wall represented the outer security perimeter of the Han empire. Yet the redrawing of frontiers has not ended, as is evident from China's irredentist territorial claims and maritime ambitions. It shows India's Arunachal Pradesh state, Spratlys, Paracels, Senkakus and Taiwan as its territories.

The emergence of Bangladesh from the 1971 India-Pakistan war buried Pakistan's hopes of militarily wresting Indian Kashmir. Consequently, Islamabad embarked on a strategy from the late 1980s to change the characterisation of the Kashmir issue from an India-Pakistan territorial dispute to a popularly-supported *jihad*, or Islamic holy war, against Indian rule.

Today the *jihad* culture has created a plethora of radical Islamic bands, many of them involved in narcotics and the export of terrorism. The Pakistan military, closely tied to such narco-terrorist forces, is loath to rein in the *jihad* culture (although 'this monster threatens to devour Pakistani society') because it wants to 'pay India back' for 1971 and *jihad* is 'a relatively cheap way to keep Indian forces tied down' (Stern 2000, 115-16).

In fact, the concept of *jihad* has no provision for a pause or a cessation or any retraction. *Jihad* is supposed to be a fight to the finish. Once you declare *jihad*, you are part of it until victory is yours or death snatches you away. Despite his efforts to project himself as a moderate, Musharraf is the first Pakistani ruler to proclaim *jihad* as an instrument of state.

Kashmir remains the focus of India-Pakistan territorial conflict. Even with China, India's territorial dispute centres on the one-fifth of the original state of Jammu and Kashmir that Beijing occupies. For more than a half-century, Kashmir has posed the single biggest problem in Southern Asia. The United States has tried hard over the years to mediate an end to the Kashmir conflict between India and Pakistan. Lack of success has prompted it more recently to switch from an overt to a quiet, behind-the-scenes role as a peace broker. While this new role conforms better to subcontinental sensitivities, America's silent diplomacy faces the very complexities and hurdles that stymied previous efforts.

The conflict between India and Pakistan is rooted in history, religion and the politics of revenge, epitomising competing visions and clashing worldviews and a divide along civilisational faultlines. Kashmir is the symbol rather the cause of the conflict. The rivalry between India and Pakistan will survive any Kashmir solution, if one could be found magically. Musharraf has admitted that a Kashmir settlement will not usher in peace in the region.

The difficulty is in defining what will bring peace to the subcontinent, whose problems are rooted in its partition. Although Pakistan was established as a homeland for the Muslims of undivided India, there are more Muslims in India today. Yet Pakistan's claim on the Indian-held Kashmir Valley is based on religion. It is easier to encourage than identify a solution to the Kashmir dispute. It is obvious that no solution in absolute terms is possible. Any compromise has to be shaped within existing realities. Yet it is the commitment to absolute solutions that is the cause of conflict, terrorism and *jihad* on the subcontinent.

In the competition between 'status quoist' India and irredentist Pakistan, the Kashmir problem is likely to fester. Kashmir is critical for both India and Pakistan. The Kashmir issue is the glue that holds together Pakistan, still in search of a national identity. The future of secular, democratic, united India is tied to its ability to hold on to Kashmir.

Pakistan will not accept any solution other than a further partition of Indian Kashmir. Pakistanis fervently believe that the creation of Pakistan remains unfinished until the Muslim-dominated Kashmir Valley (now ethnically cleansed of its Hindu population) merges with their country. Indians, however, argue that there is little rationale for India's existence as a secular state if religion were the sole basis for forming a modern nation-state or readjusting frontiers.

Militarily, it is not possible to undo the division of Kashmir into three parts held by India, Pakistan and China. Kashmir thus is likely to remain for some time to come the focal point of disputes over territory, sovereignty and nationalism. The regional players will have to learn to manage, rather than resolve, the Kashmir dispute.

As regards India and China, every high-level visit between them is a reminder that the two Asian giants have failed to settle their Himalayan frontier dispute despite the longest border-related negotiations between any two neighbours in the post-World War II period. The question to address is: why have they failed to make tangible progress in negotiations? After all, China has reached land-border agreements with all neighbours except India. The Sino-Indian border negotiations actually began even before the surprise 1962 Chinese attack on India. These negotiations were frozen post-1962 but resumed in 1981 and continue to this day. If you add the pre-1962 talks, India and China have been negotiating the border issue for more than a quarter-century.

After two decades of continuous talks, India and China took one small step forward in November 2000: they exchanged maps showing their respective military positions along the largely undisputed middle sector. The two, however, have yet to define the line of control in any sector, although it is officially called the Line of Actual Control (LAC).

India and China today are the only two large countries that still do not have an accepted border or a mutually defined line of control between them. In contrast, India and Pakistan share an internationally recognised border except in Kashmir, where they have a clearly defined and delineated Line of Control (LoC). The only ill-defined section is the small Saltoro Ridge, where the Siachin Glacier is situated, at the northernmost end of the LoC.

Defining any line of control without prejudice to rival territorial claims is only a first step. The second step is delineating the line jointly on quarter-inch-scale maps to obviate any confusion. Demarcation, the third possible step, involves putting markers on the ground.

While dragging its feet in negotiations with India, Beijing agreed in record time to settle its land borders with Russia (except for two sectors), Vietnam, Kazakhstan, Krygystan and Tajikistan. Why? Apparently it goes for a settlement when it can successfully assert its claims. A weak, rudderless Russia made more than four-fifths of the concessions to clinch the border deal, while the troubled Central Asian states also accepted the bulk of the Chinese claims.

Besides persisting with an undefined LAC with India, Beijing continues to lay claims to large chunks of Indian territory. Chinese official maps show three Indian states outside India. Arunchal Pradesh is shown as part of China, Sikkim as independent, and Jammu and Kashmir as disputed. However, the one-fifth of Kashmir that China occupies (Aksai Chin and Shaksgam Valley) is presented as Chinese. On Sikkim, China still ploughs a lonely international furrow, being the only country not to recognise its merger with India. The Chinese formulation that the border issue with India can be resolved when 'conditions are ripe' really means when the balance of power has shifted in China's favour as it did *vis-à-vis* a weak Russia and Central Asia.

THE NUCLEAR ELEMENT

India's nuclear tests in 1998, which prompted Pakistan to follow suit, were very significant, both internationally and regionally. In one stroke, India broke free from its self-imposed restraint and arrived as a nuclear-weapons state with sophisticated fission and fusion capabilities. More broadly, the tests challenged the nuclear non-proliferation regime and showed the impracticability of indefinitely maintaining a hierarchy of global power based on a five-nation nuclear monopoly. The tests shattered the belief that the exclusive, monopolistic right of the Permanent Five (P-5) to wield nuclear weapons had been safeguarded by the 1995 permanent extension of the Non-Proliferation Treaty (NPT).

India's action was a daring act of defiance. The Comprehensive Test Ban Treaty had clearly signalled to India that if it did not seize its closing opportunity to go overtly nuclear, it would remain a nuclear-threshold state, bearing the burden of an open option while not reaping its benefits. The events since then have disproved the prophets of doom who had warned that an overtly nuclear India would get so isolated and squeezed internationally that its economy would collapse and it would turn into a virtual pariah state. India actually has gotten away with just a slap on the wrist, with most of the post-testing sanctions having already been lifted. Even critics admit today that India has improved its international status, underlining the political value of nuclear weapons.

Such benefits, however, are difficult to discern in the case of Pakistan. The impact of nuclear testing has been severe on Pakistan. Pakistan's tit-for-tat tests exacted a heavy toll on the Pakistani economy, triggering a chain of sovereign default on international loans that came to a stop in December 1999 following bailout packages announced by multilateral and bilateral creditors. However, Pakistan remains in a dire economic state. According to one analyst, 'Pakistan is on the way to becoming the world's first failed nuclear state' (Ijaz 2000). The jihad-spouting generals in Islamabad seem firmly ensconced in power even though their military rule has neither halted their country's slide towards chaos nor reversed its international isolation. In fact, military rule has served as one more negative label for a country that conjures up images of fanaticism, terrorism and gun-toting mullahs. Sebastian Mallaby described Pakistan in the Washington Post as a 'Colombia with nukes and Islamic fundamentalism' (Mallaby 2000).

Economically, Pakistan's situation has improved marginally under the rule of the military, which returned to the political saddle in October 1999. Military rule, however, has scared away investors with its bellicose rhetoric and cosy ties with fundamentalists. Most of the regime's initiatives also have turned out to be barren, except for tax-collection overhaul, while the introduction of harsh Islamic banking laws has proved counterproductive. The economy currently is growing only at the same rate as population, while external debt has ballooned to US$35.5 billion, or half of its GDP. With four-fifths of the national budget being used for defence and debt servicing, hardly any development is taking place.

It is against this background that Pakistan's nuclear weaponisation poses difficult questions. Do Pakistan's travails increase, rather than decrease, the threat to regional security? Will the Pakistani military go to the extent of ratcheting up hostility with India and engaging in further adventurism to keep Pakistan from disintegrating? In other words, will a sinking Pakistan insist on sinking India too? Pakistan's continuing support to irregulars in

Indian Kashmir, its invasion of Kargil in 1999 and its role in the hijack of an Indian jetliner in late 1999 raise troubling questions about its nuclear capability.

Kargil, although a limited war between India and Pakistan, raised issues relating to the dynamics of regional nuclear deterrence. For India, the obvious lesson of Kargil was that the mere possession of nuclear weapons does not automatically deter aggression. Deterrence only flows from fully deployed nuclear forces, from delivery capabilities that can reach intended targets and penetrate defences, and most importantly from political resolve. Instead of discussing the value of deterrence or how to plug the gaps in India's deterrent posture, the officially-sponsored Indian enquiry into the Kargil invasion aimlessly recounted the evolution of the rival nuclear programs, drawing no conclusion (Kargil Review Committee 2000, 183-213).

The third and important element in the regional nuclear picture is China, both in terms of its growing nuclear arsenal and its critical support to the Pakistani nuclear and missile programs. China played a key role in compelling India to cross the nuclear threshold. It seriously miscalculated that India would put up with a Pakistan armed with Chinese nuclear-warhead blueprints and missiles in the same way New Delhi resigned itself to China's emergence as a nuclear power.

The nuclear picture has been further muddled by Washington's plans to press ahead with national missile defence (NMD) and theatre missile defence (TMD). TMD and NMD will challenge the deterrent posture of China, which currently has only two dozen US-reachable ICBMs. The rest of China's arsenal consists of weapons that can threaten the security only of its neighbours like Russia and India. To see the Chinese rattled by US missile defences will be an agreeable sight for India. The problem, however, is that Beijing's Leninist rulers, thriving on a burgeoning trade surplus with Washington, will use TMD and NMD to justify an accelerated nuclear and missile buildup.

The ensuing rapid Chinese buildup, in turn, will undercut India's modest deterrent capabilities. The asymmetry with China will increase to the extent that New Delhi will be compelled to divert more of its scarce resources to new nuclear missile projects. An Indian ICBM program in that situation will become inevitable.

The action-reaction cycle triggered by missile defences is bound to drive India closer to the United States. The first evidence of that has been provided by India itself, one of the few countries to extend instant support to President Bush's national missile defence plan. India's positive response to Bush's plan fits well with its options and interests in an Asia marked by missile buildups and a growing power disequilibrium.

India faces a difficult situation in Asia that demands deep strategic engagement with the United States. China is bound to use US missile defences to justify its already-expanding nuclear and missile arsenals. With or without such defences, India's security will be adversely affected by the increasing trans-Himalayan missile threat and Beijing's continued nuclear and missile transfers to Pakistan. But with US missile defences, China is likely to flout international norms and conventions more openly and seek new ways to deliver lethal missile blows.

Over the past three centuries, the drive for supremacy through technology has advanced from sea power (which led to colonisation of today's Third World) to air power and to space power now. National missile defence is a short form for a host of futuristic space-related technologies whose development will change the face of the world – and the nature of war.

America's heavy investment in strategic defence is a venture to secure its global dominance for decades to come.

However undesirable a new arms buildup may be, the logical progression of military technology is unstoppable in a world in which states compete fiercely and seek relative advantage. As a vulnerable state living in a dangerous neighbourhood, India is looking at missile defences strictly from the prism of national interest. Having wasted half a century mouthing didactic, internationalist and self-righteous rhetoric, India has to get on with assertively advancing its interests.

US missile defences will not threaten India's security but could yield potential strategic benefits. Missile defences are likely to help strengthen and expand US-led security arrangements. In the years ahead, the United States could potentially extend a 'missile umbrella' to its allies the way it presently holds out a nuclear umbrella. An India strategically aligned with the United States could avail itself of certain missile defence benefits in a manner to reduce its own security burden.

The nuclear factor in Southern Asia does not alter the basic military equations, whether between India and Pakistan, or India and China. Today, none of the regional players has an overwhelming conventional military superiority to clinch a decisive victory on the battlefield. Against China, India is not what it was in 1962, when it suffered a humiliating defeat. But India is not in a position to militarily defeat Pakistan in a decisive manner.

Militarily, Pakistan, with the world's eighth largest army, is now a stronger entity than it was in 1971 despite the serious political and economic problems at home. The secession of East Pakistan actually made Pakistan militarily and economically more compact. As a result of the consolidation of defence assets from two widely-separated wings into one entity, Pakistan has considerably narrowed the military gap with India. Although India is portrayed internationally as having a much larger conventional-force capability than Pakistan, that is true only in aggregate strength, not operational availability.

India does not have the conventional military power to cut Pakistan into two or to disarm it. Nor is India in a position to recover Pakistani-held Kashmir. With neither India nor Pakistan possessing the capacity to score a decisive victory on the battlefield, the possibility of a full-scale war between the two remains low. However, limited war, such as that waged in Kargil, can never be ruled out. Moreover, due to its narrow strategic waistline, Pakistan will continue to emphasise offence, including pre-emption, in its military doctrine.

The combination of a possible limited war and one side's proclivity for pre-emption raises the threat of nuclear use. It is obvious that in Southern Asia deterrence will entail more than the traditional principles. Classical nuclear deterrence theory makes no sense when dealing with a sinking state that values nuclear weapons as a shield for adventurism, as it showed in Kargil.

Pakistan has made far greater progress than India in integrating its nuclear weapons with its war-fighting strategy. Many in India still remain wedded to existential deterrence – that it is possible to deter an adversary without a fully operational nuclear force.

The Pakistan military not only fully controls the country's nuclear weapons, it is also in charge of political decision-making. In India, issues relating to nuclear command and control need to be sorted out more clearly. Kargil showed the inordinate time India took to get its act together in the absence of institutional decision-making structures and an integrated war-fighting machine. Its tardy response to conventional aggression has raised valid questions about its ability to deal with a nuclear attack. India will have to examine the potential costs of keeping its military out of policymaking and marginalising it when in both Pakistan and China the military is the most powerful institution and calls the shots.

Another aspect of the regional landscape is the dissimilar nuclear posture of each player. In an environment where India confronts one adversary with a conditional no-first-use nuclear posture, China, and another adversary with an overtly first-use doctrine, Pakistan, the unconditional no-first-use Indian doctrine demands that New Delhi build a robust, survivable capacity against a first strike.

Beliefs also play an important role in the nuclear picture. India's decision not to cross the Kashmir line of control and fight the entire Kargil war on Indian soil has left a dangerous belief in Pakistan that Pakistani nuclear weapons effectively deterred India from crossing the LoC. In other words, this means that India's nuclear deterrent is not good enough to dissuade Islamabad from committing aggression and that Pakistan's nuclear shield is so effective that the Indians did not dare to cross the line even in retaliation. Such a belief can hardly build stable deterrence.

Concluding Observations

The role of nuclear weapons is undergoing subtle but important changes in deterrence strategy. Although this transformation is a consequence of the collapse of bipolarity in international relations and the shift in military threats from the global to regional context, the trend is becoming visible now due to more recent developments. The principles of nuclear deterrence are beginning to alter in a way that could impact profoundly on the still-evolving post-Cold War security order.

How the theory and practice of deterrence are being transformed can be seen from the current US debate on an NMD system. At the core of the debate is a growing acknowledgement that deterrence in the twenty-first century cannot be pivoted on principles based on the bipolar nuclear paradigm.

Deterrence traditionally has been an offence-based posture that aims to retain a balance between mutual vulnerabilities and a capability to wreak unacceptable punishment on an aggressor. Now, national and theatre missile defences symbolise a potential shift in focus from offence to defence. Without offence being given up, deterrence is intended to be constructed on the principles of defence, calculatingly tilting the balance between mutual vulnerabilities in favour of one side.

Change is affecting the face of deterrence, but not its primary purpose. Deterrence will still centre on achieving strategic objectives, not through military victory in a nuclear conflict, but with the threat of war. Since the threat has to be realistically based on ready, deliverable nuclear weapons, the symbiosis of deterrence and use will remain the key reality of the nuclear world. The difference now is the difficulty in identifying the mechanisms for credibly executing such a threat in a post-bipolar world.

The nuclear landscape in Southern Asia will be significantly influenced by the changing face of deterrence and the emerging triangular strategic offence/defence relationship among the United States, China and Russia. In a complex world marked by conflicting trends, it is apparent that each deterrent relationship will be different from the other, premised on principles at variance with classical deterrence theory. The concept of mutually assured destruction is losing relevance. Deterrence has to be constructed on principles radically different from notions of qualitative or quantitative parity.

China has overwhelming nuclear superiority over India but its deterrent posture against the United States is centred on a capability to threaten America's East Asian allies and a few US cities. India similarly can live with nuclear disparity with Beijing, but not with an inadequate reach against dominance-seeking China.

The future of deterrence, however, remains hazy, with a lot of unanswered questions. What are the military missions for which nuclear weapons will remain relevant? What should be the right mix of offence and defence in deterrence? For deterrence to be credible, what level of force and alertness is required? How does deterrence work in relation to a state that is irresponsible and sinking (Pakistan) or is totally opaque (China), or when the two are hand-in-glove?

References

Ijaz, Mansoor (2000) 'Stop Pakistan's Fall Into Nuclear-Armed Failure'. *International Herald Tribune* May 4.

Kargil Review Committee (2000) *From Sunrise to Reckoning: The Kargil Review Committee Report*. New Delhi: Sage Publications.

Khalilzad, Zalmay, David Orletsky, Jonathan Pollack, Kevin Pollpeter, Angel Rabasa, David Shlapak, Abram Shulsky and Ashley Tellis (2001) *The United States and Asia: Toward a New US Strategy and Force Posture*. Santa Monica, CA: Rand.

Mallaby, Sebastian (2000) 'Pakistan's Palaver Turns Democracy on Its Head'. *International Herald Tribune* April 28.

Parliamentary Standing Committee on Defence (1995) *Fifth Report, Presented to the Lok Sabha on August 24*. New Delhi: Lok Sabha.

Parrenas, Julius Caeser (2001) 'Washington Could Help Southeast Asia Get Itself Together'. *International Herald Tribune* May 15.

Rice, Condoleezza (2000) 'Promoting the National Interest'. *Foreign Affairs* 79: 1 January/February.

Singh, Jaswant (1999) *Defending India*. New Delhi and London: Macmillan.

Stern, Jessica (2000) 'Pakistan's *Jihad* Culture'. *Foreign Affairs* 79: 6 November-December.

Part IV.
Social, Ecological and Human Crises

Chapter 14

Impact of the Crisis in Indonesia on Population, Migration and Refugees

Graeme Hugo
Director of the National Key Centre in Research and Teaching
in Social Applications of Geographical Information Systems
University of Adelaide
Australia

Introduction

Among all of the countries hit by the Asian economic crisis of 1997 Indonesia has been the hardest hit and the slowest to recover. By 1999 Korea's economy was growing by 10 per cent, Malaysia's by 7.5 per cent, Thailand's by 4.2 per cent and in 2000 Singapore grew by 10 per cent. However, Indonesia's economy shrank by 13 per cent in 1998, was static in 1999 and grew by 4.5 per cent in 2000. Moreover, the economic effects of the crisis have been exacerbated by political uncertainty, internal conflicts and demands for independence in some peripheral regions. An important feature of the crisis has been the uneven nature of its impact between areas and between subgroups in the society, although detailed information on its impact has been limited. This chapter focuses on one dimension of the impact of the crisis, population trends, and especially on population movements within and outside the nation.

Severe and sustained economic downturns produce a range of responses and coping mechanisms in the populations effected by them. Although Indonesia experienced a period of substantial economic growth and decline in poverty prior to the onset of the crisis (Figure 1), in the 1960s and early 1970s economic difficulties had forced large numbers of Indonesians to develop coping strategies in order to earn a living.

The onset of the crisis in 1997 also saw a range of strategies adopted by the groups most effected by the crisis (for example, see Manning and van Diermen 2000; Poppele, Sumarto and Pritchett 1999). These included sale of assets, reduced spending, increased female labour force participation, increased involvement in the informal sector, increased participation in primary production, etc. A number of these responses impinged upon population trends in the nation, especially upon population movement patterns and they are the focus of this paper. It begins with a brief assessment of the impact of the crisis on fertility and mortality. It then discusses the effects on population movement within the country, especially on that between urban and rural areas. The effects on movement in and out of Indonesia are addressed and new patterns of forced migration as a result of insecurity in the post-crisis period are examined. Finally, the initial results of the 2000 census are scrutinised to see if there is any evidence of the impact of the crisis.

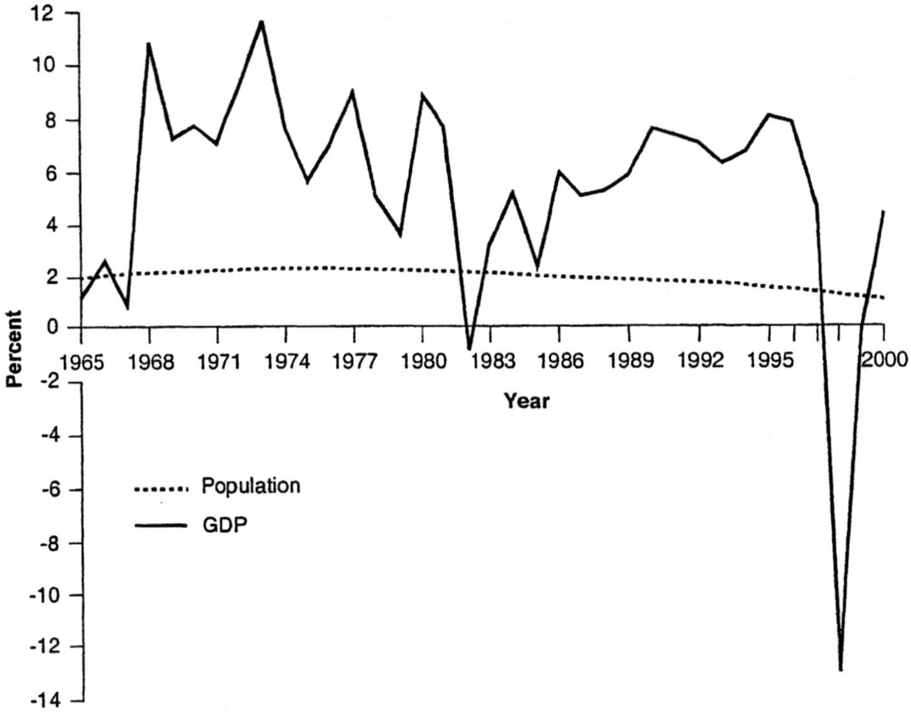

Figure 1: Indonesia: GDP and Population Rates, 1965-2000

Impacts of the Crisis

Table 1 indicates that after many years of reductions in the proportion of Indonesians living in poverty, the crisis years saw a reversal. In 1976 estimates of the population in poverty by the Indonesian government were of 40.1 per cent of the population, reducing to 28.6 per cent in 1980, 15.1 per cent in 1990 and 11.3 per cent in 1996. By 1998 this proportion had increased to 24.2 per cent and there was some improvement by 1999. While there is a great deal of controversy about the definition of poverty, these trends are indicative of the real situation. It is noticeable that while the incidence of poverty in Indonesia prior to the census was twice as great in urban as in rural areas, the increase in poverty during the crisis was slightly greater in urban than in rural areas.

Table 1: Indonesia: Number and Percentage of the Population Living in Poverty, 1990-99

	Urban		Rural		Total	
	No. (m)	%	No. (m)	%	No. (m)	%
1990	9.4	16.8	17.8	14.3	27.2	15.1
1996	7.2	9.7	15.3	12.3	22.5	11.3
1998	17.6	21.9	31.9	25.7	49.5	24.2
1999	15.8	19.4	23.2	26.1	48.0	23.4

Source: Hugo, 1999; BPS, 2000a

The impacts of the crisis on employment were of major significance. Table 2 shows that early predictions of massive increases in unemployment did not occur, although a small increase was recorded. Although undoubtedly large numbers, mainly in urban areas, lost their jobs, many were absorbed in other sectors.

Table 2: Indonesia: Levels of Unemployment and Underemployment, 1997-99

	Percent Unemployed			Percent Underemployed		
	1997	1998	1999	1997	1998	1999
Urban	8.0	9.3	10.5	21.2	22.5	23.8
Rural	2.8	3.3	3.8	44.6	45.6	46.8
Total	4.7	5.4	6.4	36.6	37.6	38.5

Source: BPS, 2000a

There was clearly some transfer from the formal to the informal sector, entry to the informal sector being much easier than that to the formal sector. However, earnings in the informal sector reduced due to the increased number of workers as well as a reduction in the spending power of the population. A distinctive feature was a reversal of the pattern prior to the crisis of decreasing numbers of workers being involved in the agricultural sector as Table 3 indicates. However, there was a reduction in significance of both industry and services. Another major characteristic of the shifts in the labour force was the increased workforce participation of women.

Table 3: Indonesia: Industry Composition of Workforce, 197-99

Sector	1997	1998	1999
Agriculture	40.7	45.0	43.6
Manufacturing	19.1	16.3	17.8
Other	40.2	38.7	38.6
Total	100.0	100.0	100.0

Source: BPS, 2000a

Clearly one of the strategies in the crisis was for families to increase the number of family members who are earning. One major impact has been a decline in real wages. Smith *et al.* (2000) estimated that real hourly wages declined by 40 per cent in the first year of the crisis, offsetting almost all of the growth in real hourly earnings of the prior decade for men, and half of that earnt by women. There were substantial increases in the proportion of workers who were own account workers and family workers. The reduction in the value of the rupiah resulted in high inflation so that in 1998 the CPI rose by 80 per cent and the price of the staple food (rice) more than doubled.

EFFECTS ON FERTILITY AND MORTALITY

National population growth in Indonesia is shaped by fertility and mortality trends, both of which underwent massive change in the two decades leading up to the crisis. The nation's population growth rate has reduced significantly as Table 4 indicates. This has been predominantly a function of a spectacular decline in fertility. Contemporary women in Indonesia are having only half as many children as their counterparts in the 1960s. The TFR[1] has declined steadily since the late 1960s when it stood at around 5.6 children per woman. This had declined to 5.2 in the early 1970s and 4.68 in the late 1970s. At the 1990 census the TFR for the 1985-90 period was measured at 3.326 and at the 1994 Indonesian Demographic and Health Survey a level of 2.856 was recorded for the previous two years. Table 5 shows this further declined to 2.78 in the next three years.

Table 4: Indonesia: Population Change, 1971-99

Year	Total Population (m)	Annual Growth Rate (%)
1970	119.21	-
1980	147.49	2.32
1990	179.38	1.98
1995	194.75	1.66
1999	207.44	1.61

Source: BPS, 2000a, 1

Table 5: Indonesia: Estimates of Fertility and Infant Mortality Change, 1967-99

Year	Total Fertility Rate	Year	Infant Mortality Rate
1967-70	5.605	1967	145
1971-75	5.200	1971	142
1976-79	4.680	1980	112
1980-85	4.055	1987	75
1983-87	3.590	1991	74
1989-91	3.022	1994	67
1991-94	2.850	1997	52
1995-97	2.780	1999	46

Source: Hugo et al., 1987; IDHS, 1998; BPS, 2000a

The processes shaping the decline in fertility are complex but are associated with significant changes in the role and status of women and in the structure and functioning of the family. This involves a move away from emotionally extended families to nuclear families and changes in the role and status of women, intergenerational relationships, selection of marriage partners and relationships between partners. These social changes have been associated with the introduction of universal education, the penetration of mass media and reduction in the significance of the family as a unit of production. The national family planning program has undoubtedly played a significant role. In 1972, only 400,000 couples were practising some form of family planning whereas in 1997, 78 per cent of currently married women had used contraception at some time. In 1997, 97.2 per cent of currently married women interviewed in the National Demographic and Health Survey indicated that they had knowledge of at least one method of family planning.

Mortality levels also have undergone significant reduction, although Indonesia still has higher mortality than several of its ASEAN neighbours. Nevertheless, infant mortality (number of children out of every 1,000 born who die before their first birthday) is now only a third of what it was three decades ago (Table 5).

The impact of the crisis on fertility and mortality is difficult to establish and the accurate estimation of levels from 2000 census data will be needed to make a definitive assessment. Initial fears were that the withdrawal of funds from the successful family planning program would see fertility rise. Moreover, the onset of political turmoil was seen as a problem. The installation of the government of Abdurrahman Wahid at the end of 1999 saw a dramatic change in the legendary government instrument of family planning – the BKKBN. It was placed under the control of the Ministry of Women's Empowerment. There were concerns that the crisis would see a decline in the availability of contraceptives and an increase in their costs. However, there was quick action by donors (Jones, Hull and Ahlburg 2000, 54) who had been gradually withdrawing from Indonesia before the crisis. It would seem that there has been a loss of flexibility in the family planning system but supplies of contraceptives have continued, although social marketing schemes have been curtailed. There is evidence of women changing from more expensive forms of contraception (for example, injectibles) to those provided free (for example, pills). The most authoritative assessment of the impact on fertility (Jones *et al.* 2000, 57) concludes that the patchy data available suggest there was little or no change in fertility. They state:

> Even if an increase in fertility came about as a result of the crisis, it would simply retard the fertility decline a few years and would no doubt be quickly reversed with efforts to reconstruct systems of contraceptive distribution. This is because all evidence on desired family size shows a consistent reduction in the numbers of children women want to bear. Widespread anecdotal evidence indicates that the anxieties produced by the crisis were, if anything, reinforcing these attitudes.

With respect to mortality there were newspaper reports in the early days of a crisis of malnutrition occurring but there is no factual evidence of this being widespread. One of the greatest concerns related to the devaluation of the rupiah making imports of medicines and drugs substantially more expensive, since Indonesia relied on overseas sources for as much as 80 per cent of total drug demand. Steps were taken, however, to subsidise drugs and some items of food, including rice. The price of drugs rose much more slowly than that of rice. Nevertheless, as Jones, Hull and Ahlburg (2000, 58) point out:

> The recent declines of infant and child death were the result of immunisation and nutritional programs and the promotion of rudimentary improvement in birth practices.

Such mass public health programs were vulnerable to both cuts to the budgets for personnel and disruption to the logistics systems providing basic supplies and drugs. Unless managed effectively, the crisis could have provoked increases in infant and child mortality.

Analysis of the 2000 census data will enable national mortality measures to be calculated and indicate whether long-term mortality declines have been arrested or even reversed.

EFFECTS ON POPULATION MOVEMENT

While it is unlikely that the crisis has impacted in a major way on trends in long-term declines in fertility and mortality in Indonesia, it has had significant effects on population movement, although again we lack representative national data to identify these changes definitively. One of the most pervasive of demographic myths in Indonesia is that it has low levels of population mobility and that most Indonesians are born, live and work, and eventually die, in a single place. This is reinforced by relatively low proportions of Indonesians being identified as migrants in census enumerations. Table 6 shows that in 1990 only one in ten Indonesians were classified as migrants, although this was nearly twice the rate two decades earlier. However, to qualify as a migrant an Indonesian had to move between provinces on a more or less permanent basis.

Table 6: Measures of Migration, 1971-95

	Migration Measure	Males	Females
1971	Percent ever lived in another province	6.29	5.06
1985	Percent ever lived in another province	8.37	7.29
1985	Percent intra-province migrants	7.04	6.75
1985	Percent five-year migrants:		
	interprovincial	2.07	1.85
	intra-provincial (between *kabupaten*)	1.97	1.89
1990	Percent ever lived in another province	10.62	9.03
1990	Percent five-year migrants: interprovincial	3.54	3.12
1995	Percent ever lived in another province	11.19	10.00
1995	Percent five-year migrants: interprovincial	2.46	2.37

Source: Indonesian Censuses of 1971 and 1990; Intercensal Survey of 1985 and 1995

In fact much more movement occurs *within* provinces and Indonesians engage in a great deal of non-permanent movement (Hugo 1975). Indonesians have long responded to a lack of income earning opportunities by engaging in some form of mobility which allows them to take advantage of opportunities elsewhere, often without having to move permanently from their present place of residence. Since the crisis impacted unevenly across Indonesia, it is likely that it will have caused significant population mobility. We will begin by considering the effects on international migration.

THE CRISIS AND INTERNATIONAL MIGRATION

Globalisation has seen an exponential increase in population movement between countries on both a permanent and temporary basis. One form of movement which has particularly expanded is that of contract labour migration whereby workers move between countries (usually from labour surplus to labour short countries) to work for a fixed period. Indonesia, having one of the world's largest labour surplus economies, became one of the major suppliers of international contract labour in the 1990s, although it entered that market later than its neighbours such as the Philippines and Thailand. Table 7 shows the official figures on overseas labour migration out of Indonesia. As will be discussed later, there is also a significant flow out of the country which does not go through the Department of Labour. Nevertheless, it will be noted in the table that there was a substantial increase in the official outflow in the 1990s. It should be noted that the figure of 517,209 people leaving in 1996-97 included 321,756 undocumented migrants (Kassim 2000) who were already in Malaysia and were regularised in an amnesty in that year. The evolution of Indonesia's overseas labour migration has been documented elsewhere (Hugo 2000a). The table shows a clear increase in the number of official OCWs following the crisis.

There were conflicting forces operating on overseas labour migration as a result of the crisis. On the one hand, 'push' factors undoubtedly increased as a result of the loss of jobs and reduction in wages in Indonesia. On the other hand, these factors and the collapse of the rupiah made it much more expensive to find the funds to finance going overseas. Nevertheless, there can be no doubt that the crisis saw an upswing in official labour migration out of the nation. Table 7 shows that outmovement in 1998-99 (that is, April 1998 to March 1999) was 75 per cent larger than that in 1997-98 and that the new higher level of outmovement has been maintained over the subsequent two years.

Some of the main features of Indonesian international labour migration before the crisis were as follows (Hugo 1995; 2000a; 2000c):

- The Middle East has been the dominant destination of official migrants (Table 7).
- Malaysia and Singapore have traditionally been important destinations for Indonesians over centuries but have increased in significance as destinations for official labour migrants in recent years.
- Other Asian nations with labour shortages (Hong Kong, Taiwan, South Korea) have become increasingly important destinations.
- Official outmigrations have been dominated by women who are predominantly domestic workers.
- Official labour migrants predominantly come from Java.
- More than a half of labour migrants going overseas are undocumented. Most of these go to Malaysia. More males than females are undocumented workers and a greater proportion of them came from the Outer Islands than is the case for official migrant workers.

Table 7: Number of Indonesian Overseas Workers Processed by the Ministry of Manpower, 1969-2001

Year (Single	Middle East		Malaysia/Singapore		Other		Total	Percent Change	Sex Ratio
Year)	No.	%	No.	%	No.	%	No.	over Previous Year	(Males/100 Females)
2000	128,975	30	217,407	50	88,837	20	435,219	+2	46
1999	154,327	36	204,006	48	69,286	16	427,619	na	41
1999-2000	153,890	38	187,643	46	62,990	16	404,523	-2	44
1998-99	179,521	44	173,995	42	58,153	14	411,609	+75	28
1997-98	131,734	56	71,735	30	31,806	14	235,275	-55	20
1996-97	135,336	26	328,991	64	52,942	10	517,269**	328	79*
1995-96	48,298	40	46,891	39	25,707	21	120,896	-31	48
1994-95	99,661	57	57,390	33	19,136	11	176,187	10	32
1993-94	102,357	64	38,453	24	19,185	12	159,995	-7	36
1992-93	96,772	56	62,535	36	12,850	7	172,157	15	54
1991-92	88,726	59	51,631	34	9,420	6	149,777	74	48
1990-91	41,810	48	38,688	45	5,766	7	86,264	3	73
1989-90	60,456	72	8,488	22	5,130	6	84,074	37	35
1988-89	50,123	82	6,614	11	4,682	8	61,419	1	29
1987-88	49,723	81	7,916	13	3,453	6	61,092	11	35
1986-87	45,405	66	20,349	30	2,606	4	68,360	23	61
1985-86	45,024	81	6,546	12	4,094	7	54,297	21	44
1984-85	35,577	77	6,034	13	4,403	10	46,014	57	79
1983-84	18,691	64	5,597	19	5,003	17	29,291	38	141
1982-83	9,595	45	7,801	37	3,756	18	21,152	18	
1981-82	11,484	65	1,550	9	4,570	26	17,604	11	
1980-81	11,231	70	564	4	4,391	27	16,186	56	
1979-80	7,651	74	720	7	2,007	19	10,378		
1977							3,675		

Five Year Planning Periods:		Target	Total Deployed
Replita VII	1999-2003*		862,838
Replita VI	1994-99	1,250,000	1,461,236
Replita V	1989-94	500,000	652,272
Replita IV	1984-89	225,000	292,262
Replita III	1979-84	100,000	96,410
Replita II	1974-79	none set	17,042
Replita I	1969-74	none set	5,264

* 1999 and 2000only

** Year in which 300,000+ Malaysian labour migrants were regularised (194,343 males and 127,413 females).

Source: Suyono, 1981; Singhanetra-Renard, 1986, 52; Pusat Penelitian Kependudukan, Universitas Gadjah Mada, 1986, 2; AKAN Offices, Bandung and Jakarta; AKAN (Antar Kerja Antar Negara); Departement Tengara Kerja, Republic of Indonesia, 1998, 14

- There are increasing numbers of 'trainees' going to Japan and Korea, many of whom 'run away' from their employers and become undocumented migrants.
- Almost all Indonesians going overseas take up unskilled, low status, low paying jobs.

Table 8 presents estimates of the numbers of Indonesians working overseas around 2000. This suggests around 2.5 million or more than 3 per cent of Indonesia's workers are currently working overseas.

Table 8: Indonesia: Estimated Stocks of Overseas Contract Workers Around 2000

Destination	Estimated Stocks	Source
Saudi Arabia	425,000	Indonesian Embassy Riyadh
United Arab Emirates	35,000	*Asian Migration News*, 30 April 1999
Malaysia	1,900,000	Kassim, 1997
Hong Kong	40,000	*Migration News*, March 2001
Singapore	70,000	*Asian Migration News*, 5 May 1999
Taiwan	18,269	*Asian Migration Yearbook,* 1999: 197
South Korea	11,700	*Asian Migration Yearbook,* 1999: 182
Japan	3,245	*Asian Migration Yearbook,* 1999: 128
Philippines	26,000	*SCMP*, 10 December 1998
Brunei	2,246	*Asian Migration Yearbook,* 1999: 125
Other	20,000	Depnaker
Total	2,551,640	

What have been the effects of the crisis on international labour migration? Although there are little or no data to establish the patterns definitively, a number of points can be made (Hugo 2000c):

- The crisis increased the pressure to migrate both in a documented and undocumented way. This led to an increase in new international labour migrants. This was facilitated by the expanding social networks created by previous migrant workers and the proliferating migration industry.
- The impact of the crisis in receiving countries (especially Malaysia) led to a tightening of the labour market. This led to an increase in deportations and increased surveillance leading to greater capture of migrant workers seeking to enter the country clandestinely. However, the effects were not as great as anticipated, largely due to labour market segmentation which ensured that unemployed Malaysians had no wish to replace Indonesians in so-called 3D (dirty, dangerous, difficult) and low paying jobs such as plantation workers, forestry workers and domestic workers.
- Many of the official migrant workers displaced in Malaysia became undocumented workers after losing their jobs and sought other work, often in the informal sector.
- There was some evidence of the increased return of migrant workers to Indonesia but this almost certainly was more than counterbalanced by increased outflows.
- One of the few sets of data available are deportation statistics provided by the Regional Development Office (Bappeda) in Samarinda, East Kalimantan which

keeps statistics on Indonesians deported from Sabah. These data are presented in Table 9 and do not indicate a major upturn in the number of deportees after the crisis.

Table 9: Undocumented Indonesian Migrant Workers Deported from Tawau (Sabah) to East Kalimantan January 1994-December 1998

Province of Origin	Jan. 1994-June 1996	1997	1998
South Sulawesi	13,402	3,890	4,674
East Nusa Tenggara	10,704	733	742
East Java	3,940	433	556
West Nusa Tenggara	4,988	54	66
Southeast Sulawesi	1,283	299	389
East Kalimantan	522	46	39
Other	1,073	33	51
Total	36,002	5,488	6,517
Males	24,101	4,374	5,064
Females	11,891	1,111	1,448
Sex Ratio	200.8	392.6	349.7

Source: Provincial Development Office of the province of East Kalimantan Samarinda

- Associated with the crisis was an outbreak of anti-Chinese violence in 1998. This led to an outflow from the country, to Singapore, Malaysia, Hong Kong and Australia, often to where other family members were already settled. Table 10 shows the figures for Indonesians entering Australia and it will be noted that the crisis saw a downturn in the numbers of Indonesian visitors to Australia as tourism and short-term business visiting shrank during the crisis. However, the numbers of long-term arrivals increased, despite the reduction in the number of Indonesian students coming to Australia during the crisis. It will be noted too that the number of Indonesians settling as permanent immigrants in Australia doubled during the crisis and undoubtedly a large proportion of these are Chinese (Hugo 2000a). Much of the movement of Chinese to elsewhere in Southeast Asia involved families staying with relatives while they watched the situation in Indonesia. In many cases the head of the family commuted to Indonesia to maintain family businesses. The extent of return to Indonesia is difficult to establish, although there have been pleas from the last two Presidents for them to return to Indonesia.
- As indicated, there has been a small decline in the outflow of Indonesian students studying abroad. For example, the numbers going to Australia fell from 11,607 in 1996-97 to 8,024 in 1997-98 but recovered to 8,767 in 1998-99.
- Before the crisis there was a substantial number of expatriates living and working in Indonesia because of the mismatch between the output of Indonesia's training and education systems and the needs of a restructuring and developing economy. There were estimated to be 67,000 foreign workers in Indonesia before the crisis but this fell drastically during the crisis so that in 1998 they numbered 35,061.

Table 10: Australia: Arrival from Indonesia. 1994-2000

	Settler Arrivals[1]	Long-Term Arrivals[2]	Visitor Arrivals[3]
1994-95	1,013	6,173	128,475
1995-96	1,793	7,376	152,890
1996-97	1,750	8,788	170,120
1997-98	1,917	9,257	128,624
1998-99	2,491	9,443	110,938
1999-2000	2,943	9,910	102,596

1. Persons migrating to Australia permanently.
2. Visitors arriving with the intention to stay in Australia for twelve months or more, and the return of residents who had stayed abroad for twelve months or more.
3. Travellers whose intended or actual stay in Australia is less than twelve months.

Source: DIMA unpublished statistics

The Crisis and Internal Migration

It is important to establish at the outset that Indonesian population mobility has increased substantially over recent decades and that there is an established history of Indonesians adopting a range of mobility strategies to adjust to changes in the labour market and cope with crises (Hugo 1978; 1982). The latter is especially the case in rural Java where, prior to the crisis, the pressure on agricultural employment led to many moving to cities on a permanent or a temporary basis to take advantage of off-farm job opportunities (Hugo 1978; Mantra 1981; Spaan 1999). In the early days of the crisis much was made of the potential for workers displaced from urban-based jobs to return to their home areas in the rural hinterland to obtain work and support from their communities of origin. This undoubtedly occurred (Silvey, 1998; Ananta 1999; Manning and van Diermen 2000; Hugo 2000b; UNSFIR 1999; Sumarto, Wetterberg and Pritchett 1999), but it did not become the urban-rural flood that some expected (Hugo 2000b). This was because:

- Many urban dwellers had become attracted to urban life and sought alternative jobs if they were displaced, especially in the informal sector.
- The capacity of rural areas to absorb an influx was limited because of the effects of El Nino, the progressive commercialisation of agriculture and the fact that indeed many rural communities had been heavily reliant on the influx of remittances from migrants in urban areas for their prosperity. This all meant that often there were no jobs to go back to in the village.

In sum, however, it is clear not only that the outflow from urban to rural areas was less than anticipated, but also that subsequent return to the city was very common. A seminar on the impact of the crisis on village development in Java (Sandee 1999, 142) concluded that there were:

> mixed reports on the significance of return migration. In some villages more than 50 per cent of the migrants had returned, while in the others the majority stayed active in the

urban economy. There were examples of rural wages being adjusted downwards to accommodate more workers. However, there was also some evidence of migrants who failed to integrate, and, consequently, had gone back to the cities. Most contributors stressed, however, that the majority of migrants remain in the cities, although the crisis is likely to have had a negative impact on their remittances.

To summarise, it appears that there has been only a limited permanent redistribution of population away from urban areas to rural areas. This is reflected in the results of the 1997 and 1998 Sakernas (Annual National Workforce Survey) which show that between the two surveys the urban population aged 15 and over grew by 5.13 per cent, while the rural population only grew by 0.92 per cent. The true extent of urban to rural distribution of population will be able to be established with the release of the full results of the 2000 census. It may well have been the case that there was a reversal of the patterns of circular migration rather than a significant permanent redistribution of the population. Prior to the crisis there was a strong pattern whereby rural-based families sent members to work for extended periods in the city to supplement their village incomes. In the crisis it seems some urban-based families sent back family members to get work in the village to supplement city incomes.

There is little known of the effect of the crisis on movement between Java and the Outer Islands. In fact, if anything, the Outer Islands fared better than Java in the crisis because:

- The sectors hardest hit by unemployment (manufacturing, construction and low level white collar jobs) are underrepresented outside Java.
- Export-oriented, resource-based industries (oil palm, oil, forestry, mining) were not effected by the crisis, indeed the devaluation of the rupiah made them more competitive.
- There were more opportunities for agricultural expansion outside Java.

Hence it may be that some Java residents would be attracted by the availability of jobs in the Outer Islands. However, there is little evidence of an increased flow.

In sum, there can be little doubt that the crisis saw an overall increase in the mobility of Indonesians as they ranged more widely in the search to earn enough to support their families. It is likely that the bulk of this increase occurred in non-permanent mobility as families sought to expand their portfolio of sources of income to cope with downturns of income in their place of permanent residence. It may have led to a dampening of longstanding trends of displacement of people from village to city. It is probable that its effects on permanent moves of population have been limited. In fact a bigger effect on such movement has been the onset of insecurity and conflict in parts of Indonesia in the wake of the crisis and the political change sweeping across the country. This is examined in the next section.

Forced Population Displacement

The last three years of the economic crisis have also seen a substantial displacement of Indonesians within the country due to conflict. It is estimated that more than a million Indonesians (Djalal 2001, 56) have been uprooted from their homes and are scattered across the country, many in 'refugee'[2] camps. Figure 2 shows the distribution of the displaced persons and their approximate numbers as reported in the media. Their movements have been associated with bloodshed in Aceh, Maluku, East Timor, Central Kalimantan and West Kalimantan. Some refugees remain in the areas of conflict. However, many of those who have been displaced are former migrants, or more often the descendants of former migrants, and some have returned to their areas of origin. However, in many of these cases they do not retain linkages with their areas of origin, so they have not been able to seek refuge in the homes of family members in their origin areas.

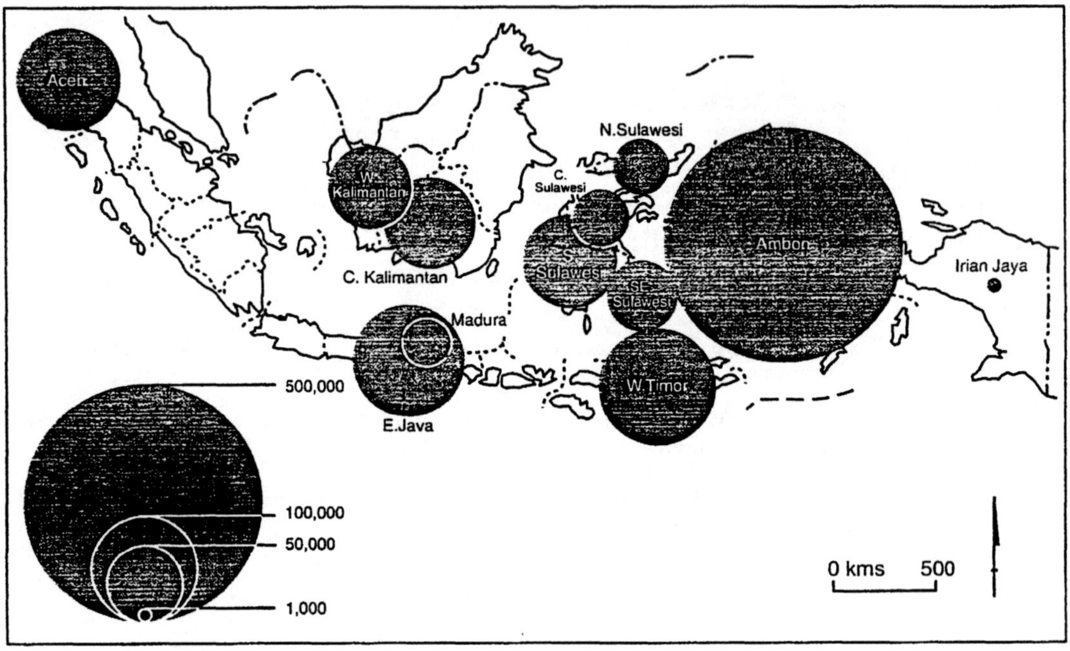

Figure 2: Distribution of Internally Displaced Persons, 2000

Aceh in Northern Sumatra has been seeking independence from Indonesia from the earliest days of the republic. In the 1950s there was a major campaign to turn Aceh into an independent Islamic state. Thereafter the separatist movement waxed and waned in influence, but since 1998 several hundred people have been killed, hundreds of public buildings burned down and more than 200,000 people displaced by fighting, although many have since returned to their homes. Nevertheless, at least a third remain uprooted. Many of those who have been displaced are from the estimated 200,000 residents of the province who are ethnically non-Acehrese (*Asian Migration News* 1999). Many of these are from Java or the descendants of people from Java who settled in the province as transmigrants or as workers on large projects such as oil and gas fields or timber mills. The displaced persons are housed in 'refugee sites' such as schools, mosques and warehouses as well as 'refugee camps' run by the government. There has also been a significant flow back to Java with a substantial camp being set up in West Java to received displaced persons. It is argued that the rebels forced the 'refugee' crisis in 1999 in order to stir up an international outcry to precipitate a withdrawal of the 7,000 army stationed in the province (Cohen 1999, 17).

In West Kalimantan there has been a history of clashes between local Dyaks and Madurese who came from their island home near East Java as transmigrants or spontaneous settlers. The centre of the conflict has been in Kabupaten Sambas, north of Pontianak, the capital. In 1997 some 20,000 Madurese moved to Pontianak and a similar number followed them in 1999 as a result of ethnic-based clashes (McBeth and Cohen 1999, 20). In early 2001 the number of displaced persons was put at 60,000 (Djalal 2001, 58). There has been a significant flow of around 20,000 of the group back to Madura and to East Java (Djalal 2001, 59), but the majority have remained in camps throughout West Kalimantan, especially near Pontianak. It has been estimated that around a half of those who went to Madura could not adjust to life back in their homeland and returned to West Kalimantan (Djalal 2001, 59).

One of the largest outflows of internally displaced persons has been from the former province[3] of Maluku where there has been a conflict which has pitted Christians against Muslims. Both the island of Ambon in the south and the northern islands have been subject to violence and movement of displaced persons. The largest flows have been out of Ambon. There is a long history of conflict between Christians and Muslims in the province, including the occasion when Christian separatists sought to break away from the new Indonesian republic in 1949. However, for most of the subsequent period there has been a local tradition of *pela gambong* (non-violence), although over this period consistent inmigration of Muslims from Southern Sulawesi has reduced the Christians' demographic dominance (McBeth and Djalal 1999, 28-30). The current violence began in early 1999 and has produced more than 3,000 deaths (*Far Eastern Economic Review* 2000a, 15) and displaced over 400,000 people. Many of those displaced from Southern Maluku have remained in camps but also there has been a significant flow back to South and Southeast Sulawesi with 100,000 leaving Ambon (Djalal 2000, 34). The insecurity in the region was exacerbated by the influx of Muslim militants from Java who declared a so-called *Laskar Jihad* (Holy War) in the region (*Far Eastern Economic Review* 2000c, 10). By late 1999 the violence had spread beyond Ambon to the islands of Buru, Ternate, Halmahera and elsewhere in Maluku (Cohen 2000, 16). As in Ambon, while the origins of the conflict do not lie in religious difference, this has quickly become an important factor in the hostility and bloodshed. A significant number of refugees from North Maluku (especially Halmahera) have fled to Menado in North Sulawesi (McBeth 2000, 17).

There have been reports of poor conditions in the camps containing internally displaced persons from Maluku. For example, in the camps in South and Southeast Sulawesi it was reported (*Jakarta Post* 1999, 2) that 'Twenty five Ambon refugees in makeshift refugee centres in Buton, Southeast Sulawesi died of cholera in recent weeks while 400 others were hospitalised with various diseases'. The humanitarian group 'Doctors Without Borders' reported a deterioration in health conditions in Maluku because of squalid conditions and lack of medical supplies (*Asian Migration News* 2000a). There have also been reports that some boats crowded with refugees from Maluku have sunk with significant loss of life. One boat licensed to carry 250 passengers sank with more than double that number on board while taking Christian refugees from Halmahera to North Sulawesi (*Far Eastern Economic Review* 2000b, 12).

There were substantial flows out of the former Indonesian province of East Timor in the aftermath of the 30 August 1999 vote for independence. The outflow included two groups. On the one hand were people from Java who filled many of the government positions and the Bugis from South Sulawesi who dominated small scale private sector economic activity. On the other hand, there were over 200,000 Timorese who were placed in camps in several parts of Indonesia but especially across the border in West Timor and near the West Timor capital of Kupang. With the restoration of order by a United Nations force there was some repatriation of the latter group. Nevertheless, there are still over 100,000 East Timorese in West Timor camps 'awaiting repatriation in the face of protests of pro-Jakarta militia groups which continue to resist the refugees' return home' (Djalal 2001, 58). Little is known about the East Timorese who were evacuated to other parts of Indonesia.

In Irian Jaya there has been a separatist movement (the OPM) ever since the former Dutch colony became part of Indonesia in 1963. This was quite weak through much of the 1980s and early 1990s but there has since been an upsurge of opposition to Indonesian sovereignty (Murphy 1999; Dolven 2000). There has been violence directed at immigrants from other parts of Indonesia (*Far Eastern Economic Review* 2000d, 14). As yet there have not been reports of massive outflows from the province, although there have been people displaced from the areas bordering Papua New Guinea (*Asian Migration News* 2000b).

In early 2001 a new outbreak of ethnic violence occurred in Central Kalimantan. In a similar situation to the problems in West Kalimantan, indigenous Dyaks have clashed with Madurese settlers and the death toll has been estimated at between 400 and 1,000 (*Asian Migration News* 2001). This has seen a massive displacement of Madurese settlers including 24,000 from Sampit, 5,000 from the capital Palang Karya and 15,000 from Samuda. Overall, some 100,000 Madurese had been settled in Kalimantan and the violence of recent times has seen a major evacuation of the group. They have been crowded into makeshift camps and some have fled back to Madura. Conditions in the camps have been poor with a lack of food and widespread disease (*Asian Migration News* 2001).

An interesting dimension of these patterns of forced movements is that they represent a reversal of flows of two of the most substantial population movements in post-Independence Indonesia. The first is that in some locations it is transmigrants from Java that have been forced to leave and enter local refugee camps or return to the area that they or their ancestors had left several decades ago. The transmigration program which aimed at resettling farm population from Java-Bali in less crowded outer island areas relocated around 6 million people in almost a century of operation, although it was stopped in 2000. The distribution of transmigrant settlers in the Outer Islands is shown in Figure 3. In some areas there have been clashes between local populations and the transmigrants but not on the scale that has been experienced in the post-crisis situation in the locations discussed earlier.

A much less well known post-Independence movement has been the diaspora from South and Southeast Sulawesi of the so-called BBM (Bugis, Butonese, Makassarese) groups. They have long been a peripatetic group (Naim 1984). For much of the last 400 years their movements and settlements have been to the west of their home area (Lineton 1975). However, since 1950 they have increasingly travelled to and settled in eastern Indonesia. Hence, as Figure 4 shows, they have settled widely throughout the Indonesian archipelago. This movement has been such that a major South Sulawesi cultural association has 8 million workers outside South Sulawesi and 7 million inside the province (Cohen and Murphy 1999, 27).

The violence in East Timor and Maluku has seen a substantial backflow of BBM to South and Southeast Sulawesi provinces. Moreover, they are a significant group in Irian where some resentment has grown up against the BBM dominating much of the small scale trade (Adicondro 1986).

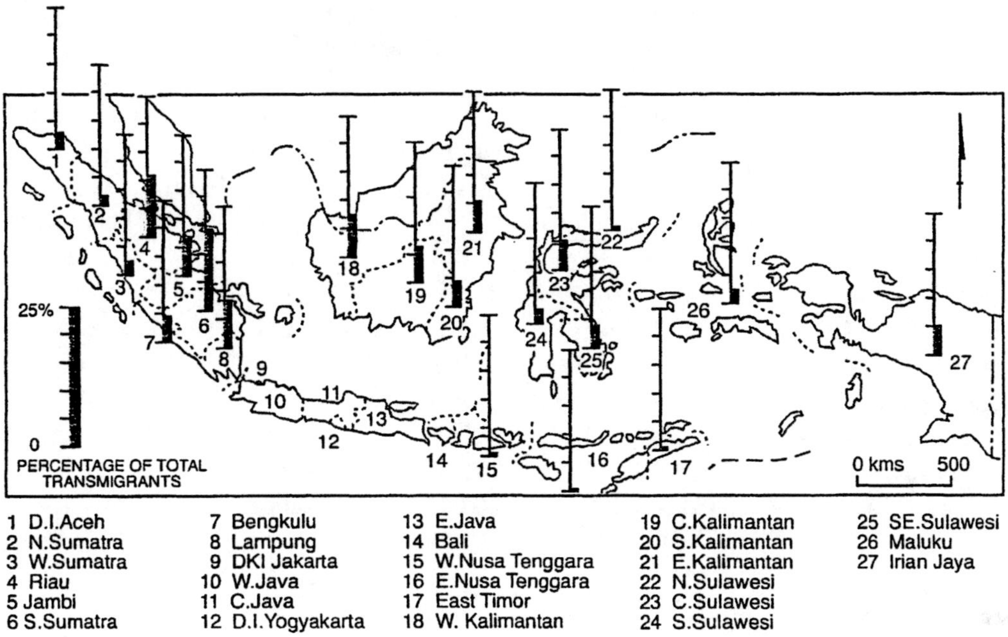

Source: Republic of Indonesia, 1993 and 1998; Pramono, 2000

Figure 3: Destination of Transmigrants, 1968-2000

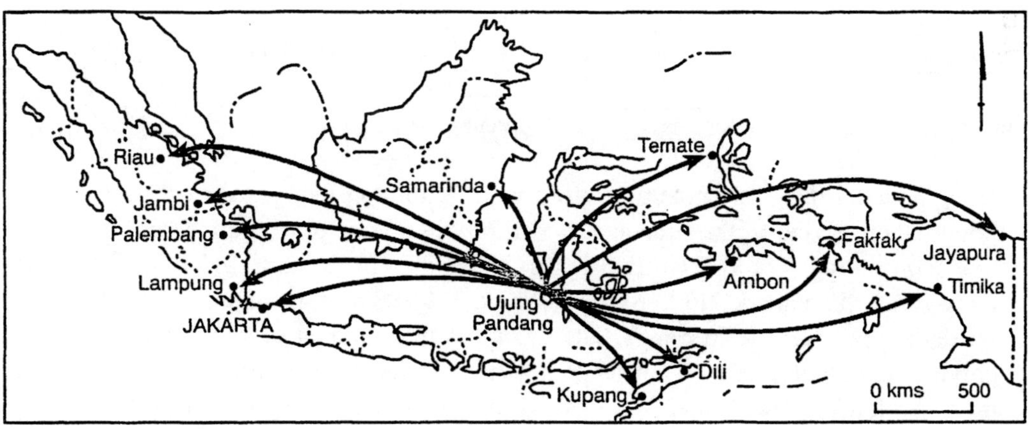

Source: Cohen and Murphy, 1999

Figure 4: Bugis Migrations from South Sulawesi

The result of these massive internal displacements of population has been the growth of camps around Indonesia to house them. Table 11 shows the numbers of inhabitants of those camps in each province.

Table 11: Internally Displaced Person (IDP) Refugee Figures by Regions (as of 21 March 2000)

Province/Region Affected	Number of Internally Displaced Housholds	Number of IDPs	Estimated Number and Percentage of Women IDPs of Reproductive Age (App. 40% from Total IDPs)	
			Number	Percentage
Aceh	2,096	8,380	3,352	1
North Sumatra	5,785	27,567	11,027	3
Riau	762	3,135	1,254	
Jambi	519	2,103	841	
South Sumatra	425	1,700	680	
West Java	2,363	9,257	3,703	1
Central Java	2,946	12,335	4,934	1
East Java	9,490	40,013	16,005	4
Bali	751	2,974	1,190	
NTB	3,239	13,013	5,205	1
West Kalimantan	12,472	68,934	27,574	7
Central Kalimantan	29	116	46	
Central Sulawesi	12,794	58,005	23,202	6
South Sulawesi	8,951	35,804	14,322	3
North Sulawesi	9,946	39,785	15,914	4
South East Sulawesi	32,513	161,226	64,490	15
Maluku	53,763	215,061	86,024	21
North Maluku	42,808	197,327	78,931	19
East Nusa Tenggara	31,040	128,427	51,371	12
Irian Jaya	4,027	16,600	6,640	2
Total	236,719	1,041,762	416,705	100
Total Coverage by UNFPA	196,437	932,364	372,946	88

Source: Indonesian Agency for Disaster Management

This indicates that early in 2001 there were 1.04 million Indonesians (0.5 per cent of the total population) living in those camps. It will be observed from Figure 5 that the IDPs are strongly concentrated in the Outer Islands, especially in Eastern Indonesia. The largest numbers are in Maluku and North Maluku, where 376,288 persons or around 19.0 per cent of the resident population are in camps. The second largest number of 161,226 (9.1 per cent of the province population) is in Southeast Sulawesi and these also are people displaced from the violence in Maluku. The 128,427 in East Nusa Tenggara are predominantly East Timorese refugees. The small numbers in Central Kalimantan will have greatly increased in the months subsequent to these figures being collected.

While there is considerable involvement of international agencies and non-government organisations in many of the camps, there are reports of poor conditions in them. In particular, crowded conditions and poor hygiene are problems. There is also a fear that there will be a spread of HIV/AIDS and other STDs in the camps.

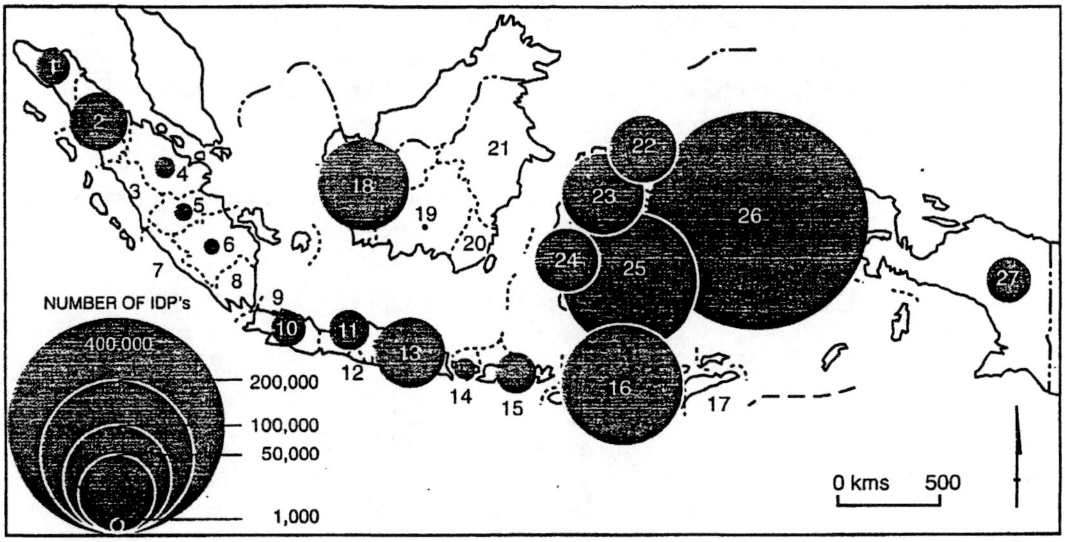

1 D.I.Aceh
2 N.Sumatra
3 W.Sumatra
4 Riau
5 Jambi
6 S.Sumatra
7 Bengkulu
8 Lampung
9 DKI Jakarta
10 W.Java
11 C.Java
12 D.I.Yogyakarta
13 E.Java
14 Bali
15 W.Nusa Tenggara
16 E.Nusa Tenggara
17 East Timor
18 W. Kalimantan
19 C.Kalimantan
20 S.Kalimantan
21 E.Kalimantan
22 N.Sulawesi
23 C.Sulawesi
24 S.Sulawesi
25 SE.Sulawesi
26 Maluku
27 Irian Jaya

Source: Indonesian Agency for Disaster Management

Figure 5: IDP/Refigee Population Figures by Regions (as of 21 March 2001)

THE PRELIMINARY RESULTS OF THE 2000 POPULATION CENSUS

The fact that Indonesia conducted a complete census in 2000 provides the opportunity to make an assessment of the impact of the crisis on population in the country. Unfortunately, at the time of writing only the most preliminary of data are available.

The first results of the 2000 census of population in Indonesia were recently announced (BPS 2001) and they put the nation's population at 203.45 million. This would suggest that the national population grew by only 1.35 per cent per annum in the 1990s compared with 1.97 per cent between 1980 and 1990. Undoubtedly, part of the decline is a function of the success of the program to reduce fertility in Indonesia. However, it is clear that there were significant numbers of people missed in the census. The fact that there were at the time of the census more than 2.5 million people away working overseas, substantially more than twice as many as in 1990, would have been influential. Moreover, the effects of the crisis may have made it more difficult to detect people living in marginal conditions in the major cities. A limited Post Enumeration Survey found that there was in fact an undercount of 6 per cent in urban areas in Indonesia. Another problem with the census arises from the fact that the unrest and insecurity in some areas prevented census takers from entering them, so their populations needed to be estimated. These areas included the *kabupatens* of North Aceh, Pidie and East Aceh in Aceh, Sambas in West Kalimantan and Puso, Central Maluku, Jayawijaya and Ambon in Maluku.

The populations enumerated in each of Indonesia's provinces are given in Table 12 and while these figures must be regarded as preliminary for the reasons given above, some comments can be made. Probably most striking in the table is the fact that DKI Jakarta's population grew by only 0.16 per cent per year compared with 2.41 per cent between 1980 and 1990. This appears to fly in the face of the commonly voiced opinion that Indonesia is experiencing rapid urbanisation and that Jakarta is one of the world's rapidly growing mega-cities.

Table 12: Indonesian Population Numbers and Change, 1980-2000

Province	Population			Annual Rate of Growth	
	1980	1990	2000	1980-90	1990-2000
Aceh	2,011,271	3,416,156	4,010,865*	2.72	1.67
North Sumatra	8,306,894	10,256,027	11,476,272	2.06	1.17
West Sumatra	3,406,816	4,000,207	4,228,108	1.62	0.57
Riau	2,168,535	3,303,976	4,733,948*	4.31	3.79
Jambi	1,445,994	2,020,568	2,400,940	3.38	1.80
South Sumatra	4,629,801	6,313,074	7,756,506*	3.09	2.15
Bengkulu	768,064	1,179,122	1,405,060	4.38	1.83
Lampung	4,624,785	6,017,573	6,654,354	2.65	1.05
SUMATRA	27,362,160	36,506,703	42,666,048		
Jakarta	6,503,449	8,259,266	8,384,853	2.41	0.16
West Java	27,453,525	35,384,352	43,552,923	2.57	2.17
Central Java	25,372,889	28,520,643	30,856,825	1.18	0.82
Yogyakarta	2,750,813	2,913,054	3,109,142	0.57	0.68
East Java	29,188,852	32,503,991	34,525,588	10.8	0.63
JAVA	91,269,528	107,581,306	120,429,331		
Bali	2,469,930	2,777,811	3,124,674	1.18	1.22
West Nusa Tenggara	2,724,664	3,369,649	3,821,794	2.15	1.31
East Nusa Tenggara	2,737,166	3,268,644	3,929,039	1.79	1.92
	7,931,760	9,416,104	10,875,507		
West Kalimantan	2,486,068	3,229,153	3,740,017	2.68	1.53
Central Kalimantan	954,353	1,396,486	1,801,504	3.88	2.67
South Kalimantan	2,064,649	2,597,572	2,970,244	2.32	1.40
East Kalimantan	1,218,016	1,876,663	2,436,545	4.42	2.74
KALIMANTAN	6,723,086	9,099,874	10,948,310		
North Sulawesi	2,115,384	2,478,119	2,820,839	1.60	1.35
Central Sulawesi	1,289,635	1,711,327	2,066,394*	2.87	1.97
South Sulawesi	6,062,212	6,981,646	7,787,299	1.42	1.14
Southeast Sulawesi	942,309	1,349,619	1,771,951	3.66	2.86
SULAWESI	10,409,540	12,520,711	14,446,483		
Maluku	1,411,006	1,857,790	1,977,570*	2.78	0.65
Irian Jaya	1,173,875	1,648,708	2,112,756*	3.41	2.60
	2,584,881	3,506,498	4,090,326		
TOTAL	146,934,948	178,631,196	203,456,005	1.97	1.35

* Including estimates.

Source: Indonesian censuses 1980, 1990 and 2000

A number of explanations, however, can be put forward for the figure, some of which relate to the crisis:

- Firstly, the undercount referred to above was undoubtedly significant. It may be that the crisis has expanded the numbers living in marginal situations and hence not easy to detect by census takers.[4]
- Secondly, it was already clear in the 1980s that Jakarta had overspilled the boundaries of DKI Jakarta and that the bulk of growth was occurring on the growing edge of the city located in the neighbouring West Java *kabupaten* of Bekasi, Tanggerang and Bogor (Hugo 1996). DKI Jakarta has in fact been 'filled up'.
- Thirdly, there is little doubt that the crisis hit harder in urban areas than rural areas and especially in Jakarta where there was a marked slowing down of construction and other activity. Moreover, this led many to return to their villages (Hugo 2000b). However, there is also evidence that many who did return to their villages also subsequently returned to the city because of a lack of village-based opportunities.

It may be that all three of these factors are of some significance in Jakarta's low growth rate over the 1990-2000 period.

The 2000 census figures in Table 12 also show some interesting patterns for other provinces. Almost all provinces had lower population growth rates in 1990-2000 than in the previous decade. There are only three exceptions. Yogyakarta was Indonesia's slowest growing province in 1980-90 but was only the fifth slowest growing in 1990-2000. This is probably due to the significant influx of so-called 'refugees' from elsewhere in Indonesia in the late 1990s, especially from Eastern Indonesia. The second province experiencing an increase in population growth rates between the 1980s and 1990s was Bali. This is an interesting case since it has had the lowest, and fastest declining, levels of fertility in Indonesia. Undoubtedly its increase in growth rates is not due to any change in fertility patterns. Indeed, other things being equal (that is, zero net migration), Bali's population growth rates would have fallen precipitously. The difference has been made up by migration. In the first place the development of the Balinese economy largely due to the expansion of tourism, led to increased job opportunities that both dampened Balinese outmigration and increased inmigration from other provinces. Table 13 shows that the number of foreign tourists increased fivefold in the decade preceding the crisis. As the premier destination of foreign tourists, Bali's economy prospered. It will be noticed, however, that one of the effects of the crisis and the ensuing political instability has been a sharp overall downturn in tourist arrivals and this will have disproportionately effected Bali.

Another factor in Bali's increase in population growth has been its role as a haven for internally displaced persons. It has been regarded as a safe haven by Chinese Indonesians fleeing violence elsewhere, especially Jakarta (Cohen 1998, 16). In addition it has received some of those displaced from Maluku, East Timor and Irian Jaya.

The most significant turnaround seeing an increase in population growth was in the province of East Nusa Tenggara. This was one of the slowest growing Outer Island provinces in the 1980s due to the fact that it was one of the nation's major outmigration provinces, especially of international contract workers, most of whom moved to Sabah (Hugo 2000b). However, in the late 1990s the province became the major destination for people moving out of neighbouring East Timor. In fact, at the time of the census there was substantial settlement of East Timorese not only in and around Kupang and along the border with East Timor but also elsewhere in the province, such as in Flores. Table 11 indicates that in 2001 there were still 128,427 in official IDP camps in the province.

Table 13: Indonesia: Foreign Tourist Arrivals, 1987-2000

1979	494,366	1987	1,060,347	1995	4,069,478
1980	566,402	1988	1,301,049	1996	4,258,136
1981	598,715	1989	1,625,965	1997	5,185,200
1982	592,016	1990	2,177,566	1998	3,767,700
1983	638,855	1991	2,584,570	1999	3,920,300
1984	700,910	1992	3,060,197	2000*	3,084,100
1985	749,351	1993	3,403,138		
1986	825,035	1994	4,006,312		

* January-September only.
Source: BPS, 2000b

Elsewhere substantial declines in population growth rates were recorded. As with the national data, the decline in fertility rates was a major factor in these declines, but it is apparent that the variation in provincial growth rates is due to more than interprovincial variation in fertility and fertility decline, although such elements are significant. Interprovincial migration, some of it influenced by the crisis, has been influential. One major question relates to the balance between Java and the Outer Islands. Table 14 shows that there was a consistent increase in the proportion of the nation living outside Java over the last century, although Java in 2000 still had 59.2 per cent of the national population living on 6.8 per cent of the national land area. It will be noted, however, that the increase in the population living outside Java was slower in the 1990s than in the 1970s and 1980s.

Table 14: Indonesia: Number of People Living in Java and Its Proportion of the Indonesian Population, 1900-2000

Year	Number	Percent
1900	29,000,000	72.0
1920	34,984,000	71.0
1930	41,718,000	69.0
1961	62,993,000	64.9
1971	76,102,000	63.8
1980	91,269,528	62.1
1990	107,581,296	60.2
2000	120,429,331	59.2

There are several possible reasons for the slowdown:

- A decrease in the differential in fertility between the Outer Islands and Java. For all of the post-Independence period fertility has been higher in the Outer Islands.

- A decrease in migration from Java to the Outer Islands.
- An increase in migration from the Outer Islands to Java.

The first of these factors can largely be discounted but the slowdown in transmigration in the 1990s and its eventual closing down[5] in 2000 may have been influential. Of greater significance may be the fact that Indonesia has pursued an economic policy which has encouraged foreign investment in manufacturing and export of manufactured goods since the late 1980s, replacing a policy heavily dependent on expanding exports of raw materials. Clearly the earlier policy favoured development in the Outer Islands and the later one development in Java, since Java is the main location of manufacturing activity. This could have led to both a dampening of the spontaneous outflow from Java and also encouraged movement into Java from the other islands. What is also clear, however, from the previous section is that the forced migration associated with the insecurity and conflict of Aceh, West Kalimantan, Maluku, East Timor and Irian Jaya has produced a flow of former migrants and their families back to Java from areas of conflict in the Outer Islands.

Examination of population growth patterns in Java indicates that by far the greatest growth has occurred in West Java, whose population grew twice as fast as for Java as a whole and almost four times faster than the other four Java provinces. This is clearly a function of the overspill of Jakarta into West Java but also reflects the development of the province as a whole as one of the main locations of manufacturing activity in Indonesia. The reductions in growth rates in the other Java provinces are a function both of declining fertility and continuing outmigration to West Java and selected Outer Island areas.

The highest population growth rates were recorded in areas which continued to benefit from substantial development of resource exploitation (Riau, South Sumatra, Central and East Kalimantan and Irian Jaya). In Riau the development of Batam Island as an independent manufacturing area and overflow area of neighbouring Singapore has been important as has continued oil, plantation and forestry activity. Elsewhere mining, oil, timber and plantation development has attracted immigrants. Southeast Sulawesi also had a high rate of population growth. In the past this has been due to it being a significant transmigration site but in the late 1990s the influx of returnee displaced persons from Ambon may have been a factor (Table 12).

Traditional areas of heavy outmigration in the Outer Islands continued to experience low population growth. West Sumatra, for example, as the homeland of the peripatetic Minangkabau had the second lowest population growth rate in the country between 1990 and 2000. South Kalimantan, South Sulawesi and North Sumatra as the homelands of the Banjarese, Bugis-Butonese-Makassarese and Bataks respectively, all highly mobile groups, had low and reducing rates of population growth. Lampung, as the premier destination of transmigrants for many decades, was one of Indonesia's major immigration provinces up to 1990 but it has largely been 'filled up' and its population growth in the 1970s was well below the national average, suggesting a net outmigration occurred in the 1990s for the first time in the twentieth century.

The most substantial reduction in growth rates, however, was in the province of Maluku. This reflects the fact that this province was the destination of substantial numbers of settlers from South Sulawesi and, to a lesser extent, Java in the 1970s, 1980s and early 1990s. However, as described earlier, conflict between Christians and Muslims in the late 1990s has seen an exodus from the province. In Aceh the outmovement associated with the conflict also influenced population growth, although many of those internally displaced remained in camps in the province. The same is the case in West Kalimantan.

In sum, the preliminary 2000 Indonesian population census figures do indicate that the crisis, or more particularly the political insecurity and conflict which has followed the onset of the crisis, has had some influence on population growth in the various provinces. It is not yet possible to see whether it has influenced the patterns of population development in smaller regions and whether it has altered the balance between rural and urban populations and the longstanding trend towards urbanisation.

Conclusion

Indonesia's economic crisis has been deeper and more longstanding than that elsewhere in the Asian region. Its effects have been exacerbated by the El Nino in 1997 and more recently by political instability, the outbreak of separatist movements and inter-group violence in some peripheral parts of the country. Undoubtedly the impacts of all of these forces on population have been considerable, especially on population mobility. Having said that, however, it is clear that the population impacts of the crisis have not been as dramatic as was being predicted by many at the onset of the crisis. While the definitive measurement of the population impact must await the publication of the full details of the 2000 census, it would seem that the effects on the fertility and mortality levels in Indonesia have been small, if any. Similarly, it would seem that in terms of permanent displacement of population the effects of the crisis have been quite small, although the forced internal displacements accompanying regional conflicts and insecurity have been significant. The most widespread population impacts of the crisis have been in the area of non-permanent movements. Overseas labour migration has increased, as has internal temporary movements. The latter has taken on some new directions with more movement being directed toward rural areas, although many of those moving subsequently returned to urban areas. This points to considerable resilience on the part of Indonesians in dealing with the negative economic effects of the crisis. A great deal of resourcefulness has been shown in adapting to the downturn and an increase in the area over which they range in search for income earning opportunities is one of the main coping strategies employed.

References

Adicondro, G.J. (1986) *Datang Dengan Kapal, Tidur Di Pasar, Buang Air Di Kali, Pulang Naik Pesawat*. Yayasan Pengembangan Masyarakat Desa Irian Jaya: Jayapura.

Adioetomo, S.M., D. Handayani, N. Wiyono, S.H. Hatmadji and N. Otobe (2000) 'Gender Dimensions of the Economic Crisis and Employment in Urban Informal and Rural Sectors in Indonesia'. *SEAPAT Working Papers*, No. 6.

Ananta, A. (1999) *Internal Population Mobility During Indonesian Crisis*. Mimeo.

Asian Migration News (1999) December 2.

—— (2000a) January 15.

—— (2000b) December 15.

—— (2001) February 16-28.

Biro Pusat Statistik (BPS) (2000a) *Welfare Indicators*. Jakarta: BPS.

—— (2000b) *Indonesia in Figures*. Jakarta: BPS.

—— (2000c) *Laporan Perekonomian Indonesia 2000*. Jakarta: BPS.

Cohen, M. (1998) 'Loot Thy Neighbour'. *Far Eastern Economic Review* July 30.

—— (1999) 'Captives of the Cause'. *Far Eastern Economic Review* September 2.

—— (2000) 'Spite Islands'. *Far Eastern Economic Review* January 20.

Cohen, M. and D. Murphy (1999) 'Swept Away'. *Far Eastern Economic Review* April 8.

Djalal, D. (2000) 'The Great Divide'. *Far Eastern Economic Review* February 24.

—— (2001) 'Strangers in Our Own Land'. *Far Eastern Economic Review* January 18.

Dolven, B. (2000) 'A Rising Drumbeat'. *Far Eastern Economic Review* November 18.

Far Eastern Economic Review (2000a) July 6.

—— (2000b) July 13.

—— (2000c) July 15.

—— (2000d) October 12.

Frankenberg, E., D. Thomas, and K. Beegle (1999) 'The Real Costs of Indonesia's Economic Crisis: Preliminary Findings from the Indonesian Family Life Surveys'. *Rand Labour and Population Programs Working Papers Series*.

Hugo, G. (1975) *Population Mobility in West Java, Indonesia*. Thesis submitted for degree of Doctor of Philosophy, Department of Demography, Institute of Advanced Studies, Australian National University.

—— (1978) *Population Mobility in West Java*. Yogyakarta: Gadjah Mada University Press.

—— (1982) 'Circular Migration in Indonesia'. *Population and Development Review* 8: 1.

—— (1995) 'Labour Export from Indonesia: An Overview'. *Asean Economic Bulletin* 12.

—— (1996) 'Urbanisation in Indonesia: City and Countryside Linked'. In J. Gugler, ed., *The Urban Transformation of the Developing World*. New York: Oxford University Press.

—— (1999) 'Indonesia'. In T.R. Leinbach and R. Ulack, eds, *Southeast Asia: Diversity and Development* New Jersey: Prentice Hall.

—— (2000a) 'The Crisis and International Population Movement in Indonesia'. *Asia and Pacific Migration Journal* 19: 1.

—— (2000b) 'The Impact of the Crisis on Internal Population Movement in Indonesia'. *Bulletin of Indonesian Economic Studies* 36: 2.

—— (2000c) 'Labour Migration from East Indonesia to East Malaysia: Recent Trends'. *Revue Europeenne des Migrations Internationales* 16: 1.

International Labour Organisation (ILO) (1999) *Indonesian Strategies for Employment-Led Recovery and Reconstruction: Main Report*. Jakarta, ILO.

Jakarta Post (1999) April 7.

Jones, G.W., T.H. Hull and D. Ahlburg (2000) 'The Social and Demographic Impact of the Southeast Asian Crisis of 1997-99'. *Journal of Population Research* 17: 1.

Kassim, A. (2000) 'Recent Trends in Migration Movements and Policies in Malaysia'. Paper presented at the Japan Institute of Labour Workshop on International Migration and Labour Markets in Asia, Tokyo, Japan, January 26-28.

Lineton, J. (1975) '"Pasompe Ugi": Bugis Migrants and Wanderers'. *Archipel* 10.

McBeth, J., and M. Cohen (1999) 'Dayak Destruction: New Ethnic Violence Erupts in Kalimantan'. *Far Eastern Economic Review* April 1.

McBeth J., and D. Djalal (1999) 'Tragic Island'. *Far Eastern Economic Review* March 25.

McBeth, J. (2000) 'Beyond the Pale'. *Far Eastern Economic Review* January 20.

Manning, C., and P. van Diermen, eds (2000) *Indonesia in Transition: Social Aspects of Reformasi and the Crisis*. Singapore: Institute of Southeast Asian Studies.

Mantra, I.B. (1981) *Population Mobility in Wet Rice Communities*. Yogyakarta: Gadjah Mada University Press.

Murphy, D. (1999) 'The Next Headache'. *Far Eastern Economic Review* April 29.

Naim, M. (1984) *Merantau: Pola Migrasi Suku Minangkabau*. Yogyakarta: Gadjah Mada University Press.

Poppele, J., S. Sumarto, and L. Pritchett (1999) *Social Impact of the Indonesian Crisis: New Data and Policy Implications*. Social Monitoring and Early Response Unit (SMERU): Semarang.

Pramono, D.S. (2000) Penangan Internally Displaced Persons (IDPs) Sebagai Akibat Terjadinya Konflik Sosial dengan Tindak Kekerasan. Makalah disampaikan dalam Simposium Nasional Pokok-Pokok Masalah Kebijakan Terkini Mengenai Mobilitas Penduduk Urbanisasi dan Transmigrasi. Jakarta, May 25-26.

Romdiarti, H., T. Handayani and S. Rayahu (1998) Aplikasi Jaring Pengamon Social Bidang Ketenagakerjaan: Beberapa Isu Penting Dari Hasil Kajian Cepat di Propinsi Jawa Barat, PPT. Jakarta: LIPI.

Sandee, H. (1999) 'The Impact of the Crisis on Village Development in Java'. *Bulletin of Indonesian Economic Studies* 35: 1.

Silvey, R.M. Forthcoming. 'Migration Under Crisis: Household Safety Nets in Indonesia's Economic Collapse'. *Geoforum*, Special Issue on the Crisis.

Smith, J.P., D. Thomas, E Frankenburg, K. Beegle and G. Teruel (2000) 'Wages, Employment and Economic Shocks: Evidence from Indonesia'. Draft Paper. Santa Monica: RAND Corporation.

Spaan, E. (1999) *Labour Circulation and Socio Economic Transformation*. PhD Thesis, Rijksuniversiteit Groningen.

Sumarto, S., A. Wetterberg and L. Pritchett (1999) 'The Social Impact of the Crisis in Indonesia: Results from a Nationwide Kecamatan Survey'. Jakarta: World Bank.

United Nations (1998) *National Population Policies*. New York, United Nations.

United Nations Population Fund and Australian National University (1998) *Southeast Asian Population in Crisis*. New York: UNFPA.

United Nations Support Facility for Indonesian Recovery (UNSFIR) (1999) 'The Social Implications of the Indonesian Economic Crisis: Perceptions and Policy. Jakarta: UNSFIR.

Urip, S. (1998) Dampak Krisis Ekonomi Tertedap Ketenaga Derjaan dan Migrasi. Jakarta: BPS Labour Force Division.

ENDNOTES

[1] The TFR (Total Fertility Rate) is the average number of children women would bear if they went through their childbearing years conforming to the age-specific fertility pattern of the given year. Hence it indicates approximately the average total number of children women are having at a particular point in time.

[2] The term refugee is commonly used in Indonesia to identify this group, but they do not fit the UN Convention definition of a refugee which only applies to people who are forced to leave their own country. They are more correctly designated 'internally displaced persons'. No other country in Asia currently has more internally displaced persons.

[3] It has recently been divided into two separate provinces.

[4] One explanation for the undercount is the fact that the earlier censuses have been carried out in two stages. The first is a complete enumeration collecting only 3-4 pieces of information and the second was of a sample of less than 5 per cent and collected more detailed information. In 2000 it was a single detailed enumeration and the argument is that a larger number of census takers had to be involved and the quality of them diluted.

[5] Undoubtedly the decision to stop transmigration was influenced by the crisis since it was an expensive program.

Chapter 15

From the Grassroots: The Continuing Impact of Crisis on Export Crops, Farmers and Forests in Outer Indonesia

Lesley Potter
Geographical and Environmental Studies
Adelaide University
Australia

Introduction

It is argued that Indonesia has experienced three crises – economic, ecological and political – during the momentous four years since the onset of the Asian 'meltdown' in 1997. Although the 1997-8 El Nino drought and the La Nina floods which followed it have subsided, the effects of the economic and political crises continue to be felt, with far-reaching impacts across the country. This chapter examines the present economic position and coping strategies of farmers producing export crops in parts of Sumatra, Sulawesi and Kalimantan (Map 1). Some of these people live near or inside the remaining forests, so the pressures on the forests also become a relevant focus.

The chapter falls into two parts, beginning with general discussion of the three crises and their effects in outer Indonesia, then narrowing to two sets of case studies. The first of these examines the current position of four commodities: oil palm, rubber, coffee and cocoa, and the communities which produce them. It draws on field work carried out during the past two years in Riau, South Sumatra and South Sulawesi. The second group of case studies examines the present situation of Riau's forests and forest dwellers. A general section on community coping strategies draws this material together, followed by an overall conclusion.

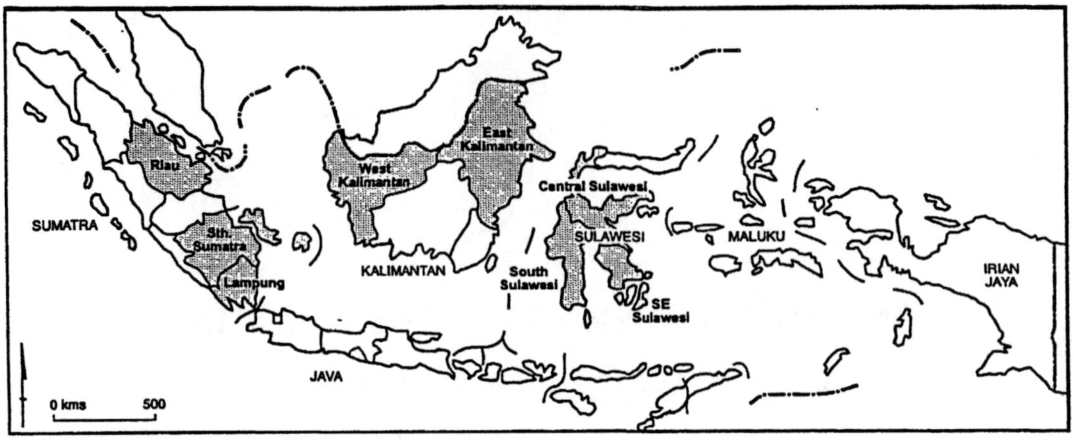

Map 1 – Indonesia: Provinces (shaded provinces mentioned in text)

'KRISMON'[1] – A JAVANESE CRISIS?

Early reports of the impact of the economic crisis on Indonesia tended to concentrate on the situation in Java, especially Jakarta, where its results were very obvious. The closure of many factories and construction projects meant a substantial reduction in employment, the effects of which were extremely painful for thousands of people. Displaced factory workers either moved into the informal sector or returned to their villages, largely in rural Java, putting more pressure on those communities. To many observers, the crisis was largely a Javanese one. This was also the finding of a World Bank 'quick' survey implemented in September-October 1998 in each of the country's 4000 subdistricts, which examined the severity of various dimensions of crisis impact – education, employment and other social areas, including coping strategies (Wetterberg *et al.* 1999). Wetterberg *et al.* also concluded that the crisis was more severe in urban than in rural areas, largely because of the magnitude of the disruption to people's lives and the level of *relative* change which had occurred. While recognising that problems existed in traditionally poor regions of eastern Indonesia, the recommendation was for crisis relief to be targeted to Java and to specific urban areas. It was noted that regions outside Java producing export crops were comparatively less affected.

Export crops are of increasing importance to the Indonesian economy. The country is the world's largest producer of pepper; it is second only to Malaysia in oil palm and Thailand in rubber, third in the world in cocoa and fourth in coffee. With the exception of oil palm with its strict processing requirements,[2] the bulk of these commodities are produced by smallholders. Even oil palm is moving increasingly to smallholder production, albeit mainly under estate supervision. Cocoa and oil palm have been the 'glamour' crops of the five, with vast expansion in area over the past ten years. Cocoa is largely concentrated in Sulawesi, oil palm in Sumatra and West Kalimantan, though spreading into most other regions. Prices for export crops are also highly variable depending on world markets, so those who plant them must be prepared for the risks involved.

As the value of the Indonesian currency (the rupiah) declined during the economic crisis, farmers producing certain export crops found that prices for these commodities increased markedly. They thus experienced some months of windfall gains, especially in 1998, when the crisis was at its height. The diagram comparing an index of local commodity prices with an index of farmer costs published in Sunderlin *et al.*, (2001, 769) illustrates this well. The 'boom' lasted from about December 1997 to November 1998, after which prices dropped to more moderate levels with the partial recovery of the currency. For pepper, coffee and cocoa, prices remained well above farmer costs, which included food (especially rice) and other basic expenditures. Oil palm and rubber also experienced price rises during this time, but their net impact was not as great. By October 1998, the index price for palm oil had slipped below that of rice; with rubber, this had happened as early as June, as international rubber prices were sliding downwards (Figure 1). Other commentators on the crisis such as Evans (1998) and Booth (1999) also noted that outer island farmers were better off than their counterparts in Java, which was correct while the windfall lasted, but very commodity and district specific. The press made much of the good fortune of cocoa farmers in South and Southeast Sulawesi, who were able to afford the Haj pilgrimage (*Suara Pembaruan* 1998), while there were stories of traffic jams in small coffee towns of South Sumatra, with farmers all driving newly acquired vehicles (fieldwork, July 1999). A recent book (Gerard and Ruf 2001), also focuses on commodities during the Indonesian crisis, with a series of case studies carried out in late 1998 and the first half of 1999. The authors analyse the kinds of purchases made during the period of windfall profits by cocoa farmers in Sulawesi and coffee farmers in Bengkulu (Ruf and Yoddang, 2001a; 2001b; Ruf *et al.*, 2001). Stories of enhanced spending capacity continue for pepper, the price of which has remained reasonably high, though lower than in the boom period (*Jakarta Post* 2001e).

It must be remembered, however, that commercial farmers are very reliant on inputs such as fertiliser and sometimes weedicides and pesticides. All inputs increased in price as a result of the low rupiah. While the government attempted to subsidise fertiliser, there are reported cases of some large companies (especially oil palm estates) managing to commandeer supplies, so that small farmers missed out. Anecdotal evidence suggests a reduction in fertiliser use by many farmers, which seems to have impacted on yields.[3] The Chair of the Indonesian Palm Oil Producers' Association claimed that because of the crisis, insufficient fertiliser had been used in that industry since 1999 (Derom Bangun 2001). Finding sources of credit was also difficult for farmers as a result of bank failures.

Sunderlin *et al.* (2001) document a study of 1050 households in five outer island provinces (Riau/Jambi and Lampung in Sumatra, West and East Kalimantan, and Central Sulawesi) undertaken between June and August 1999. The households interviewed across 30 villages were a particular subset of commodity producers, that is, those living close to forest margins. Results indicate that, apart from pepper growers and to a much lesser extent, producers of oil palm, most farmers felt that they were worse off in the period July 1998-June1999 than in the equivalent period of 1996-97. While providing many insights, such a survey underestimates the financial cushion of the windfall for large numbers of coffee and cocoa farmers who were not pioneers on the forest margin. It was also slanted towards rubber growers (32 per cent of the sample), whose experience was certainly negative, as rubber prices by mid-1999 were at a 30-year low.

The author interviewed rubber producers in Riau and South Sumatra in July 1999 and found the low prices had forced many to seek work elsewhere. It was the case, however, that local producers who were land-rich fared better than Javanese newcomers trying to get a foothold in the industry. Many South Sumatran coffee producers were continuing to do quite well, but again, it was poorer Javanese tenants or share croppers, especially recent migrants, who were not succeeding, as they tried to work heavily eroded soils (Potter 2000). On the other hand, Angelsen and Resosudarmo (1999) found that in Central Sulawesi it was new settlers (Balinese or Bugis) with the resources to open forest land, rather than poor locals, who were able to profit most from the cocoa boom there. In South Sumatra the Javanese newcomers were resource poor; in Central Sulawesi the migrants possessed tractors and chainsaws. In both studies resources held prior to the boom, together with land availability and quality (preferably with secure tenure) appear to have been the factors determining success.

It is argued that the impact of the economic crisis was delayed for certain commodity producers in Outer Indonesia, but it has now arrived in most regions.[4] The new crisis is partly a global one, as world market prices for several of Indonesia's major commodities, especially coffee and oil palm, have fallen drastically (Denny and Bellos 2001, 28; World Bank, 2001a).[5] Rubber prices made a slight recovery during 2000 from their trough in 1999, but have then trended downwards again (Figure 1). Farmers have wistful memories of the better times, which makes their present plight appear even more serious.

THE ECOLOGICAL CRISIS

In 1998 the province of East Kalimantan was certainly not enjoying a boom, as it was still suffering from the effects of the extreme El Nino drought. The drought had brought crop failures and fanned extensive fires in Kalimantan and Sumatra during 1997, but in East Kalimantan it remained dry through the normal rainy season up to April 1998. Further large scale burning took place in that province in the first four months of the year. Ironically, most of the fires in both years were shown to have been set largely by companies clearing land for new oil palm and pulp plantations. Many of these did not eventuate, as firms subsequently became bankrupt or reduced their operations (Casson 2000a). There is also evidence of deliberate burning of forests to increase the legal availability of land classified as 'production forest', in which cropping was only permitted if the forest was degraded (Potter and Lee 1999). Deliberate burning of village gardens by an oil palm company seeking to take over the land was also observed in East Kalimantan (Goenner 1998). While the drought there was exceptionally severe, the smoke and haze from the previous year's fires had affected the fruit yield and quality of oil palm crops throughout the producing districts of Sumatra and Kalimantan in 1998 (*Oil World* 1998). As happens often after a severe El Nino, the climatic crisis continued in the form of serious floods as the opposite La Nina system became established. Heavy rain is detrimental to coffee and pepper crops, causing losses in South Sumatra and Lampung (*Jakarta Post* 1999); cocoa output in Sulawesi was also affected (Lewa Pardomuan 1999). The rains were followed by locust infestation in a number of districts, including West Kalimantan and Lampung (*Akcaya* 1999; *Kompas* 1999). In these regions also, the prosperity accompanying the high commodity prices was short-lived.

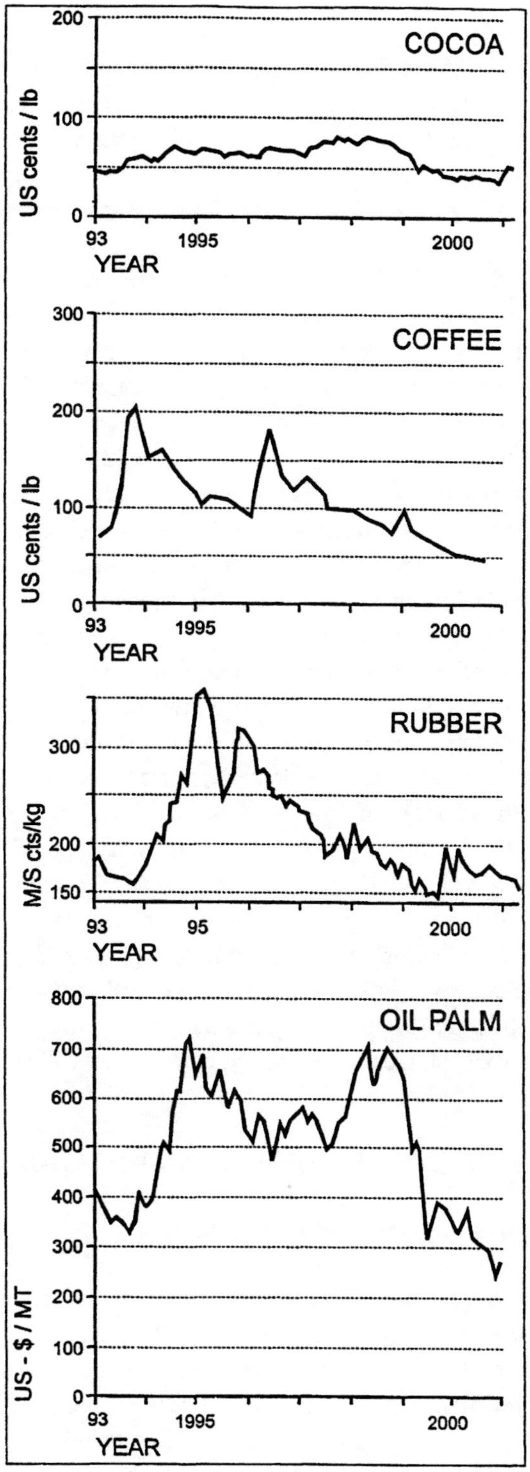

Source: ICCO (2001); Denny and Bellos (2001); INRO (2001); Oilworld (2000)

Figure 1: Fluctuations in world prices for four commodities, 1993-2001 (N.B. different units employed)

The Political Crisis

The third crisis to impact on Indonesia during the past four years has been a political one. The original economic 'meltdown' brought the collapse of the Suharto regime, which was followed by *'reformasi'*, the first steps towards democracy – but also instability. This instability continued during the temporary Habibie regime and through the Wahid Government's period in office. As noted by the World Bank, in reference to environmental impacts of this instability:

The authority of the center over regional affairs, including natural resource extraction...virtually disappeared with the fall of the Suharto government in May 1998. Removal of central control over natural resources, biased and limited though it had been before the change of government, led to virtually no control at all, and illegal logging and mining spiralled upward. (World Bank 2001b, i)

The transition to regional autonomy, which began legally on 1 January 2001, has been made more uncertain and frustrating because of lack of clarity in defining the responsibilities of each level (district, province and centre), and delays by the central government in issuing regulations, especially in the important areas of fiscal responsibility and transfers of resource income to the districts. Following the successful breaking away of East Timor, some provinces, such as Aceh and Papua, continue to fight for full independence rather than accept any form of autonomy. Violent inter-ethnic and inter-religious conflicts, and displaced and refugee populations, have created exceptional problems in a number of other regions, such as Maluku, West Timor and parts of West and Central Kalimantan. Outbreaks of violence create obvious disruption to normal activities, especially agriculture. In Aceh (Sumatra), ongoing violence between those in support of independence and the Indonesian military has led to large-scale abandonment of arabica coffee plantations, many of which were in remote mountain areas (*Straits Times* 1999). By July 2001, 80 per cent of oil palm and rubber companies in Aceh had also ceased operation (*Bisnis Indonesia* 2001). Ethnic tensions over land in 1999 led to the relinquishing of cocoa holdings in Luwu, South Sulawesi by Christian Toraja. The Toraja had successfully grown cocoa on the plains for some years, but the land was now claimed by an Islamic group. The migrants were eventually forced to retreat to their mountain heartland after their houses were broken down (Potter 2000).

Impacts of the Economic Crisis

Continuing Economic Problems of Large Firms

Among Indonesia's largest conglomerates hit hard by 'krismon', none has been more important than the Salim group. With more than 100 companies, this conglomerate was among the biggest debtors of the Indonesian Bank Restructuring Agency (IBRA). Among its interests were 25 oil palm plantations totalling 267,776 ha, claimed to be the largest area of oil palm in the world planted by one enterprise (Jakarta Post 2001c). The plantations, scattered across Sumatra, Kalimantan and Sulawesi, have recently been sold to a Malaysian firm, Guthrie Bhd, despite protests from a number of sources. Some members of the parliament believed that the land was undervalued and that the entire process had not been conducted openly. In Malaysia, some observers believed that Guthrie had bid too much for the plantations, as 44 per cent of the land was not yet planted. Others argued that it was a sensible move, as land and wage costs were three times higher in Malaysia. One Malaysian industry executive commented 'It's prime land and very, very cheap' (Jayasankaran and Dhume 2001, 45). Authorities in Riau, site of a number of the plantations, were annoyed that they had not been consulted. The then Vice-President Megawati complained that the Salim Group had previously agreed to sell 70 per cent of the land to local farmers. The farmers, operating small plots of oil palm on the estates, have been uncertain of their future. Guthrie has indicated that they envisage no problems with the smallholders, who will continue working on the estates and will receive 10 per cent of the land (New Straits Times 2001). About 57 per cent of the crop is immature and in dire need of refinancing, while wages need to be paid to 43,000 employees (Business Times 2001). This sale gives Malaysian interests an even bigger share of Indonesia's oil palm area than they previously controlled (now about 1.6m ha or 54 per cent) (Casson 2000a, Appendices 2, 3).

Other oil palm companies with multiple holdings, such as PT Bakhrie Sumatra Plantation, and PT London Sumatra ('LonSum'), continue to post large losses, despite attempts at restructuring. They blame low commodity prices and the weakening rupiah, which has increased their international liabilities (Krisna Maharani 2001; Jakarta Post 2001f). LonSum's plantation in Kutai, East Kalimantan, centre of protracted disputes with local people, lies abandoned. The trees are bearing fruit, which is simply rotting as there is no processing plant. The company has no funds to build one and there is no other factory in the district. Members of a local cooperative who had purchased land from the company to plant oil palm see their investment as now useless. In desperation they are looking to the local district leader to solve their problems (Casson 2000b). The pulp and paper giants, Indah Kiat Pulp and Paper (part of the Sinar Mas conglomerate) and Riau Andalan Pulp and Paper (belonging to Raja Garuda Mas) are equally cash strapped and heavily in debt (Barr 2000). Sinar Mas owes US$11.6 billion, one third of which is pulp and paper debt (Soraya Permatasari 2001). There are many negative impacts of the liabilities of such large firms on both the environment within which they operate and on local people, which will be analysed further in the Riau case study.

Performance of the Rupiah

Once the currency had recovered from its battering in mid-1998, it entered a period of relative stability during the following two years, with rates to the US dollar being around Rp7,500 to Rp8,500. This provided reasonably cheap exports from Indonesia but high costs for imported components. From August 2000 the rupiah's value began to slide again, and it has been above Rp9,000 to the dollar since December, reaching Rp11,642 in May 2001 and Rp11,350 in June (WHO International Exchange Rates). This monetary instability is largely a result of political uncertainties regarding the future of the Wahid Government. Given the low international prices prevailing for most of Indonesia's agricultural commodity exports, it might provide some breathing space for farmers. Domestic demand for commodities such as palm oil-based cooking oil has dropped, however, as purchasing power has been eroded with the continuing slide in the rupiah (Derom Bangun 2001).

Globalisation and Commodity Prices

World prices for a number of agricultural commodities have not been in Indonesia's favour during the past two years and several have continued to trend downwards. Crude palm oil averaged only US$247 per metric ton in the first quarter of 2001, compared with $344 in the corresponding period of 2000 (and over $700 during 1998) (Figure 1). Robusta coffee went from an average of 109 to 69 US cents per kilogram between 2000 and 2001, while rubber dropped from 69 to 59 cents (World Bank, 2001a).[6] These kinds of prices are bad news indeed for many farmers in Sumatra, where these commodities are of great importance. Because of the fluctuations in the rupiah and the transaction chains between the farm gate and the eventual point of sale, prices at the farm gate will reflect these trends, but will be enhanced when the rupiah is low and decline when the currency recovers.

In seeking 'painless' strategies to tide itself over the present difficulties, Malaysia has been burning palm oil as fuel to reduce stocks and engaging in a massive replanting programme (*Jakarta Post* 2001d; *Business Times* 2001). The King of Thailand is promoting palm oil mixed with diesel as fuel for motor vehicles (BBC 2001). Despite some discussion over the use of CPO as fuel, Indonesia has not adopted any of those initiatives, though replanting is a looming problem for the older, government-owned estates. It has agreed to join with Malaysia in joint marketing efforts to counter competition from soybean. Attempts to stockpile coffee among all major world producers to force up prices have not been successful. One way out for coffee is to seek new markets. In Indonesia, coffee is scarcely drunk by poor people: were living conditions to improve, such a market might be developed locally. Against those trends, cocoa prices, after falling in 1999 and 2000, have begun to rise again (ICCO 2001). In Sulawesi, the main centre of cocoa production, the fear is that yields will be reduced very considerably as a result of pests, especially the pod-borer, which has been spreading through the island, despite efforts to halt it. Many growers will thus be unlikely to benefit from the price rise.

Levels of Poverty and Well-Being

All studies have indicated increased poverty as a result of the economic crisis, the main arguments being about the ways of measuring poverty and the levels reached, which have varied enormously (Booth 1999). Booth acknowledges the impact of high earnings from export crops during the 'boom' in reducing rural poverty, but suggests that these were to some extent offset by rapid increases in the costs of basic foodstuffs, especially rice. Poverty lines in Indonesia are based on consumption of food and other basic commodities. One interesting new paper (Suryahadi and Sumarto 2001) introduces the concepts of 'chronic' and 'transient' poverty, and identifies those households 'vulnerable' to poverty. 'Transient' poverty refers to those just above the poverty line, who could easily fall below it, while those in 'chronic' poverty are below the line. 'Vulnerability' to poverty is the risk that a household will become poor in the near future, where its consumption levels are quite variable. The general conclusions, comparing chronic and transient poverty and vulnerability between 1996 and 1999, were that poverty had definitely increased, especially in rural areas (up from 20.4 to 34.5 per cent), while urban poverty rose from 7 per cent to 16.8 per cent. Vulnerability had also increased, from 23.8 per cent to 42.5 per cent in rural areas. Across regions, while poverty remained highest in Eastern Indonesia (Papua, East Nusa Tenggara), in 1999 Lampung had 38 per cent of its population 'poor' and a high 48 per cent 'vulnerable'. Comparable figures in 1996 were 17.3 per cent and 20 per cent. This is an enormous increase and partly reflects the geographical position of Lampung, the southernmost province of Sumatra and a short ferry ride from Java. The province has received large numbers of Javanese, both as transmigrants in earlier times, and now as 'overflow' of displaced people from Java and Jakarta. The provinces from which case studies are drawn in the second half of this chapter (Riau, South Sumatra and South Sulawesi) tended to have moderate to low levels of both poverty and vulnerability in 1999, but all showed big increases in these measures since 1996 (Figure 2).

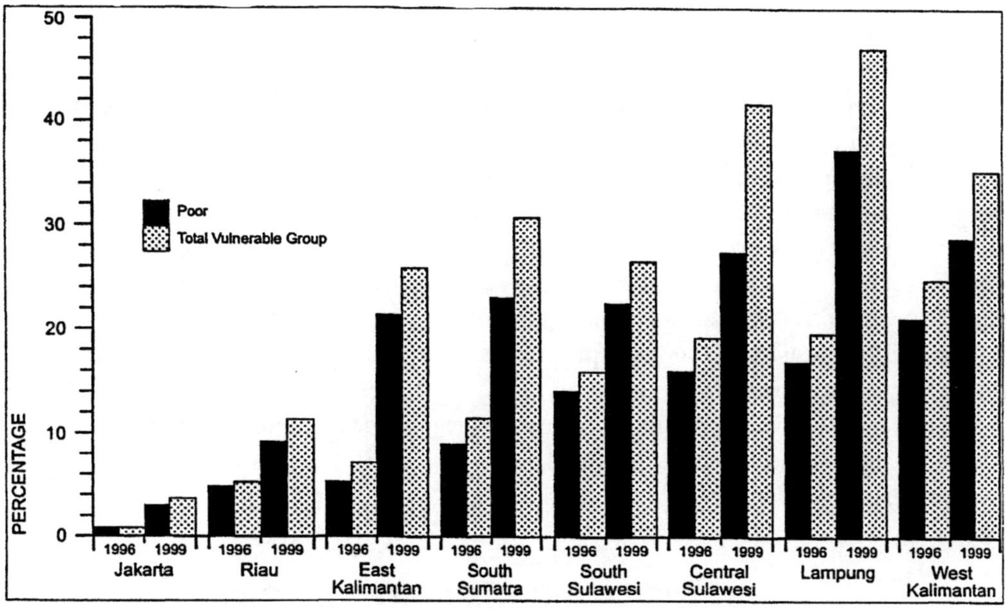

Source: Asep Suryahadi and Sudarmo Sumarto (2001)

Figure 2: Measures of the 'poor' and the 'vulnerable' by province, selected provinces 1996 and 1999

Concepts such as 'vulnerability' emphasise the changing nature of poverty and the fact that households can go into and out of poverty quite quickly. This can certainly happen to households exposed to global commodity prices, especially if they are specialising in only one kind of commodity.

IMPACTS OF THE POLITICAL CRISIS

Reformation and Breakdown of the Rule of Law

Local people throughout Indonesia have been happy to shake off the authoritarian structures of the Suharto period. They are no longer fearful of repercussions from the police or the army when they openly defy regulations they had long felt to be unjust. For example, land once belonging to villages was taken by the Suharto regime and classified 'protected forest', to which the villagers had no legal access. People argue that they had never approved this transfer, so that if they now take the land back, that is only righting a wrong. They also argue that they need the land in order to grow food. Many have the same argument about land now occupied by large companies producing oil palm or pulpwood. Villagers claim that they were cajoled or bullied into surrendering the land which should now be returned. There is increasing anarchy in rural districts, especially those with large numbers of estates or with national parks or protected forests. To date, there have been no effective controls put into place to counter these tendencies.

Regional Autonomy

In a title to a recent paper, Wihana Kirana Jaya and Howard Dick have referred to regional autonomy as 'the latest crisis' (Wihana and Dick 2001). While they do not justify their use of the term 'crisis', they argue that under the new decentralised system, the central government is mainly interested in removing the power of the provinces, rather than giving up its own power. If responsibility is devolved to the districts, which are weaker and still largely dependent on the centre for funding, then the latter can still wield a great deal of influence. McLeod (2000) has a similar argument. These statements are of interest, especially as Megawati Sukarnoputri, who has replaced Wahid as President, has stated several times that she does not approve of regional autonomy. The new system is undoubtedly still in its infancy and the big question of controlling some activities of local populations has scarcely been tackled. Any attempt to dismantle regional autonomy at this stage is likely, however, to meet with local resistance.

IMPACTS OF THE CRISIS ON EXPORT CROP AGRICULTURE: CASE STUDIES

Oil Palm and Rubber in Riau

Riau province in Central Sumatra is now Indonesia's leader in its area of oil palm planted, though not yet in CPO production, as much is still immature.[7] There are three basic arrangements under which the crop is produced: on older government-owned estates, with transmigrant (usually Javanese) smallholders; on private estates, with or without smallholders, some of whom may be local; and in independent cooperatives of local smallholders. All smallholders working on estates must use specified amounts of fertiliser, the price of which has tripled since the crisis. Prices for their fruit are set by estate factories, so they find themselves squeezed. If independent smallholders try to reduce fertiliser application on Riau's poor soils, their yields and the quality of their fruit are likely to suffer. Estate factories can refuse to process poor quality fruit.

The industry is currently beset by disputes between private estates and local communities. The origin of some of these disputes relates back to the efforts of companies to establish themselves in particular districts, especially to obtain access to adequate amounts of land.[8] Procedures with which companies have had to comply to receive their planting licences have been slow, complicated and centralised. Estate management would often try to short-circuit the process by making 'deals' with local leaders. They usually failed to negotiate adequately with village interests and would at times resort to intimidation to secure land. Village efforts to reclaim such land since *reformasi*, or even to force 'rogue' companies to leave the province, have not so far been successful. Sporadic violence and theft of fruit continue.[9] Despite the present low prices of palm oil products, local people still want to grow the 'golden crop'. They would prefer not to do it through the estates but to organise cooperatives, a move supported by district officials. However, smallholders so far are still dependent on the large estates for processing their fruit. What is lacking is a system of independent 'mini-factories', which cooperatives could use for processing. With the prevailing low prices and deteriorating road surfaces in many areas, estate factories will sometimes refuse to collect fruit from smallholders, as they argue that it is uneconomic for them to do so (Potter and Badcock 2001b).

Rubber is grown in more remote parts of the province, particularly in the south. Some swidden cultivators from the minority Talang Mamak group, who live inside and around the boundaries of the Bukit Tigapuluh National Park, have only recently begun planting the crop in their fallows. Farmers who have been in the industry longer find themselves with more land in production, but in debt to rubber buyers who supply them with basic food and other goods. When more than one kilogram of rubber is needed to pay for a kilo of rice, they are in a losing situation.[10] The low returns from rubber have led them to look for alternative crops and they perceive oil palm to be the answer. Much oil palm has been planted on old rubber land, but more is replacing forest. Villagers are being encouraged to sell off their traditional forests for a small return by operators connected to urban interests, who loan them chainsaws and heavy machinery. The theory is that the deforested lands will be turned into oil palm cooperatives, but this is not guaranteed, as farmers need capital for such ventures. Selling timber is a useful source of much needed ready cash, so people are tempted into cutting their forests (Potter and Badcock 2001a).

Coffee in South Sumatra

The hilly lands in the south of South Sumatra and extending into Lampung have traditionally been used to plant coffee, often on steep slopes. Erosion can be severe when new gardens are being established, but this declines once the trees have grown. Many systems exist with various combinations of coffee and different shade or fruit trees, sometimes developing into complex agroforests with multiple layers of trees. Most coffee grown is *robusta*, with the better-priced *arabica* on higher ground. Several local ethnic groups are involved, together with Javanese. All have different systems, the Javanese often working as tenants or share croppers. In the boom period, many local farmers opened extra coffee land. Now they are unable to pay for its management, so hire share croppers to assist them (spraying one hectare with weedicides, for example, costs Rp300,000 and must be done four times per year). During the 1998 boom, prices for coffee were up to Rp17,000 per kilo: they are now only Rp2,000 to Rp3,000, which is below the cost of production.[11] Farmers would like to diversify into other crops, especially pepper, but are hampered by lack of access to credit. They cannot afford to buy fertiliser, using instead the husks from the coffee berries, but yields tend to be low (1 to 2 tonnes per hectare). Many children have been forced to leave school to help their parents with the crop – that is, those who remain in the district. In one village, almost all the able-bodied adults were away working elsewhere. Farmers noted that petty crime had increased: they no longer kept many chickens, as they feared they would be stolen. There were complaints that government response to the situation has been quite inadequate; a few pepper seedlings have been supplied, but farmers really need credit and advice on suitable alternatives (fieldwork, March 2001, Lahat and Muara Enim districts).

Cocoa in Sulawesi

Cocoa has been the dominant crop in Central, South and Southeast Sulawesi since about 1989, with an especially rapid rate of expansion after 1995. It is almost entirely a smallholder crop, which, tradition has it, was brought to Sulawesi by migrants who had worked on cocoa estates in Sabah.[12] The high prices prevailing in 1998 brought a further rush to put land under cocoa. Critics observed, however, that there was inadequate care of the crop during the boom period. Farmers were too busy enjoying themselves, 'building new houses and buying electronic goods' (Lewa Pardomuan 1999). Erosion was reducing soil fertility, yields were low and the preparation of the harvest for market, especially fermentation, was considered inadequate. As the price of cocoa declined in 1999, some growers began to seek alternatives, such as cloves, but most stayed with cocoa. Costs of fertiliser and insecticide also rose, so their application was reduced.[13] A major concern was the spread of the pod-borer. That worm-like pest recently migrated from Central to South and Southeast Sulawesi and has been estimated to be increasing its coverage of the cocoa lands by 25 per cent each year. Some observers were already predicting losses of 20-30 per cent in South Sulawesi and even higher in Central, totalling $1 billion per year (Mackay 2000). A low cost strategy has been recommended to stop the advance by regular pruning (to break the life cycle of the pest), with composting and frequent and regular harvesting to stimulate pod production. This has the added advantage of providing a regular income for growers. US-funded development agency ACDI/VOCA plans to spend $1 million to train 20,000 smallholders in these techniques (*Jakarta Post* 2001b).

Despite the problems, people are keen to plant cocoa. As one observer writes from Polmas in South Sulawesi: 'What is really interesting is the tenacity with which people are adopting the crop: no matter what the condition or suitability of the land, cocoa is being planted. The lure of the weekly cash income is so strong' (Branford-Bowd 2001).

IMPACTS ON FORESTS AND FOREST PEOPLE (CASE STUDIES FROM RIAU)

Fibre Demands of Pulp and Paper Companies

Riau province is in the unique position of having two large pulp and paper companies within its boundaries, Indah Kiat and RAPP. Both these firms are part of heavily indebted conglomerates (Sinar Mas and Raja Garuda Mas), which have invested in enormous capacity for their pulp and paper operations, so are looking for ways to make the highest profits while at the same time cutting expenditure. Unfortunately for Riau's forests, the cheapest source of fibre to feed the mills is 'mixed tropical hardwood', or timber from natural forests. Although both companies have plantation programs using fast-growing *Acacia mangium*, only about one million m^3 is being used so far from plantation sources, all by Indah Kiat. The annual fibre demand of the two companies is estimated at 11 million m^3. The maximum annual outturn of *legal* timber from Riau's forests has been calculated to be 6 million m^3, the total demand for wood around 16 million m^3 (Dephutbun 1999). Barr's comment is apt for the Riau situation: 'To date, Indonesia's pulp mills have relied heavily on unsustainable, and in many cases, illegal sources of fiber, much of which is obtained through the clear-cutting of natural forests' (Barr 2000, 2). While theoretically both companies control sufficient land to meet their requirements from plantations in another few years, in reality this is unlikely. Their planting programs are behind schedule, and the economic crisis set them back further. The plantations themselves are exposed to claims from local interests and some have been burned (Potter and Badcock 2001b). Because the companies continue to rely on natural timber, this is tacit encouragement to illegal loggers to provide it, and to the companies to turn a blind eye to its origins. It has been estimated that all legal supplies of mixed tropical hardwood within an economic distance of the mills will be gone by 2005 (Jaako Poyry, quoted in Barr 2000). One may only conclude that the presence of these two mills spells disaster for Riau's forests, although the companies provide employment for thousands of workers. For district administrations, such companies are virtually beyond control. To date they have provided no local taxes, their taxes continuing to be received by the central government.

'Illegal' Logging and Sawmilling: The Organisers and the Participants

As in other provinces, 'illegal' logging is booming in Riau. This has come about partly because the market for all kinds of timber is so huge, because timber provides cash income to families suffering as a result of the crisis (especially from low rubber prices), and because there is a hunger among ordinary people to benefit from previously forbidden forests. Aside from the demand from the pulp and paper plants, numbers of sawmills, many of them illegal, process logs for sale as sawn timber. Markets are in the capital, Pekanbaru, in the cities of nearby provinces, and in Java. Much of this timber comes from 'village forests', which local people claim as their own. Technically most still fall under forestry department jurisdiction or form part of an abandoned timber concession. They are supported by 'operators', urban or local entrepreneurs who provide them with machinery to expedite clearing. They are sometimes encouraged to cut new roads and move the machines into other forested areas, such as national parks. The insidious aspect of these activities is that everybody benefits, even if on a small scale. Local administrators themselves, including forestry department employees, are often involved and will drop in at sawmills for 'petrol money'. Police stop logging trucks along the roads, but let them pass after receiving payment. Controlling illegal and unsustainable forest conversion presents huge challenges for the newly autonomous districts (Potter and Badcock 2001b).

Encroachment on Parks and Protected Areas

These encroachments can go as far as the complete clearing of a forest, or they can take the more usual form of a gradual removal of valuable resources, such as marketable timber, rattan and other non-wood products, and poaching of aquarium fish and animals, especially the Sumatran tiger. While economic need may be claimed for some of these incursions, with genuinely poor local people involved, others are well organised, their major beneficiaries more likely to be outsiders, sometimes from outside the province.

In one case of a 'protection' forest which suffered complete destruction, but victory for traditional claimants, the situation is complex. Bukit Betabuh forest lay in steep country athwart the border between Riau and West Sumatra. On the West Sumatra side, it was not classified as protection forest, and in 1998 was being worked by illegal loggers, who, perhaps unknowingly, crossed over into Riau and began removing trees. When this incursion was noted and no government sanctions were forthcoming, local villagers, who claimed the forest as traditional land, began invading it and clearing small plots for rubber and food crops. They then began a lengthy process of negotiation to obtain the land legally, but in the interim, the forest was regarded as no longer 'off-limits' and many others arrived to engage in an orgy of logging. A belated government attempt to seize chainsaws resulted in the burning of the forestry post. The process was described by one forestry officer as 'the euphoria of reformation'. In this case the people were permitted to keep their rubber plots and the land has been re-classified as a 'social forest', but there is scarcely a tree remaining. With its poor, stony and eroding soils, the re-establishment of a tree cover in Bukit Betabuh is obviously a priority.

Coping Strategies of Households during Economic Crisis

There are similarities in behaviour among the small farmers in the two sets of case studies discussed above. When prices of export crops fall, they will attempt to cut costs by using family labour (if necessary taking children out of school), reducing inputs such as fertiliser, and sometimes leaving the district, either permanently or seasonally, to seek work in the towns. There are cases of people walking off their land in the coffee belt of South Sumatra, or selling out to urban buyers. These strategies will have a negative impact on the development of the districts concerned, because they perpetuate a low yielding, impermanent type of farming and eventually absentee ownership. On the other hand, farmers now recognise the advantage of mixed cultivation, hence their search for pepper seedlings. In Sulawesi there has also been experimentation with other crops and crop combinations. People saw the low labour demands of cocoa as an advantage, but they are now realising that defeating the pod-borer requires more attention to be given to cocoa cultivation. In neither region has there been much help forthcoming from government agencies: people have basically been left to work out their own solutions. Provided that the project being set up by ACDI/VOCA works well, an opportunity has been provided to place the Sulawesi cocoa industry on a sounder footing. The enthusiasm of the Sulawesi cocoa-growers for their crop is matched by the 'oil palm fever' (*demam sawit*) which has gripped the southern districts of Riau. Village forests are being exchanged for a future in oil palm which may never eventuate. People believe, perhaps mistakenly, that this crop will solve all problems, so they are willing to take the risk. Meanwhile the sale of timber is providing cash to satisfy immediate needs to an extent that rubber cannot match. Such behaviour reflects the 'frontier' mentality of so much that is happening in Riau.

CONCLUSION

This paper has explored the triple crises which have affected Indonesia – economic, ecological and political – particularly from the point of view of smallholder farmers growing export crops in Sumatra, Sulawesi and Kalimantan. The conclusion is that those farmers who escaped the economic crisis in 1998 have now found it catching up with them, mainly as a result of low global commodity prices. If these low prices encourage mixed farming systems, instead of monocultures, then that will be a useful outcome. Despite the downturn, farmers are placing their hopes on cocoa and oil palm, with coffee and rubber financially unviable at present. While local people in those provinces are generally not 'chronically poor', they may be vulnerable to poverty, as their consumption patterns become more variable as a result of globalisation. The impacts of the economic crisis include the heavy levels of debt incurred by large rural conglomerates. These have proved problematic, both in their effects on the environment (especially the forests) and on local people. The political crisis has spawned the culture of '*reformasi*', with people now being brave enough to challenge existing laws and boundaries, and to stake claims to government forests and company lands alike. A big challenge to regional administrations will be to meet the legitimate aspirations of the people while being able to restore the rule of law against the forces of anarchy.

REFERENCES

Akcaya (Pontianak daily newspaper) (1999) 'Pemda Ketapang nyatakan perang terhadap hama belalang' ('Ketapang administration declares war on grasshoppers'). April 9.

Angelsen, A., and I.A.P. Resosudarmo (1999) '*Krismon*, Farmers and Forests: The Effects of the Economic Crisis on Farmers' Livelihoods and Forest Use in the Outer Islands of Indonesia'. Unpublished manuscript, Center for International Forestry Research (CIFOR), Bogor, May.

Barr, C. (2000) 'Profits on Paper: The Political-Economy of Fiber, Finance and Debt in Indonesia's Pulp and Paper Industries'. Forthcoming chapter in Christopher Barr, *Banking on Sustainability: A Critical Assessment of Structural Adjustment in Indonesia's Forest and Estate Crop Industries*. CIFOR and WWF, Macroeconomics Program Office (November).

BBC (2001) May 31.

Booth, A. (1999) 'The Impact of the Crisis on Poverty and Equity'. In H.W. Arndt and H. Hill, eds, *Southeast Asia's Economic Crisis: Origins, Lessons and the Way Forward.* Melbourne: Allen and Unwin.

Branford-Bowd, R. (2001) Personal Communication April 17.

Bisnis Indonesia (2001) July 12.

Business Times (Malaysia) (2001) 'Guthrie Said to Have Started Payment on Indon Estates'. June 13.

Casson, A. (2000a) *The Hesitant Boom: Indonesia's Oil Palm Sub-Sector in an Era of Economic Crisis and Political Change*. Occasional Paper No. 29, Center for International Forestry Research, Bogor.

—— (2000b) 'Decentralization of Policy Making and the Administration of Policies Affecting Forests in Kutai Barat, East Kalimantan'. Draft report to CIFOR, October

Denny, C., and A. Bellos (2001) 'Burning Issues for Coffee Growers'. *Guardian* May 15.

Derom Bangun (2001) 'Palm Oil Production to Dip This Year'. *Jakarta Post* March 30; March 31.

Dephutbun (Kantor Wilayah Kehutanan dan Perkebunan) (Department of forestry and estate crops) (1999) *Potensi dan distribusi sumberdaya kehutanan dan perkebunan di daerah Kabupatan/Kota Se-Propinsi Riau (Potential and distribution of the resources of forestry and estate crops in the districts/towns of Riau Province*). Pekanbaru: Kantor Wilayah Propinsi Riau Departemen Kehutanan dan Perkebunan.

Evans, K. (1998) 'Survey of Recent Developments'. *Bulletin of Indonesian Economic Studies* 34: 3.

Gerard, F., and F. Ruf, eds (2001) *Agriculture in Crisis: People, Commodities and Natural Resources in Indonesia, 1996-2000*. Richmond: Curzon Press.

Goenner, C. (1998) 'Forest Fires in Kecamatan Jempang, Kutai: Some Observations from the Field'. *Report for SFMP (Promotion of sustainable forest management systems in East Kalimantan) and GTZ.*

ICCO (International Cocoa Organization) (2001) 'ICCO Monthly and Annual Averages of Daily Prices of Cocoa Beans, 1971-2001' *<http://www.icco.org/prices>*

Indonesian Observer (2001) 'Locals Burn Truck Fully Loaded with CPO'. May 20.

INRO (International Rubber Organization) (2001) 'Daily Market Indicator Price, Monthly Averages Oct 1980-March 2001' *<http://www.jaring.my/inro/dmip.html>*

Jakarta Post (1999) 'Indonesian Pepper Exports Predicted to Drop 40 Per Cent'. July 29.

—— (2000) 'IBRA to Sell Salim's Oil Palm Plantations Soon'. November 25.

—— (2001a) 'Indonesia Tops World's Pepper Exports'. January 17.

—— (2001b) 'U.S. Grants $1 Million to Combat Cocoa Pest'. February 1.

—— (2001c) Feburary 14.

—— (2001d) March 31.

—— (2001e) 'Pepper Farmers Laughing Their Way to the Bank'. May 2.

—— (2001f) 'BSP Takes Hit on Low Commodity Prices'. June 21.

Jayasankaran, S., and Sadanand Dhume (2001) 'Malaysia: Betting the Farm'. *Far Eastern Economic Review* April 26.

Kompas (1999) 'Belalang juga menyerang Lampung dan Sumba Barat' ('Grasshoppers Also Attack Lampung and West Sumba'). July 15.

Mackay, I. (2000) 'Proceedings from the Sustainable Cocoa Production Workshop'. Makassar June 13-14 (summary).

Maharani, Krisna (2001) 'London Sumatera rugi Rp141.9 M' (London Sumatra Loses Rp141.9 billion). *Detikcom* June 6.

McLeod, R. (2000) 'Survey of Recent Developments'. *Bulletin of Indonesian Economic Studies* 36: 2.

New Straits Times (2001) 'Guthrie Plans to Refinance Bridging Loan'. June 28.

Oil World (1998) 'Insufficient World Supplies of Palm Oil'. December 11.

—— (2000) 'Monthly Crude Palm Oil Prices and Competitiveness cif Rotterdam'. 43: 51/52.

Pardomuan, Lewa (1999) 'Rains Seen Cutting Jakarta Cocoa Output by 30 Per Cent' *<http://www.expressindia.com>* July 26.

Permatasari, Soraya (2001) 'Indonesia Says Will Pressure Sinar Mas on Debts'. *Reuters* March 30.

Potter, L. (2000) 'Rural Livelihoods and the Environment at a Time of Uncertainty: The Situation Outside Java'. In C. Manning and P. van Diermen, eds, *Indonesia in Transition: Social Aspects of Reformasi and Crisis*. Singapore: ISEAS.

Potter, L., and J. Lee (1999) *Oil Palm in Indonesia: Its Role in Forest Conversion and the Fires of 1997/98*. Jakarta: WWF Indonesia.

Potter, L., and S. Badcock (2001a) '*Reformasi* and Riau's Forests'. *Inside Indonesia* Jan-March.

—— (2001b) 'The Effect of Indonesia's Decentralisation on Forests and Estate Crops: Case Study Of Riau Province, The Original Districts of Kampar and Indragiri Hulu'. *Report to CIFOR* (June).

Ruf, F., and P. Ehret (1996) 'Why a Cocoa Boom in Sulawesi?'. In W. Clarence-Smith, ed., *Cocoa Pioneer Fronts Since 1800: the Role of Smallholders, Planters and Merchants*. London: MacMillan.

Ruf, F., and Yoddang (2001a) 'Cocoa Migrants from Boom to Bust'. In Gerard and Ruf, *Agriculture in Crisis*.

—— (2001b) 'From Migration to Motorisation: How Market Liberalisation Has Benefitted Coffee Farmers'. In Gerard and Ruf, *Agriculture in Crisis*.

Ruf, F., Yoddang and Waris Ardhy (2001) 'Transmigrants and the Cocoa Windfall: "Paradise is Here, Not in Bali"'. In Gerard and Ruf, *Agriculture in Crisis*.

Straits Times (Singapore) (1999) 'Aceh Violence Hurts Coffee Production'. October 8.

Suara Pembaruan (1998) 'Kakao komoditas penyalamat petani Kolaka di masa Krismon' (Cocoa the commodity which saves Kolaka farmers in the time of the monetary crisis.) December 26.

Sunderlin, W., A. Angelsen, I.A.P. Resosudarmo, Ahmad Dermawan and Edy Rianto (2001) 'Economic Crisis, Small Farmer Well-Being, and Forest Cover Change in Indonesia'. *World Development* 29: 5.

Suryahadi, Asep, and Sudarno Sumarto (2001) 'The Chronic Poor, the Transient Poor and the Vulnerable in Indonesia Before and After the Crisis'. *Working Paper from the SMERU Research Institute*, Jakarta, May.

Wetterberg, A., Sudarno Sumarto and Lant Pritchett (1999) 'A National Snapshot of the Social Impact of Indonesia's Crisis'. *Bulletin of Indonesian Economic Studies* 35: 3.

Wihana, Kirana Jaya and H. Dick (2001) 'The Latest Crisis of Regional Autonomy in Historical Perspective'. In G. Lloyd and S. Smith, eds, *Indonesia Today: Challenges of History*. Singapore: ISEAS.

WHO International Exchange Rates *<http://whqmarcopolo.who.int/exchrate/ExRetrieve.asp>*

World Bank (2001a) *Indonesia: Environment and Natural Resource Management in a Time of Transition*. Washington, DC: The World Bank.

World Bank (2001b) 'Commodity Price Data Pinksheet – April 2001' *http://www.world bank.org*.

ENDNOTES

[1] 'Krismon' is a common Indonesian acronym for 'Krisis monetar', the economic or monetary crisis.

[2] Fruit must be processed within 24 hours of picking, or it will spoil.

[3] Ruf and Yoddang, however, noted increased spending on fertiliser among cocoa farmers (Ruf and Yoddang, 2001).

[4] The exception is pepper, which continues to reward its growers handsomely. At its peak in 1998, the price of a kilogram of pepper was Rp90,000, a huge increase over Rp4,000 to Rp6,000 a year earlier. Current prices are around Rp20,000 (*Jakarta Post* 2 May 2001). However, increased production in Indonesia (which accounts for 30 per cent of the world's supply) and in Vietnam, were expected eventually to lead to a decline (*Jakarta Post* 17 January 2001).

[5] Global over-production, especially the entry of Vietnam as a large producer, together with a huge stockpile, is the reason for the slide in coffee prices to a 30-year low. In the case of palm oil, competition from soya and other vegetable oils in some of palm oil's main markets, such as India, seems to be the problem.

[6] These figures for rubber refer to Singapore prices, which is the standard now used, in preference to Malaysian.

[7] Oil palm needs at least three years to begin to fruit and around five years to become fully productive.

[8] 5000 ha is needed for a viable operation which supports its own processing plant.

[9] In one recent confrontation, an attempt was made by a village to charge vehicles of one infamous company Rp5 million per month for the use of village roads. When the company refused to pay (claiming 'pure extortion'), the truck and its load of CPO was burned (*Indonesian Observer* 20 May 2001).

[10] In July 1999, rubber was selling in the district at the extremely low price of Rp600 to Rp700 per kilo. By April 2000 it had risen to Rp1300-Rp1600, still only half the cost of a kilo of rice (fieldwork).

[11] In this area, rice costs Rp2,500 per kilo, cooking oil Rp3,000 and sugar Rp4,000 (fieldwork, March 2001).

[12] Both Toraja and Bugis claim that it was their people who brought cocoa from Sabah to Sulawesi (Potter, 2000), but Ruf and Yoddang (2001a) and Ruf and Ehret (1996) mention only the Bugis.

[13] It should be noted that Ruf and Yoddang (2001a) did not find a reduction in fertiliser use, nor a neglect of cocoa holdings in their study area.

Chapter 16

THE INDONESIAN MULTI-LAYERED CRISIS AND ITS IMPACT ON WELLBEING

Sri Moertiningsih Adioetomo[1]
Director of the Demographic Institute
Faculty of Economics
University of Indonesia

1. INTRODUCTION

The Indonesian economic crisis dates from 4 August 1997, when the Central Bank released its control over the value of the rupiah. The foreign exchange rate fluctuated significantly. The price of the rupiah plummeted from Rp2,316 per US dollar before the crisis, to Rp16,000 in early 1998, when Dr. Habibie was appointed President. It then stabilised at Rp7,000 during 1999, but then rose to Rp9,550 by the end of 2000. The fluctuations were a response not only to the economic situation, but also to the political and social unrest following the fall of Suharto. The price of basic needs skyrocketed, especially during the first year of the crisis, and when the government increased the electricity tariff in April 2000 and released the oil subsidy in October 2000. While there was optimism that the crisis would be over quickly, it continued well into the new millennium.

This chapter attempts to summarise the major impacts of the crisis on the Indonesian community. The impacts have been substantial and it is suggested that the crisis should be conceptualised as being multi-layered. It utilises a range of data sources to assess the effects of the crisis on living costs, poverty, health and nutrition, education, fertility, employment, retrenchment and also discusses some of the effects of the crisis from the perspective of gender.

2. General Impacts of the Crisis

The political crisis came to a head with severe riots in Jakarta and other cities in May 1998, leading to considerable loss of life and destruction of property. Suharto finally stepped down and was replaced by Habibie, while the IMF disbursed some of the agreed US$6 billion to rescue the Indonesian economy. The deterioration caused by the fluctuations in the exchange rate and the crisis of confidence *(krisis kepercayaan)* has affected the entire society. However, the effects have been different for different regions and different groups. Regions with natural resources or where agricultural exports are booming as a result of the devaluation of the rupiah have done well and in some cases they have demanded greater autonomy, as have others with longstanding political grievances against the central government.

The euphoria of democracy following the downfall of Suharto led to demonstrations and protests opposing corruption and demanding good governance. There was also an invasion of farmland or golf courses claimed to have been wrongfully expropriated from their owners, as well as looting of grain godowns and fishponds. This continued even after President Abdurrahman Wahid was elected. The social unrest was worsened by political conflict among the elite. This led to further deterioration of the general wellbeing of the population, including the fear of bomb blasts for which nobody claimed responsibility.

The weaker rupiah has led to a high inflation rate and reduced purchasing power, especially among the poor. From a base of 100 in 1996, by May 1998 the consumer price index increased to 183 for food, 168 for health, 138 for education and 147 for transport and communication. Overall the CPI increased to 157, meaning that prices have risen by an average of 50 per cent since the crisis began. The Central Bureau of Statistics estimated that the poverty line rose from Rp38,246 per capita per month for urban areas and Rp27,413 for rural areas in 1996 to Rp52,473 for urban and Rp41,558 for rural areas in 1998. Early estimates suggested that the number of people under these poverty lines increased from 11 per cent or 22 million people in 1996 to 40 per cent or 80 million people in 1998 (*Kompas* 1998). However, revised estimates using different measures and new data indicated the number of poor people was 49.5 million people or 24.23 per cent of the total population (BPS and UNDP 1999; Irawan 2000).

The depreciation of the value of the rupiah by five times caused the collapse of some manufacturing industries, bank and financial services, construction and property businesses. Businessmen and even the government have difficulty in obtaining working capital or opening letters of credit to import goods or raw materials because of a lack of confidence among foreign creditors about the ability of the Indonesian businessmen to repay debts. The soaring prices of imported raw materials prevented some manufacturers from obtaining them. This has led to low production and accordingly to displacement of labour or reduction of working hours, fringe benefits and other workers' compensation. Displacement of workers was also substantial following liquidation of banks and a decline in other supporting activities such as transportation, construction, trade and services. On the other hand, demand for goods and services was reduced due to declining purchasing power.

3. Government Responses

The crisis has had a serious impact on the government administration. By September 1998, the contraction in the economy was 16.5 per cent, leading to a drastic decline in government tax and other revenue. On the other hand, government expenditure increased drastically because of increasing prices, and a policy to subsidise prices of basic needs like fuel, education and drugs (including contraceptives).

Social Safety Nets (SSNs)

In coping with declining purchasing power, the government established some social safety nets. During the first year of the crisis, the government, supported by donor agencies, managed to allocate substantial funding to the social sector. This was embedded in the CRP (Community Recovery Program) and SPSDP (Social Protection Sector Development Scheme). These programs aimed to help directly the people in need. Detailed guidelines of activities to disburse the money were prepared. The CRP was initiated by the National Planning Bureau (BAPPENAS) and was supported financially by the World Bank, UNDP, CIDA and others, to rescue the most affected group, that is, the poor. Civil society led and coordinated the CRP and acted as the channel for distribution of the resources. CRP worked to alleviate poverty by providing short term assistance to those people unable to continue their daily social and economic activities because of the impact of the crisis. This was supposed to be implemented through: 1) proactively plugging gaps in the social safety net; 2) giving immediate response to poor communities most affected by the crisis; 3) establishing synergy between the civil society, government and the private sector in Indonesia, together with the international community, for improved response to needs. The CRP involved decentralisation of resources and decision-making processes, strong involvement of civil society, and transparency. The activities were focused on increasing food security, continuing the provision of social services (education, health, and family planning), and job creation and income generation. The CRP program was oriented toward helping women and children, the most vulnerable groups in the society affected by the crisis. The government developed varieties of social safety net schemes. Among others were: 1) the subsidised rice program (OPK rice program); 2) the SPSDP-scholarship and school block-grant; 3) the Health and Nutrition Sector Development program (HNSDP or JPS-BK); 4) the Labor intensive employment program.

In the fiscal year 1998-99, the OPK rice program (Special Price of Rice Program) was established to target poor families throughout Indonesia and was continued through the next fiscal year. The program aimed at assisting poor families to meet their fundamental needs, by providing 20 kg of rice per family every month at a subsidised price of Rp1000 per kg (the market price was Rp2500 per kg). A study of a sample of villages found that 80 per cent of families in the target area were receiving subsidised rice in December 1999 (Demographic Institute 2000). However, most of these families (93.1 per cent) did not receive the full amount of 20 kg of rice. Among other reasons for this was that some village headmen attempted to spread the rice over a larger number of families by reducing the ration. The second problem lies in the fact that many of the families could not afford to pay Rp20,000 at one time. Availability of cash was a problem in several areas. This program was expanded to cover the influx of internally displaced persons in East Nusatenggara and West Kalimantan. However, there were complaints about the poor implementation of the program and the low quality of the rice produced.

Another scheme called JPS-BK (social safety net for the health sector) aims at maintaining and improving health and nutrition, especially of the poor. This program contains two types of activities. Firstly, it provides direct services for the poor, which include: 1) basic health services; 2) basic obstetric gynaecology; 3) nutrition improvement services; 4) preventive and curative measures relating to communicable diseases; 5) referral services. The second supports: 1) stabilisation of the system to monitor the security of food and nutrition; 2) JPKM (insurance); 3) revitalisation of the *Posyandu* (village integrated health services); 4) socialisation of the program; 5) training for the providers. This program is being conducted by issuing health cards to poor families. About 39 per cent of the 10 million health cards (or 92 per cent of the target) produced during January-October 2000 have been utilised. In May 2000 pregnant mothers, delivering mothers, and post-natal mothers who were receiving basic maternal health services, reached 71 per cent, 49 per cent and 44 per cent respectively of the targets (Irawan *et al.* 2001). Like many other SSN programs, this one also suffered from difficulties in reaching the targeted people.

One concern at the onset of the crisis was that children may drop out of school to save money and to enter the workforce. To keep children in school and to increase their chances of continuing to higher education, a scholarship scheme was implemented. Block grants were given to the schools to manage their day-to-day operations. The individual scholarship was distributed to both boys and girls. However, since studies had found that when resources are scarce it is the boys who are given preference to continue schooling over girls, this program selectively favoured girls. The block grant (DBO school operational funds) is given to any public or private school with a minimum of 90 students for primary school, 60 for special school, and 60 for lower and upper secondary school. The amount of the block grant was Rp2 million for primary school, Rp4 million for lower secondary school and Rp10 million for upper secondary school. The use of this funding is limited to cover necessary expenses in running the school.

Research found that 89.1 per cent of reports on the implementation of the program matched the real situation. Hence between 87.2 and 94.05 per cent of the reported beneficiaries did actually receive the scholarship (Demographic Institute *et al.* 2000b). Some students who did not receive SSN funds said that the funds were used by the school to pay for overdue fees. The block grant seems to have been distributed effectively, with 99.8 per cent of the reported beneficiaries actually receiving grants to help in school operations.

A variety of public labour-intensive programs was also launched to help the people most affected by the crisis. These were targeted to poor and unemployed men and women. The public works program (*Padat Karya Program*), was designed to provide job opportunities for around 400,000 unemployed persons with an 80:20 male-female composition. Although this program was reported as successful by achieving 80 per cent of its disbursement, it was also criticised for mis-targeting beneficiaries (Irawan *et al.* 2001).

There are many other schemes designed to help the poor with employment creation, but a general problem lies with the lack of data that clearly indicates the location of the poor. Such data is greatly needed for timely and appropriate distribution of assistance to the target beneficiaries. The government of Indonesia immediately faced two major challenges: 1) lack of a systematic and effective social sector strategy to assist the poor with various crisis-affected problems; 2) non-existence of an early monitoring system relating to social concerns, notably in relation to the availability of reliable and timely poverty statistics – both at the aggregate and individual levels (Irawan *et al.* 2001).

4. The Impact of the Crisis on Indonesian Wellbeing

4.1 The Upsurge of the Consumer Price Index

The impact of the crisis on daily lives is seen in the rapid increase of the consumer price index (CPI). By May 1998, 9 months after the first indication of crisis, the overall CPI had increased to 157 compared with a base of 100 in 1996. This increased further to 205 in May 1999, remained somewhat stable during the rest of 1999, but again increased in late 2000 when it reached 217. Hence the crisis has had a prolonged impact on Indonesian living standards, with average prices of basic needs increasing to more than double compared with the situation before the crisis. The increase in the price of food impacted especially on the poor. During the first year of the crisis (up to June 1998) the price of food doubled and almost tripled during the first quarter of 1999. The CPI for food went down to 250 during the first year of Wahid's presidency, but then rose again after mid 2000 because of the increase in the electricity tariff and the abolition of the fuel subsidy in October 2000 as a condition of IMF funding (Table 1).

Table 1. Upsurge in Consumer Price Index, 1998- 2000

Items	May 1998	August 1998	Dec 1998	May 1999	August 1999	Dec 1999	May 2000	August 2000	Nov 2000
Overall	157	189	199	205	200	199	207	212	217
Food									
Staple food or cereals	167	275	306	293	278	306	255	258	251
Meats and other products	162	213	235	253	250	235	237	246	261
Fresh fish	151	199	227	269	264	227	261	268	263
Eggs, milk and other products	208	244	254	265	259	254	232	230	239
Herbs and spices	203	262	283	287	175	283	249	208	218
Fats and oils	216	276	237	252	218	237	207	203	193
Housing	137	154	159	164	165	159	174	177	183
Fuel, Electricity and Water	125	126	127	129	128	127	138	139	153
Clothing	176	226	220	230	226	220	243	247	250
Health services and drugs	152	161	172	182	187	172	196	198	202
Education	126	136	137	137	145	137	153	187	193
Books/stationery and other equipment	180	222	227	228	234	227	238	256	256
Transport cost	148	163	167	171	171	167	185	190	199
Vehicle spare parts and other supports	167	194	201	201	200	201	203	205	207

Source: BPS: *Warta IHK 44 Kota*, May and August 1998-1999.
BPS: *Indikator Ekonomi*, May, August, and November 2000.

Note : 1996=100

The cost of commodities which have a high import component (especially medical services and drugs) and clothing increased more than 2.5 times by the end of year 2000. Costs of education, transportation and housing also increased, but not as rapidly as those of other basic needs, the price of these commodities having doubled. During the era of the crisis, the value of the rupiah fluctuated widely. However, the prices of basic needs did not decrease but increased steadily until the end of 2000. This upsurge in price indices has caused suffering, especially among those who were already poor, and the new poor (those who slipped below the poverty line and those who were retrenched from work).

Housewives often suffer more than other family members. In Indonesia wives are often in charge of household expenditure. Husbands are expected to give their earnings to be managed by the wives (Adioetomo and Eggleston 1998). It is the women's responsibility to provide daily food and household services and even pay education, health and transport costs for the children. The declining purchasing power because of rapid price increases and the loss of income in cases where the breadwinner of the house has been laid-off is a real burden for the women.

Box 1: The Impact on the Daily Expenditure

Focus group discussions with a group of wives in a rural area in Krawang (West Java) and with a group of husbands with low incomes (Rp250,000-Rp300,000 a month) in urban fringe Jakarta (Depok) were conducted in June 1998. Similar patterns were found: before the crisis a family with two to four children normally spent about Rp5,000 on daily food including rice and meat (chicken). They even said that before the crisis they were still able to save money for emergencies. But after the crisis they had to spend Rp10,000 for daily food, often without being able to buy any source of protein. Beside rice, the increasing price of oil and other ingredients of cooking have made life more difficult. They said that if they were lucky (got an extra job) they were able to buy meat once a month. The price of other sources of protein, such as fish, eggs, tofu and soya bean cake, that were usually less expensive than the price of chicken, have doubled, and become unaffordable. The situation was even worse after August 1998 when the price of rice increased to Rp3,500-Rp4,000 per kilogram, which made families with a monthly income of Rp200,000 hardly able to survive.

The price of milk powder has increased 4 times because almost 100 per cent of its ingredients are imported. However, normally babies of these informants are breast-fed by their mothers, and when they are weaned, they are given adult food with no milk in their food intake. Only some informants in the urban areas said that they had stopped buying milk for their small children and replaced it with water. A serious impact was found from an in-depth interview in urban Jakarta. A family has to fast on Tuesdays, because it is the day when the husband is off from work. The husband works in a gas station with Rp200,000 monthly salary plus Rp10,000 daily expenses to cover his transport and lunch. But actually the whole family depends on this Rp10,000 to cover their daily food expenses.

Transport costs increased sharply so that parents are not able to give children extra pocket money; instead they must walk everywhere. But this increases their appetites, causing an increase in household consumption of rice. Most informants stated that education of children is very important and had to be continued. However, a wife in Jakarta said that her second daughter had not been able to continue to high school, because she had to pay Rp330,000 for entry at the Economic High School (SMEA). She added that the money has to go to the first child (also a girl) to finish her high school.

Cost of health and family planning services seems not to be a big issue for many people. This was because of the sporadic nature of these services. They still are able to borrow from relatives, friends and neighbours or from their office to meet such expenses. The women in Krawang said if they have no other source, they borrow from a money lender and pay interest. Most of the informants or informants' wives said they are using an injection to control fertility. Before the crisis they had to pay Rp5,000 to get the injection, but now the cost of the injection and its service is Rp10,000. When they had no money for the injection, they borrowed the money, or changed to the pill that is cheaper (Rp1,000 per strip). Most of the informants said that they tried carefully not to have more children because life would be even more difficult with more children. A husband from Depok said that they had no-one to borrow money from for re-injection so they abstained to avoid pregnancy. 'But not more than one week', they said.

4.2 Size, Structure, Composition and Trends of Poverty

Before the 1970s Indonesia was one of the world's poorest countries with income per capita of only US$50. It was estimated that 60 per cent or 70 million people lived under the poverty line. Development programs, especially agricultural intensification, introduced by the New Order Government from the early 1970s, was able to reduce the number of poor people to 33 per cent or 47.2 million people in 1978 (World Bank 1990), 22 per cent or 35 million people in 1984, and to 17.4 per cent or 30 million in 1987. This was paralleled by a decline in income inequality, and a decreasing number of malnourished people. The mean caloric intake increased annually by 6 per cent. In the 1990s, 27 million people (16 per cent) were considered to be poor, but before the crisis the population living under the poverty line declined to only 22 million people or 11 per cent of the 198 million people. In 1987 the geographic distribution of poor people in Indonesia was 66 per cent in Java, 11.2 per cent in Sumatra, 2.5 per cent in Kalimantan, 9 per cent in Sulawesi and 11.3 per cent in other eastern parts of Indonesia (World Bank 1990, Table 2.3, 31). Except for the Eastern Islands, which had a preponderance of the poor, the distribution of poverty matched the distribution of the population. Java, the most densely populated island occupied by two-thirds of the population, had the highest concentration of poor people. The poorest districts in Java were upland areas, particularly the limestone hills of Central and East Java; Madura; areas relatively further away from urban areas; and fishing villages along the coast of West and East Java.

The economic crisis seems to have dissipated much of the success and achievements of the past three decades in the space of just one year. The real income per capita has fallen substantially. Some economists have suggested that the Indonesian economic situation is now similar to that in the mid-1970s, with income equivalent to US$350 per capita. However, it is unrealistic to use a dollar figure converted at present exchange rates to measure the decline in real incomes of the bulk of the population.

Java was the first island hit by the crisis. Construction, manufacturing, property and the banking and financial sectors were most severely affected by the crisis and these are disproportionately located in Java. Displaced workers mostly come from these sectors. The dramatic rise in unemployment added many new poor to the already large numbers of poor people in Java before the crisis. On the other hand, agricultural products for export, such as cocoa plantations, cloves, coffee and fisheries such as prawns and lobsters are booming because of their increased international competitiveness due to the depreciation of the rupiah. These products are concentrated in South Sulawesi, North Sulawesi, Lampung and some areas in the Eastern Islands; in these areas the impact of currency crisis is minimal.

4.3 The Impact of the Crisis on Health and Nutrition

Evidence from surveys and studies looking at the impact of the economic crisis on the health of the adults and children have been confusing with no consistent pattern found (Gardner and Amalia 1999). It was widely argued that the crisis would lead to an increased number of children suffering from malnutrition. The increase in food prices, especially of milk and other sources of protein including soybean cakes and tofu, would lead to a deterioration in children's nutrition, and therefore the infant and child mortality rate was expected to increase. Even if death did not occur, severe malnutrition among young children was potentially devastating, because its irreversible effects on the children could lead to a 'lost generation'. These children would survive with a low intellect and a high risk of morbidity because of a lack of essential micro-nutrients important to develop their intellectual and bodily resistance during childhood.

Such expectations were not clearly answered by the data derived from the field. The Indonesian Family Life Survey Data 1997 and 1998 reported that the proportion of malnourished children under nine years old decreased significantly, meaning that their health status in 1998 was better than before the crisis took place (Frankenberg *et al.* 1999). But this study reported a large drop in the proportion of children using any health service in the month preceding the survey between 1997 and 1998 (from 25.8 per cent to 19.9 per cent). This fall is related mostly to the reduction in the use of *Posyandu* (health post) and *Puskesmas* (clinic). A more detailed examination of those aged under five from the IFLS data revealed that the proportion of malnourished babies (under one year) has actually increased (MisCicih 2000). This was consistent with studies by Jahari *et al.* (1999) using the *Susenas* (National Social Economic Survey) 1998. Jahari *et al.* (1999) concluded that aggregate data might not be able to provide information on the real problem. It is clear, however, that there was a serious problem among children in the younger age group.

Further confusing results emerged from research on the use of adult health services. The 1997 and 1998 IFLS data found a large drop in the use of out-patient health services by adults in the same communities between 1997 and 1998 (from 14.4 to 13.3 per cent), characterised by a statistically significant reduction in the use of public health services, private doctors and paramedic services. Data from the *Susenas* do not quite comform to these findings, mainly because of different measures applied. The proportion of women using health services declined very sharply, probably due to the timing of the survey which was taken during the fasting period, where most people do not seek health services.

The media reported that severely malnourished babies were found in many places in Indonesia such as West Sumatra, West Java and Central Java. Many of these babies finally died of malnutrition. The question arises: what is the extent of this situation? In the past three decades, Indonesia has been very successful in increasing the health status of its people. The infant mortality rate declined sharply from 145 deaths per 1000 births in 1971 to 47 per 1000 births in 1997. Some researchers and health specialists argued that the increasing trend in malnutrition among babies actually had a significant impact on the infant mortality rate in that it stalled the decline in the IMR, but confirmation must await the next round of the Demographic and Health Survey (IDHS, 1997).

One thing is certain: the increasing number of poor people and the increasing costs of health services and drugs will affect the affordability of, and willingness of the population to pay for, health services. Delaying the decision to seek help from doctors and paramedics is a common coping mechanism in this situation. It is therefore threatening the quality of human resources in the near future.

There have been a range of health interventions to help people cope with the deteriorating economic situation. However, the implementation of the health SSN program has been hampered by the lack of reliable data showing the location of those in need. Before the crisis we were satisfied with the data available from CBS, because it was obtained from a reliable sampling design. However, this did not allow us to locate specific areas and groups in need. The only micro information available is the BKKBN Family Welfare data. This, however, contains severe defects.

4.4 Education

During the previous three decades of development the Indonesian government has provided education for most primary school age children (7-12 years old). However, not all of these children finished their primary schooling or continued to secondary education. During the fiscal year 1997-98 (August 1997), of about 4.8 million children who entered primary schools, only about 2.8 million would continue to junior high school, and about 1.8 million children would enter senior high school. The enrolment rate for children aged 13-15 years in junior high school increased from 36 per cent in 1994 to 45 per cent in 1997, and the rate for 16-18 year-olds increased from 24 per cent to 30 per cent (GOI 1998). The proportion of children unable to progress to secondary education declined during the first four years of the sixth Five-Year Development Program, from 43 per cent in 1994 to 29 per cent in 1997. Under this increasing trend in education enrolment, the government's plan to achieve compulsory nine-year education by the year 2003 seemed to be reasonable. Meanwhile the percentage of children who finished junior high school but were not able to continue in high school remained stable at 10 to 15 per cent. The percentage of those finishing high school who did not progress to tertiary education was very high, 52 per cent in 1997-98.

The decrease in purchasing power, the loss of income, and the loss of jobs reduced parents' ability to send their children to school. The decision of parents to pay for education costs competes with satisfying daily food needs. To maintain school enrolment and avoid further dropouts the government eliminated school fees and distributed the SSN for education disbursement. But school fees are not the only expense that parents have. They must provide school uniforms, books and stationery, transport costs and money for school refurbishment.

Prices of these commodities have gone up rapidly, though not as fast as the increase in the cost of food (Table 1).

The 1993 Indonesia Life Survey (IFLS) reported that family income is an important determinant of whether children were enrolled in school (Serrato and Melnik 1995). Families with higher incomes were more likely to be able to pay schooling costs. Those belonging to the poorest quintile have the least ability to afford higher education. The 1993 IFLS data did show, however, that enrolment in primary school is almost universal.

In the early stages of the crisis, most informants interviewed in FGDs and in-depth interviews stated that they did not want their children to drop out from school. But the cost of education other than school fees had gone up very rapidly, making it more difficult for parents to send their children to school. Studies conducted in 10 *kabupaten* in Indonesia by the World Bank reported very little indication of an increase in dropout rate. School administrators said that children were kept at school, but there was evidence of delaying school payments. A relatively stable enrolment rate was also found in the 1998 and 1999 National Socio-Economic Survey (a sample of 200,000 households), 6 and 22 months after the economic crisis first hit Indonesia. Figures derived from these surveys show that the percentages of children enrolled at the three levels of education remained stable across age, sex and residence (Table 2). However, these findings have to be interpreted cautiously. Other studies, comparing the 1997 *Susenas* with other data derived from the 'Mini-*Susenas*' collected in December 1998 found a slight decrease in enrolment rate of high school students, especially among the lowest income group (BPS and UNDP 1999).

Even before the crisis, the initial cost to enter the first year of each level of education (contributions for schools management, building refurbishment, school uniforms, etc.) was a major barrier for parents wishing to send their children to school. The crisis has made this problem more severe. From the FGDs and in-depth interviews conducted in mid-June 1998 (one year after the onset of the economic crisis), it was found that the cost to enrol in a public primary school was Rp80,000 – a daunting amount for those facing poverty. The longitudinal data from the 1997 and the 1998 IFLS support this argument by showing that the percentage of primary school children who were not in school increased by 1.0 per cent for boys and by 2.8 per cent for girls. The difference is greatest between the lowest and the highest income group being 4.8 per cent compared with 0.9 per cent respectively. Contrary to the common belief that the urban population was hit harder than rural people, these data showed that it was rural parents and their children who suffered more because of the crisis. Some 3.3 per cent of eligible rural children compared with 2.2 per cent of those from urban areas were not enrolled at primary school in 1998 (Frankenberg *et al.* 1999). In addition, a similar pattern was also found in dropouts from primary school. Girls and children of the poor families have a higher risk of not entering or not finishing primary school. This situation was worse for high school children.

Even though the gender gap in Indonesia is disappearing among primary school students and decreasing among the higher education levels (Oey-Gardiner 1998), when resources are limited, boys are still given a higher priority in education. Conversely, in Malaysia, boys were the first to drop out from school in this type of context to work to help support the family. The crisis clearly threatens the government's target to achieve universal nine years of education by 2003.

Table 2. Population 7 Years of Age and Over Attending School by Age Group, Sex, and Residence

Level of Education	Percent attending school							
	1995		1997		1998		1999	
	Male	Female	Male	Female	Male	Female	Male	Female
Primary School (7-12 years) :								
Urban	97.1	97.1	97.1	97.7	97.4	97.8	97.3	97.7
Rural	93.2	93.6	93.6	94.6	94.1	94.1	93.8	94.6
U+R	94.5	94.7	94.7	95.6	95.4	95.4	95.0	95.7
Lower secondary (13-15 years) :								
Urban	88.5	84.7	84.7	87.1	89.2	88.0	89.0	87.1
Rural	71.1	68.3	68.3	70.5	70.8	70.4	73.7	73.5
U+R	77.2	74.3	74.3	76.7	77.3	77.0	79.3	78.7
Upper Secondary (16-18 years) :								
Urban	66.75	58.13	58.13	64.2	70.4	65.0	69.7	67.9
Rural	37.21	30.08	30.08	34.7	37.2	35.2	38.6	37.3
U+R	48.95	41.93	41.93	47.4	50.4	48.0	51.5	50.8
University (19-24 years) :								
Urban	23.43	17.10	-	-	-	-	23.8	19.1
Rural	5.96	3.18	-	-	-	-	6.36	4.36
U+R	13.49	9.07	-	-	-	-	14.27	11.24

Source: 1) BPS, 1995
2) BPS, 1999

In the long run, the problem of a large number of unskilled human resources with minimal education in Indonesia remains unsolved. In addition, the impact of the crisis on the quality of education and quality of children's development are also being questioned. The lower capacity of parents to provide food for children hamper the children's intellectual development. The increasing price of basic needs and the capability of school to provide extra income for teachers have threatened the sustainability of education.

4.5 The Impact on Contraception

In-depth interviews conducted in mid-June 1998 indicated that parents (especially mothers) tried very hard not to have more children, because they knew that having more children means more costs. New options were sought to obtain contraceptives. Officials from the Family Planning Bureau tried to motivate community groups to develop schemes to help poor people to maintain contraceptive use. For example, in West Java there is a movement called *'rereongan sarumpi'* (togetherness for helping others), providing a discount scheme for the poor to obtain contraception injections. Midwives appear to have become more flexible with payment when they give contraceptive services to clients, most of whom were choosing injectable types of contraception (Adioetomo and Brooks 1998). Comparing results of the 1997 and 1998 IFLS showed that the prevalence of contraceptive use remained constant at 54.7 per cent, both before and during the first year of the economic crisis. However, the dynamics of contraceptive use changed. Women tended to switch to cheaper and more accessible forms of contraception, that is, from injectables to pills, which not only cost less per month, but also are easily obtained from the nearest family planning cadres without incurring travel costs (Demographic Institute 1999).

Midwives interviewed in a Safe Motherhood baseline survey in Central and East Java reported shortages of contraceptive supplies, especially pills. Injectables have been available mostly from the private sector even before the crisis and became unaffordable to poor clients (Demographic Institute 2000). A shortage in pill supply inspired the UNFPA in Jakarta to seek international help to supply contraceptives. A monitoring survey in 11 provinces has shown that the donor providing pills has successfully increased the availability of contraceptives (64 per cent of clients interviewed at the village level were using the donor-provided pills). However, they are not reaching the target population, that is, the poor (Demographic Institute 2001). Further, clients are being made to pay for these pills when they were supposed to be distributed free.

4.6 Employment

This crisis has led to contraction in many economic activities. The share of construction in the 1998 GDP declined by 30 per cent, finance by 15.1 per cent, and trade/hotel/restaurants by 6.1 per cent. The manufacturing sector maintained a constant share of GDP because some of the multinational factories are still producing for export, taking advantage of the low rupiah, but its percentage share of the workforce decreased from 17.3 to 15.7 between 1997 and 1998. The sector recovered in 1999 to 17 per cent. Other sectors have shown a decline in the number of workers, especially in construction and services, but, in 1999, manufacturing activities seemed to have recovered to pre-crisis levels (Tables 3, 4, 5).

Table 3. Percentage of Labour Absorbed by Sector, Urban Areas

Main Industry	1997	1998	1999
Agriculture	7.88	11.07	10.89
Mining and Quarrying	0.85	0.87	0.84
Manufacturing	17.27	15.70	17.38
Utilities	0.59	0.32	0.48
Construction	6.04	5.26	4.87
Trade	31.27	31.05	31.70
Transport	7.49	7.45	7.34
Finance	1.87	1.76	1.62
Service	26.72	26.52	24.88
Others	0.01	0.00	0.00
Total	100.00	100.00	100.00

Table 4. Percentage of Labour Absorbed by Sector, Rural Areas Indonesia

Main Industry	1997	1998	1999
Agriculture	57.94	62.86	61.71
Mining and Quarrying	1.11	0.71	0.80
Manufacturing	10.59	9.02	10.44
Utilities	0.11	0.09	0.06
Construction	4.30	3.36	3.26
Trade	13.87	12.91	12.89
Transport	3.44	3.30	3.24
Finance	0.19	0.15	0.19
Service	8.44	7.60	7.40
Others	0.00	0.00	0.00
Total	100.00	100.00	100.00

Table 5. Percentage of Labour Absorbed by Sector, Urban and Rural Areas

Main Industry	1997	1998	1999
Agriculture	40.73	44.96	43.21
Mining and Quarrying	1.02	0.77	0.82
Manufacturing	12.89	11.33	12.97
Utilities	0.27	0.17	0.21
Construction	4.90	4.02	3.85
Trade	19.85	19.18	19.74
Transport	4.83	4.74	4.74
Finance	0.77	0.70	0.71
Service	14.72	14.14	13.76
Others	0.00	0.00	0.00
Total	100.00	100.00	100.00

The 1998 National Labour Force Survey *(Sakernas)* reported that during the first year of the crisis, more men than women lost jobs in the formal sector and more men than women entered the informal sector in 1998. This was more apparent in urban than rural areas. But in 1999 employment in the urban formal sector seemed to recover, as is indicated by an increase of 3.6 per cent of men working in this sector when compared with 1997, and 6 per cent for women (Tables 6, 7, 8). The influx of men into the informal sector is still apparent in 1999. The recovery is not seen in the rural areas, because the number of workers in the formal sector continued to decline (by 3.66 per cent) in 1999. This again contradicts the belief that urban people were hardest hit by the crisis. In fact this finding supports the argument that the crisis has hit people throughout Indonesia, in both urban and rural areas. The expectation that women are the last to be hired and the first to be laid off was not proven; rather, women's workforce participation increased during the crisis (Oey-Gardiner 1998).

Table 6. Percentage Change of Working Population Aged 15 Years and Above, by Work Status, Urban Areas, 1997-1999

Work status	1997-1998			1997-1999		
	Men	Women	Total	Men	Women	Total
Informal sector						
Self-employed	13.24	5.11	10.39	21.70	18.91	20.72
Self-employed with family workers	6.95	7.98	7.29	6.64	17.51	10.23
Unpaid family worker	14.55	14.36	14.42	22.77	19.24	20.29
Total working in informal sector	11.42	8.74	10.31	17.15	18.71	17.79
Formal sector						
Employer	6.03	5.80	5.99	52.77	59.99	54.04
Employee	-4.05	1.09	-2.37	1.10	4.86	2.32
Total working in formal sector	-3.55	1.20	-2.03	3.63	6.09	4.42

Source: *Sakernas* 1997, 1998, and 1999

Table 7. Percentage Change of Working Population Aged 15 Years and Above, by Work Status, Rural Areas, 1997-1999

Work status	1997-1998			1997-1999		
	Men	Women	Total	Men	Women	Total
Informal sector						
Self-employed	1.66	-4.29	-0.34	6.10	-2.04	3.37
Self-employed with family workers	7.73	17.84	10.01	1.66	12.06	4.00
Unpaid family worker	11.56	5.68	7.23	7.00	-2.91	-0.30
Total working in informal sector	6.06	5.46	5.80	4.10	0.11	2.40
Formal sector						
Employer	4.79	-5.73	2.76	63.61	211.81	92.23
Employee	-9.96	-2.20	-7.70	-11.41	-2.99	-8.96
Total working in formal sector	-9.08	-2.33	-7.15	-6.97	4.59	-3.66

Source: *Sakernas* 1997, 1998, and 1999

Further analysis of the 1998 *Sakernas* found that 4.28 million people said that they had stopped working or changed jobs between August 1997-August 1998. Among them 3.3 million stopped or changed work from the formal sector, and the rest (945,700 workers) were in the informal sector (Adioetomo, Riyanto and Wiyono, 2000). The number of men who stopped working or changed jobs was twice that of women (2.8 million compared with 1.4 million). Compared with men, women's employment seems to be more stable. In urban areas, the percentage of men who stopped or changed work after July 1997 was higher (10.52 per cent) than that of women (8.14 percent) (Table 9).

The percentage of men who were laid off after July 1997 was also higher at 14.27 compared with 12.47 for women. The informal sector clearly operated as a safety net during the economic crisis, with the percentage of men and women that were compelled to stop or change work from the urban informal sector being only 3.86 per cent. Women's work in the formal sector was more stable than that of men's. Half of the men who stopped working after July 1997 had already found another job. Half of them were able to go back to the formal sector while the rest had to find work in the informal sector. On the other hand, only 25 per cent of women who stopped working were able to find another job, half in the formal sector, and the rest in the informal sector. Thirty-five per cent were still looking for work while the rest were out of the labour market. However, when women were forced out of the informal sector they were not likely to go back into the labour market.

Table 8. Percentage Change of Working Population Aged 15 Years and Above, by Work Status, Urban and Rural Areas, 1997-1999

Work status	1997-1998			1997-1999		
	Men	Women	Total	Men	Women	Total
Informal sector						
Self-employed	5.54	-1.00	3.32	11.33	5.30	9.28
Self-employed with family workers	7.60	15.33	9.49	2.49	13.45	5.18
Unpaid family worker	12.06	6.94	8.31	9.63	0.31	2.81
Total working in informal sector	7.34	6.21	6.86	7.22	4.34	6.00
Formal sector						
Employer	5.37	-0.63	4.26	58.51	144.68	74.46
Employee	-6.89	-0.36	-4.86	-4.91	1.41	-2.95
Total working in formal sector	-6.22	-0.36	-4.44	-1.49	5.43	0.62

Source: *Sakernas* 1997, 1998, and 1999

The data show that re-employed workers tend to go back to the sector where they worked before the crisis. This is seen especially in urban agriculture for women, although less for men; the manufacturing sector for both men and women; and in the construction sector for men. Urban-based agriculture acted as a safety net for workers expelled from other sectors. Some 12 per cent of the men who stopped working in the manufacturing sector, and 16 per cent of those expelled from the construction sector changed their jobs to the urban agricultural sector. There was a large number who shifted from other sectors to trade and services (most of them to the informal sector).

In summary, then, the crisis has induced movement of workers between sectors. Urban agriculture (which is in the informal sector) and trade and services have been able to accommodate the workers who were expelled from other sectors after July 1997. More than half of men and women who changed jobs stated that their new working conditions in the formal sector are no better than formerly, in terms of income, facilities, health cover, work safety or transport facilities. Fewer women than men have better or the same payment, facilities in the workplace, and transport facilities when moved from the formal or the informal sector. Thus, as in other areas, women are disproportionately affected by the crisis.

Table 9. Population 10+ Years Who Stopped Working After July 1997, by Sex, Employment Status and Work Status in 1998, Urban Areas, Indonesia, Labour Force Survey, 1998

Population 10+	*Condition in August 1998*					Stopped/ changed work after July 97	Never Stopped Work	Number and Per cent from all employed in July 97
	Formal Sector	Employed Informal Sector	Total	Seeking work	Not in the labour force			
Stopped work after July 97								
Male	335,082	334,498	669,580	471,151	191,438	1,332,169	11,329,074	12,661,243
	25.15	25.11	50.26	35.37	14.37	100		10.52
Female	90,586	90,230	180,816	241,940	260,572	683,328	7,715,954	8,399,282
	13.26	13.2	26.46	35.41	38.13	100		8.14
Male and	425,668	424,728	850,396	713,091	452,010	2,015,497	19,045,028	21,060,525
Female	21.12	21.07	42.19	35.38	22.43	100		9.57
Stopped work from formal status after July '97								
Male	290,893	258,347	549,240	425,749	149,584	1,124,573	6,757,255	7,881,828
	25.87	22.97	48.84	37.86	13.3	100		14.27
Female	81,061	74,438	155,499	222,194	176,993	554,686	3,912,562	4,467,248
	14.61	13.42	28.03	40.06	31.91	100		12.42
Male and	371,954	332,785	704,739	647,943	326,577	1,679,259	10,669,817	12,349,076
Female	22.15	19.82	41.97	38.59	19.45	100		13.60
Stopped work from informal status after July '97								
Male	44,189	76,151	120,340	45,402	41,854	207,596	4,571,819	4,779,415
	21.29	36.68	57.97	21.87	20.16	100		4.34
Female	9,525	15,792	25,317	19,746	83,579	128,642	3,803,392	3,932,034
	7.4	12.28	19.68	15.35	64.97	100		3.27
Male and	53,714	91,943	145,657	65,148	125,433	336,238	8,375,211	8,711,449
Female	15.97	27.34	43.32	19.38	37.3	100		3.86

Notes: tabulated from *Sakernas* 1998

A high proportion of factory workers are migrants, mostly from West, Central and East Java. Daily construction workers and many informal sector workers are circular migrants from areas surrounding the big cities of Jakarta and Surabaya. These workers tended to return to their place of origin when they lost their jobs. However, job opportunities in rural areas were very limited. There is a tendency for husbands to stay in big cities, while their families went back to rural areas. This increased the pressure in rural areas. However, there is also a tendency for young people and agricultural labourers to migrate to urban areas because of a lack of job opportunities in rural areas. This has increased competition in the informal sectors. Displaced female workers tend to go home, and therefore they become invisible in urban areas where the *padat karya* (labour intensive) program was implemented. Besides losing income, female workers laid off from urban industry face social problems when they go back to their place of origin.

Box 2: Displaced from Their Place of Origin

Hujaenah, a girl of 17 years, from Serang was laid off from a footwear manufacturer. She is a technical secondary school graduate. Being a factory worker, she was seen as having good prospects. Hujaenah earned Rp300,000 a month. Half of it was sent to her parents for food and the cost of schooling for her two younger siblings. She said she is not ashamed of being laid off, because there are a lot of other people experiencing the same fate. But what is very difficult for her is that her peer group at home does not want to accept her as one of them, because she was labelled as a factory-city girl. Although this is an individual story, it is very likely that other girls being laid off also feel similarly and are treated similarly. This social cost adds to the economic cost of those being laid off.

There was also concern among policymakers that many young women worked to support their parents or pay for the education of their siblings. Many of them were forced to seek employment as sex workers, but demand for such services has decreased, while it also involved exposure to the risk of STDs including HIV/AIDS.

Box 3: Female Sex Workers

A sex worker in a low class area of Jakarta has five children being cared for by her parents in rural Central Java. She said that she had to work as a sex worker to pay for the education of her children. Before the crisis she brought home Rp500,000 a month but afterwards she could only bring Rp100,000 home. 'There are still many visitors, but they do not have money', she said. She tried to gain employment as a domestic worker before, but the salary was only Rp50,000 a month.

One of her younger friends said that she worked at a factory before but chose to become a sex worker because the income was 10 times higher. However, her income decreased to only Rp300,000 per month (from Rp500,000) because of the economic crisis. Visitors who demand their services have declined. It involves a long wait to get a customer and sometimes there are only one or two clients a week.

4.7 Migrant Workers

The Ministry of Manpower registered half a million workers working in other countries. However, it is believed that this statistic is an underestimate since there are many more illegal migrants working.

One impact of the crisis on migrant workers was that some destination countries were also hit by the economic crisis, such as Malaysia, which is the biggest recipient of Indonesian migrant workers. The Malaysian immigration officers stopped giving visa extensions for migrant labourers. Exceptions were migrant workers involved in the plantation industry (agricultural industry) and other export oriented industries. By January 1998, Malaysia sent home 9,000 workers, and it was reported that they would be sending home another 2 million migrant workers, 600,000 of whom were from Indonesia (*Suara Pembaruan* 1998). However, they were not successful in repatriating such large numbers. A violent riot was reported when Malaysian troops tried to return 500 workers from Aceh in northern Sumatra.

More than half of Indonesian migrant workers are female, and work as domestic helpers in Brunei Darussalam, Hong Kong, Malaysia, Singapore, Saudi Arabia and the United Arab Emirates (Table 10). Their services are still very much in demand and are not affected by the economic crisis in Asia.

Table 10. Number of Registered Overseas Workers from Indonesia Sent Abroad in 1997-2000

Destination Countries	1997	1998	1999	2000
Asia Pacific				
Brunei Darussalam	2426	5337	6477	4019
Hong Kong	2019	14809	12762	5841
Japan	3245	3434	3388	3058
South Korea	8390	7119	11078	6396
Malaysia	317685	95033	169177	170067
Singapore	31928	42031	34829	20456
Taiwan	9445	14109	29372	41620
Others	245	702	685	92
Total	375317	182574	267768	251549
America				
USA	576	2149	3300	1256
Others	160	299	219	205
Total	736	2448	3519	1461
Europe	577	1214	1696	359
Middle East & Africa				
Saudi Arabia	116844	177404	131157	108734
Arab Emirates	9062	15452	17584	9120
Others	137	1081	5895	5228
Total	126374	193937	154636	123082
Grand Total	502977	380173	427619	376451

In rural areas where job opportunities are virtually absent, working abroad as domestic helpers is seen as a major opportunity for a family to survive. The increase in the foreign exchange rate has increased women's motivation to work as migrant workers in other countries, especially in Saudi Arabia and other Middle Eastern countries. The remittances help their family in the area of origin to survive. However, the fact that many of these workers are married mothers raises concerns about childcare. Fathers are not used to looking after children. Usually children of these migrant workers are left with their grandmothers who usually are poor and uneducated. The nutrition of these children is often neglected. Consideration must also be given to the protection of these workers from physical as well as sexual abuse by their overseas employers.

Box 4: The Role of Female Migrant Workers

From a visit to two areas in Rural West Java, it is found that although problems of abuses and violence against domestic helpers remain, many women want to go to Saudi Arabia. An ex migrant worker said she could save Rp40 million by working only 16 months. This is a huge amount of money. However, most workers spend the money, for example, buying a house, rather than using it as working capital for the future. She is preparing to go again, leaving her children and husband behind. Another domestic helper who works in Singapore, said that her monthly salary Sin$300 is equivalent to Rp1.8 million rupiah. The remittance of income to their families in the village means a lot, especially in this era of severe economic pressure.

In this difficult time, promoting migrant workers to go abroad seems to be one alternative to help rescue the rural families left behind. However, the issues of violence and abuse, and the responsibilities for childcare, health and nutrition of the children left by their mothers have to be taken seriously.

4.8 The Impact on the Family and Community

Even though the status of Indonesian women has improved, their role, especially that related to housework and child-rearing activities, has not changed substantially. Even before the crisis, wives felt compelled to work for additional family income if their husbands' income was not sufficient to cover daily expenses. Many women earn more than their husbands, but working wives always stated that they only 'help' their husbands *(bantu-bantu suami)* because of their cultural orientation (Adioetomo and Eggleston 1998).

The economic crisis has led to more women entering the workforce for family survival, but they are also expected to be responsible for domestic work and child rearing. Coping strategies of displaced workers are different between men and women. The overburdened women, the frustrated husbands and the sharp fall in family purchasing power are a source of conflict in the family. Divorce rates are expected to increase. Further, there is potential for domestic violence. It is thought that reports on domestic violence levels are underestimated, and so far very few have been reported in the media. NGOs, however, reported mass systematic rapes at the time of the May 1998 riots, but the government was slow in responding. Only very recently did the Ministry of Women's Affairs and the President admit that such violence had taken place.

5. Summary

The economic crisis in Indonesia has become a prolonged multi-layered crisis to most Indonesians. It affects all aspects of their lives, from prices of basic needs, decline in purchasing power, education, health and nutrition, employment and even family relations. There are, however, a few overarching points that can be made:

- The crisis has impacted upon very large numbers of people, not only in urban areas but also in rural areas. It is not just an 'urban crisis'.
- In coping with problems in the decline in purchasing power, the government faces the problem of a lack of reliable micro data, preventing it from effectively targeting the poorest groups in order to help meet their basic needs.
- The data do not indicate a substantial downturn in education enrolments, but surveys show some falls in particular income and residence groups. A similar pattern applied in the impact of the crisis on nutrition. This suggests that the real effects of the crisis can only be appreciated by breaking down aggregate information according to meaningful groups and areas.
- Women's employment levels remained stable in the crisis.

REFERENCES

Adioetomo, Sri Moertiningsih and Siswanto Agus Wilopo (1998) 'Impact on Population and Reproductive Health in Indonesia'. *Southeast Asian Population in Crisis. Challenges to the Implementation of the ICPD Programme of Action.* New York: UNFPA and Australian National University.

Adioetomo, Sri Moertiningsih and Elizabeth Eggleston (1998) 'Helping Husband, Maintaining Harmony: Family Planning, Women's Work and Household Autonomy'. *Journal of Population* 4: 2.

Adioetomo, Sri Moertiningsih and Roy Brooks (1998) 'Potential Financing and Promotion Options for Future Contraceptive Use'. A Monograph Report submitted to the Policy Project/Futures group/USAID, Jakarta.

Adioetomo, Sri Moertiningsih, Dwini A. Riyanto and Nur Hadi Wiyono (2000) 'Economic Crisis, Employment and Gender in the Urban Informal Sector. *Gender Dimensions of the Economic Crisis and Employment in Urban Informal and Rural Sectors in Indonesia.* SEAPAT Working Papers 6. ILO-Manila.

Adioetomo, Sri Moertiningsih, Triasih Djutaharta and Lilis MisCicih (2000) 'Proyeksi Penduduk Dengan Memperhitungkan Dampak Krisis' ('Incorporating the Impact of Economic Crisis on Population Projection'). Paper presented at Workshop on the Impact of Crisis on Health, Ministry of Health, Lembang, West Java.

BPS (Biro Pusat Statistik) and UNDP (1997) *Keadaan Angkatan Kerja di Indonesia: Sakernas.* (The Situation of the Indonesian Labour Force: National Labour Force Survey). Jakarta.

—— (1997) *Indikator Kesejahteraan Rakyat.* (Social Welfare Indicators). Jakarta.

—— (1998) *Keadaan Angkatan Kerja di Indonesia: Sakernas.* (The Situation of the Indonesian Labour Force: National Labour Force Survey). Jakarta.

—— (1998) *Indeks Harga Konsumen di Ibukota Provinsi Indonesia (1996=100).* (Consumer Price Index in Capital Cities of Indonesia). Jakarta.

—— (1998) *Indikator Kesejahteraan Rakyat.* (Social Welfare Indicators). Jakarta.

—— (1999) *Indeks Harga Konsumen di Ibukota Provinsi Indonesia (1996=100).* (Consumer Price Index in Capital Cities of Indonesia). Jakarta.

—— (1999) *Indikator Kesejahteraan Rakyat.* (Social Welfare Indicators). Jakarta.

—— (1999) *Crisis, Poverty and Human Development in Indonesia, 1998*. Jakarta: Biro Pusat Statistik.

—— (1999) *Keadaan Angkatan Kerja di Indonesia: Sakernas*. (The Situation of the Indonesian Labour Force: National Labour Force Survey). Jakarta.

—— (2000) *Indikator Ekonomi: Buletin Statistik Bulanan: Bulan Mei*. (The Economic Indicators: Monthly Statistics Bulletin, May, November). Jakarta.

—— (2000) *Indeks Harga Konsumen di Ibukota Provinsi Indonesia (1996=100)*. (Consumer Price Index in Capital Cities of Indonesia). Jakarta.

—— (2000) *Indikator Kesejahteraan Rakyat*. (Social Welfare Indicators). Jakarta.

Demographic Institute Faculty of Economics University of Indonesia (1999) 'The Impact of Economic Crisis on Family Planning and Health (Based on the IFLS 1997 and IFLS 1998)'. A Report Submitted to the Policy Project and National Family Planning Coordinating Board. Jakarta.

—— (2001) 'Monitoring the Distribution of CIDA DonorProvided Pills in 11 Provinces of Indonesia'. A report submitted to the UNFPA-CIDA.

Demographic Institute Faculty of Economics University of Indonesia, The World Bank and Ministry of Finance (2000a) *Laporan Verifikasi Pelaksanaan Program Operasi Pasar Khusus (OPK) – Beras Untuk Laporan Bulan April dan Mei 2000*. (Report on the Verification Study on the Implementation of Subsidised Rice Program. April-May) Jakarta.

—— (2000b) *Laporan Verifikasi Pogram JPS Bidang Pendidikan (Beasiswa dan DBO). Untuk Laporan bulan April – Mei 2000* (Report on the Verification Study on the Implementation of Education Social Safety Net – Scholarship and Operational Financial Support. April-May 2000). Jakarta.

—— (2000c) *Laporan Verifikasi Pogram JPS Bidang Kesehatan. Untuk Laporan bulan April – Mei 2000* (Report on the Verification Study on the Implementation Health Social Safety Net. April-May 2000). Jakarta.

Departemen Tenaga Kerja RI (2000) *Laporan Bulanan*. Jakarta. Direktorat Jenderal Pembinaan dan Penempatan Tenaga Kerja. (Monthly Report).

Frankenberg, Elizabeth M., Duncan Thomas and Kathleen Beegle (1999) *The Real Cost of Indonesia's Economic Crisis: Preliminary Findings from the Indonesia Family Life Survey*.

Gardner, Michelle and Lila Amalia (1999) 'An Analysis of Conflicting Crisis-Related Research Results'. *Frontiers in Reproductive Health Cooperative Agreement*. Jakarta: The Population Council.

GOI (Government of Indonesia) (1998) *Lampiran Pidato Kenegaraan Presiden Republik Indonesia di Depan Sidang Dewan Perwakilan Rakyat, 15 Augustus 1998. Pelaksanaan Tahun Keempat REPELITA VI*. (Annex to the Presidential Speech in Front of the House of Representative Meeting, 15 August 1998. Implementation of the 4th year of the REPELITA VI.) Jakarta.

Irawan, Puguh (2000) *Analysis Sensitivitas pada Pengukuran Kemiskinan: Fenomena Kemiskinan Sementara Selama Krisis Ekonomi di Indonesia* (Sensitivity Analysis of Poverty Measurement. How to Distinguish Transient from Chronic Poverty During the Economic Crisis). In Proceedings of Widya Karya Nasional Pangan dan Gizi VII (Workshop on Food and Nutrition VII). Jakarta, February 29 – March 3. Jakarta: National Institute of Science.

Irawan, Puguh B., H. Romdiati, U. Suhaimi and Erman Rahman (2001) 'Social Safety Nets Analysis and Recommendations : Prospects in Indonesia', draft.

Jahari *et al.* (1999). Nutritional Status of Underfives in Indonesia During the Period of 1989 to 1998 (draft), Jakarta. Indonesia.

Kompas (1998) '*Kurs Rupiah terhadap US$*'. July 9.

—— (1997-2000).

MisCicih, Lilis Heri (2000) *Nutritional Status of Under Five Years Old Before and During The Crisis.* A paper submitted to the National Institute of Science. Jakarta.

Ministry of Education and Culture (1998) *Statistik Pendidikan: Susenas (Education Statistics).* Jakarta.

—— (1999a) *Dampak Krisis Ekonomi pada Pendidikan Dasar: Penelitian di Sepuluh Kabupaten di Indonesia (The Impact of Economic Crisis on Primary Education in Indonensia*). Jakarta. Badan Penelitian dan Pengembangan. Laporan No. 01-0599. (Agency for Research and Development, Report No. 02-599).

—— (1999b) *Dampak Krisis Ekonomi Terhadap Pendidikan Dasar di Indonesia: Hasil Survei di Sekolah-sekolah.* (The Impact of Economic Crisis on Primary Education in Indonensia). Jakarta: Badan Penelitian dan Pengembangan. Laporan No. 02-599. (Agency for Research and Development, Report No. 02-599).

National Development Planning Bureau (2000) *Renewing Poverty Reduction Strategy in Indonesia.* Jakarta.

Oey-Gardiner, Mayling (1997) 'Educational Development, Achievment and Challenges'. In Hull and Jones, eds, *Indonesia Assessment. Population and Human Resources.* RSPACS, ANU and ISEAS. Singapore: ISEAS.

—— (1998) 'Gender Differentiated Impact of the Crisis on Indonesian Labor Market'. Paper presented at the AIT-ILO joint research.

Serrato, Carl and Glenn Melnik (1995) 'The Indonesian Family Life Survey: Overview and Descriptive Analysis of the Population, Health and Education data'. Mimeo.

Suara Pembaruan (1998) January 5.

World Bank (1990) *Indonesia Strategy for a Sustained Reduction in Poverty: A World Bank Country Study.* Washington DC: World Bank.

ENDNOTES

[1] The author wishes to thank the UNFPA, New York and Jakarta; Australian National University, Demography Program RSSS, Canberra for their sponsorship and collaboration to develop the first version of this paper (UNFPA, 1999) and to Dewi Prihastuti for providing inputs for the new evidence.

INDEX

C

D

E

I

J

N

O

Q

R

S

T

U

V

W